DAY TRIPS IN DELMARVA

Revised and expanded
2nd edition

by Alan Fisher

RAMBLER BOOKS

Baltimore

DAY TRIPS IN DELMARVA, 2nd edition

by Alan Fisher
Maps and photographs by the author

Rambler Books
1430 Park Avenue
Baltimore, MD 21217

ISBN 0-9614963-6-3

CONTENTS

MAP 1 – The Delmarva Peninsula

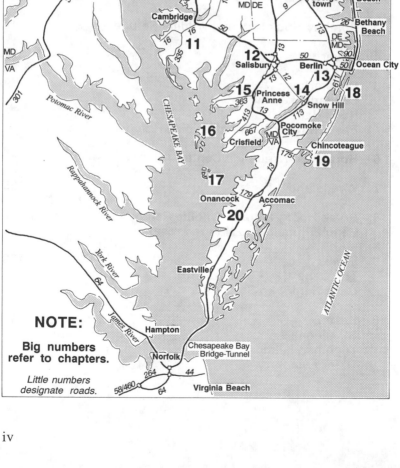

NOTE:

Big numbers refer to chapters.

Little numbers designate roads.

PREFACE

THE DELMARVA PENINSULA is the landmass — intriguing on a map and just as intriguing in reality — that separates Chesapeake Bay from Delaware Bay and the Atlantic Ocean. It consists of southern Delaware and the Eastern Shore of Maryland and Virginia: hence *Del-Mar-Va*, a term of commercial origin that came into use during the first quarter of this century. Recognizing that the Delmarva Peninsula is large and that many visitors will be coming from beyond its bounds, I have included in this book only places that I think are worth driving a considerable distance to see — in short, the best of Delmarva. I have tried to provide variety: car tours combined with short walks and longer hikes; wildlife refuges and wild beaches; the peninsula's two major cities (Salisbury and Dover) and also its historic river ports, agricultural market towns, and bayside villages. Many of the places and itineraries described here provide outstanding opportunities for bicycling as well as car touring (as, for example, along the C. & D. Canal embankment roads) and for canoeing (as at the Pocomoke River, where canoes can be rented locally). Smith and Tangier islands, of course, are not only fascinating in themselves but also provide the occasion for a pleasant ride on the mail boat or one of the tourist excursion boats.

Because it is anticipated that readers will be driving from different places to reach the sites described here, the directions outline different avenues of approach. Necessarily, there is much repetition, so focus on the set of directions that applies to you and skip the others.

Most of this book's commentary on social history and natural history is general in character. It is intended to be read ahead of time and consists of pertinent essays rather than specific observations about this or that structure or feature seen along the way — although there is that too. Each chapter stands on its own, but I hope that the cumulative effect is a fairly comprehensive introduction to Delmarva's land, history, and wildlife.

The following people helped me with this book by reviewing different chapters and making suggestions: Bronwen Anderson, Maggie Briggs, Paul D. Daly, Ann B. Horsey, Ben Hren, Michael J. Kennedy, Larry G. Points, John D. Schroer, and Madeline Thomas. Joanne Doyle researched the word *Delmarva*. And Penny Firth and David Knapp posed for the cover. Many, many thanks.

Alan Fisher

7

COMFORT AND SAFETY

PLEASE READ THIS. It is customary, in guidebooks such as this, to include a catalog of cautions about possible nuisances and hazards. Such matters do not make for scintillating reading, but really, I think that you will be glad to have read here about a few potential problems, so that you can avoid them, rather than learn about them through uncomfortable (or even dangerous) experience. Please also read the introductory matter for each excursion before you go.

Many of the excursions described in this book include rural walks, some fairly long. You will have more fun if you allow ample time to linger along the way. I usually carry a small knapsack containing insect repellent, sunscreen (especially for the beach), a sandwich or snack, a drink, perhaps a bathing suit and towel, and an extra layer of clothing, such as a sweater or rain parka. Wear shoes that you do not mind getting muddy or wet. For longer walks, you should always be prepared for bad weather, particularly during the colder part of the year. Personally, I think that late fall, winter, and early spring are the best times for exploring Delmarva's many marshy wildlife areas, because at that time of year there are no mosquitoes, no heat, no crowds, and abundant waterfowl.

Hunting is sometimes allowed at the wildlife management areas described in this book. Even many of our national wildlife refuges have brief hunting periods in order to control deer populations. Where appropriate, I try to alert you to the possible risk from hunting, but for precise information on hunting schedules, call the telephone numbers provided in the introductory material to the various chapters. And if you go walking in areas where hunting is underway, wear a bright orange vest or jacket.

During winter, all too often drownings occur when people fall through the ice after venturing out onto frozen ponds, rivers, or the shelf of ice that sometimes extends from shore into Chesapeake Bay or even the ocean. I am sure that you have heard this before; everybody has. And yet each winter a few more people die in this manner. Don't be one of them; stay off the ice. And tell your kids.

Other sound advice that is ignored with puzzling regularity concerns lightning. If you are at the beach or some other exposed area and a lightning storm approaches, return to your car immediately. That is the

9

safest place to be — safer even than a small shelter. And if a storm arrives before you get back to your car, hunker down in a low spot. Don't worry about getting wet or feeling stupid as you crouch there with the rain pouring down. Clearly it is better to get wet and yet be safe than to try to stay dry by huddling under a beach umbrella, an isolated tree or pavilion, or some other target for lightning.

Because the car tours in this book are too long for most bicyclists and occasionally make use of major highways, they are not intended to double as bicycle tours. Nonetheless, most of the chapters describe shorter opportunities for bicycling — but not for children. Bicycling on roads is risky enough for adults, and in my experience children lack the discipline to stay steadily as far to the right as possible and to ride single file. Two other major rules for bicycling are to get off the road before dusk and to wear a helmet.

Several of the outings described here are at the beach. Some of these beaches are lifeguarded; others are not, and clearly the latter require more vigilance and caution if you go swimming. At lifeguarded beaches you might be discouraged, or even prohibited, from using buoyant mats or floats, but at unguarded beaches there may be no one to tell you about the hazards of these devices. Briefly, they can provide a false sense of security to poor swimmers, particularly children. Some of these items can deflate suddenly, or the occupant can be knocked off by a wave or blown out to sea by a strong wind. The fact is that drownings have been associated with these devices. Also, when there is surf, be conservative in judging what you and your children can handle.

Where the trails described here follow roads for short distances, walk well off the road on the shoulder to minimize the risk of being hit by a car, and use caution, especially at dusk or after dark, where the routes cross roads. Studies show that in poor light conditions, motorists typically cannot even see pedestrians in time to stop, so your safety depends entirely on you.

Finally, about ticks. Virtually all parks and wildlife refuges in the mid-Atlantic region now post warnings about ticks and Lyme disease. The chances of being bitten by a tick are minimal if you stick to wide, well-maintained trails. But if you walk through tall grass or brush, you can easily pick up ticks, which are active from early spring through autumn, or even during mild weather in winter. Some ticks may carry Lyme disease, which can cause swelling of the knees and hips, arthritis, and other disorders. The main carriers of Lyme disease are tiny deer ticks (about the size of a caraway seed in spring and summer, slightly larger in fall and winter). One simple precaution is to wear long pants and a long-sleeved shirt and to tuck your pant legs into your socks and your shirt into your pants in order to keep ticks on the outside, where you can pick them off. Spray your clothes, especially your shoes, socks, and pant legs, with insect repellent containing DEET (N-diethylmetatoluamide) applied according to the directions on the label. If your clothes are light colored, it will be easier to spot any ticks that may get on you. Inspect yourself occasionally during your outing and when you return to your car. And when you get home, wash your clothes and examine your body closely. Pay particular attention to your lower legs, the backs of your knees, your groin, back, neck, and armpits, which are all places where ticks are known to bite.

If you are bitten by a tick, remove it immediately. Grasp the tick with sharp-pointed tweezers, as near to your skin as possible, and gently but firmly pull straight out until the tick comes off, then blot the bite with alcohol. Some authorities say to save the tick in alcohol for identification and to make a note of when you were bitten. If the tick's mouthparts break off and remain in your skin, call your doctor to have the pieces removed. Research suggests that ticks must feed two days in order to transmit Lyme disease, so there is a fairly big margin of safety if you remove the tick promptly.

The main early symptom of Lyme disease is a circular, slowly expanding red rash, often with a clear center, that may appear a few days or as long as two months after being bitten by an infected tick. Flu-like symptoms are also common, perhaps accompanied by headache, swollen glands, a stiff neck, fever, muscle aches, nausea, and general malaise. If you develop any of these symptoms after being bitten by a tick, see your doctor promptly so that one of a variety of blood tests can be conducted. Don't put if off, because Lyme disease in its early stages is easily treated with some antibiotics.

1

SOUTH CHESAPEAKE CITY
THE CHESAPEAKE AND DELAWARE
CANAL
DELAWARE CITY
FORT DELAWARE STATE PARK

As shown on **Map 2** on page 19, the **Chesapeake and Delaware Canal** cuts across the narrow neck of land at the northern end of the Delmarva Peninsula, linking the head of Chesapeake Bay at the Elk River with the Delaware River about 25 miles below Wilmington. A stupendous volume of earth dredged from the waterway has been heaped along the banks, creating high bluffs that slope steeply down to the ribbon of water that parts the land. Running along the bluffs are dirt roads, in some places arranged one above the other, and now and then interconnected, like the tiers and ramps of an open pit mine.

Exploring these roads by car, by fat-tired all-terrain bicycle, or on foot is great fun and provides by far the best way to view the canal and to appreciate the immensity of this engineering project. For cyclists, an easy and enjoyable outing is to ride 20 miles round-trip along the south bank of the canal between Chesapeake City and St. Georges, keeping pace with gargantuan freighters that pass through the waterway. For a more rugged outing, try the high roads along the canal's north bank. **Map 4** on page 23 attempts to show all the roads in schematic outline. The embankment roads are open daily from dawn until dusk, but before you go, please read the discussion starting on page 22. The canal (and the canal museum at South Chesapeake City) are managed by the U.S. Army Corps of Engineers; telephone (410) 885-5622. Parts of the canal embankment and of the land and marsh farther back from the canal constitute the C. & D. Canal Wildlife Management Area, which is administered by the Delaware Department of Natural Resources and Environmental Control, Division of Fish and Wildlife; telephone (302) 834-8433.

Near the western end of the canal is **South Chesapeake City**, a small and picturesque canal town that retains much of the appearance of its nineteenth-century origins. (See **Map 3** on page 21.) In the few blocks of the old business district are concentrated a variety of antique shops, country stores, restaurants, and bed-and-breakfast establishments. Located just outside South Chesapeake City is the outstanding **C. & D. Canal Museum**, which is open Monday through Saturday from 8 A.M. to 4:15 P.M. and Sunday from 10 to 6. The biggest annual event at South Chesapeake City is Canal Days, held the last Saturday in June. For information about this and other festivals, house tours, and the like, call the Cecil County tourism office at 1-800-232-4595.

Near the eastern end of the waterway is another old canal town, **Delaware City**, from which a passenger ferry operates to **Fort Delaware State Park** on Pea Patch Island in the Delaware River. Built immediately before the Civil War, massive Fort Delaware is open from 11 A.M. to 6 P.M. on weekends and holidays from the last weekend in April through the last weekend in September. The boat that leaves Delaware City at 4 P.M. is the latest in the afternoon that will allow you sufficient time to see the fort. Pets are prohibited. The ferry and fort are managed by the Delaware Department of Natural Resources and Environmental Control, Division of Parks and Recreation; telephone (302) 834-7941. On some evenings in summer, there are ferryboat cruises on the Delaware River or the C. & D. Canal, and at the end of October there are usually two fall foliage cruises. Call for schedule information and details.

THE CANAL ERA got underway in this country toward the end of the eighteenth century and reached its peak in the 1830s and '40s, when many hundreds of miles of waterways were built in the eastern states to transport bulk products to and from the major cities. Then canal construction and use tapered off as most of the waterways were supplanted by the newly-developed railroads. In a few cases, however, some of the most successful canals, originally built early in the nineteenth century, are still in operation today, and, indeed, have been enlarged repeatedly over the years so that they now carry infinitely more tonnage than the old canals ever did. Among these still-flourishing works is the Chesapeake and Delaware Canal, now one of the busiest canals in the world.

The idea for such a canal goes back to the first century of European settlement in the Chesapeake region. In 1661 Augustine Herman, a surveyor and maker of an excellent map of Maryland and Virginia (for which Cecilius Calvert, second Baron Baltimore and the proprietor of Maryland, granted him 4,000 acres in the "farr remote, then unknown wilderness" in 1662), outlined the possibility of a canal linking the head of Chesapeake Bay with the westernmost meander of the Delaware River. The idea was considered several times in the eighteenth century, but not surprisingly, nothing came of the proposal during the colonial period, when Great Britain was more interested in promoting trade *with* the colonies than *among* them.

After the War of Independence and more than a decade of desultory negotiations, the canal got its start in 1799, when Pennsylvania, Maryland, Delaware, and the federal government agreed to join together to purchase stock in the Chesapeake and Delaware Canal Company. Five possible routes were surveyed — the most northerly linking the Elk River with the Christiana River at Wilmington and the most southerly making use of the Chester River — before a route was finally selected. Excavation of the canal began in 1804, but funds were quickly spent and work came to a stop in 1806. Not until 1824 was a reorganized canal company able to muster financial support in the form of new subscriptions for stock to resume work on the waterway, which opened for navigation in 1829.

As first constructed, the canal was nearly 14 miles long, 66 feet wide at the water line, 36 feet wide at the bottom, and 10 feet deep. Near the canal's midpoint, up to 77 vertical feet of earth in a swath 366 feet wide had to be excavated by hand. Water level in the canal was 14 feet above sea level. Boats were raised to, and lowered from, the canal by locks, each measuring 100 by 22 feet. There was a high lock at Chesapeake City at the western end of the waterway and a pair of locks — one at St. Georges and another at Delaware City — near the eastern end of the canal. Barges, mostly carrying coal and lumber, were pulled by tow lines harnessed to mules or horses that followed a towpath along the canal bank. Later, steam tugs took over the task of pulling or pushing barges through the narrow waterway. Other vessels using the canal included passenger packets, floating stores, and an occasional itinerant showboat making a tour of the river towns of Chesapeake Bay. The Baltimore and Philadelphia Steamship Company even built a fleet of narrow, shallow-draft, propeller-driven boats that closely fit the canal locks and provided through passage between the two metropolises.

Because water was constantly lost from the canal through evaporation, leakage, and locking boats in and out at each end, water in the canal had to be replenished. At first this was done exclusively from

several streams that flowed into the canal and by water released from Lums Pond (a man-made reservoir north of the canal, and now a state park). But these sources proved to be inadequate, so water at the Chesapeake level (which on average is slightly higher than the Delaware River) was lifted up to the canal. The C. & D. Canal Museum occupies the former pump house, built in 1837 and still containing a huge waterwheel and a pair of handsome rocker-beam steam engines installed in 1851. The wheel's buckets scooped up water from a channel linked to the tidal boat basin at Back Creek and dumped the water out into an appendage of the higher canal.

Because passage through the canal and more particularly through the locks was limited to boats of shallow draft and narrow beam, the towns at each end of the waterway became thriving transfer points where cargo was unloaded from larger vessels, warehoused, and reloaded onto canal boats, and *vice versa*. So-called arks — large, ungainly barges used to float bulk cargo down the Delaware and Susquehanna rivers — were even dismantled at Delaware City and Chesapeake City and sold for timber (some of it used in local buildings) because the arks could neither pass through the canal nor be taken back upstream.

By the beginning of the twentieth century, the canal no longer accommodated the growing commerce of the mid-Atlantic region, so in 1906 President Theodore Roosevelt (a promoter, too, of the Panama Canal) appointed a commission to study the possibility of a federal takeover and enlargement of the Chesapeake and Delaware Canal. In 1919 the canal was purchased by the federal government, which undertook the Herculean task of lowering the canal to tidewater, thus eliminating the need for locks and pumps. Also, the waterway was widened to 90 feet, its depth increased to 12 feet, and its east entrance relocated to Reedy Point. This work was completed in 1927, and although the result was a much more efficient (and toll-free) canal, the improvements led to the rapid decline of Chesapeake City and Delaware City, where boats no longer had reason to stop. And, of course, a large part of Chesapeake City along the north bank was taken for the canal.

During the Great Depression of the 1930s the canal's width and depth were more than doubled as a project of the Works Progress Administration. And during the 1950s and early '60s, the canal was enlarged yet again to its present width of 450 feet (measured at the bottom) and depth of 35 feet, thus accommodating ocean-going cargo ships. Vessels as large as 958 feet long and 106 feet wide have passed through the canal. Presently the U.S. Army Corps of Engineers is planning to deepen the canal to 40 feet, although there is controversy over whether a deeper canal might harm wildlife by increasing salinity in the upper Chesapeake Bay or by covering good habitat with eighteen million cubic yards of dredged silt.

≈   ≈   ≈   ≈

AUTOMOBILE DIRECTIONS: Cutting across the isthmus that separates the upper end of Chesapeake Bay and the Delaware River, the Chesapeake and Delaware Canal more or less defines the northern boundary of the Delmarva Peninsula. (See **Map 1** on page iv in the Table of Contents, and also **Map 2** at right.) Go first to South Chesapeake City and the C. & D. Canal Museum, located near the western end of the canal, where Route 213 crosses the waterway.

To South Chesapeake City from Interstate 95 north of Delmarva: Interstate 95 passes about 8 miles north of the C. & D. Canal, but there is no direct exit onto Route 213. So if you are coming from the direction of Baltimore on Interstate 95, take Exit 100 for Route 272 toward the town of North East. Near the bottom of the exit ramp, fork right toward North East and follow Route 272 south 1.5 miles to Route 40. Turn left (east) onto Route 40 and go 6.6 miles, then turn right (south) onto Route 213.

If, however, you are coming from the direction of Wilmington on Interstate 95, take Exit 1A for Route 896 south toward Middletown. From the bottom of the exit ramp, follow Route 896 south 3 miles to Route 40. Turn right (west) onto Route 40 and go 4.6 miles, then turn left (south) onto Route 213.

Once you are on Route 213, follow it south 5.8 miles to and across the C. & D. Canal. At the first opportunity after crossing the high bridge, turn right for Route 286 toward the Chesapeake City Historical District and C. & D. Canal Museum. Immediately bear right again, pass under the bridge, then turn left onto George Street (Route 286). Go 0.3 mile to an intersection with Second Street, then turn right and go one block to Bohemia Avenue. This is **South Chesapeake City**, shown on **Map 3** on page 21.

To South Chesapeake City from the Chesapeake Bay Bridge: Follow Route 50/301 across Kent Island. At the point where Route 50 and Route 301 split, continue straight on Route 301 northbound for 31.8 miles to an intersection with Route 313. Turn left and follow Route 313 for 2.5 miles to a traffic light in Galena, and from there continue straight north on Route 213 for 14.2 miles toward Elkton. Immediately before the high bridge over the C. & D. Canal, exit to the right for Route 286 toward the Chesapeake City Historical District, the

MAP 2 — Chesapeake and Delaware Canal

MAP 2 — Chesapeake and Delaware Canal

DELAWARE RIVER

Fort Delaware State Park

Fort DuPont

Reedy Point

Rte. 9

Port Penn

branch canal

Delaware City

Rte. 9

Rte. 9

Rte. 72

Rd. 411

North St. Georges

South St. Georges

Rte. 13

Rte. 1

Exit 142

Rte. 1

Rte. 13

Rtes. 1 & 13

Rte. 7

Rte. 13

Grove Rd.

Lorewood

Rte. 1

Rte. 896

Rte. 13

Rte. 71

Exit 152

Kirkwood

Kirkwood - St. Georges Rd.

North Summit Marina

Rte. 72

Lums Pond State Park

Summit

Rd. 63

Rtes. 71, 301, & 896

Rtes. 71 & 301

5

4

3

miles

2

Rte. 40

Rte. 896

Rte. 71

Rte. 75

Rte. 286

Rd.

Churchtown

1

Rte. 285

Chesapeake and Delaware Canal

Rte. 286

Old Telegraph Rd.

MD|DE

0

MD|DE

Elkton

Rte. 213

North Chesapeake City

South Chesapeake City

Back Creek

Rte. 286

Rte. 342

Rte. 310

Rte. 213

Bohemia River

Rte. 40

Elk River

19

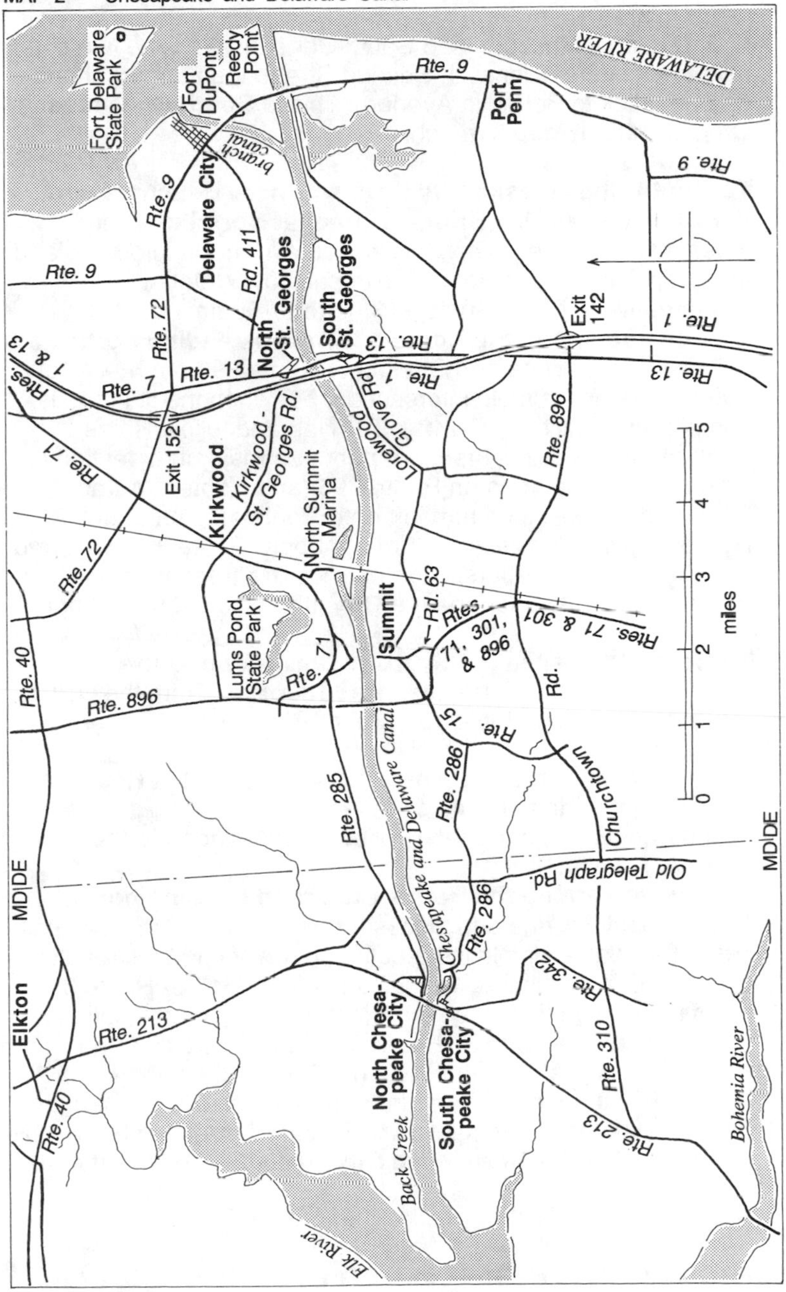

C. & D. Canal Museum, and South Chesapeake City. Go 0.4 mile to an intersection with Second Street, then turn right and go one block to Bohemia Avenue. This is **South Chesapeake City**, shown on **Map 3** at right.

To South Chesapeake City from southern Delmarva and the Chesapeake Bay Bridge-Tunnel at Norfolk: After crossing the bridge-tunnel, follow Route 13 north into Maryland and past Salisbury to Route 1 north at Dover, Delaware.

Alternatively, follow Route 113 north to Route 1 past Dover.

Once you are on the Route 1 toll road heading north, follow it past Smyrna and Odessa to Route 896 north. (As of 1998, this was a simple intersection; but when the toll road is completed, it will be Exit 142.) Turn left and follow Route 896 north about 3.5 miles, then turn right at a major intersection in order to continue north on Route 896 (and Routes 71 and 301). Go 2 miles, then turn left onto Route 15 south. Follow Route 15 just 0.8 mile, then turn right onto Route 286 west and go 3.7 miles to the intersection of Second Street and Bohemia Avenue in **South Chesapeake City**, shown on **Map 3** at right.

To South Chesapeake City from Salisbury and the Delaware and Maryland seashore resorts: From the vicinity of Salisbury, follow Route 13 north to Route 1 past Dover, Delaware.

From Ocean City and Bethany Beach, go west to Route 113 and follow it north to Route 1 past Dover.

And from Rehoboth Beach, follow Route 1 north to the vicinity of Dover.

Once you are on the Route 1 toll road heading north, follow it past Smyrna and Odessa to Route 896 north. (As of 1998, this was a simple intersection; but when the toll road is completed, it will be Exit 142.) Turn left and follow Route 896 north about 3.5 miles, then turn right at a major intersection in order to continue north on Route 896 (and Routes 71 and 301). Go 2 miles, then turn left onto Route 15 south. Follow Route 15 just 0.8 mile, then turn right onto Route 286 west and go 3.7 miles to the intersection of Second Street and Bohemia Avenue in **South Chesapeake City**, shown on **Map 3** at right.

≈　　　≈　　　≈　　　≈

FROM SOUTH CHESAPEAKE CITY TO THE C. & D. CANAL MUSEUM: The bold line on **Map 3** shows the way. From the

MAP 3 – South Chesapeake City

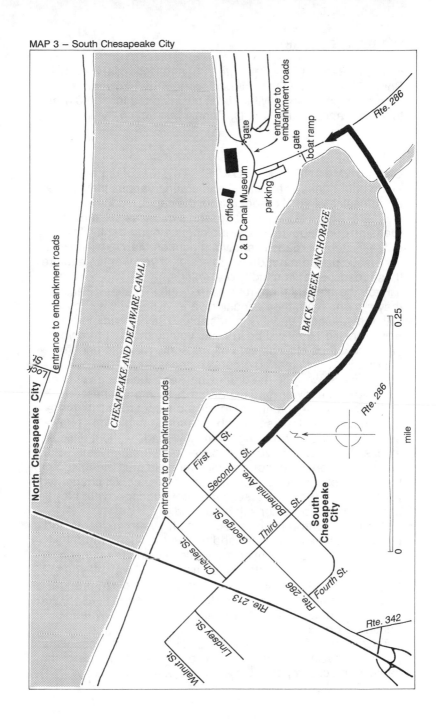

corner of Second Street (Route 286) and Bohemia Avenue in South Chesapeake City, follow Second Street downhill away from the high bridge. With a boat basin on the left, go 0.4 mile to the entrance to the C. & D. Canal Museum on the left.

≈　　≈　　≈　　≈

CANAL EMBANKMENT ROADS: A system of dirt roads runs along both banks of the canal and around various plateaus and diked basins of spoil dredged from the canal. At the canal's midpoint, where the cut is deepest, as many as six tiers of roads rise one above the other along the north bank. The entire system of roads is shown at right on **Map 4**, which is a schematic diagram not drawn to scale. If you want to explore these roads, bear in mind two warnings.

First, the embankment roads are rough in places. Because they are unpaved, their condition varies with the weather and with the seasons, and it is impossible to say ahead of time what condition they will be in when you go there. From year to year, the Corps of Engineers allows some roads to become overgrown while clearing others as necessary to do maintenance work on the drains that keep the slopes stable. In general, the lower roads near the canal are the best maintained, while the higher roads are sometimes little more than rutted Jeep tracks through man-made badlands. I have seen ordinary cars traveling on the low roads without difficulty at all seasons (and have often driven over them myself). But I have also seen Jeep-type vehicles mired in mud along some of the more obscure roads distant from the canal. Of course, you will have to judge for yourself whether your car or your bicycle can handle the conditions that you find.

Second, **hunting** is permitted along the embankments and plateaus at times during fall and winter; telephone (302) 834-8433 for the precise hunting schedule. During the hunting season, stay on the roads, out of the hunters' way. If you are bicycling or walking during this period, wear a blaze-orange vest or jacket. However, even during the hunting season, you can avoid hunters altogether by going on Sunday, when hunting is prohibited.

There are several places to enter the system of embankment roads. Focusing first on the roads along the south side of the canal, one access point (usually open only on weekdays

MAP 4 – Schematic diagram of the C & D Canal embankment roads

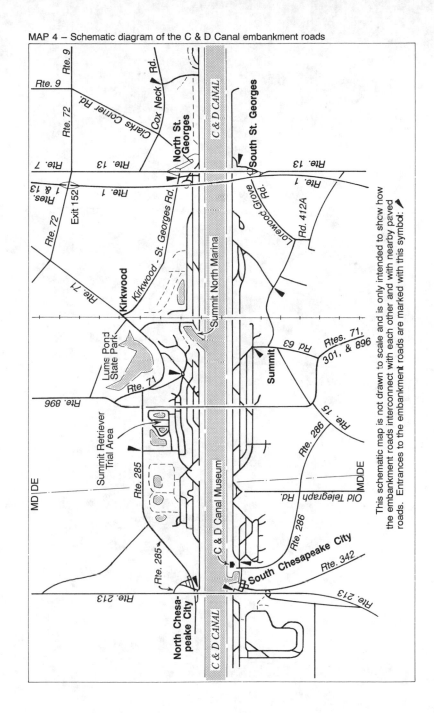

This schematic map is not drawn to scale and is only intended to show how the embankment roads interconnect with each other and with nearby paved roads. Entrances to the embankment roads are marked with this symbol: ➤

23

before 3:30 P.M.) is by the C. & D. Canal Museum just outside South Chesapeake City. From the museum's parking lot, follow a driveway up past the stone museum and through a gate in a chainlink fence.

Another entrance (one that is always open) is at the village of Summit, which is located midway along the south bank of the canal. Summit can be reached from the C. & D. Canal Museum as follows: After exiting from the museum compound through the main gate, pass the road that leads right toward South Chesapeake City. Go 3.3 miles on Route 286, then turn left at an intersection and continue 0.8 mile to Route 896. Turn right onto Route 896, but go only 0.7 mile, then turn left toward Summit on Road 63. Go 0.8 mile to the entrance to the Delaware C. & D. Canal Wildlife Management Area, where you can descend a series of ramps to the edge of the canal.

As shown on Map 4, the embankment roads can also be entered (or exited) at South St. Georges.

An entirely different section of dirt roads west of South Chesapeake City can be entered by descending from the corner of Second Street and Charles Street in the old canal town.

The embankment roads along the north side of the canal can be entered at several points shown on Map 4. These embankment roads are split into two sections (east and west) separated by an arm of the old canal at Summit North Marina. At North Chesapeake City, the western section of roads can be entered at the foot of Lock Street. At North St. Georges, the eastern section of roads can be entered under the Route 13 bridge where North Main Street joins the Kirkwood - St. Georges Road.

≈   ≈   ≈   ≈

DELAWARE CITY and FORT DELAWARE STATE PARK:
As shown on **Map 2** on page 19, near the eastern end of the C. & D. Canal is Delaware City, formerly the waterway's terminus on the Delaware River before the canal's outlet was moved south to Reedy Point. The town is still served by the relatively narrow Delaware City Branch Canal, which follows the old route, now lowered to sea level. The canal's only surviving lock (it is not in service) is located at Delaware City, which better than any other place provides a glimpse of what the C. & D. Canal looked like during the nineteenth century.

The town, too, retains much of its nineteenth-century architecture and atmosphere, particularly along Clinton Street and the adjacent streets to the north. Delaware City is also the embarkation point for the passenger ferry operating to **Fort Delaware** on Pea Patch Island in the middle of the Delaware River. Finally, adjacent to Delaware City is **Fort DuPont State Park**, entered off Route 9 just south of the old Delaware City Branch Canal (and north of the present day shipping canal). Compared to Fort Delaware, however, Fort DuPont is of minor interest.

To reach Delaware City, use Map 2 to navigate from wherever you end up after exploring the canal's embankment roads. Go to the intersection of Route 9 and Clinton Street in Delaware City, and then follow Clinton Street to its end at the waterfront. The parking lot and ferry dock for Fort Delaware State Park are on the right near the end of Clinton Street.

Fort Delaware on Pea Patch Island was built by the federal government in order to guard the water approach to Wilmington and Philadelphia. The island was the site of earthworks during the War of 1812 and of a masonry fort built on inadequate foundations in 1819 and torn down in 1833. Work on yet another fort began in 1848, but it was not finished for nearly a dozen years. Equipped with guns and manned at the outbreak of the Civil War, the massive pentagonal fortress was said to be the strongest bastion on the East Coast. As still seen today, its high, moated walls were sheathed in granite. On the two sides facing downstream, cannon concealed within vaulted brick chambers (or casemates) fired through openings (embrasures) arranged on two levels, with yet a third tier of smaller guns mounted atop the walls. The photograph at left shows the fort's western side, with many openings for small arms.

In March of 1862 the fort's commander was warned by Secretary of War Edwin Stanton that the Confederate ironclad *Virginia*, which was based at Norfolk, might try to run passed the fort to attack Philadelphia. This threat, however, evaporated when the *Virginia* was destroyed by her commander as the Confederates abandoned Norfolk in May. Even before then, the possibility of a raid by Southern ships up the Delaware River was considered to be so remote that Fort Delaware was used to house 258 Confederate prisoners who arrived in April.

For the rest of the Civil War, Fort Delaware and Pea Patch Island served as a prison camp. Barracks were built outside the fort's walls, and by July of 1862, there were about 3,000 captured Confederate soldiers on the island guarded by fewer than 300 Union troops. Eventually, barracks for 10,000 prisoners and a hospital for 800 patients were built. Following the battle of Gettysburg in July of 1863, the prisoner population on Pea Patch Island reached a peak of 12,595, and after that fluctuated between 6,500 and 9,300 for the duration of the war. Confederate officers — at times numbering as many as 160 — were held within the fort itself, as were some political prisoners.

In the prison camp's crowded conditions, mortality from epidemics of smallpox, dysentery, and other diseases was high, totaling about 2,700 men during the war. In just October of 1863, 12.5 percent of the prisoners died. On July 26, 1863, Dr. S. Weir Mitchell of Philadelphia visited the vermin-infested camp (which he termed an "inferno") and summarized what he saw there:

> A thousand ill; twelve thousand on an island which should hold four . . . ; twenty deaths a day of dysentery and the living having more life on them than in them. Occasional lack of water and thus a Christian (!) nation treats the captives of its sword.

More than two months later the Union surgeon at the fort wrote to his superior that "the mortality to me is fearful and it is melancholy proof . . . of the unfitness of this wet island as a depot for large numbers of men." However, Confederate prisoners continued to be brought to the island in droves following each large battle and held there until they were either paroled after taking an oath of allegiance to the United States of America or exchanged for Union soldiers held by the South.

The Civil War provided the impetus for such rapid improvements in naval ordnance that by the end of the conflict Fort Delaware and other forts like it were obsolete. Their high masonry walls were intended only to protect against smoothbore guns mounted on wooded ships, which presumably would be sunk or repelled before such forts suffered much damage. But the development of rifled artillery with greater range, accuracy, and penetrating power than the old smoothbores raised the spectre that works like Fort Delaware could be reduced quickly to rubble from a great distance, as in fact occurred during the Civil War at several masonry forts guarding Southern seaports, albeit the damage there was inflicted by land-based siege guns. But it was not long before guns of similar power were mounted on battleships. In 1869 Major General John Gross Barnard, who during the Civil War had directed the construction of a ring of sixty-eight low, earthen forts surrounding Washington, D.C., recommended that Fort Delaware be supplemented by a modern fort on each side of the Delaware River, as was subsequently done at the end of the century by construction of Fort Mott on the New Jersey bank and Fort DuPont on the Delaware bank.

At the same time, work began in 1897 on reinforced-concrete revements for three 12-inch coastal defense rifles within the old walls of Fort Delaware. The difference between these emplacements and the older part of the fort emphasizes the tremendous changes that occurred in the field of armaments during the second half of the nineteenth century. The new guns were mounted on carriages that allowed them to be lowered — or to "disappear" — behind the revetment walls for loading. Elevators raised the shells and powder from the ammunition chambers below. Batteries of smaller guns were built outside the walls.

Fort Delaware was garrisoned during World War I and again following the entry of the United States into World War II, but it was abandoned by all but a searchlight squad in 1943 after Fort Miles at Cape Henlopen became the main center for the defense of the Delaware River. Declared surplus property, Pea Patch Island was leased in 1945, then turned over to the state of Delaware in 1948. In 1951 the fort, by then severely vandalized, was made a state park, largely as a result of lobbying by the Fort Delaware Society, a non-profit organization that maintains a museum and gift shop at the fort and which continues to work for the fort's restoration.

Also on Pea Patch Island is a short trail leading upriver from the fort to an observation tower overlooking one of the region's largest heron nesting areas.

2

ODESSA and vicinity

The 60-mile car tour outlined in this chapter (and shown on **Map 6** on page 39) explores some of the back roads of northeastern Delmarva. Along the way, the tour visits colonial manors, eighteenth-century merchant houses, old churches, Victorian villages, and other oases of the past scattered throughout the rich agricultural landscape that for more than three centuries has formed the foundation of most commercial activity in this region. The route starts (and ends) at the village of **Odessa**, Delaware, shown on **Map 5** on page 37. Under the auspices of **Historic Houses of Odessa**, two sumptuous houses, both furnished to reflect life in the late eighteenth and early nineteenth centuries, are open to the public. Historic Houses of Odessa also features the **Brick Hotel Gallery**, which exhibits an outstanding collection of Victorian Belter furniture. The houses and gallery are open March through December on Tuesday through Saturday from 10 A.M. to 4 P.M., and on Sunday from 1 to 4. They are closed Mondays, Easter, July 4, Thanksgiving, December 24 and 25, and all of January and February. Yet another house, built about 1700, is open Friday and Saturday during March through October. Historic Houses of Odessa is administered by Winterthur Museum; telephone (302) 378-4069. "Christmas in Odessa" is an annual open house when many old private residences may be toured as well. Sponsored by The Women's Club of Odessa, the open house is held on the first Saturday in December.

The car tour eventually leads to **Smyrna**, where there are many old houses, one of which is operated by the Duck Creek Historical Society as the Smyrna Museum, open on Saturdays from 1 to 4 P.M.

The car tour also passes the **Allee House** southeast of Smyrna at Bombay Hook National Wildlife Refuge (which is featured in Chapter 3 as well). The Allee House is a distinguished colonial farmhouse that has been restored to its eighteenth-century appearance. It is open each Saturday and Sunday in spring and fall from 2 to 5 P.M.; telephone (302) 653-9345 for information.

Although they are rarely open, two old churches that are discussed in this chapter are well worth visiting, even if only to view from the outside. Those who want to see the insides must plan carefully. Services are held at **Old Drawyers Presbyterian Church** north of Odessa *once annually* on the first Sunday in June, and the public is welcome. **Old Bohemia Church** near Warwick, Maryland — one of the oldest permanent Catholic churches in the English colonies — is open from 1 to 5 P.M. on the third Sunday of April, May, September, and October. Mass is celebrated at 4 P.M. (Should Easter fall on the third Sunday of April, Old Bohemia Church is open the following Sunday.)

Finally, bicyclists may enjoy a ride of 32 miles round-trip along scenic Route 9 between Odessa and Bombay Hook, as discussed at the beginning of the tour directions on page 36.

IN THE SECOND QUARTER of the seventeenth century, the tidewater region along the Delaware River was settled by Swedes, Finns, and a few Dutchmen under the direction of the New Sweden Company, organized in 1637. By mid-century New Sweden had a European population of about three hundred people concentrated at Fort Christiana (now Wilmington) and Tinicum Island (now part of Philadelphia). In 1655 the straggling Swedish colony was overawed by a Dutch force sailing from New Amsterdam (New York). Dutch rule, however, was brief; in 1663 the English seized New Amsterdam, and the following year gained control of the region along the Delaware River.

Odessa (originally called Cantwell's Bridge) got its start as a small village about sixty years after the English took over the Delaware region. Among those Englishmen receiving spoils of conquest was Captain Edward Cantwell, first Sheriff of New Castle County, who acquired a large estate on the Appoquinimink River that had been confiscated from a former Dutch official. In 1731 Cantwell's son Richard obtained permission to erect a toll bridge over the Appoquinimink, and Cantwell's Bridge evolved into a stopping place for people traveling between the Delaware River and Chesapeake Bay.

In about 1760 David Wilson opened a general store at Cantwell's Bridge, and from it he sold all manner of supplies, tools, and household goods to farmers in the surrounding district. Wilson's activity did much to make Cantwell's Bridge a center of agricultural trade and a local port for shipping out grain.

In 1765 land at Cantwell's Bridge was purchased by William Corbit, a member of the third generation of a prosperous Quaker family that had lived in New Castle County since 1717. After learning the tanning trade as a young man in Philadelphia, Corbit opened a tannery at Cantwell's Bridge in 1767. Two years later his sister married David Wilson, who had a large Georgian house built for himself and his new wife on Main Street next to his store. Wilson's master builder/architect was John May, who in turn was hired by William Corbit to build a still grander house, finished in 1774 and apparently based on the best of what Corbit had seen in Philadelphia. The house is shown in the photograph on page 30. With its generous but balanced proportions, five-bay facade, stone lintels, central hall, and interior paneling, the Corbit House is said by architectural historians to be one of the best examples of the Georgian style in Delaware.

In 1817 there were about thirty houses at Cantwell's Bridge, all on the south side of Main Street. Four years later the land to the north was laid out into lots and streets, and the following year the Brick Hotel was built at the corner of Main and Second. The Corbit House, the Wilson House, and the Brick Hotel are now all open to the public under the auspices of Historic Houses of Odessa.

Cantwell's Bridge reached its peak of prosperity during the second quarter of the nineteenth century. In his *History of Delaware* (published in 1888), J. Thomas Scharf wrote:

> In 1825 Cantwell's Bridge was a place of considerable importance. . . .
> At this time Cantwell's Bridge was the principal grain market for the
> surrounding country. Grain was conveyed here for shipment from all points
> within a radius of twelve or fifteen miles. Six large granaries, holding about
> thirty thousand bushels, standing on the bank of the Appoquinimink, were
> often completely filled, which delayed the purchase of grain until some of it
> was shipped to Philadelphia. From 1820 until 1840 there were shipped from
> this town four hundred thousand of bushels of grain annually. . . . During the
> busiest seasons, six sloops made weekly trips to Philadelphia, and three
> coasting schooners went to Boston and the East, besides a large number of
> transient vessels.

In 1855 the town's name was changed to Odessa after the large Russian grain port on the Black Sea. At about the same time, however, the newly-constructed Delaware Railroad bypassed the town by more than three miles to the west, a circumstance that led to an economic decline at Odessa as shippers relocated their businesses to be near the railroad. By the beginning of the twentieth century, Odessa's big granaries had disappeared from her rotting wharves, and the town was served by only one small steamer making two trips weekly to Philadelphia.

Compounding Odessa's difficulties was a trauma affecting the entire region. In the last quarter of the nineteenth century the "yellows" — a form of blight — ruined the extensive peach orchards that by then provided the main crop of southern Delaware (whose state flower is the peach blossom).

Odessa's decline as a mercantile center has been complete, and today it is almost wholly residential in character. Although it lies astride Route 13, it has the air of a quiet village, where dozens of handsomely restored houses, barns, and gardens provide a glimpse into a seemingly idyllic past — a scene not entirely accurate, since many of today's residences on Main Street formerly housed (at least in part) trade establishments and professional offices. Still other commercial structures, including the Corbit tannery and the Wilson store, have been removed altogether.

The leading figure in Odessa's program of architectural restoration was H. Rodney Sharp, who in 1938 bought the Corbit House from a descendant of William Corbit. Sharp restored the Corbit house, then went on to acquire and restore — or in some cases, tear down — other dilapidated structures nearby. His work included moving the Collins-Sharp House, now located at the corner of Second Street and High Street, to Odessa from the shore of the Delaware River near Taylors Bridge. Using material left over from some of his restoration projects, he even built a new old house, called Left Overs, next to the Brick Hotel. In 1959 Mr. Sharp gave the William Corbit House (now called the Corbit-Sharp House) to Winterthur Museum, and in 1966 he gave Winterthur the Brick Hotel, after restoring its exterior. The David Wilson House (now the Wilson-Warner House) was similarly given to Winterthur by Wilson's descendants, one of whom — Mrs. E. Tatnall Warner, Wilson's great-granddaughter — had opened the house as a museum.

Finally, on High Street at the intersection with Second Street is the oldest public library in Delaware. The Corbit-Calloway Memorial Library was established in 1847 by the will of Dr. Daniel Corbit. Its Delaware Room is an outstanding resource for anyone interested in Delaware history.

≈ ≈ ≈ ≈

AUTOMOBILE DIRECTIONS: The car tour shown on **Map 6** on page 39 starts at Odessa, Delaware, which is located where Route 299 crosses Route 1 and Route 13 about 7 miles south of the Chesapeake and Delaware Canal and 23 miles north of Dover. (See **Map 1** in the Table of Contents.)

To Odessa from northernmost Delmarva and Interstate 95 southwest of Wilmington: From Interstate 95 take Exit 4A for Route 1 south, and stay on Route 1 past a quick succession of exits. Follow Route 1 about 16 miles to Route 299 for Odessa and Middletown. (As of 1998, this intersection is simply a crossroads at a traffic light, but when the Route 1 toll road is completed, the off-ramp for Route 299 will be Exit 136.) Turn left onto Route 299 east and follow it into Odessa to the Brick Hotel Gallery on the left.

To Odessa from the Chesapeake Bay Bridge: After crossing the bridge, follow Route 50/301 across Kent Island. At the point where Route 50 and Route 301 split, continue straight on Route 301 northbound for about 43 miles, then turn right at an intersection with Route 299 eastbound toward Middletown. Follow Route 299 east for 4 miles through Middletown to Odessa and the Brick Hotel Gallery on the left.

To Odessa from southern Delmarva and the Chesapeake Bay Bridge-Tunnel at Norfolk: After crossing the bridge-tunnel, follow Route 13 north into Maryland and past Salisbury to Route 1 north at Dover, Delaware.

Alternatively, follow Route 113 north to Route 1 past Dover. **Once you are on the Route 1 toll road heading north**, follow it past Smyrna to Route 299 for Odessa and Middletown. (As of 1998, this intersection is simply a crossroads at a traffic light, but when the Route 1 toll road is completed, the off-ramp for Route 299 will be Exit 136.) Turn right onto Route 299 east and follow it into Odessa to the Brick Hotel Gallery on the left.

To Odessa from Salisbury and the Delaware and Maryland seashore resorts: From the vicinity of Salisbury, follow Route 13 north to Route 1 past Dover, Delaware.

From Ocean City and Bethany Beach, go west to Route 113 and follow it north to Route 1 past Dover.

And from Rehoboth Beach, follow Route 1 north. Continue as Route 1 becomes a toll road at Dover.

Once you are on the Route 1 toll road heading north, follow it past Smyrna to Route 299 for Odessa and Middletown. (As of 1998, this intersection is simply a crossroads at a traffic light, but when the Route 1 toll road is completed, the off-ramp for Route 299 will be Exit 136.) Turn right onto Route 299 east and follow it into Odessa to the Brick Hotel Gallery on the left.

≈　　　≈　　　≈　　　≈

HISTORIC HOUSES OF ODESSA: Start at the **Brick Hotel Gallery**, which fronts on Main Street but is entered around the corner on Second Street. At the Brick Hotel you can buy a ticket that enables you to visit not only the gallery, but also the **Corbit-Sharp House** and the **Wilson-Warner House**, which are adjacent to each other across Main Street, and the **Collins-Sharp House** (if it is open) at the corner of Second Street and High Street. If time permits, seeing all four is well worthwhile.

After you have toured the houses and their gardens, you may enjoy walking up and down Main Street and High Street east of Route 13, where many other old houses have been restored. (See **Map 5** at right.)

≈　　　≈　　　≈　　　≈

CAR TOUR: The bold line on **Map 6** on page 39 shows the route followed by a 60-mile car tour, which circles counter-clockwise to the south of Odessa. A shorter excursion for bicyclists is to follow the tour route *backwards* from Odessa along scenic Route 9 to the **Allee House** at Bombay Hook, then return the way you came, for a round trip of 32 miles. To nearly double the length of your trip, you can go farther south on Route 9 to the **John Dickinson Plantation**, described in Chapter 4. Bicyclists should bear in mind, however, that although Route 9 is not a major road, it is used by cars traveling at high speeds.

From the Brick Hotel Gallery in Odessa, follow Route 299 (Main Street) west 0.3 mile to the intersection at a traffic light with the northbound lanes of Route 13, and there turn right. Follow Route 13 north only 0.9 mile, then turn left into the entrance for Old Drawyers Presbyterian Church, which overlooks (toward the back) Drawyers Creek.

The congregation that eventually built **Old Drawyers Presbyterian Church** was formed late in the seventeenth century. In 1708 the Presbytery at Philadelphia directed the minister at New Castle (at that time the site of the only Presbyterian church in Delaware) to preach "once a month on a week day" to the "persons about Apoquinimy." The next year the minister was instructed to supplement his weekday preaching with a sermon "once a quarter on Sunday." Land at Drawyers Creek

MAP 5 – Odessa

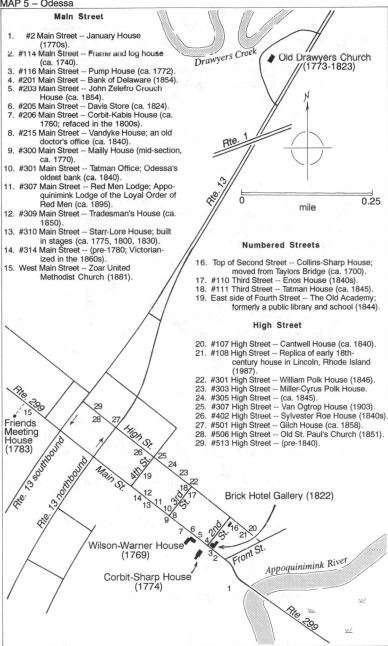

Main Street

1. #2 Main Street -- January House (1770s).
2. #114 Main Street -- Frame and log house (ca. 1740).
3. #116 Main Street -- Pump House (ca. 1772).
4. #201 Main Street -- Bank of Delaware (1854).
5. #203 Main Street -- John Zelefro Crouch House (ca. 1854).
6. #205 Main Street -- Davis Store (ca. 1824).
7. #206 Main Street -- Corbit-Kabis House (ca. 1760; refaced in the 1800s).
8. #215 Main Street -- Vandyke House; an old doctor's office (ca. 1840).
9. #300 Main Street -- Mailly House (mid-section, ca. 1770).
10. #301 Main Street -- Tatman Office; Odessa's oldest bank (ca. 1840).
11. #307 Main Street -- Red Men Lodge; Appoquinimink Lodge of the Loyal Order of Red Men (ca. 1895).
12. #309 Main Street -- Tradesman's House (ca. 1850).
13. #310 Main Street -- Starr-Lore House; built in stages (ca. 1775, 1800, 1830).
14. #314 Main Street -- (pre-1780; Victorianized in the 1860s).
15. West Main Street -- Zoar United Methodist Church (1881).

Numbered Streets

16. Top of Second Street -- Collins-Sharp House; moved from Taylors Bridge (ca. 1700).
17. #110 Third Street -- Enos House (1840s).
18. #111 Third Street -- Tatman House (ca. 1845).
19. East side of Fourth Street -- The Old Academy; formerly a public library and school (1844).

High Street

20. #107 High Street -- Cantwell House (ca. 1840).
21. #108 High Street -- Replica of early 18th-century house in Lincoln, Rhode Island (1987).
22. #301 High Street -- William Polk House (1846).
23. #303 High Street -- Miller-Cyrus Polk House.
24. #305 High Street -- (ca. 1845).
25. #307 High Street -- Van Ogtrop House (1903).
26. #402 High Street -- Sylvester Roe House (1840s).
27. #501 High Street -- Gilch House (ca. 1858).
28. #506 High Street -- Old St. Paul's Church (1851).
29. #513 High Street -- (pre-1840).

Drawyers Creek

Old Drawyers Church (1773-1823)

Rte. 1

Rte. 13

N

0 mile 0.25

Friends Meeting House (1783)

Rte. 299

Rte. 13 southbound

Rte. 13 northbound

High St.

4th St.

3rd St.

2nd St.

Main St.

Front St.

Brick Hotel Gallery (1822)

Wilson-Warner House (1769)

Corbit-Sharp House (1774)

Appoquinimink River

Rte. 299

was purchased in 1711 and a wooden meeting house was built. With John May serving as master builder, the present church was built in the Georgian style starting in 1773. Old Drawyers was closed in 1861 after the construction of a new Presbyterian church in Odessa, since torn down. In 1895 a nondenominational group called The Friends of Old Drawyers was organized to care for the church, which belongs to the Presbytery of New Castle.

CAR TOUR continued (Map 6): Leave Old Drawyers Church by turning right onto Route 13. Follow Route 13 south less than a mile to an intersection at a traffic light with Route 299 in Odessa, and there turn right (west) toward Middletown — but almost immediately pull over to the side of the road next to Odessa Memorial Park, across from the white and blue signs for the **Appoquinimink Friends Meeting House.** Although he was not a Quaker, David Wilson built this meeting house in 1783 for his wife's Quaker congregation. The small brick meeting house is set back about a hundred yards from Route 299 behind the Zoar United Methodist Church, which was established in 1881. The simple, intimate meeting house is worth seeing, if only to look through the windows. Next to the meeting house is the Corbit family graveyard.

From the Friends Meeting House, follow Route 299 west about 3 miles to Middletown.

The history of **Middletown** is in some ways the obverse of Odessa's. In 1816 there were only a few houses at Middletown, but after 1855, when the Delaware Railroad was built immediately west of the village, Middletown grew fast, as reflected in its stock of Victorian structures along Main Street. (Note the mansard roofs and ornate facades with hooded windows and bracketed eaves.) Soon the town supplanted Odessa as the center of the surrounding farming district, a role it has retained to the present day.

CAR TOUR continued (Map 6): From the center of Middletown, continue west on Route 299 to the intersection — located 0.4 mile beyond the railroad — with Route 301. Turn left onto Route 301 and follow it for 2.4 miles, passing, along the way, two large "peach mansions" on the left — **Cochran Grange** (built about 1840) and **Hedgelawn** (1856).

"Peach mansion" is a term used by historians of Delaware architecture to describe a number of somewhat ostentatious houses built during the middle of the nineteenth century by farmers made wealthy

MAP 6 — Car tour from Odessa

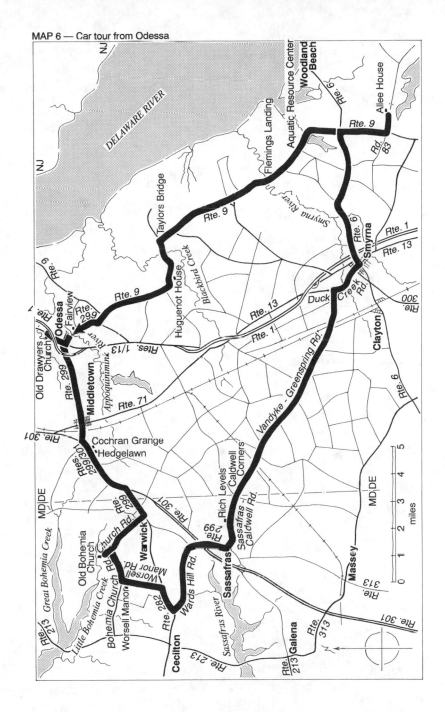

by growing peaches, at that time a new cash crop. Cochran Grange is basically a Georgian house with Greek Revival and Italianate features added to the exterior. The original owner of Cochran Grange was John Price Cochran, a leading farmer and fruit grower who was Delaware's governor from 1875 to 1879. Cochran eventually owned fifteen farms totaling about four thousand acres west of Middletown, and during his life he gave a farm to each of his six sons, one of whom built the Italianate Hedgelawn. And just down the road on the right (opposite a large brick house, but not easily seen from the highway) is Summerton, built in about 1850 by another Cochran son.

CAR TOUR continued (Map 6): As noted above, follow Route 301 south for only 2.4 miles (during which Route 301 is congruent with Route 299), then bear right to follow Route 299 west toward Warwick. Go 1.2 miles as Delaware Route 299 becomes Maryland Route 282, then turn right onto Church Road in the village of Warwick. Follow Church Road 1.8 miles to an intersection with Bohemia Church Road, and from there continue straight toward the church, visible a few hundred yards ahead. Pass in front of the church and bear right to park by the rectory museum, which is open on the same days as the church.

Old Bohemia Church, more properly called St. Francis Xavier Church, was built about 1790 as part of a Jesuit mission established here in 1704 under the leadership of the Reverend Thomas Mansell. At first Old Bohemia was the only Catholic mission in Delmarva and southeastern Pennsylvania, but its influence diminished over the following sixty years as other missions were established in Pennsylvania and at Cordova, Maryland (northeast of Easton). After the Diocese of Wilmington was established in 1868, a conventional parish structure was introduced to the Delmarva Peninsula, and in 1898 the Jesuits relinquished the Old Bohemia mission to the Bishop of Wilmington.

Old Bohemia included not just a church but also a self-sufficient plantation of 1,200 acres, complete with a gristmill and sawmill, a kiln for making bricks, a blacksmith shop, barns, and a wharf on Little Bohemia Creek. Developed by the early priests, the plantation generated income to support the Jesuits' missionary and educational activities, including an academy run at the plantation during the second half of the eighteenth century. Among the students at Bohemia Academy were John Carroll, the first American Catholic bishop and archbishop, and his cousin Charles Carroll of Carrollton, signer of the Declaration of Independence.

The interior of Old Bohemia Church burned in 1912 but was rebuilt. Presently, the church and plantation are being restored by the Old Bohemia Historical Society, Inc. in cooperation with the Diocese of Wilmington.

CAR TOUR continued (Map 6): Follow the driveway back to the first intersection, and there turn right onto Bohemia Church Road. Go 1.2 miles, then turn left onto Worsell Manor Road. After only 0.3 mile pass Worsell Manor on the right; it is a private residence just barely visible from the road.

In 1683 Charles Calvert, third Baron Baltimore and the proprietor of Maryland, granted Major Peter Sayer, a prominent Catholic, a tract of one thousand acres called **Worsell Manor**. The plantation later came into the possession of James Heath, who died in 1731 and is buried on the property. On May 14, 1773, Daniel Heath had as his guest for the night George Washington, who was taking his stepson Jackie Custis to King's College, New York (now Columbia University). And why, you ask, would Washington choose a route through this remote place to go north? At that time, the main north-south road — the Upper King's Road — lay through this part of Delmarva, running from the harbor at Rock Hall (which was served by ferry from Annapolis) to Chestertown and on through Warwick and Middletown to Wilmington and Philadelphia.

CAR TOUR continued (Map 6): Continue on Worsell Manor Road to a T-intersection with Route 282, and there turn right. Go 1 mile, then turn left onto Wards Hill Road. Continue as straight as possible for 3 miles to a junction with Route 301. Cross Route 301 and follow Route 299 for 0.8 mile to the hamlet of **Sassafras**, site of the **Old Rehoboth Methodist Protestant Church**, built in 1859 by a black congregation but now abandoned. Turn left by the church onto the Sassafras - Caldwell Road. After only 1.2 miles, pass a large house on the left.

Called **Rich Levels**, this painted brick house was built in the middle of the eighteenth century as a two-story structure. About a century later the third story with hipped roof was added. Inside, this private residence has a central hall with a handsome stairs and paneled rooms on the first two floors. The name Rich Levels is derived from the region, locally called The Levels, and said to be among the best farmland in Delmarva.

CAR TOUR continued (Map 6): From Rich Levels, continue on the Sassafras - Caldwell Road for 1 mile to a five-way intersection called Caldwell Corners, and from there continue as straight as possible for 8.6 miles. (For most of this distance, you will be following the Vandyke - Greenspring Road.) At a T-intersection with Duck Creek Road, turn right and go 1.1 miles. This is part of the Lower King's Road, which ran south from New Castle to Smyrna and Dover, and remained the main road until the DuPont Highway (Route 13) was built between 1912 and 1924. Cross Glenwood Avenue (Route 6/300) at a traffic light and continue straight on Main Street about 0.3 mile to the center of Smyrna at the Four Corners. Take the time to park and to walk up and down Main Street and Commerce Street, where there are many houses, stores, and a few hotels dating from the late eighteenth, nineteenth, and early twentieth centuries.

The history of **Smyrna** somewhat resembles that of Odessa. The town, which at first was called Duck Creek Cross Roads, grew up around the Four Corners of what are now Main and Commerce streets, where in 1768 Samuel Ball, a Quaker merchant from Philadelphia, purchased fifteen acres and erected a general store. A combination sawmill, gristmill, and bolting mill was already located on Duck Creek a mile north of the crossroads. Immediately to the south of the crossroads was another gristmill on Mill Creek, and to the east was Duck Creek Landing, to which ships could navigate from the Delaware River.

During the second half of the eighteenth century, coastal sloops and schooners carrying grain sailed regularly from the landing for Philadelphia and New York. By 1790 large ships were being repaired and built at Duck Creek Landing. At that time the crossroads was a stage coach stop and had a post office, several taverns, a Methodist meeting house, and over fifty houses. In 1806 the name of the town was changed to Smyrna (a Turkish port and site of one of the "seven churches which are in Asia" in the Bible).

By the 1850s, when Smyrna entered its most prosperous half-century, as many as seven vessels per day sailed from Smyrna Landing during the height of the grain shipping season. At harvest time, the roads to Smyrna were clogged with teams hauling wagons loaded with grain and peaches. A substantial business district of Victorian buildings grew up around the Four Corners and new industries — principally canneries and fertilizer plants — were established.

In the twentieth century, however, Smyrna encountered a series of difficulties. As was the case at Odessa, the Delaware Railroad had bypassed the town two miles to the west, where Smyrna Station eventually developed into the rival town of Clayton. Grain output declined and the blighted peach crop failed utterly. Competition from the railroad, the siltation of Duck Creek, and the trend toward ever larger vessels turned Smyrna Landing into a forgotten backwater. When Route 13 reached Smyrna in 1923, it bypassed the Four Corners. Smyrna has managed to adapt, however, and today the town is a center, on a modest scale, for light manufacturing. Retailing has flourished along DuPont Highway (Route 13) so that now it too has been bypassed by the new Route 1 toll road immediately to the east.

As already noted, there are many old houses and commercial structures in Smyrna. At 11 South Main Street is the **Smyrna Museum**, thought to have been built about 1790. The **Enoch Spruance House** at 21 East Commerce Street grew in sections, starting with the part farthest to the right, which was built late in the eighteenth century. The ground floor was used as a bank, with living quarters for one of the bank's officers above. The "simplified Regency" **John Cummins House** is across from 115 North Main Street. Cummins was Smyrna's leading merchant in the first quarter of the nineteenth century. A little annex to one side was Cummins' office. The house was built about 1820, at a time when Cummins was one of the biggest grain merchants in Delaware and a delegate to the state's General Assembly. Cummins' schooners sailed to Philadelphia, New York, and Boston loaded with grain and returned with manufactured goods, which he wholesaled to crossroads stores throughout lower Delaware and into Maryland.

CAR TOUR continued (Map 6): At the intersection of Main Street and Commerce Street in the center of Smyrna, turn left (east) onto Commerce Street and go 0.2 mile to the junction with Route 13. Cross Route 13 and follow Route 6 east 5.2 miles to a crossroads with Route 9, and there turn right. Follow Route 9 south 1.7 miles to the entrance to the Allee House on the left. Turn left and follow the driveway 0.6 mile to the Allee House.

The **Allee House** was built about 1753, probably by Abraham Allee, the son of John Allee, a Huguenot emigre who first acquired land at Bombay Hook in 1706. Wealthy by inheritance, Abraham Allee was elected to the General Assembly in 1726, was made a Justice of the Peace in 1738, and in 1749 was appointed to the prestigious position of Chief of the Kent County Rangers, or that is, mounted militia riflemen. The exterior brickwork of the Allee House is in Flemish bond with a few decorative glazed headers. The interior of the house is surprisingly elegant, with paneling on the end wall of the main room.

CAR TOUR continued (Map 6): From the Allee House, turn right out the entrance and follow Route 9 north 1.7 miles back to the crossroads with Route 6. From there continue north on Route 9 for 12.9 miles; follow the route signs closely so as not to be shunted off Route 9 onto some other road. After 1.6 miles, you will reach the **Delaware Aquatic Resource Education Center** on the right, where there is a good boardwalk out into the tidal salt marsh. In another 2.3 miles you will pass Flemings Landing on the Smyrna River (formerly called Duck Creek); a glimpse of the river here will perhaps make it easier to believe that coasting schooners used to ascend to Smyrna Landing farther upstream. Later you will reach Taylors Bridge, where there is a high cast-iron navigational beacon built in the mid-1800s for the nearby Delaware River and where the road turns sharply left. About 1.5 miles beyond this turn, Route 9 passes an old farmhouse atop a knoll on the left several hundred yards from the road (which itself bends left at this point).

This is the **Huguenot House**, built in 1711 by Elias Naudain, whose father, also named Elias, had fled from France to England when the Edict of Nantes (which granted religious freedom to Protestants) was revoked in 1685. The younger Elias Naudain came to Delaware, then part of Pennsylvania, in about 1708 and acquired large landholdings. In 1715 he was recorded as being one of the elders of Old Drawyers Church. About 0.5 mile beyond the Huguenot House, also on the left, is another old house, of which the front part (built sometime between 1812 and 1835 by one of Naudain's descendants) is appended to a still older rear section.

CAR TOUR continued (Map 6): Finally, at an intersection where Route 9 turns abruptly right, continue straight west on Route 299. After only 0.2 mile, turn right at a T-intersection and follow Route 299 for 1.2 miles across the Appoquinimink River and back into Odessa, where the car tour ends.

About half a mile before entering Odessa, Route 299 passes a handsome Georgian house on the right called **Fairview**, built in 1773 for Captain (later Major) James Moore, who served during the Revolutionary War. Like the Corbit and Wilson houses in Odessa, Fairview is the work of masterbuilder John May, and shows the same elegant simplicity outside and fine woodwork and paneling inside.

3

BOMBAY HOOK NATIONAL WILDLIFE REFUGE

Containing about 25 square miles, **Bombay Hook** in Delaware is one of the largest national wildlife refuges on the Atlantic coast's migratory flyway. The area open to visitors is shown on **Map 7** on page 51. Bird watching here is made easy by more than 11 miles of rock-grit roads that overlook a vast expanse of tidal marsh and large freshwater ponds. There are several short foot trails leading to observation towers or other vantage points. Walkers can also simply follow the refuge roads (but first please read the discussion starting at the bottom of page 53). If you have a fat-tired or hybrid bicycle that can handle the sometimes loose, gravelly surface, the refuge roads also provide good bicycling.

The refuge is open daily from sunrise to sunset. Dogs must be leashed. Deer hunting is permitted on a few days each fall, and on those rare occasions part of the refuge is closed to non-hunters, so you may want to call ahead of time. The visitor center, which features exhibits and a video, is open year-round Monday through Friday from 8 A.M. to 4 P.M., and also — in spring and fall — on Saturday and Sunday from 9 to 5. The **Allee House**, a small but handsome colonial house that has been restored to its eighteenth-century appearance, is open free of charge during spring and fall on Saturday and Sunday from 2 to 5 P.M. The refuge is managed by the U. S. Fish and Wildlife Service; telephone (302) 653-9345.

FROM THE DIKE ROAD at Bombay Hook, salt marsh stretches east to the horizon. Sinuous tidal creeks meander through the marsh, eventually connecting with Delaware Bay, which is out of sight beyond the marshy flats. Bordering the dike road to the west is a chain of large freshwater impoundments, and inland from them are low, swampy woods and farm fields, used in part to grow food for ducks and geese.

Taken altogether, the saltwater and freshwater marshes, tilled and fallow fields, woods, and ponds provide a wide diversity of habitats and the opportunity to see many bird species. A bird list showing seasonal fluctuations is available at the refuge visitor center.

The best bird watching is at the several ponds (or pools, as the management calls them). Here immense rafts of Canada geese, snow geese, and various species of ducks and other waterfowl congregate from late September through early December, reaching a peak at the end of October and beginning of November. Particularly stirring is the sight and sound of wave upon wave of geese — at times seeming to fill the sky with a huge vortex of birds — returning to the refuge at dusk after feeding during daylight in farm fields. Some waterfowl stay through the winter or are present again as they pass northward late in winter.

By lowering weirs in spring, the pools are partially drained to create mud flats and shallow water suitable for migratory shorebirds and waders. Thousands of sandpipers, plovers, and larger birds such as herons, egrets, ibises, American avocets, greater and lesser yellowlegs, dunlins, and dowitchers, provide interest at a time of year when the waterfowl population is relatively sparse. Many of the shorebirds return in August, and a few species, notably black-necked stilts and willets, stay through June and July to breed in the refuge. Of course, the usual birds of forest and field are also present during summer. And in fall the weirs are raised again so that the pools slowly refill to suit migratory waterfowl.

Land at Bombay Hook was first acquired by the federal government in 1937, three years after passage of the Migratory Bird Hunting Stamp Act provided a reliable stream of funds to buy refuge land. Under the hunting stamp act, waterfowl hunters are required to buy a revenue stamp annually. As bird watching has grown in popularity, refuge entrance fees have also helped to generate funds for the purchase, maintenance, and periodic enlargement of our national wildlife refuges.

Of the approximately 16,000 acres at Bombay Hook National Wild-life Refuge, all but 25 percent are tidal salt marsh. Estuaries such as Delaware Bay are a typical setting for salt marsh formation — and, indeed, satellite images of the bay show that nearly its entire coast is lined by marshes, often extending two or three miles inland. Where rivers meet the sea — and we are talking here not just of major rivers like the Delaware but also of many small streams like the Leipsic and Smyrna rivers near Bombay Hook — the sediments that have been carried downstream settle out. As the sediments accumulate in the river mouths or farther offshore in the estuary, they form mud flats that are exposed at low tide and that gradually are colonized by marsh grasses spreading from the shore. The dense, grassy carpet slows and filters the muddy tidewater that twice daily inundates the marsh, thus further contributing to the deposition of sediments. Thick layers of peaty mud develop, bound in a matrix of partially decomposed roots and leaves of marsh grasses.

As long as the marsh is flooded by the tide, upward growth of the surface continues because of the ongoing processes of sedimentation and peat formation. But as the marsh builds vertically toward the high water level, less material is washed onto the surface and upward growth slows. The limit is about a foot above average high water. At that level only storm tides or the highest tides of the year during spring and fall cover the marsh, so that there is no longer enough deposition to raise the level of the marsh appreciably. To some extent, the accumulation of dead and decaying salt grass builds up the surface. But at the same time, the underlying peat is continually decomposing, which causes the surface of the marsh to settle back toward the level of the yearly high tides. The marsh is thus in equilibrium among the processes of deposition, plant growth, compaction, and decay, which altogether produce a remarkably level surface.

There are, however, some slight differences in elevation, which are reflected in different varieties of plant life. At Bombay Hook the short *Spartina patens* (commonly called saltmeadow cordgrass or saltmarsh hay) and *Distichlis spicata* (salt grass) dominate the high marsh that is flooded only during the year's highest tides or storm surges. The far taller *Spartina alterniflora* (seven or eight feet high and vernacularly called saltmarsh cordgrass) occupies lower areas that are inundated during every high tide.

Salt marshes are extraordinarily productive. Their shallow sunlit waters permit photosynthesis to take place at a very rapid rate. Great quantities of algae and animal microorganisms are produced. Algae are even able to grow during the winter. According to John and Mildred Teal, authors of *Life and Death of the Salt Marsh*, the grasses and algae capture up to 6 percent of the solar energy falling on the marsh during the year, compared to 2 percent for a corn field at its peak. The algae in turn consume only 10 percent of their energy intake, passing 90 percent along to the myriad animals that feed on them. An acre of salt marsh yields about ten tons of organic material yearly, compared to fifteen tons for wheat fields (including stems and leaves) and four tons for the very best hay fields.

Coastal marshes are prime feeding and breeding grounds not only for migratory waterfowl but also for fish. Worms, shrimp, shellfish, and baitfish thrive on the algae and rotting vegetation. In turn, the young of larger fishes find food and protection in these rich nurseries. According to the Teals, two-thirds of the value of the commercial harvest of fish and shellfish caught on the East Coast comes from species that spend at least part of their life cycle in coastal and estuarine marshes. Such areas are about ten times as productive of fish as the coastal waters of the continental shelf, and about one hundred times more productive than the open ocean.

In recent years attention has focused also on the importance of freshwater wetlands, which in Delmarva's level terrain often occur as low, soggy woods, meadows, and farm fields lying immediately inland from coastal marshes, as, for example, in the vicinity of Bombay Hook's Finis Pool, fed by Finis Branch. Freshwater wetlands soak up immense quantities of storm runoff during periods of rain and flood, then slowly release it over a period of weeks or months. In this way they help to replenish groundwater and serve also as natural reservoirs and filters for streams that eventually flow into coastal marshes and estuaries.

≈   ≈   ≈   ≈

AUTOMOBILE DIRECTIONS: Bombay Hook National Wildlife Refuge is located in Delaware about 7 miles northeast of Dover, where Delaware Bay narrows and becomes the Delaware River. (See **Map 1** on page iv in the Table of Contents.)

To Bombay Hook from northernmost Delmarva and Interstate 95 southwest of Wilmington: From Interstate 95 take Exit 4A for Route 1 south, and stay on Route 1 past a quick succession of exits. Follow Route 1 more than 29 miles to Exit 114 for Route 13 and South Smyrna. At the bottom of the exit ramp, bear right and then right again onto Route 13 north, and follow it 0.7 mile to the intersection with the Smyrna-Leipsic Road (Road 12). Turn right to follow the Smyrna-Leipsic Road 4.6 miles. Curve right as the road merges with Route 9, then go only 0.2 mile on Route 9 before turning left onto Whitehall Neck Road (Road 85) toward Bombay Hook National Wildlife Refuge. Follow Whitehall Neck Road 2.5 miles to the refuge visitor center on the left.

To Bombay Hook from the Chesapeake Bay Bridge: After crossing the bridge, follow Route 50/301 across Kent Island.

MAP 7 – Bombay Hook National Wildlife Refuge

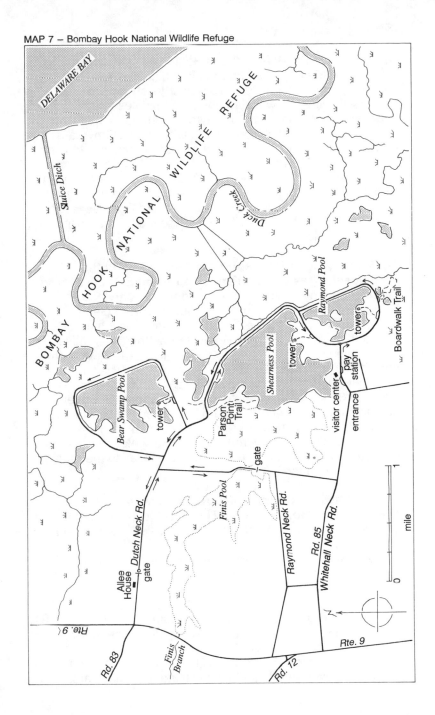

At the point where Route 50 and Route 301 split, continue straight on Route 301 northbound for 20.5 miles to an intersection with Route 300. Turn right (east) toward Sudlersville and follow Route 300 for 21.6 miles to a T-intersection with Route 13 in Smyrna. Turn right and follow Route 13 south 1.1 miles, then turn left onto the Smyrna-Leipsic Road (Road 12), where a sign points the way toward Bombay Hook National Wildlife Refuge. Follow the Smyrna-Leipsic Road 4.6 miles. Curve right as the road merges with Route 9, then go only 0.2 mile on Route 9 before turning left onto Whitehall Neck Road (Road 85) toward Bombay Hook. Follow Whitehall Neck Road 2.5 miles to the refuge visitor center on the left.

To Bombay Hook from southern Delmarva and the Chesapeake Bay Bridge-Tunnel at Norfolk: After crossing the bridge-tunnel, follow Route 13 north into Maryland and past Salisbury to the intersection with Route 9 toward Georgetown and Lewes. Follow Route 9 east to the intersection with Route 113, and there turn left onto Route 113 north. (Alternatively, this junction can be reached by taking Route 113 north from the junction with Route 13 near Pocomoke City, Maryland.)

Follow Route 113 north past Milford. Continue north as Route 113 merges with Route 1. As you approach Dover, bear right to take Route 9 north toward Leipsic and Little Creek. Follow Route 9 for 13 miles, then turn right onto Whitehall Neck Road (Road 85) toward Bombay Hook National Wildlife Refuge. Follow Whitehall Neck Road 2.5 miles to the refuge visitor center on the left.

To Bombay Hook from Salisbury and the Delaware and Maryland seashore resorts: The first objective is to get onto combined Route 1/113 north of Milford, Delaware, heading toward Dover.

From the vicinity of Salisbury, take Route 13 north, then route 9 east to Route 113 north, which eventually merges with Route 1 north of Milford.

From Ocean City and Bethany Beach, go west to Route 113 and follow it north to the merge with Route 1 near Milford.

And from Rehoboth Beach, follow Route 1 north to the merge with Route 113 near Milford.

Once you are on Route 1/113, follow it north. As you approach Dover, bear right to take Route 9 north toward

Leipsic and Little Creek. Follow Route 9 for 13 miles, then turn right onto Whitehall Neck Road (Road 85) toward Bombay Hook National Wildlife Refuge. Follow Whitehall Neck Road 2.5 miles to the refuge visitor center on the left.

≈　　　≈　　　≈　　　≈

TOURING BOMBAY HOOK BY CAR OR BICYCLE: Map 7 on page 51 shows the refuge roads, which provide excellent vantage points for bird watching. An Auto Tour pamphlet, giving commentary that is keyed to numbered signs along the way, is available at the visitor center.

After paying the entrance fee at the visitor center or at the pay station on the main tour route, follow the system of dike roads around the various pools and to the western spurs at the **Allee House** and Finis Pool. Please drive slowly; note that some of the roads are one-way.

≈　　　≈　　　≈　　　≈

WALKING AT BOMBAY HOOK: Several short foot trails are shown on **Map 7** on page 51. The **Boardwalk Trail** is about 0.5 mile round-trip, and the **Parson Point Trail** (which is sometimes closed in order to enable eagles to roost or nest undisturbed) is 1 mile round-trip. For both these trails, there are pamphlets available at the visitor center providing information that is keyed to numbered posts. The other refuge trails lead a few hundred yards to various observation towers.

Serious hikers may find it more satisfying to park their cars at the visitor center or one of the tower lots and then walk on the dike road. The safest place to do this is where the road is one-way; walk facing the oncoming traffic in order to minimize the risk of being hit by a car. The **road around Raymond Pool** is one-way and forms a circuit 2 miles long. The **road around Bear Swamp Pool** forms a 3-mile circuit and is less frequented by cars, but a short part of it is two-way. Walking on the road is best during late fall, winter, and early spring, when mosquitoes are absent, birds abundant, and excessive heat merely a memory.

4

DOVER

As the seat of Kent County, the capital of Delaware, and the state's second-largest city, **Dover** offers a week's worth of day trips. At its center is the historic district, shown on **Map 8** on page 65. Concentrated in this area are the **Delaware State Visitor Center**, the **State House**, the two **Meeting House Galleries**, and the **Johnson Victrola Museum**. All of these sites are Delaware State Museums. Also here are the **Sewell C. Biggs Museum of American Art**, **Woodburn** (the governor's official residence), **Wesley Church**, **Christ Church**, the state office buildings, including **Legislative Hall**, and many old houses clustered around **The Green**. Each of these sites is discussed separately on pages 63-68. Some historic buildings that are shown on the map but not listed here may be open to the public during Old Dover Days, held the first weekend in May. For information telephone the Delaware State Visitor Center at (302) 739-4266.

Near Dover are other attractions: **The Delaware Agricultural Museum and Village**, **Dover Downs**, the **Dover Air Force Base Museum**, the **John Dickinson Plantation**, the River Trail at the **St. Jones Preserve**, **Barratt's Chapel**, and **Killens Pond State Park**. All are shown on **Map 9** on page 69 and are discussed separately on pages 68-77.

IN THE MIDDLE DECADES of the seventeenth century, when Delaware was still a Dutch colony, all the region below Bombay Hook was administered from Hoornkill, later called Horekill or Whorekill and now Lewes. Great Britain seized control of Delaware from the Dutch in 1664, and a few years later settlers began to claim land along the St. Jones River and other small but navigable tidal creeks in the region midway between the villages of New Castle and Whorekill. The settlers came not only from areas north and south along the Delaware coast but also from Maryland, where good, unpatented land on navi-

At left: Chamber of the House of Representatives at
the State House, courtesy of Delaware State Museums.

gable water was becoming scarce. In 1680 a petition was directed to Governor Andros from people "living and ambitious to abide under the sunshine of yor Honors Government Inhabetinge in the upland part of the Whorekill County." The petitioners described "the great greivances Hazards and perils both by land and water that wee undergoe in going to the Whorekill Court," the "want of commodacons of man or beast," the "unpassable, dangerous waies," the "perillous Creeks," and the "hazardous large Marshes." They concluded by requesting the creation of a new court "to be held in some convenient place in St. Jones Creeke." Sixty-four men signed the document, adding a note at the end: "The shipe goeing away, wee had nott time to gitt ye rest of there names, butt we think there may be about 100 tithabell," meaning taxpayers in the region.

The request was promptly granted, and in 1680 old Whorekill County was divided into two parts, of which the northern was called St. Jones (changed to Kent a few years later). The seat of the new county was a place called Towne Point at the mouth of the St. Jones River, where the court met in the house of one of the justices. Working under the Lieutenant Governor and the provincial Assembly, the court of each county was the center of local government, not only adjudicating cases but also collecting taxes, administering decedents' estates, appointing special trustees to transact county business, and issuing patents for land.

The annual court of Kent County continued at Towne Point until 1689 or '90, when it moved inland to a tavern located at the head of navigation on the St. Jones River, where the King's Highway (a rough track) crossed the creek. In 1694, however, the court never sat because two of the justices refused to use the tavern any longer. The next year county trustees purchased two hundred acres nearby for a new town. It was to be called Dover and would have a county court house and jail, as had been ordered (but without immediate result) in 1683 by William Penn, who held not only Pennsylvania under a grant from King Charles II but also Delaware under a 10,000-year lease from the Duke of York.

Even after the purchase of land for Dover, the town was slow to develop. In 1697 a court house was erected, and also stocks and a whipping post, but not until 1717 was the county's property laid out into lots around The Green. In 1722 the court house was sold and a new one erected on the site of the present State House. South of The Green was Church Square, reserved for the established Anglican church. Church Square was relocated in 1734 to the site where Christ Episcopal Church now stands. West of The Green was Meeting House Square for the use of the region's numerous Presbyterians, descended mostly from Scotch-Irish immigrants and a smaller number of Huguenots. This square is now occupied by the Meeting House Galleries. In 1751 construction of a public market house was authorized at Dover, but it was never built. At that time, the county was still seeking to sell lots from the original Dover tract. Nonetheless, the town became the chief business center for Kent County, which in 1760 had a population of about seven thousand people, of whom the vast majority lived on farms. Before the American Revolution, the General Assembly of Delaware met at New Castle, but after the British seized control of the Delaware River in September and October of 1777, the legislature convened for the fall session at Dover, as had already been arranged the prior spring. The British abandonment of Philadelphia in June 1778 ended the period of greatest danger for Delaware, but the Assembly continued at Dover for two years, then met successively at Wilmington, Lewes, Dover, New Castle, and again Lewes as each community pressed its claim to be made the state capital. Centrally located, Dover was at last selected permanently in 1781.

During the war, Delaware provided the Continental Army with only one regiment, but it was among the army's best. One of the regiment's companies carried a number of fighting cocks that were said to be the offspring of a blue hen, and so the Delaware soldiers came to be called the "Blue Hen's Chickens." On the home front, the Delaware militia under Brigadier General Caesar Rodney kept Tory agitation in check. Occasionally the militia mustered in response to raids by small boats that, operating under the protection of a British warship posted at Cape Henlopen, ascended Delaware creeks to loot farms and landings. For four years Caesar Rodney also served as the President of revolutionary Delaware, working to provide Washington's army with food and military supplies. Rodney's revolutionary zeal is further demonstrated by a famous incident. Learning on July 1, 1776, that the deliberations of the Continental Congress, to which he was a delegate, were reaching a head while he was at Dover on public business, Rodney rode overnight (despite rain, chronic asthma, and cancer) to Philadelphia to cast his vote for independence.

After the war, and after the unsatisfactory start of nationhood under the Articles of Confederation, the Delaware Assembly became the first state legislature to ratify the federal Constitution. The unanimous vote was held December 7, 1787 at the Golden Fleece tavern, one of two Dover hostelries used by the legislature. To provide permanent accommodations for itself, the Assembly in 1786 had asked the government of Kent County to share the new court house it was planning to build. The arrangement was accepted and a building fund was established, supported by fees for marriage and tavern licenses. When those sources proved inadequate, a state lottery was established to swell the building fund. The State House, as it is called, was finished in

1792. Located at the east end of The Green, it is now an outstanding museum showing the court, the legislative chambers, and a few offices. Following the Revolution, Dover grew steadily. Its residents included prosperous attorneys, doctors, merchants, bankers, and owners of large farms in the region. In 1785 Dover's population was approximately six hundred. According to one observer, the town had about a hundred houses, "principally of brick," and considerable trade with Philadelphia, to which small, shallow-draft sloops sailed via the Delaware River from landings on the St. Jones River and nearby Little Creek. In 1812 the Dover Canal Company, with a capital of $30,000, tried to improve navigation on the St. Jones, but without much success. There was also stagecoach service via the old King's Highway.

In 1829 Dover was incorporated by the General Assembly. Among the first acts of the town commissioners were the purchase of forty good fire buckets, six ladders, and four fire hooks, the sinking of new wells, the erection of a hay scales behind the State House, the paving of intersections of the principal streets, and the installation of lamp posts and lamps. In 1856 the Delaware Railroad reached Dover from the north, accelerating the town's development as a depot and market center for the surrounding agricultural region. Steamboat service, however, was less satisfactory; boats commonly ran on an "as needed" basis. One attempt at a regular water and stagecoach route linking Philadelphia, Dover, Seaford, and Norfolk failed.

Although a slave state, Delaware on the eve of the Civil War had a large population of free blacks. Many whites had long favored voluntary manumission of slaves, but stopped short of supporting equal rights. At the outbreak of the war, the state opposed secession and promptly answered President Lincoln's call for troops to uphold the Union. In southern Delaware, however, there were many sympathizers with the Confederacy. In March 1862, Maryland troops arrived at Dover and other towns to disarm pro-southern units of the local militia. At the request of the Republican governor during the elections of 1862 and '64, federal troops served as guards at polling places, supposedly to preserve order but actually, it was charged, harassing known Democrats. After the war, Delaware's General Assembly refused to ratify the Thirteenth, Fourteenth, and Fifteenth amendments to the U.S. Constitution, and at times the federal Circuit Court had to supervise elections to prevent disenfranchisement of blacks. As in Virginia and Maryland, segregation was codified in Delaware and remained law until the middle of the twentieth century.

While northern Delaware became increasingly industrialized following the Civil War, the economy of southern Delaware stayed largely agricultural. Wheat and corn, previously the main crops, were surpassed by peaches, pears, melons, and strawberries after arrival of the railroad made it easy to ship these more valuable but perishable commodities to market. Vegetables, including sweet potatoes and Irish potatoes, were important as well. Most manufacturing had an agricultural base. In 1870 the Dover Flouring Mill on the St. Jones River was a modern roller mill that stood where a succession of grist mills had been in operation for nearly a hundred years. Stites & McDaniel, one of a series of tanneries, operated at Dover from 1865 to 1880. Peach brandy and later rye whiskey were distilled at Dover by a family named Levy. Canning and packing plants proliferated, and so did mills making wood products, such as fruit baskets, ship timbers, and doors and window sashes. Food processing equipment and fruit evaporators were manufactured. The biggest business at Dover was Richardson & Robbins, founded in 1855 and engaged in canning fruit, vegetables, meat, and seafood. Still going a century later, the Richardson & Robbins plant was purchased in 1954 by the William Underwood Company, which used the facility until 1975 to make "Red Devil" brand meat spreads. Located at 89 Kings Highway north of The Green, the former plant is now occupied by the Delaware Department of Natural Resources and Environmental Control. In 1867 Richardson & Robbins purchased the Dover Gas Works, which had been established in 1859 to make gas from resin and later from coal. Gas was used for manufacturing and also for street and interior lighting until Dover turned to electricity at the end of the century. Another local milestone was construction of the Kent County Court House in 1873 after Delaware finally purchased exclusive title to the 1792 State House.

In the twentieth century, Dover has become a sprawling city of about 30,000 residents (as of 1998), compared to 3,329 in 1900. Kent County, excluding Dover, has a population of about 95,000. Built between 1912 and the early '30s, Routes 13 and 113 put the state capital within an hour's drive of all of southern Delaware.* Route 13 through Dover has since become the city's main street. In the early 1930s the new Capitol Square was laid out and Legislative Hall was built. The

---

*Route 13 (the DuPont Highway) was completed through Delaware in 1924. It was built largely at the individual initiative and expense of Thomas Coleman du Pont, who had been president of the DuPont Company until he sold all his shares and went into politics. In 1921 the Delaware governor appointed du Pont to the United States Senate to fill a vacancy arranged specifically for him. The four-lane DuPont Highway was a pioneering motor road, and until it was built, road communications between Dover and Wilmington were often impassable each winter.

expansion of state government during the century has, of course, bolstered Dover's growth. In 1941 Dover Air Force Base opened, and it too has fed the local economy. Agriculture remains important (sales of Kent County farm products gross well over $100 million annually), but now there is a huge service sector, particularly in the area of banking and credit cards. Presently the area's largest employers are state government (excluding education), Dover Air Force Base, MBNA America Bank, federal, county and municipal government, the University of Delaware, Wilmington Trust Company, Delmarva Power & Light, Acme Markets, Sears, PNC Bank, the Alfred DuPont Institute (a pediatric clinic), Kent General Hospital, J.C. Penny, Playtex, Bell Atlantic, Kraft Foods, Blue Cross/Blue Shield, and Delaware State University. Harness racing and slot machines at Dover Downs draw visitors from throughout the state and beyond, as do also the large tax-free shopping malls. And yet at the heart of all this, retaining the appearance of the eighteenth and nineteenth centuries, is Dover's historic downtown, site of the museums and other places described starting on page 63. And near Dover are other attractions described on pages 68 through 77.

≈   ≈   ≈   ≈

AUTOMOBILE DIRECTIONS: Dover, Delaware is located near the northern end of the Delmarva Peninsula, where Route 113 meets Route 13. The Route 1 toll road passes through the eastern edge of the city. (See **Map 1** on page iv in the Table of Contents, and also **Map 9** on page 69.) The directions below take you first to the **Delaware State Visitor Center**, which is located in the same building as the **Sewell C. Biggs Museum**. Near the Visitor Center are other sites in historic downtown Dover shown on **Map 8** on page 65 and discussed starting on page 63. Outlying sites are discussed beginning on page 68, and in each case directions are provided from the Delaware State Visitor Center.

To Dover from northernmost Delmarva and Interstate 95 southwest of Wilmington: From Interstate 95 take Exit 4A for Route 1 south, and stay on Route 1 past a quick succession of exits. Follow Route 1 south past Smyrna and past Exit 104 for North Dover. After going through a toll plaza, continue on Route 1 for 3.1 miles, then take Exit 95 for South Dover. At the bottom of the exit ramp, turn right onto Route 113 north. Go 1 mile, then turn left onto Court Street toward historic downtown Dover. Follow Court Street 0.6 mile straight across Route 13 and past Legislative Hall to an intersection with Legislative Avenue. Continue straight one block on Duke of York Street. Cross Federal Street and go straight into the driveway for the **Delaware State Visitor Center** and **Sewell C. Biggs Museum**.

Alternatively, you can approach Dover from the north via Route 13. After passing the **Delaware Agricultural Museum and Village** (which you may want to see now rather than return to later) continue 2 miles, then turn right onto Court Street just beyond the intersection with Route 113. Follow Court Street 0.4 mile past Legislative Hall to an intersection with Legislative Avenue. Continue straight one block on Duke of York Street. Cross Federal Street and go straight into the driveway for the **Delaware State Visitor Center** and **Sewell C. Biggs Museum**.

To Dover from the Chesapeake Bay Bridge: After crossing the bridge, follow Route 50/301 across Kent Island. At the point where Route 50 and Route 301 split, continue straight on Route 301 northbound for about 18 miles, then turn right onto Route 302 toward Barclay and Dover. Follow Route 302 east 8.9 miles, then turn right onto Route 454 toward Dover. Follow Route 454 south for 2.2 miles to the state line in the town of Marydel. As you enter Delaware, Route 454 becomes Route 8. Follow Route 8 east 12.1 miles, then (after passing an intersection with Route 15) fork right toward Loockerman Street and historic downtown Dover. Go 0.9 mile, then turn right onto Federal Street. Pass E. North Street, then turn right into the driveway for the **Delaware State Visitor Center** and the **Sewell C. Biggs Museum**.

To Dover from southern Delmarva and the Chesapeake Bay Bridge-Tunnel at Norfolk: After crossing the bridge-tunnel, follow Route 13 north about 73 miles to the intersection (near Pocomoke City, Maryland) with Route 113, and there turn right onto Route 113 north toward Berlin and Ocean City. Follow Route 113 across Route 50 and into Delaware. Eventually, north of Milford, merge with Route 1 and continue north toward Dover. (As you approach Dover, you will pass **Barratt's Chapel** and — 5.4 miles north of it — Route 9 near the **John Dickinson Plantation**, the **St. Jones Preserve**, and the **Dover Air Force Base Museum**. Obviously, it may be convenient to stop by these places now rather than return to them later. See Map 9 on page 69.)

For historic downtown Dover, continue north on Route 1/113 past Dover Air Force Base. At Exit 95, where Route 1 and Route 113 split, stay to the right in order to follow Route 113 north toward Dover. After passing an intersection with Route 10, go 2 miles, then turn left onto Court Street. Follow Court Street 0.6 mile straight across Route 13 and past Legislative Hall to an intersection with Legislative Avenue. Continue straight one block on Duke of York Street. Cross Federal Street and go straight into the driveway for the **Delaware State Visitor Center** and **Sewell C. Biggs Museum**.

To Dover from Salisbury: Follow Route 13 north. On the outskirts of Dover, cross Route 10. Continue 3.4 miles, then turn left onto Court Street toward historic downtown Dover. (If you pass Loockerman Street or Route 8, you have gone too far.) Follow Court Street 0.4 mile to an intersection with Legislative Avenue next to Legislative Hall. Continue straight one block on Duke of York Street. Cross Federal Street and go straight into the driveway for the **Delaware State Visitor Center** and **Sewell C. Biggs Museum**.

To Dover from the Delaware and Maryland seashore resorts: Take either Route 1 or Route 113 north to the point where they merge near Milford, and from there continue north on Route 1/113 toward Dover. (As you approach Dover, you will pass **Barratt's Chapel** and — 5.4 miles north of it — Route 9 near the **John Dickinson Plantation**, the **St. Jones Preserve**, and the **Dover Air Force Base Museum**. Obviously, it may be convenient to stop by these places now rather than return to them later. See Map 9 on page 69.)

For historic downtown Dover and the Delaware State Visitor Center, continue north on Route 1/113 past Dover Air Force Base. At Exit 95, where Route 1 and Route 113 split, stay to the right in order to follow Route 113 north toward Dover. After passing an intersection with Route 10, go 2 miles, then turn left onto Court Street. Follow Court Street 0.6 mile straight across Route 13 and past Legislative Hall to an intersection with Legislative Avenue. Continue straight one block on Duke of York Street. Cross Federal Street and go straight into the driveway for the **Delaware State Visitor Center** and **Sewell C. Biggs Museum**.

≈   ≈   ≈   ≈

SEEING DOVER: Map 8 on page 65 shows the historic district and government campus at the center of town. The best place to start sightseeing is the **Delaware State Visitor Center**, located on Federal Street at the intersection with Duke of York Street. The staff can answer any questions you may have about places and events; telephone (302) 739-4266. There are two exhibit galleries at the visitor center itself, and also a museum shop. You are, of course, welcome to park in the visitor center lot, but the limit is one hour, so you may be better off parking on the street, especially if you plan to tour the historic district on foot. The Visitor Center is open Monday through Saturday from 8:30 A.M. to 4:30 P.M and on Sunday from 1:30 to 4:30. It is closed state holidays.

Sharing the building with the Delaware State Visitor Center is the **Sewell C. Biggs Museum of American Art**. This mid-sized museum (fourteen galleries) emphasizes paintings, sculpture, furniture, and silver of the Delaware Valley region. The building itself consists of a modern wing appended to the former Kent County Levy Court House, built in 1858 as a fireproof structure to house government records. The museum is open Wednesday through Saturday from 10 A.M. to 4 P.M. and on Sunday from 1:30 to 4:30. It is closed Monday, Tuesday, and state holidays. Telephone (302) 674-2111.

While you are at the Delaware State Visitor Center, be sure to ask the staff about touring the nearby **State House**, which should be high on anyone's list of things to see in Dover. Built in 1792 as the Delaware Capitol, it was restored in 1976. Now a museum, the State House includes a court, legislative chambers (see page 54), the governor's room, and county offices as they appeared late in the eighteenth century. The State House is open Tuesday through Saturday from 10 A.M. to 4:30 P.M. and on Sunday from 1:30 to 4:30. It is closed Mondays and state holidays.

The staff at the Visitor Center can also help you by telephoning to **Woodburn**, a handsome Georgian house located on the King's Highway a few blocks north of downtown. Woodburn was built about 1790 on a ten-acre parcel at the outskirts of Dover, which at that time was still a small village clustered around The Green. Woodburn is now the governor's official residence. On weekdays, especially during summer and fall when there are few government-related events at

Major sites are identified on Map 8 and are discussed on pages 63, 66, and 68. The sites designated by small numbers on Map 8 are discussed briefly below. Most of these buildings are private and are not open to the public.

1 Rose Cottage at 102 S. State Street was built in the 1850s or early '60s by the Rev. Thomas Bradford in a style called Cottage Gothic that was, in part, an outgrowth of the Romantic Movement in literature and art. The house has shallow Tudor arches on the porch and ornamental bargeboards dripping from the gables and eaves. Active in real estate, the Rev. Bradford laid out the surrounding neighborhood, which has much Victorian architecture.

2 The John Bullen House at 214 S. State Street was constructed in the late 1770s by master-builder Bullen for himself. Showing Flemish bond brickwork, it is now occupied by the Delaware Made General Store. Visitors are, of course, welcome.

3 This corner site was the location of the Golden Fleece Tavern, where in 1787 the Delaware General Assembly, meeting "in convention" for purposes of Article VII, ratified the U.S. Constitution, making Delaware the first state to do so.

4 Built in 1728, the Ridgely House at 7 The Green is laid in Flemish bond with glazed headers. This is the oldest house on The Green.

5 The two houses at 15 and 21 The Green were built in the mid-19th century. James Kirk, a printer, lived at #15 and did business at #21.

6 The Delaware Supreme Court Building at 55 The Green was constructed in 1909.

7 The Sykes Building at 45 The Green was the home of Dr. James Sykes, a state senator and Acting Governor of Delaware in 1801–02. The house was built in about 1812. With its flat, five-bay facade (in the main section) and minimum of ornamentation, it is an austere example of the Federal style.

8 The small building at 43 The Green is a late 18th-century remnant of the Bell Tavern complex, most of which stood just to the west at the corner with State Street.

9 The Kent County Courthouse was built in 1875 on a site occupied by an early courthouse and then, from 1723 to 1863, by the Bell Tavern.

10 The Century Club at 40 The Green was originally the Dover Baptist Church, built in 1852.

11 With its projecting central tower, mansard roof, dormers topped with pediments, and general decorative exuberance, The Wilds-Frame House at 34 The Green shows the Second Empire Style that was fashionable in the 1870s.

12 The Old Farmers Bank Building at 30 The Green occupies a site where a prior bank building opened in 1807.

13 Built about 1740 and remodeled in the 19th century, the house at 26 The Green was one of the homes of Caesar Rodney, leader during the Revolutionary period.

14 The Hughes Jackson House at 10 The Green was built in about 1860. Its symmetrical facade, tall windows, widely spaced cornice brackets arranged in pairs, and low-pitched, projecting hip roof are characteristic of the so-called Italianate style that was popular in the middle of the 19th century — and that is seen in a number of houses facing The Green.

15 The McDowell-Collins Store at 408 S. State Street was built in the early 19th century.

16 The Loockerman-Bradford House at 419 S. State Street was built in the mid-18th century in the Georgian style by Vincent Loockerman, a Dover merchant. The frame wing to the south was added in the 19th century. Sharing a party wall on the north side is 417 S. State Street, built in 1790 by John Bell II, whose family ran the tavern at State Street and The Green.

17 The King Dougall House at 426 S. State Street is typical of the establishments that lined State Street in the late 18th century. The larger section was Dougall's house; the smaller part to the north was his store.

18 The Richard Wilson House at 438 S. State Street was built in 1723. Richard Bassett, a signer of the U.S. Constitution and governor of Delaware from 1791 to 1801, lived here.

19 The John Banning House at 527-529 S. State Street was built in about 1766. Following the Revolution, Banning was treasurer of Delaware. During the 19th century, the house was the Dover Academy.

20 The Townsend Building (various state agencies).

21 The Hall of Records (visitors are welcome).

22 The Tatnall Building (offices of the governor and lieutenant governor).

23 Colonel John Haslet Armory.

24 The Jesse Cooper Building (vital statistics).

25 The Timothy Hanson House (circa 1730).

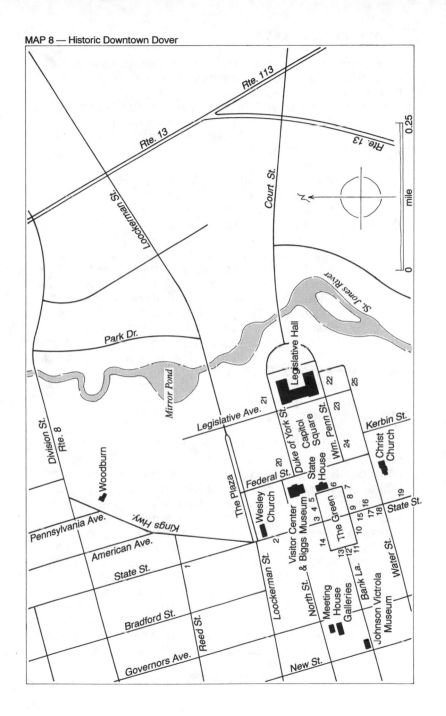

MAP 8 — Historic Downtown Dover

Woodburn, you may be able to tour the house on the spur of the moment. Alternatively, you can arrange in advance for a tour by calling (302) 739-5656.

At the center of Dover's historic district is **The Green**, laid out by order of William Penn in 1717. A walk around The Green, and also north and south for a few blocks along State Street, is well worthwhile. Some of the buildings are discussed briefly on page 64 in a format keyed to Map 8.

A block west of The Green are the **Meeting House Galleries** on Governors Avenue. One of these two buildings is a 1790 Presbyterian Church now containing exhibits on Delaware archaeology. The other is the church's 1880 Sunday school building, which contains the furnishings, tools, stock — in short, the complete paraphernalia — of four commercial establishments from the first decades of the twentieth century. There is a general store, a woodworker's shop, a drugstore, and a print shop. The Meeting House Galleries are open Tuesday through Saturday from 10 A.M. to 3:30 P.M. They are closed Sundays, Mondays, and state holidays.

Behind the Meeting House Galleries (and open on the same schedule) is the **Johnson Victrola Museum** at the corner of Bank Lane and New Street. Eldridge Reeves Johnson founded the Victor Talking Machine Company at Camden, New Jersey in 1901. Already he had been making wind-up, constant-speed motors for phonographic pioneer Emile Berliner, whose patents and business he bought. Johnson eventually had other factories in England and Germany and sales and distribution offices around the globe. The depiction of Nipper the dog peering into a Victrola horn became a world-famous trademark. It transcended technological progress, continuing in use even after amplifiers were shrunk and put inside the cabinets, and it is still in use today on compact disks. In the mid-1920s Victor started making plug-in, combination Electrolas-Radiolas. In 1929 — three years after Johnson retired — the company was bought by RCA, which was already supplying the radio components. Because Johnson had been raised and educated in Delaware, his son chose Dover as the site for a museum that he built in memory of his father and gave to the state. At the museum you can see a succession of Victor machines and hear them play old Victor records. For the best sound quality, ask the attendant to close the lid or cabinet doors.

About two blocks north of The Green on State Street is

Wesley United Methodist Church. Its congregation was organized in 1778, partly in response to the preaching of Freeborn Garrettson, a lay missionary whose powerful exhortations helped to spread Methodism in southern Delaware. Showing the Gothic Revival style, the present church was built in 1850 to replace the original structure, which stood at another site.

South of The Green on Water Street is **Christ Episcopal Church.** The central part — originally a simple, rectangular meeting house with the door in the middle of the south wall — was started in 1734 but not finished until the 1760s. For half a century after independence from England, the church deteriorated because of the loss of tax support and growing competition from Methodism. In 1840 Alfred Lee, the first Bishop of Delaware, wrote the local parish to say that during an upcoming visit he would prefer to preach in the State House or some other building rather than the church, which he had heard was a refuge for wild animals, including snakes. But in the second half of the nineteenth century, major repairs and renovations were made, including installation of the richly colored, neo-Gothic windows seen today. Yet other alterations were made in the early and mid-twentieth century.

Finally, east of the Delaware State Visitor Center is **Capitol Square**, around which are arranged many of the present-day state office buildings. The Capitol building or **Legislative Hall** was completed in 1933. It is open weekdays (except state holidays) from 9:30 A.M. to 4:30 P.M. To join a tour of Legislative Hall, telephone (302) 678-8724.

≈   ≈   ≈   ≈

OTHER SITES IN THE DOVER AREA: The places described below are shown on **Map 9** at right. In each case there are directions from the Delaware State Visitor Center in historic downtown Dover.

≈   ≈   ≈   ≈

The Delaware Agricultural Museum and Village is located just north of Dover on Route 13. The exhibits reflect farm life on the Delmarva Peninsula during the last 150 years, during which grain, peaches, produce, milk, and poultry have been leading commodities. Many old structures have been moved

MAP 9 — Dover area

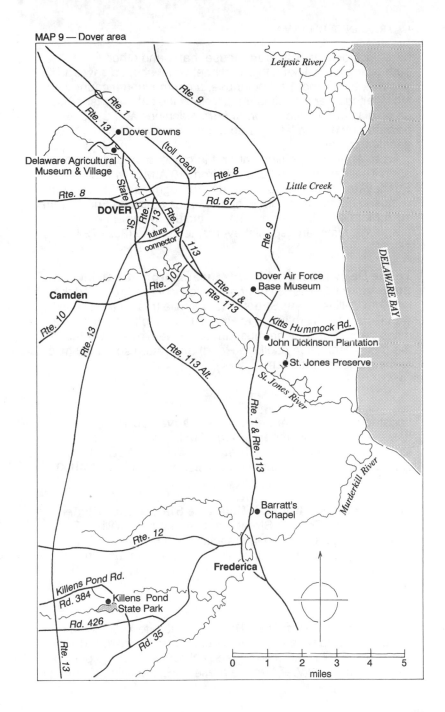

here, including an 1893 farmhouse, barn, and other outbuildings, a blacksmith and wheelwright shop, a saw and gristmill, a one-room schoolhouse, a church, and a country store, altogether providing a marvelous look at the past. Also on display are a succession of farm machines and devices powered by human labor, draft animals, steam engines, and gasoline motors.

From April through December, the museum and village are open Tuesday through Saturday from 10 A.M. to 4 P.M and on Sunday from 1 to 4. From January through March, the village is closed but the museum is open Monday through Friday from 10 A.M. to 4 P.M. For information, including current exhibits, programs, films, and special events, telephone (302) 734-1618.

To the Delaware Agricultural Museum from the Delaware State Visitor Center: Turn right onto Federal Street and then left onto William Penn Street. Go 0.5 mile to an intersection with Route 13. Turn left onto Route 13 and follow it north 2.2 miles. After passing the museum on the left, make a U-turn at the next intersection (College Road) and return south 0.2 mile to the museum entrance.

≈   ≈   ≈   ≈

Located north of Dover on Route 13, **Dover Downs** has harness racing November through April. And, yes, there are slot machines year-round. There is also one NASCAR race in June and another in September. Telephone (302) 674-4600 for information.

To Dover Downs from the Delaware State Visitor Center: Turn right onto Federal Street and then left onto William Penn Street. Go 0.5 mile to an intersection with Route 13. Turn left onto Route 13 and follow it north 2.4 miles, then turn right into the racetrack.

≈   ≈   ≈   ≈

The Dover Air Force Base Museum is located southeast of Dover off Route 9 near the intersection with Route 1/113. The aircraft on display include trainers, fighters, and cargo planes dating from World War II to the present. Especially poignant (if that adjective can apply to a bomber) is a B-17G Flying Fortress, carrying a crew of ten men squeezed on top of one another in the thin-skinned fuselage and Plexiglas turrets. Dover Air Force Base is open Monday through Saturday from 9 A. M. to 4 P.M. It is closed major holidays. On the first and third Friday and Saturday of each month, a giant C-5 Galaxy may be on hand and open for tour, if one is available. On the third Saturday during the period April through October, there are demonstrations of one kind or another. For information telephone (302) 677-5938.

To the Dover Air Force Base Museum from the Delaware State Visitor Center: Turn right onto Federal Street and then left onto William Penn Street. Go 0.5 mile to an intersection with Route 13. Cross Route 13 and then — after just 0.1 mile, turn right onto Route 113. Follow Route 113 south toward Milford 4.7 miles. At first stay right in order to avoid exiting at Route 10, but then move to the left lane to exit for Route 9. Go a hundred yards to Route 9 itself, then turn left and follow Route 9 north 0.7 mile to the entrance for the Dover Air Force Base Museum. Follow the signs 0.5 mile to the museum itself.

≈   ≈   ≈   ≈

The John Dickinson Plantation, administered by Delaware State Museums, is the childhood home of one of the leading figures of the Revolutionary period. The plantation is located southeast of Dover near the intersection of Route 9 and Route 1/113. The house was built in 1740 by Dickinson's father, Judge Samuel Dickinson, who with his second wife moved from Talbot County, Maryland after giving up his land there to the children of his first marriage. Samuel died in 1760 and is buried on the Dickinson Plantation. After part of the original house burned in 1804, John Dickinson rebuilt it. As an adult John lived in Philadelphia and later in Wilmington, but he called the plantation the Home Place. It was managed by a series of tenant-overseers whose rights and obligations were spelled out in elaborate leases. Dickinson also had five other farms along the St. Jones River, similarly leased. At the Home Place he reserved a few rooms for his own use during occasional visits to check on his properties. There are now a group of reconstructed outbuildings near the house, showing plantation life at the end of the eighteenth century. By then

Dickinson had freed his slaves, some of whom stayed on as small tenants receiving various privileges in exchange for specified work or goods.

The plantation is open Tuesday through Saturday from 10 A.M. to 3:30 P.M., and Sunday from 1:30 to 4:30. It is closed Mondays and state holidays, and also Sundays in January and February. In addition to the house and farm buildings, there is an excellent visitor center that provides background material. Costumed guides give tours, answer questions, and demonstrate farm tasks. For information telephone (302) 739-3277.

John Dickinson lived from 1732 to 1808. The son of well-to-do Quakers (though not, as an adult, an active Quaker himself), he was educated at home by his parents and a series of tutors. After studying law in England, he established a rich practice in Philadelphia. During the period leading up to the American Revolution, he became a leader of the conservative Whigs, who deplored British taxation and coercion and yet sought a peaceful settlement with the mother country. In 1765 Dickinson wrote a pamphlet opposing the Sugar Act and the Stamp Act, and he helped draft petitions to the king asking for relief. In response to the Townshend Acts in 1767, Dickinson supported the colonial non-importation agreements, and he wrote his *Letters from a Farmer in Pennsylvania*, pointing out, in a respectful and loyal tone, that the customs duties imposed by Parliament were inconsistent with established English constitutional principles. The *Letters* made Dickinson one of the best-known men in the American colonies. A member of the First and Second Continental Congresses, he wrote many official documents, including the original draft of the Articles of Confederation. As chairman of the Pennsylvania Committee of Safety and Defense, he organized the commonwealth's first battalion of troops, and yet at the same time he worked until the last moment for reconciliation with England on American terms. Although known now as "The Penman of the Revolution," Dickinson spoke passionately and courageously against adoption of the Declaration of Independence and refused to sign the document on the grounds that it would lead to a protracted war — in some ways a civil war — for which the colonies were not yet prepared militarily or financially. After briefly retiring to Delaware, Dickinson served as an officer in the local militia and was eventually commissioned a brigadier general. In 1779 Delaware returned him to Congress, and the next year he served as Governor of Delaware, and after that as Governor of Pennsylvania for four years. A champion of the rights of the smaller states, he represented Delaware to the Annapolis and Philadelphia conventions in 1786 and '87, where during the Constitutional debates he advocated creation of the Senate to counterbalance the House of Representatives. After the framers approved the federal Constitution, Dickinson (signing himself "Fabius") wrote articles urging its adoption by the states, as was done first by Delaware.

To the John Dickinson Plantation from the Delaware State Visitor Center: Turn right onto Federal Street and then left onto William Penn Street. Go 0.5 mile to an intersection with Route 13. Cross Route 13 and then — after just 0.1 mile, turn right onto Route 113. Follow Route 113 south toward Milford 4.7 miles. At first stay right in order to avoid exiting at Route 10, but then move to the left lane to exit for Route 9. Go a hundred yards to an intersection with Route 9 itself, and there continue straight on Kitts Hummock Road. After just 0.2 mile, turn right into the plantation.

≈   ≈   ≈   ≈

The St. Jones Preserve provides an opportunity to walk through farmland, marsh, and woods bordering the St. Jones River — although during the hunting season, you may find the entrance at Kitts Hummock Road closed. The mile-long River Trail starts at the parking lot and ends at a late seventeenth-century house called Kingston-Upon-Hull on the bank of the river, where there was once a landing for shipping out crops. At the end of the eighteenth century, this property was one of six farms, altogether totaling about 3,500 acres, owned by John Dickinson between Dover and the mouth of the St. Jones. You may be able to pick up a guidebocklet to the River Trail at the Dickinson Plantation visitor center, but in any case the route is self-evident. Particularly interesting is the trail's first quarter mile, which crosses a marshy arm of the St. Jones River on a long boardwalk.

To the St. Jones Preserve from the Delaware State Visitor Center: Turn right onto Federal Street and then left onto William Penn Street. Go 0.5 mile to an intersection with Route 13. Cross Route 13 and then — after just 0.1 mile, turn right onto Route 113. Follow Route 113 south toward Milford 4.7 miles. At first stay right in order to avoid exiting at Route 10, but then move to the left lane to exit for Route 9. Go a hundred yards to an intersection with Route 9 itself, and there

continue straight on Kitts Hummock Road. After 0.6 mile, turn
right and follow the entrance road to the parking lot and
trailhead.

≈   ≈   ≈   ≈

Barratt's Chapel is located about 11 miles southeast of Dover
on Route 1/113. Shortly before the American Revolution,
Methodism began to spread from England to America. Sent by
John Wesley, a few ordained Anglican clergymen of the
Methodist persuasion came to the colonies and gained
adherents by speaking in private houses and in the open. The
Methodist message was spread also by lay preachers,
especially after the outbreak of war prompted all the Methodist
clergy except the Rev. Francis Asbury to return to England.

In 1780 the Methodist Society of Kent County, Delaware built
a meeting house on land donated by Philip Barrett. Four years
later, after the Revolutionary War was over, Wesley sent the
Rev. Thomas Coke to find Asbury and to organize Methodism
in the new nation. At Barratt's Chapel on November 14, 1784,
Coke and Asbury met during a service attended by a thousand
people who overflowed the building. After the service the two
leaders made plans for a conference that was convened a few
weeks later near Baltimore to found the Methodist Episcopal
Church. By 1800 Methodism was the leading religion on the
Delmarva Peninsula.

Barratt's Chapel, a simple, handsome structure shown at left,
is now a museum. It is open Saturday and Sunday from 1:30
to 4:30 P.M.

**To Barratt's Chapel from the Delaware State Visitor
Center:** Turn right onto Federal Street and then left onto
William Penn Street. Go 0.5 mile to an intersection with Route
13. Cross Route 13 and then — after just 0.1 mile, turn right
onto Route 113. Follow Route 113 south toward Milford 10.3
miles. At first stay right in order to avoid exiting at Route 10,
but eventually move left in order to cross to the chapel on the
far side of Route 113.

≈   ≈   ≈   ≈

Killens Pond State Park is located about 12 miles south of
Dover. Trails, including a 2.6-mile circuit around the pond, are

shown on **Map 10** at right. You can get started by taking the Pondside Nature Trail from the main parking lot. Although this trail is not always within sight of the water, you should have no difficulty walking around the pond.

Killens Pond State Park is open daily year-round from 8 A.M. to sunset. Dogs must be leashed. Park facilities include water slides, ball fields, rental cabins, and a campground. The park is administered by the Delaware Department of Natural Resources and Environmental Control, Division of Parks and Recreation; telephone (302) 284-4526 for information.

To Killens Pond State Park from the Delaware State Visitor Center: Turn right onto Federal Street and then left onto William Penn Street. Go 0.5 mile to an intersection with Route 13. Turn right onto Route 13 and follow it south 12.3 miles, then turn left onto Killens Pond Road. Go 1.2 miles, then turn right into Killens Pond State Park and follow the entrance road 0.7 mile to a large parking lot.

MAP 10 — Killens Pond State Park

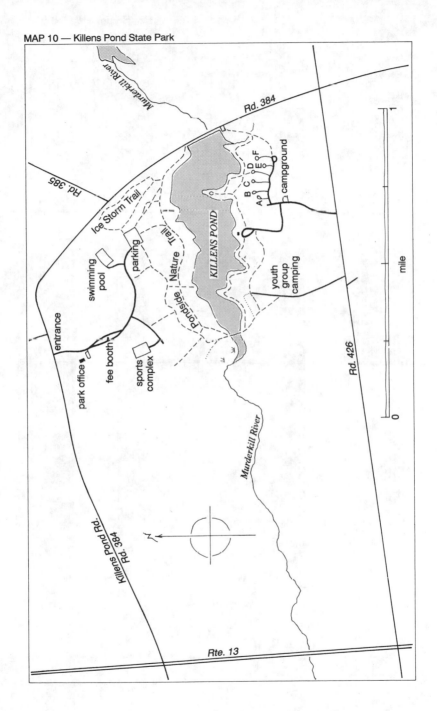

5

CHESTERTOWN
CHESAPEAKE FARMS
ROCK HALL
EASTERN NECK NATIONAL WILDLIFE
REFUGE

The 60-mile car tour outlined on **Map 12** on page 88 links the chief points of interest in southwestern Kent County, Maryland. **Chestertown**, the county seat, is an old port far up the Chester River. Its historic district retains nearly two dozen eighteenth-century houses, and its High Street and side streets have many restaurants and specialty shops. **Map 11** on page 85 provides an architectural overview. The town's main annual celebration is the Tea Party Festival, held on the Saturday of Memorial Day weekend. Another big occasion is the Chestertown Wildlife Exhibition and Sale at the end of October. For information on house tours, see page 87.

Several of Chestertown's historic buildings are open throughout the year. **The Geddes-Piper House**, now the headquarters of the Historical Society of Kent County, is open Monday from 9 A.M. to 3 P.M. and Wednesday and Thursday from 9 A.M. to noon. During the period May through October, the house is also open on Saturday and Sunday from 1 to 4 P.M. Telephone (410) 778-3499 for information. The **White Swan Tavern** at 231 High Street is a meticulously restored eighteenth-century inn now providing bed-and-breakfast accommodations and a very pleasant Afternoon Tea from 3 to 5 daily; telephone (410) 778-2300. Built in 1903, the **Imperial Hotel** at 208 High Street is another outstanding example of historic restoration, with a much-praised restaurant; telephone (410) 778-5000.

On the way from Chestertown to Rock Hall is the 3,300-acre **Chesapeake Farms**, where the DuPont Corporation researches and showcases techniques for sustainable agriculture and wildlife management; telephone (410) 778-8400. **Map 13** on page 89 shows the self-guided tour road, which is open from February 1 through October 10, although sometimes the road remains closed late into spring because of snow or excessively wet conditions.

Rock Hall, with its several boat basins, is a center for commercial fishing and recreational yachting. (See **Map 14** on page 91.) The modest **Rock Hall Museum** is open Wednesday, Thursday, Friday, and Sunday from 2 to 4:30 P.M. and on Saturday from 10 A.M. to noon. The **Waterman's Museum** is open daily from 10 A.M. to 6 P.M.

And finally, south of Rock Hall is **Eastern Neck Island**, a major wildlife refuge providing good walking and excellent bird watching, especially for waterfowl during fall and winter. Roads and trails are shown on **Map 15** on page 94. Bicyclists may enjoy riding on the 4.5 miles of roads within the refuge; other possibilities for bicycling are described at the beginning of the tour directions on page 87. The refuge is open daily from 7:30 A.M. (or earlier for the trails at the island's northern end) to half an hour after sunset; dogs must be leashed. **Please note** that from mid-September through November, the refuge occasionally is closed on Monday or Friday to permit hunting in order to control the deer population. Eastern Neck National Wildlife Refuge is managed by the U.S. Fish and Wildlife Service; telephone (410) 639-7056.

CHESTERTOWN WAS FOUNDED in 1706, when nine port commissioners, appointed by the colonial governor, purchased 100 acres and laid out the streets of the new town (originally called, in fact, New Town) around the Kent County courthouse, which had already existed there since 1698. During the eighteenth century, Chestertown became a prosperous port and one of Maryland's leading municipalities, surpassed in population only by Annapolis and, about two decades before the Revolution, by Baltimore. Chestertown's more successful merchants built substantial — and in some cases magnificent — houses fronting on the river from which the town derived its name and reason for being.

The Chester River reaches far inland to the heart of a rich agricultural region, where by the mid-1700s wheat and corn and corn-fed livestock were replacing tobacco as the chief exports. The river carried ships that sailed directly to and from Great Britain and more particularly the West Indies, where sugar so dominated the economy that most food for the

Caribbean plantations was imported. During the latter 1700s, Chestertown became the center of Maryland's West Indies trade, exchanging grain and salt pork for sugar, molasses, rum, salt, and that rarest of commodities in the tidewater region, cash, chiefly in the form of Spanish coins. Either individually or in partnerships, Chestertown's leading merchants acquired locally-built ships suitable for coastal trade southward to the Caribbean or northward to New England, which was another major market for Eastern Shore grain. And through Chestertown passed one of the main roads used by travelers going up and down the Atlantic seaboard. The route led north by post road across Delmarva to Wilmington and Philadelphia, and south by packet sailing from nearby Rock Hall to Annapolis.

By the standards of eighteenth-century Maryland, Chestertown was not only a center of commerce but also a cosmopolitan center of culture. Horse races, hunts, fancy suppers, balls, amateur theatricals, and also dramatic and operatic performances by traveling companies were held there. The Kent County Free School was established in Chestertown in 1723. In 1782 Washington College was chartered, with a private endowment of £10,000.

A glimpse of Society as known to one well-connected Chestertown girl is provided by a letter, dated January 2, 1787, from Molly Tilghman to her friend Polly Pearse:

> There was a Ball the night after Christmas which was much indebted to the Majors of Queen Anne's, the formidable Clealand, the woeful looking Emory and the handsome Smyth. Mrs. Galloway flashed upon them in her Muslin attended by her admiring spouse in his Rock of Gibraltar Coat. They had 16 couple and spent a very agreeable Evening. The play came next night which afforded a few unexpected incidents. Some Bucks of true spirit which was increas'd by good Liquor, broke open one of the Windows to the great dismay of the Ladies. As to the Play, it exceeded no one's expectations. However, the Eyes of the Audience were oblig'd by a vast display of fine Cloaths and Jewels, which more than made up for any faults in the acting. [One player] really looked very handsome, he wore Mat Tilghman's white sattin waistcoat &c, a black star brilliant with paste and fourteen black and white feathers. Last night it was again repeated with the addition of the Irish Widow. The Ball gave such a spring to the Spirit of our Beaux they have made up a Subscription for Assemblies and the first is to be to-morrow night.

Revealing a rather different perspective on these and other doings in Chestertown is a 1786 diary entry of the Rev. Francis Asbury, who had arrived in America as an itinerant Methodist missionary in 1771 and had, by the end of the Revolution, become the leader of Methodism in the new nation: "I preached . . . in the afternoon and at night in

Chestertown. I always have an enlargement in preaching in this very wicked place." The Methodists at Chestertown were proud of the fact that their brick meeting house, which was built at the beginning of the nineteenth century and still stands today (but is not used as a church), occupied a position equal in prominence to the Episcopal Church on the other side of the town square.

Although not in the vanguard of Maryland's resistance to the British taxes and coercion that led up to the Revolution, Chestertown was not far behind, especially when viewed in the context of the conservative Toryism that characterized much of the Delmarva Peninsula. Because British restrictions on the wheat trade threatened, or at least dampened, the prosperity of wheat growers and exporters, Chestertown was predisposed toward independence. And like nearly all colonial ports, Chestertown opposed the duty on tea. In an action modeled on the Boston Tea Party, a group of Chestertown citizens boarded the brigantine *Geddes*, belonging to Collector of Customs William Geddes, on May 13, 1774, and emptied its tea into the river. (In Annapolis a tea ship was burned by a screaming mob.) At about the same time some of the leading men of Kent County shared the cost of sending a cargo of flour to the people of Boston, whose port had been declared closed by act of Parliament until such time as the city paid for the tea dumped there.

During the Revolution, the Rev. Samuel Keene of what is now Chestertown's Emmanuel Episcopal Church was one of a very small minority of Anglican clergymen in Maryland who took the oath of allegiance to the new government. In 1780, however, after only one year as rector, he resigned his position because his parishioners failed to pay his annual salary of eight hundred bushels of wheat. (Before the Revolution, the church had been supported by a yearly head tax of five pounds of tobacco.) Keene's place was taken by the Rev. William Smith, who previously had been the first Provost of the College of Philadelphia, now the University of Pennsylvania. At Chestertown, Smith not only founded Washington College but also convened a meeting to reorganize Anglicanism in the former colonies. The name Protestant Episcopal Church of America was adopted, and the work of reorganization was subsequently carried forward by a state convention of which Smith was president. However, proposals that the Christian religion receive tax support as had the established Church of England were rejected by the Maryland legislature.

After the Revolution, the rise of Baltimore as a major international port led to a corresponding decline at other tidewater towns of the upper Chesapeake. Baltimore had ample waterpower for industry and for milling flour. Its growth was fueled by proximity to a vast agricultural hinterland to the west and north and by water access to the world. The effect on Chestertown was the same as elsewhere in Maryland: the town's economic horizons shrank until they extended no farther than Baltimore, to which Kent County's agricultural products were sent by small sloops and later by steamboat. Following the Civil War, which saw a Union garrison occupy Chestertown and men from Kent County fighting for opposing sides, the railroad reached Chestertown from the north, and since then much of the town's commerce has been channeled through Wilmington and Philadelphia.

Today the town remains what it has been for nearly two centuries: the seat of local government, a quiet college town, a regional retailing center with some manufacturing, and a place for transshipping farm products and supplies. It has, too, a well-to-do population of retirees and weekend residents.

≈　　≈　　≈　　≈

AUTOMOBILE DIRECTIONS: Chestertown is located in northern Delmarva on the Chester River. (See **Map 1** on page iv in the Table of Contents.) The car tour to Rock Hall and Eastern Neck shown on **Map 12** on page 88 starts at Chestertown, so you should go there first.

To Chestertown from northernmost Delmarva and from Interstate 95 near Newark, Delaware: From I-95 take Route 896 south across Route 40 and over the Chesapeake and Delaware Canal. From there, follow Route 301 south, passing straight through an intersection where Route 896 bears left. In all, follow Route 301 south into Maryland for about 24 miles to the intersection with Route 544. (You will know that you are drawing near this intersection after passing Route 291.) Turn right (west) onto Route 544 toward Chestertown and go 9.2 miles to a T-intersection with Route 213. Turn right (north) onto Route 213 toward Chestertown and go 1.9 miles across the Chester River and into Chestertown itself. Turn left onto Route 289 (Cross Street) at the first traffic light. Go two blocks to the intersection with High Street next to the town square.

To Chestertown from the Chesapeake Bay Bridge: After crossing the bridge, follow Route 50/301 across Kent Island. At the point where Route 50 and Route 301 split, continue straight on Route 301 northbound for 5.8 miles to the exit for Route 213 north toward Centreville. From the top of the ramp,

1 Built in the 1740s, the Custom House reflects Chestertown's status as a colonial port of entry. It features Flemish bond brickwork and glazed headers on the Water Street side.

2 This 1857 house on the corner is a fine example of an "Italian villa." Popular in the mid-19th century, the Italianate style is typified by such features as a full-width porch, side- and top-lighted door, hooded windows, corner pilasters, large cornice brackets, low-pitched, projecting hip roof, roof-top lantern, and overall symmetry.

3 The front part of this imposing house on the corner was built in the 2nd quarter of the 18th century. Thomas Ringgold, a wealthy merchant, added a rear section with grand stairs in 1767.

4 Pre-revolutionary Georgian house on the corner.

5 Late 18th-century house Victorianized in 1880s.

6 & 7 Originally a single residence (ca. 1743).

8 Frame house with brick end walls for the chimneys (2nd quarter of the 18th century).

9 Originally a single residence (ca. 1776-1796), this house has brick end walls like #8.

10 Simplified Italianate store (mid-19th century).

11 The fieldstone foundation and Flemish bond main section (ca. 1735-1750) reflect the age of this old and much-altered store/dwelling.

12 Imperial Hotel (1903).

13 Chester Theater (1928).

14 This Second Empire or Beaux Arts style corner building was built in 1886 by merchant/druggist Colin Stam for his business. The upper floors had rooms for public and private gatherings.

15 Italianate commercial building (pre-1877).

16 Bank building (1929) in Neo-Classic style.

17 White Swan Tavern (mid-18th century).

18 This late 19th-century storefront was the subject of litigation upholding the power of Chestertown's Historic District Commission to regulate external changes to buildings.

19 Volunteer firehouse (ca. 1908).

20 Railroad station (ca. 1905).

21 Former Methodist Church (1859).

22 Janes Methodist Episcopal Church (1914).

23 Showing a pair of arched, 2nd-floor windows typical of the Renaissance Revival style, this commercial building was erected after 1910, when most of its block burned.

24 The exuberant Queen Anne style popular at the end of the 19th century is seen in the roof zone of this building; the rest has been refaced.

25 This Italianate style residence (mid-1800s) has a bracketed cornice, corner pendants, hooded windows, and a full-width porch.

26 A "telescope" house, built in sections at different periods (mid-section is late 18th-century).

27 Tradesman's house (1771-1783).

28 A member of the wealthy Ringgold family built this house in the 2nd quarter of the 1700s.

29 Christ Methodist Church (1887) illustrates the "High Victorian" Gothic Revival style.

30 Like the neighboring church, this late 19th-century house shows Victorian Gothic traces.

31 Symmetrical residence (1877) with various 19th-century decorative features: hooded windows, bracketed eaves, hip roof, and ironwork.

32 Originally a public school (1901), this building strains the Colonial Revival style with its Palladian (tripartite) dormer windows, gambrel roof, Flemish bond brickwork, and stone trim.

33 The U.S. Post Office (1935) is in the Federal Revival style, with keystoned lintels, an elegant portico, and only a single -- yet tall -- story.

34 Former Methodist meetinghouse (1801-03).

35 Corner house (late 1700s or early 1800s).

36 Rockwell House, formerly a tavern, shows modest Italianate features (1850s).

37 Emmanuel Episcopal Church (1772) was built in the Georgian style, with the entrance at the center of a symmetrical five-bay facade facing High Street; it was greatly altered in the 1880s.

38 Italianate courthouse (1860) facing High Street.

39 Former Masonic Temple (early 1830s).

40 & 41 Just two of many offices on Lawyer's Row (second half of the 19th century).

42 Former shop, now an office (late 19th century).

43 The Geddes-Piper House (1780s) is home of the Historical Society of Kent County. At the time this impressive townhouse was built, the land around it was vacant.

44 Italianate house (ca. 1877) with slender pilasters, bracketed cornice, side-lighted door, and full-width porch popular in the mid-1800s.

45 Brick house in Flemish bond (ca. 1735-1750).

46 Mirror image of contemporaneous #44.

47 Front section dates from 1780s; rear ca. 1740.

48 John Nicholson, commander of the Continental sloop Hornet , built this house in the 1780s.

49 Much-altered house dating from the 1770s.

50 Simplified Italianate house (ca. 1867).

51 Former parsonage for Christ Methodist Church showing subdued Gothic elements (1896).

52 Blend of Gothic and Italianate details (ca. 1880).

53 Simplified Italianate house on corner (1860s).

54 Late 19th-century residence.

55 Queen Anne style corner house (mid-1880s), with varigated colors, textures, and materials.

56 Much-altered house dating from mid-1700s.

57 Late 19th-century features on ca. 1916 house.

58 The Frisby House (ca. 1766) was originally the only house on the town side of its Water Street block. The front wall is in all-header bond.

59 The front of this house is in all-header bond; the north wall in Flemish bond with glazed headers (2nd quarter of the 18th century).

60 Late 19th-century double residence with Colonial-Revival porches and other details.

61 Known as Watkins House, the land for this particularly old house was a wedding gift from the Ringgolds to their new son-in-law, Essau Watkins, in 1739. The brickwork is Flemish bond with glazed headers.

62 River House was built just after the Revolution and shows many elegant details, such as the high, stone-capped foundation and stone belt separating the first and second stories, Flemish bond brickwork on the street front, keystoned lintels, slender pilasters at the corners, and an elaborately carved cornice.

63 Built in about 1870, this house shows conservative Italianate features, such as a side- and top-lighted door, hooded windows, and a shallowly pitched roof with heavily bracketed eaves.

64 Built about 1796, this house was modified to fit the popular Italianate style in the mid-1800s.

65 Widehall (ca. 1770) was built by Thomas Smythe, a merchant and shipbuilder whose wealth is reflected in the generous proportions, all-header bond brickwork, large windows, and other fine details of his house. The flat, five-bay Georgian facade was conservative for a period when other mansions in bigger towns featured projecting entrance pavilions.

84

MAP 11 — Chestertown

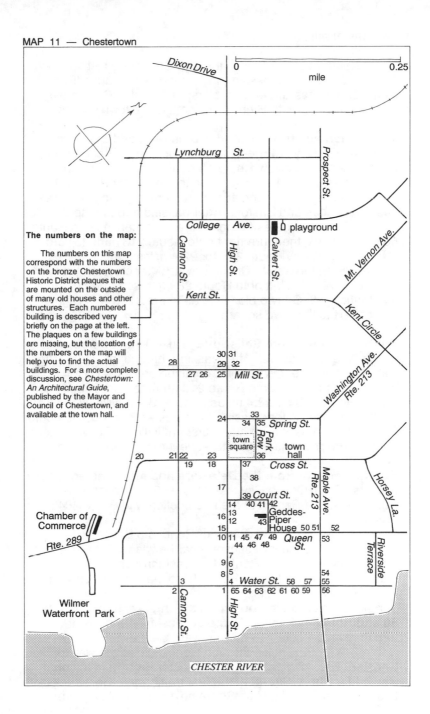

follow Route 213 for 18 miles through Centreville all the way to Chestertown. After crossing the Chester River, turn left onto Route 289 (Cross Street) at the first traffic light. Go two blocks to an intersection with High Street next to the town square.

To Chestertown from southern Delmarva and the Chesapeake Bay Bridge-Tunnel at Norfolk: After crossing the bridge-tunnel, follow Route 13 north into Maryland and past Pocomoke City and Princess Anne to the exit for Route 50 westbound near Salisbury, and from there take Route 50 west past Cambridge and Easton. After passing through the intersection with Route 404 near Wye Mills, continue on Route 50 for 1.5 miles, then turn right onto Route 213 north toward Centreville. Follow Route 213 for 22.4 miles through Centreville all the way to Chestertown. After crossing the Chester River, turn left onto Route 289 (Cross Street) at the first traffic light. Go two blocks to an intersection with High Street next to the town square.

To Chestertown from Salisbury: Take Route 50 west past Cambridge and Easton. After passing through the intersection with Route 404 near Wye Mills, continue on Route 50 for 1.5 miles, then turn right onto Route 213 north toward Centreville. Follow Route 213 for 22.4 miles through Centreville all the way to Chestertown. After crossing the Chester River, turn left onto Route 289 (Cross Street) at the first traffic light. Go two blocks to an intersection with High Street next to the town square.

To Chestertown from the Delaware and Maryland seashore resorts: From Ocean City take Route 50 west past Salisbury, Cambridge, and Easton to the intersection with Route 404 near Wye Mills.

Alternatively, from the vicinity of Rehoboth Beach, follow Route 1 north to the intersection near Lewes with Route 404 westbound, then follow Route 404 west through Georgetown and across Route 113 and Route 13 to the intersection with Route 50 near Wye Mills.

In either case, **once you are at the intersection of Route 50 and Route 404**, follow Route 50 west for 1.5 miles, then turn right onto Route 213 north toward Centreville. Follow Route 213 for 22.4 miles through Centreville all the way to Chestertown. After crossing the Chester River, turn left onto Route 289 (Cross Street) at the first traffic light. Go two blocks to an intersection with High Street next to the town square.

≈   ≈   ≈   ≈

TOURING CHESTERTOWN ON FOOT: Use **Map 11** on page 85 to explore Chestertown. The most interesting part is High Street and its side streets between the river and Mill Street. The Historical Society of Kent County's **Geddes-Piper House** is located on Church Alley just off Queen Street, and the **White Swan Tavern** and **Imperial Hotel** are on Main Street between Queen and Cross streets. Most of the other old buildings noted on the map are private residences and so are not open to the public, but annually on the third Saturday in September many are included on a candlelight tour sponsored by the historical society. Similarly, on a Saturday in mid-December many houses are open to benefit a local educational charity; telephone the Kent County Chamber of Commerce at (410) 778-0416 for information on these and other local events. Flyers and brochures describing events and attractions (including music, theater, art exhibits, antique and crafts shows, lectures, and sports) are available at the Chamber of Commerce office in the old railroad warehouse at 400 South Cross Street, and also in the town hall on North Cross Street and at Scottie's Shoes and Newsstand at 307 High Street.

≈   ≈   ≈   ≈

CAR TOUR OF SOUTHWESTERN KENT COUNTY: This 60-mile car tour is shown by the bold line on **Map 12** on page 88. The route from Chestertown to Rock Hall is also good for bicycling, provided that you bear in mind that Route 289 at the beginning and Route 20 at the end are used by cars traveling at high speeds. Unfortunately, the side trip through Chesa-peake Farms is never open to bicyclists. I suggest that bicyclists return from Rock Hall to Chestertown via the same route along the Ricauds Branch and Pomona roads as they took on the way to Rock Hall, for a round trip of 30 miles. A shorter bicycle excursion is to start at Rock Hall and ride down to Eastern Neck Island and back on Route 445 for a round trip of 18 miles. Again, cars here go as fast as on any other open road, but because Route 445 dead-ends at Eastern Neck Island, traffic is usually light.

From the intersection of High Street and Cross Street in Chestertown, follow Cross Street (Route 289) south. Go 4.3 miles as the road leads past the train depot, along the Chester River, and through farmland. At an intersection where Route

MAP 12 — Car tour of southwesern Kent County

MAP 12 — Car tour of southwesern Kent County

CHESAPEAKE BAY

Rte. 298

Rte. 514

Rte. 213

Rte. 291

Caulks Field Rd.

Fairlee

Rte. 20

Chester-town

Rte. 21

St. Paul's Episcopal Church

Ricauds Branch - Langford Rd.

Airy Hill Rd.

Rte. 289

Sandy Bottom Rd.

Chesapeake Farms

Chesapeake Farms

Langford

Rte. 664

Pomona Rd.

Swan Creek

Rte. 445

Rte. 20

Rte. 446

West Fork

East Fork

Pomona

Rte. 661

Rock Hall

Rte. 288

Rte. 289

Rte. 445

Grays Inn Creek

Langford Creek

CHESTER RIVER

Corsica River

Eastern Neck National Wildlife Refuge

0   1   2   3   4   5
miles

Rte. 301

Kent Narrows

Rte. 50/301

Rte. 50

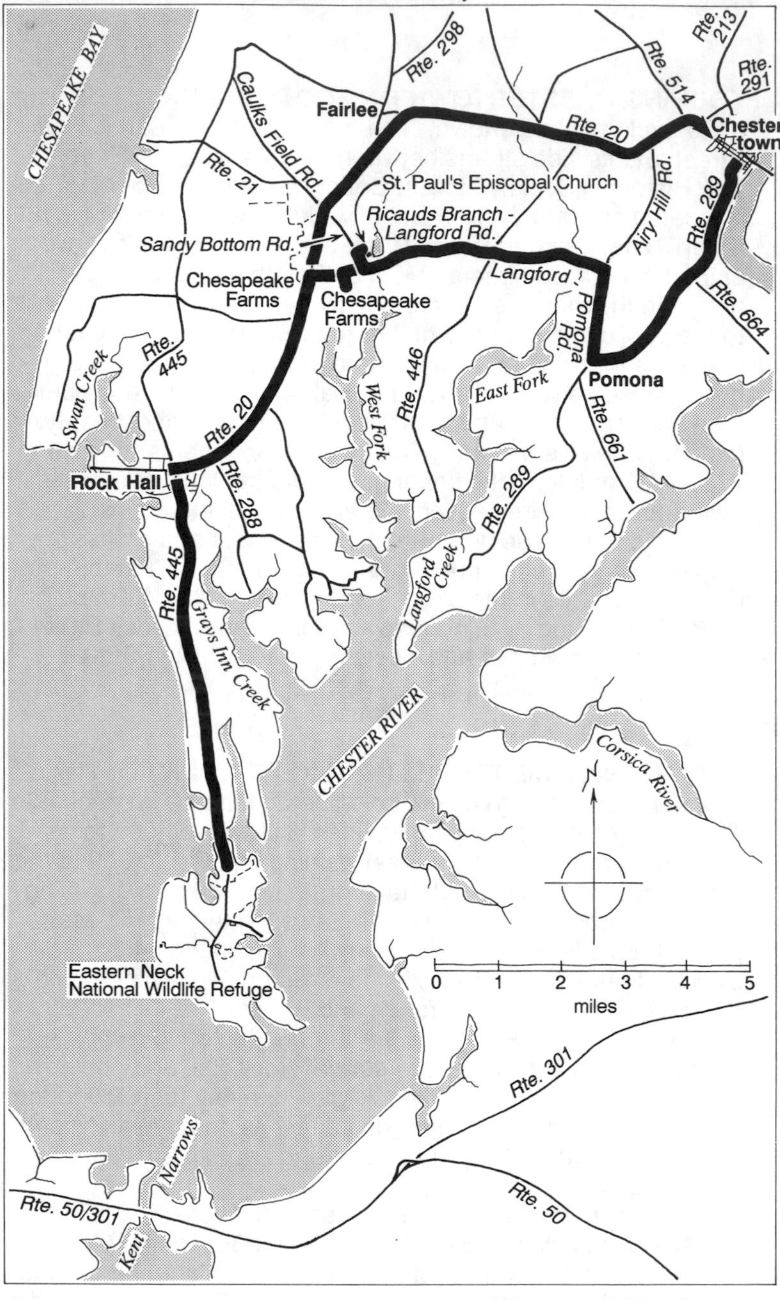

MAP 13 — Chesapeake Farms

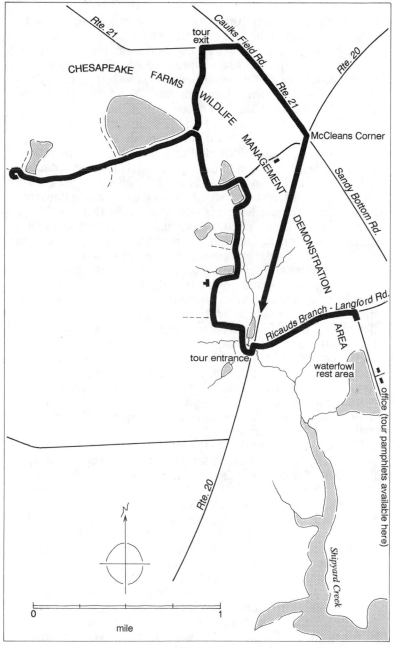

289 veers sharply left, turn right onto Pomona Road. After 1.4 miles, bear left to continue on Pomona Road where Airy Hill Road goes straight. Go 1.9 miles, then cross Route 446 and continue on Ricauds Branch Road. Go 2.3 miles, then turn right onto Sandy Bottom Road, which leads 100 yards to **St. Paul's Episcopal Church** on the right. The first church here was established in 1692; the present structure was built in 1713-15. Although you may find the church closed, the churchyard and cemetery are well worth visiting.

To continue toward Rock Hall on the car tour, return 100 yards to the intersection of Sandy Bottom Road and Ricauds Branch Road. Turn right and go only 0.3 mile, then turn left into **Chesapeake Farms**, which is open daily during daylight hours. Chesapeake Farms is operated by the DuPont Corporation to research and demonstrate how best to use its products in combination with different agricultural practices to produce good yields, low pollution, and better habitat for wildlife. From October through March, thousands of ducks and geese congregate on a pond to the right of the farm road, opposite the office. (During summer the pond is drained and the soil disced to reduce bacteria and the risk of waterfowl diseases.) From February 1 to October 10, a self-guided car tour leads past various habitats, each demonstrating different farming or wildlife management techniques. The 6-mile tour route is shown by the bold line on **Map 13** on page 89 and is further indicated by roadside signs. For an informative commentary keyed to numbered signs along the way, pick up a free tour pamphlet at the Chesapeake Farms office or at the entrance to the tour road.

To continue toward Rock Hall (or to take the Chesapeake Farms tour), turn left out the farm entrance and go 0.5 mile, then turn left onto Route 20. For the Chesapeake Farms tour, turn right immediately; at the end of the tour, you will return to this spot. For Rock Hall, continue straight 4 miles to the intersection of Route 20 and Route 445, and from there use **Map 14** at right to tour Rock Hall by car. The **Rock Hall Museum** is located in the municipal building on South Main Street (Route 445) and is open Wednesday, Thursday, Friday, and Sunday from 2 to 4:30 P.M. and on Saturday from 10 A.M. to noon. Displaying a potpourri of old photographs, tools, Indian artifacts, and other miscellaneous items, the museum has somewhat the atmosphere of the cluttered roadside curiosity shops that one sees here and there in Delmarva. The small but excellent **Waterman's Museum** at Haven Harbour

MAP 14 — Rock Hall

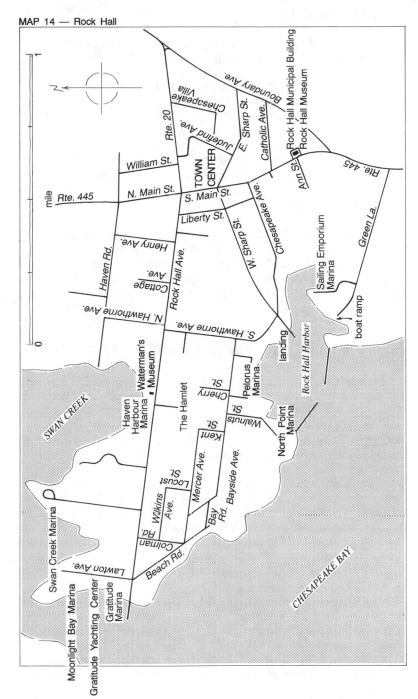

Marina (site also of the Ditty Bag) is located on Rock Hall Avenue and is open daily from 10 A.M. to 6 P.M. At Rock Hall Harbor are several seafood restaurants, including the Waterman's Crabhouse and Store at the Sharp Street wharf. At the intersection of South Main Street and Sharp Street, the America's Cup Cafe and Durdings Store define the center of town and show some of the attractive restoration that has occurred in Rock Hall. Just up Main Street is a used-book store with a courtyard of smaller stores behind it. A large antique shop is located on East Sharp Street opposite the fire house, and another antique shop is on South Main Street in the old parsonage next to Rock Hall United Methodist Church.

As noted above in the discussion on Chestertown, in the eighteenth century **Rock Hall** was the Eastern Shore terminus of a ferry sailing to and from Annapolis. Before the growth of Baltimore and the development of a good post road through Havre de Grace at the end of the century, the route through Rock Hall and Chestertown was a major line of travel between the North and the South. George Washington crossed the bay by the Rock Hall ferry several times, and his aide-de-camp Colonel Tench Tilghman (brother of Molly Tilghman, whose letter was quoted earlier) passed through Rock Hall on his way to Philadelphia to tell the Continental Congress of the British surrender at Yorktown.

Ever since the Chesapeake Bay oyster fishery boomed during the decades following the Civil War, Rock Hall has been — at least until recently — a community primarily of watermen. Large fleets of skipjacks worked the deep water and crowds of tong boats moored over the shallow oyster beds off Rock Hall. Seafood plants for processing and packing oysters, rockfish, crabs, and soft-shell clams lined the principal harbor, from which operated not only scores of independent watermen but also a charter fleet for recreational fishermen. Some people have even facetiously suggested that the town's name derives from the abundance of rockfish hauled ashore there. (More plausibly, the name is thought to be derived from a colonial manor house called Rock Hall.)

As commercial fishing in Chesapeake Bay has declined, however, Rock Hall's waterfront packing houses and workboats have in large part been replaced by harborside condominiums and marinas filled with pleasure boats. The value of waterfront land for expensive residences, restaurants, and marinas has, in fact, become so great — and the fortunes of commercial fishing so relatively low — that in 1989 the state of Maryland felt compelled to buy one of the seafood packing plants fronting on Rock Hall's harbor in order to prevent the building from being sold for residential development. Now the state leases the building to a seafood processing company, so that Rock Hall's remaining watermen will still have a local market for their catch. October through March, the parade of oyster boats returning to Rock Hall shortly after 3 P.M. is a fine sight. Clams are harvested year-round, crabs from April through November, and rock fish from late August through mid-November.

CAR TOUR continued (Map 12 — from Rock Hall to Eastern Neck National Wildlife Refuge): From the intersection of Route 20 and Route 445 in Rock Hall, follow Route 445 (Main Street) south 6 miles to the bridge leading to Eastern Neck Island. Use **Map 15** on page 94 to tour the national wildlife refuge.

At 2,285 acres, **Eastern Neck National Wildlife Refuge** is relatively small compared to the other national wildlife refuges of the Delmarva Peninsula. Nonetheless, its fields and numerous coves and ponds form an important feeding and resting place for migrating and wintering waterfowl. In particular, from October through March, thousands of Canada geese, mute and tundra swans, diving ducks and puddle ducks can be seen here, reaching a peak in November. Because of the diversity of habitat, including woods, hedgerows, farm fields, marshes, swamps, and shallows, a wide variety of other birds are also present during their appropriate seasons. Nesting species include bald eagles. A bird list of about 250 species seen at Eastern Neck is available at the refuge office.

May through September, picnicking and crabbing are permitted at the refuge's Ingleside Recreation Area. You may also want to consider renting a skiff from East Neck Boat Rentals just north of the refuge.

As noted by an historic marker at the southern end of the refuge road, Eastern Neck Island was the site of **Wickliffe**, the home of Major Joseph Wickes, who settled here in 1658. Wickes was a member of the provincial assembly, a justice of the peace, and ultimately Chief Justice of the Kent County Court, which sometimes met at Wickliffe.

WALKING AT EASTERN NECK ISLAND: As shown by **Map 15** on page 94, there are several short foot trails at the national wildlife refuge. None is very long, but taken altogether, these short trails add up to a highly satisfactory excursion.

Start at the **Tubby Cove Boardwalk**, which leads a few hundred yards to two observation towers, one of which is accessible by wheelchair. This and the vicinity of the bridge leading to Eastern Neck Island are the best spots from which to view waterfowl.

MAP 15 — Eastern Neck National Wildlife Refuge

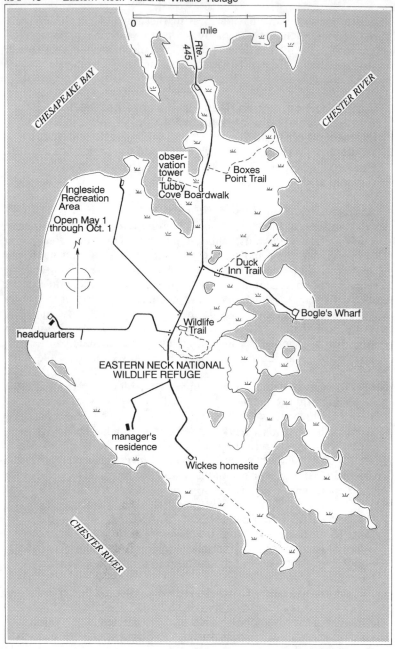

The Boxes Point Trail is 1.2 miles round-trip. Park in the Tubby Cove lot, then follow the refuge road 175 yards back toward the bridge. The trailhead is on the right.

The Duck Inn Trail is 1 mile round-trip. The trailhead is on the road leading to Bogle's Wharf. A parking lot is opposite the trailhead. The sleepy public landing at Bogle's Wharf, incidentally, was once a place where packet boats and steamboats called until as recently as 1924.

The Wildlife Trail is about 0.5 mile long. This circuit is the least interesting of the various Eastern Neck trails.

CAR TOUR continued (Map 12 — from Eastern Neck Island to Chestertown): From Eastern Neck Island, follow Route 445 for 6 miles back to Rock Hall. At the intersection with Route 20, turn right. Follow Route 20 for 13 miles to Chestertown, where the car tour ends.

≈　　≈　　≈　　≈

DIXON'S FURNITURE AUCTION near Chestertown is so large that it is almost a place — or at least an institution. The auction (which is by no means limited to furniture) occurs every Wednesday starting at 9 A.M. on the auction house grounds located east of Chestertown on Route 544 about half way between Route 213 and Route 301. (See **Map 1** on page iv in the Table of Contents.) Winning bidders must pay immediately in cash. Telephone (410) 928-3006.

6

HORSEHEAD WETLANDS CENTER

Located near the Kent Narrows in Maryland, **Horsehead Wetlands Center** is shown on **Map 16** on page 102. The Center comprises 310 acres of woods, meadow, marsh, and ponds. Special features include a collection of resident North American waterfowl, a visitor center, bird blinds that overlook several ponds, observation towers, and some short trails. Apart from the resident waterfowl, about two hundred species of birds have been seen here. This privately run wildlife refuge also rents canoes for exploring Marshy Creek just to the north. The Center is open daily (except Thanksgiving, Christmas Eve, Christmas Day, and New Year's Day) from 9 A.M. to 5 P.M. Pets are prohibited.

Horsehead Wetlands Center is managed by The Wildfowl Trust of North America, which is a non-profit corporation founded in 1979 and dedicated to education, conservation, and research. In 1981 the Trust purchased the Horsehead peninsula. For information about seasonal attractions and the Center's educational programs and special events, telephone (410) 827-6694 or (800) 226-8272. Or you can write to The Wildfowl Trust of North America, P.O. Box 519, Grasonville, MD 21638-0519.

Regarding the name "Horsehead," tilt Map 16 to the right.

THE RESIDENT WATERFOWL at Horsehead Wetlands Center provide the opportunity to see many birds up close. Under such conditions, plumage is the obvious way to tell one species from another. But in the wild, other traits are just as important, particularly when distance, haze, glare, twilight, or even molting obscure characteristic patterns of color. What follows, then, is a brief discussion of several key factors (in addition to plumage) that help to identify waterfowl in the wild. For a more comprehensive discussion of bird identification, see Chapter 8.

The distinction between dabblers and divers is basic to identifying ducks, and is in turn closely allied to habitat preference. Black ducks, gadwalls, pintails, wigeons, wood ducks, fulvous whistling ducks, shovelers, and several varieties of teal feed by dabbling at food that is floating on the surface of the water, or by upending their bodies in order to reach with their heads down to the bottom while their tails point in the air. Not surprisingly, dabblers prefer shallow marshes, ponds, and streams, and if that is the sort of environment where you are watching birds, you will know beforehand what species of ducks you are most likely to see. In contrast, redheads, canvasbacks, ring-necked ducks, scaup, goldeneyes, buffleheads, ruddy ducks, mergansers, scoters, and oldsquaws feed or escape from danger by diving, often to considerable depths. They are typically found on larger, deeper lakes, rivers, and bays. Harlequin ducks and eiders also feed by diving, and with oldsquaws, scoters, and red-breasted mergansers are seen along Delmarva's seacoast in winter. To complicate matters, however, many diving ducks breed in marshes, and most surface-feeders occasionally dive. You should also keep in mind that there are some strong divers that are not strictly classified as waterfowl, including loons, grebes, and cormorants, all of which may be seen along Delmarva's shores. Coots both dabble and dive, and gallinules feed on the surface.

The distinction between surface-feeding ducks and diving ducks is reflected in a few physical adaptations. Since diving requires more propulsive force than does dabbling or tilting in shallow water, divers typically have bigger feet than surface-feeders, and their legs are located nearer their tails. These adaptations make them strong swimmers but awkward on land. In contrast, the smaller feet of surface-feeders enables them to walk and run well on land, so that ducks seen feeding in farm fields are almost certainly surface-feeders (often mallards, pintails, or wigeons).

One easily observed difference between surface-feeding ducks and diving ducks has to do with the way that they take flight. Surface-feeders take off nearly vertically, seeming to jump from the water. Divers, however, are heavier in relation to their size, and in consequence they can only become airborne by first pattering along the surface for a considerable distance, like a seaplane gaining speed and taking off. An exception, however, is the bufflehead, a diver that jumps from the water like a surface-feeding duck.

In his booklet for bird watchers and hunters called *Ducks at a Distance*, naturalist Bob Hines outlines a checklist of identification traits to which observers can refer at different ranges. Even when ducks are far away, their flocking patterns on the water or in the air can be observed. For example, some species, such as wigeons, eiders, canvas-backs, redheads, and scaup, gather in large rafts on the water, especially during winter. When in flight, a few species (such as black ducks, mallards, pintails, and ring-necked ducks) are characterized by loose, random formations, while other species (such as gadwalls, wigeons, shovelers, teal, and scaup) usually fly in tight bunches. Mergansers and eiders fly in Indian file, low over the water, while canvasbacks and scoters fly in wavy lines and irregular V's, shifting back and forth between the two. During migration, many geese and swans, of course, fly in V formation.

Other characteristics of flight include various maneuvers that are typical of different species of waterfowl. For example, when descending to land, pintails zigzag down from high flight before leveling off near the surface of the water or the ground. Most ducks fly more or less straight, but flocks of wigeons, teal, scaup, and sometimes shovelers twist and turn irregularly as a unit, giving the impression of great speed as they fly low over the water or marsh. Although some species are, of course, swifter than others (canvasbacks are the fastest ducks), actual speed is hard to estimate and is not very useful in distinguishing one sort from another. But some ducks — the small ruddy duck, for example — beat their wings perceptibly faster than other species.

As with flight, idiosyncrasies of swimming distinguish certain waterfowl. The ruddy duck, which cannot walk on land, often swims with its tail cocked vertically. Mute swans typically swim with their necks held in an S-curve, whereas the posture of tundra swans tends to be more straight-necked. Among swimmers that are not strictly classified as waterfowl, coots and gallinules pump their heads back and forth while swimming. Common loons and cormorants float very low in the water, so that often it is difficult to see more than their heads and necks, with occasional glimpses of the top of their backs.

At mid-range it is sometimes possible, even in poor light conditions, to identify waterfowl simply by their silhouettes. For instance, unlike other ducks, pintails and oldsquaws have long needle-pointed tails; in addition, pintails have long, slender necks. Some profiles show highly distinctive features, like the disproportionately large, spatulated bills of shovelers or the swept-back crests of wood ducks and most mergansers. Of course, the long necks and great size of the various species of swans and geese seen in the Chesapeake region immediately distinguish them from all ducks. However, except for gross differences — as between the small ruddy ducks and teal at one extreme and the large, stocky eiders at the other — comparative size is of limited usefulness in identifying ducks.

As noted at the outset, plumage is basic to identification, but only if you have time to examine the birds in good light either up close or through binoculars or a telescope. Even then, plumage can be confusing due to the fact that nearly all ducks lose their body feathers twice each year. When drakes shed their bright plumage after mating and enter what is called eclipse, they resemble the comparatively drab females of the species for a few weeks before assuming a motley, messy look as they return to breeding plumage. After the summer molt, shovelers and blue-winged teal may remain in eclipse even into winter.

As outlined by Roger Tory Peterson in his *A Field Guide to the Birds*, patches of color on the wings are a particularly important aid to identification because ducks shed their wing feathers only once each year, and even then, wing colors remain constant. When the birds are flying, bold patterns of light and dark on either surface of the flapping wings may be conspicuous. For example, the contrasting pattern of a very dark body with flashing white wing linings helps to identify the black duck. In flight, the wigeon has a white *belly* and large white patches on each forewing, while the common eider has a white *back* and white forewings. And so on, in a manner that only much practice can master. Peterson's field guide includes a particularly good collection of black-and-white drawings showing how ducks appear in flight from below and from the side.

On a more detailed level, the upper side of a duck's wing features a great variety of smaller insignia. On most surface-feeding ducks, the speculum is a bright, often iridescent patch of color on the top trailing edge of each wing near where it joins the body. It provides a name, for example, to the green-winged teal. Unfortunately, shovelers and blue-winged teal (both of which show a pale blue patch on the *forward* edge of their wings) also have a green speculum. The speculum of black ducks is violet, gadwalls white, mallards blue, and pintails brown.

Even in pre-dawn darkness and other abysmal light conditions, some accomplished birders and hunters can identify waterfowl solely by their calls, although those of us who prefer to remain in bed may be tempted to dismiss such claims as just so much quackery. For what it is worth, I merely note here that different field guides employ an amazing variety of terms to describe duck calls, including *croak, peep, growl, grunt, twitter, purr, meow, moan, wheeze, squeak,* and *squeal*. Some authors are even given to mimicry. Hines, for example, has a rich vocabulary that starts with the basic *kwek-kwek* and goes on to *kack-kack, kaow, woh-woh, took-took, hoo-w-ett, cr-r-ek, squak, speer-speer,* and *kow-kow-kow-kow*. Clearly, however, something is lost in translation. For instance, while Hines hears oldsquaws, which are among the most vocal of ducks, say *caloo-caloo*, Peterson hears *ow-owdle-ow* and *owl-omelet* . This babble of ducktalk raises the issue of what the various species are perceived to say once they migrate northward into French-speaking Quebec province and southward into Mexico. (For a relevant discussion, see Noel Perrin's suggestively-titled "Old MacBerlitz Had a Farm," which appeared in the *New Yorker* for January 27, 1962.)

Finally, for one of the ultimate niceties in the truly enjoyable pastime of bird watching and bird identification, some authorities say that a few ducks (particularly goldeneyes, also called whistlers) can be identified just by the singing, swishing, or rushing sounds made by their wings.

$\approx$ $\approx$ $\approx$ $\approx$

AUTOMOBILE DIRECTIONS: Horsehead Wetlands Center is located in Maryland near the village of Grasonville, 6 miles east of the Chesapeake Bay Bridge and within sight of the high bridge over the Kent Narrows. (See **Map 1** on page iv in the Table of Contents.)

To Horsehead Wetlands Center from northern Delmarva and Interstate 95 near Newark, Delaware: From I-95 take Route 896 south across Route 40 and over the Chesapeake and Delaware Canal. From there, follow Route 301 south, passing straight through an intersection where Route 896 bears left. In all, follow Route 301 south into Maryland for about 47 miles to the merger with Route 50 just beyond Queenstown. After merging with Route 50, continue only 0.6 mile, then take Exit 45B. At the top of the exit ramp, turn left onto Winchester Creek Road toward Nesbit Road, then immediately turn left onto Nesbit Road toward Route 18. Go 0.3 mile, then at a T-intersection turn right (west) onto Route 18 toward Grasonville. Follow Route 18 for 1.6 miles, then turn left onto Perry Corner Road. Go 0.5 mile, then turn right into the entrance of the Wildfowl Trust's Horsehead Wetlands Center. Follow the road 1.1 miles to the parking lot.

To Horsehead Wetlands Center from the Chesapeake Bay Bridge: After crossing the Bay Bridge, follow Route 50/301 for 5 miles to and across the high bridge at the Kent Narrows, then take Exit 43B (the third exit after the Kent Narrows Bridge) for Chester River Beach Road. At the top of the exit ramp, turn right toward Route 18, then turn left (east) at a T-intersection onto Route 18 in Grasonville. Follow Route 18 east only 0.2 mile, then turn right onto Perry Corner Road. Go 0.5 mile, then turn right into the entrance of the Wildfowl Trust's Horsehead Wetlands Center. Follow the road 1.1 miles to the parking lot.

MAP 16 — Horsehead Wetlands Center

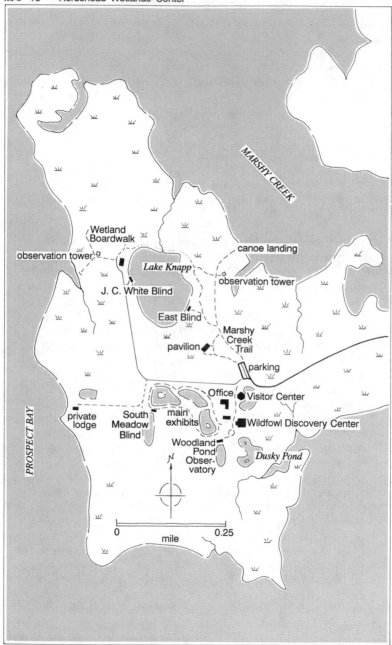

To Horsehead Wetlands Center from southern Delmarva and the Chesapeake Bay Bridge-Tunnel at Norfolk: Follow Route 13 north into Maryland and past Pocomoke City and Princess Anne to the exit for Route 50 westbound near Salisbury, and from there take Route 50 west through Cambridge and Easton. After passing through the intersection with Route 404 near Wye Mills, continue on Route 50 for 8 miles, then take Exit 45B (which is located immediately after the merger with Route 301). At the top of the exit ramp, turn left onto Winchester Creek Road toward Nesbit Road, then immediately turn left onto Nesbit Road toward Route 18. Go 0.3 mile, then at a T-intersection turn right (west) onto Route 18 toward Grasonville. Follow Route 18 for 1.6 miles, then turn left onto Perry Corner Road. Go 0.5 mile, then turn right into the entrance of the Wildfowl Trust's Horsehead Wetlands Center. Follow the road 1.1 miles to the parking lot.

To Horsehead Wetlands Center from Salisbury and the Delaware and Maryland seashore resorts: Follow Route 50 or Route 404 west to the intersection of these two roads near Wye Mills. From there continue west on Route 50 for 8 miles, then take Exit 45B (which is located immediately after the merger with Route 301). At the top of the exit ramp, turn left onto Winchester Creek Road toward Nesbit Road, then immediately turn left onto Nesbit Road toward Route 18. Go 0.3 mile, then at a T-intersection turn right (west) onto Route 18 toward Grasonville. Follow Route 18 for 1.6 miles, then turn left onto Perry Corner Road. Go 0.5 mile, then turn right into the entrance of the Wildfowl Trust's Horsehead Wetlands Center. Follow the road 1.1 miles to the parking lot.

≈   ≈   ≈   ≈

WALKING AND BIRD WATCHING AT HORSEHEAD WETLANDS CENTER: The Center's buildings, ponds, trails, and other features are shown on **Map 16** at left.

After stopping by the **Visitor Center** and **Wildfowl Discovery Building,** and after touring the nearby ponds and resident **Wildfowl Exhibits,** you may want to wander farther afield. As shown on Map 16, two blinds overlook Lake Knapp at the center of the refuge. The **J. C. White Blind** and the **Wetland Boardwalk** are reached by a rutted road leading west. The **East Blind** is reached by the **Marshy Creek Trail,** which ends at the canoe landing near an observation tower.

7

WYE ISLAND

Linked to the mainland by a short bridge, **Wye Island Natural Resources Management Area** in Maryland consists of 2,450 acres of farmland and woods to which the public is welcome for low-impact activities like picnicking (no fires, however), hiking, and fishing. The island is shown on **Map 17** on page 113. One of the island's chief attractions is the rare opportunity to rove through an agricultural landscape, skirting tilled areas and a few waterfowl sanctuaries that are posted as off limits. If you have a field dog, or perhaps yourself have the ranging, searching instincts of a field dog, here you can have a field day. (But first please read the note about **hunting** at the bottom of page 115). For those, however, who prefer well-defined paths, there are three trails (none longer than 1.5 miles round-trip), plus a dirt road through the western half of the island that provides up to 6 miles (round-trip) of excellent walking. If you have a fat-tired bicycle that can handle the sometimes loose, gravelly surface, the road is good for bicycling, too. Bicyclists may also enjoy riding on Carmichael Road, Cheston Lane, and Stagwell Road, which pass through an attractive farmscape immediately to the north of Wye Island. Although traffic on these dead-end roads is likely to be light, bicyclists should still be prepared for cars traveling at high speeds.

Wye Island is open all day year-round. Camping, however, is prohibited, except by youth groups. The island is managed by the Maryland Department of Natural Resources, primarily to provide wildlife habitat and for agricultural experimentation in conjunction with the University of Maryland's nearby Wye Research and Education Center. For inquiries about Wye Island, telephone (410) 827-7577.

WYE ISLAND shows the Eastern Shore of Maryland at its best. Located in an area of historic plantations and large farms, the island consists mainly of cultivated fields separated by hedgerows, woodlots, and the arms of tidal creeks. There is nothing spectacular here, just a mellow, quiet beauty that fortunately has been preserved by public acquisition of the area in 1976, just as the eastern third of the island (the part comprising William Paca's Wye Hall Farm) was being sub-divided into thirty-five pieces ranging in size from fifteen to seventy-five acres. Some of these parcels were in fact sold and remain in private ownership, as is evident from a few large houses that have been built.

Along Carmichael Road on the way to Wye Island are several his-toric markers noting that English settlement in this area dates back to the mid-1600s. Not for a moment, however, should it be thought that the mature agricultural landscape seen today in any way resembles the Maryland of that time, when the Chesapeake region was one of the frontiers of the New World and its English inhabitants were essentially pioneers in a wilderness, all growing one crop — tobacco — for export to Great Britain.

The vast majority of tobacco planters in seventeenth-century Mary-land were men of modest means, each cultivating a few acres cleared from the woods that covered all of the region's arable land to the water's edge. Every planter tried to acquire as much land as he could at his first patent, and the size of most early plantations substantially exceeded the fifty-acre headright quota, but the land actually cultivated was far less. Three acres of tobacco was about the upper limit for even the hardest worker. Settlers who had capital at the time of their immi-gration brought with them indentured laborers (termed "servants") with whom to claim more land and to cultivate larger fields. Still other freemen who worked alone or with their sons used the profits from their first successful harvests to acquire more land and indentured servants as quickly as possible. Some seventeenth-century writers condemned the system of indenture, but others agreed with one observer who wrote, "The work of their servants and slaves is no other than what every common freeman does." Another observer similarly noted that many masters and their sons worked alongside their bondsmen.

More than three-quarters of the immigrants to the Chesapeake region in the 1600s came as indentured servants, required by their contracts (called articles of indenture) to work for a number of years in exchange for having their passage to the New World paid by merchant recruiters, who then sold the servants to planters who could afford them. Some recruiters dealt in servants on a large scale, but most servants were transported by numerous merchants and mariners primarily engaged in other business and who had perhaps been requested by their agents and customers in the Chesapeake region to supply a few indentured labor-ers. Even if no such request had been received, merchants and ship masters knew that transporting a bondservant for resale in Maryland or Virginia was a safe speculation. In this way, even many of the smaller planters of the tidewater region acquired one or two indentured servants. Eventually, the system of indenture became so commonplace that local statutes governed the practice in cases where there were no individualized contracts. Typically, upon completion of his or her term of servitude (often five years for adults, longer for minors), each servant was paid freedom dues consisting of various items, such as new clothes, tools, and even land early on when ample land was still available. For women, the end of their indenture meant marriage to their pick of a multitude of suitors (men outnumbered women by nearly three to one) and in all probability the continuation of a workaday life not unlike what they had known as servants. For men the end of servitude meant the opportunity to set up for themselves as small tobacco planters.

The flow of indentured immigrants to Maryland and Virginia in the mid-1600s reflected depressed economic conditions in England. A variety of factors — rapid population growth, the consolidation of farms and their conversion from cultivated fields to pasture and orchards, and finally the disruption in commerce caused by the Thirty Years War and the English Civil War — all combined to create widespread unemployment in England. In consequence, many young people, mostly with family backgrounds in farming and textile manu-facture, and mostly between the ages of fifteen and twenty-four, chose to go as indentured servants to the Chesapeake region, where there was at least the certainty of gainful employment and the touted prospect of becoming planters after their servitude was over.

From the 1630s through the 1650s, when tobacco prices were high and free land was available, many indentured laborers who had com-pleted their terms of servitude did indeed manage to set up immediately as small growers on good land. But by 1660, or somewhat later in the remote regions of Maryland's lower Eastern Shore, most land suitable for growing tobacco had already been claimed and so became some-thing that had to be purchased from a prior owner. Under these less favorable circumstances, some newly-freed indentured servants took up less desirable land that did not offer much opportunity for economic advancement. Other former servants often got a start by tenant farming for established landowners — perhaps even their former masters — before eventually accumulating the means to become freeholders in their own right. Still others became hired workers or sharecroppers, typically living as members of a freeholder's household, but these men rarely improved their status, even after years of laboring. Toward the end of the century, economic prospects for former bondsmen dimmed still further as rising land prices and periodic slumps in the tobacco economy condemned most freed servants to the perpetual status of landless, voteless, voiceless tenants, sharecroppers, or hired hands — if, that is, they chose to stay in the tidewater region.

As economic opportunity declined in the Chesapeake region, so too did the flow of indentured servants willing to immigrate from England, where by the closing decades of the 1600s the economy was recovering and employment among the poor was rising. In consequence, the practice of importing African slaves became an increasingly common way to supply labor to the tidewater plantations. Once started, the conversion to slaves was speeded by the perceived anomaly of working whites and blacks together, and also by the advantages of owning slaves, who, of course, never became free and whose children too belonged to the master. After 1698, when the African slave trade was thrown open to all English firms that wished to engage in the traffic, slaves were transported to the tidewater region in great numbers.

While the rush of English immigration to Maryland lasted, however, the population grew from somewhat more than 100 in 1634, when the *Ark* and the *Dove* arrived at St. Mary's River, to 8,000 settlers in 1660, 15,000 in 1675, and 25,000 in 1688. From freed servants and other immigrants of slender resources came the bulk of pioneer planters, each drudging with his ax and his hoe to grow tobacco, which he traded for necessary implements and for a very few luxuries — perhaps sugar and occasionally rum. Inventories of probated estates only rarely list money. Rather, what means an individual had was in the form of tobacco, livestock, and land. The inventories show that the typical planter made every possible article that he could with his own hands: bowls and cups from dried gourds, trenchers and plates from slabs of wood, benches and bedsteads from hewn logs, and mattresses from corn shucks. In addition to cultivating tobacco, he tended for his own use a cornfield, a vegetable garden, and possibly an orchard that he had planted. He supplemented his diet by hunting and fishing. Nearly every planter family kept a few chickens, cows, and pigs (usually allowed to roam freely in the woods) and perhaps provided board and lodging to an unmarried sharecropper or hired hand. Most planters were illiterate — they signed their names with an X or some other mark — and very few had even a single book.

Because tobacco rapidly exhausted the soil, the typical planter was always clearing new land. The best land could grow tobacco for about eight years, but poor, sandy soil would support tobacco for only three years, after which the exhausted fields might be planted in corn for a few years more and then left fallow for a decade or two. As one seventeenth-century traveler noted, "As fast as the ground is worn out with tobacco and corn, it runs up again in underwoods; and in many places of the country that which has been cleared is thicker in woods than it was before the clearing." Scattered at intervals through the forest and overgrown fields were small houses, many of them ramshackle or even abandoned by planters who had moved to be nearer new fields.

The houses of the seventeenth-century planters were small wooden boxes. Most had only one room, shared by the master, servants, and lodgers alike. More prosperous planters might have houses of two or three rooms and perhaps a separate dwelling for servants, and a very few planters had houses with as many as six rooms. All structures were framed with wooden posts sunk into the ground. Covering the frame were boards, more often split than sawn, chinked with mud. As for the interior walls, "The best people plaster them with clay," explained two visiting Dutchmen in 1680, but some dwellings were so wretchedly constructed "that if you are not so close to the fire as almost to burn yourself, you cannot keep warm, for the wind blows through every-where." The houses were of one story, often with an earthen floor. Windows had shutters or perhaps panes of oiled paper, but no glass. Chimneys were usually of wood daubed with mud. Roofs were at first of thatch; later shingles were used. In 1686 a visiting Frenchman observed that even the wealthier planters lived in simple structures of this kind, and added, "They build also a separate kitchen, a house for the Christian slaves [or that is, indentured servants], another for negro slaves, and several tobacco barns, so that in arriving at the plantation of a person of importance, you think you are entering a considerable village."

The larger plantations were at first the only places where more than a few people lived together. The rush to acquire land and to grow tobacco so thoroughly dispersed the population that towns did not begin to develop until the final decades of the 1600s, a half-century after the first settlement in Maryland. Even then the early towns were merely minor outposts with a few trading establishments, where tobacco was gathered together for transshipment. There might also be a courthouse, a church, and a customs house where the colonial government collected import and export duties, its principal form of revenue. Another reason why towns and even roads were slow to develop was that the extensive system of tidal rivers made them unnecessary. "Noe country can compare with it," reads one enthusiastic report on the Chesapeake region. "The number of navigable rivers, creeks, and inlets, render it so convenient for exporting and importing goods into any part thereof by water carriage." Early each winter or spring, ships arrived in the Chesapeake from Great Britain and ascended the rivers, sailing from one plantation to the next to trade clothing, tools, and other manufactured goods for tobacco packed in barrels called hogsheads. Along with good soil, a good waterfront location — as, for example, along the Wye River — was one of the prime considerations in picking land for settlement and cultivation. Only as good waterfront land became unavailable did planters begin to penetrate the interior.

Hard work, command of bound or hired labor, and ownership of fertile waterfront land were not the only ingredients for prosperity in the Chesapeake region. Gloria L. Main, in her book *Tobacco Colony*, points out that good health, or more precisely, a long life, was also an important factor. With its vast marshes and suffocatingly hot summers, the tidewater region was a very unhealthful climate for most English settlers. Malaria often weakened the immigrants and left them in no condition to survive the dysentery, typhoid fever, pneumonia, and influenza that were also common. In Maryland during the middle of the seventeenth century, white male immigrants who reached age twenty-two (many died earlier) could expect to remain alive only into their early forties. A mere third of the marriages in seventeenth-century Maryland lasted as long as a decade before one or the other spouse died. In southern Maryland between 1658 and 1705, sixty-seven percent of married men and widowers who died left children who were all of minor age, while only six percent left all adult children. Consequently, the life of the typical planter was often cut short before he had accumulated more than very modest assets to pass on to the wife and children who may have survived him.

By living to old age, however, some planters were able to accumulate expertise and wealth over a protracted period. The first generation of successful planters eschewed spending their profits on consumption goods and instead invested in more and more land and laborers, while continuing to live in a manner that was spare, unostentatious, and frugal. In this way a few planters — perhaps one in twenty — rose to something like affluence by the standards of the time, and a still smaller number laid the foundations for major family fortunes. As the result of marriage gifts and bequests (which fathers commonly distributed well before their deaths), the children of such long-lived planters started adult life with a huge advantage over those without similar patrimony.

Gradually, however, mortality rates among settlers declined during the seventeenth century, and by way of explanation some historians have pointed to the increased consumption of cider, beer, rum, and pure water from deep wells, as opposed to the polluted and sometimes even slightly brackish surface water drunk by the early settlers. The popular notion at the time was simply that the survivors had become "seasoned," or that is, had adjusted to the new environment, but historians with a medical bent point out that the local diseases were such that no lasting immunity was possible, thus again suggesting that sanitation improved. Some historians have gone so far as to argue that the decline in mortality diminished economic opportunity for newly-freed indentured servants. During the middle third of the seventeenth century, the lottery of longevity had favored a few, who acquired sizable and sometimes even very large landholdings. Had the likelihood of an early death continued to be the norm, such holdings would have been without long-term consequence, because much land would soon have become available for redistribution as the descendants of big landowners died young like most other people. But instead, improved sanitation and lengthening life expectancies enabled families that already had much land to retain it permanently, shutting out newcomers.

It has also been suggested that increased longevity speeded the conversion to a slave labor force, inasmuch as permanent slaves became preferable to temporary servants once it was observed that the slaves, who were more expensive to acquire than servants, were likely to survive as long-term assets. Furthermore, it became worthwhile to do with slaves what was not worthwhile with short-term bondsmen, namely to teach them a variety of valuable skills, such as carpentry, coopering, shipbuilding, and blacksmithing, that would then remunerate the master throughout each slave's lifetime and enable the plantation to become more self-sufficient and profitable.

The stratification of society and the emergence at the top of a wealthy elite was reinforced by a pattern of wide fluctuations in the price of tobacco during the seventeenth century. At first tobacco prices were high because of the limited output, but later, as production soared and the tidewater region was wracked by periodic, precipitous drops in the price of tobacco, many growers who had not yet acquired an adequate cushion of spare capital failed, and their crops, land, and other useful assets were bought by those who were already wealthy. In particular, two periods of deep depression from 1686 to 1696 and from 1703 to 1716 eroded the holdings of the middle stratum of planters and drove away to Pennsylvania and the Carolinas (where good land was still available at low prices) the poor, the young, and the newly-freed indentured servants.

In other ways also wealth begot more wealth. Tobacco planters with adequate capital were in a position, especially after about 1680, to diversify into other fields, such as trade, moneylending, shipping, or the practice of law. Wealthy planters corresponded with English consignment houses for the sale of their tobacco, thus obtaining higher prices than did those smaller growers who simply sold their crops locally. Well-capitalized planters purchased imported goods — cloth, shoes, hats, tools, nails, salt, and other necessities — for resale at a markup of about fifty percent to the numerous smaller planters. These merchant-planters sold their goods on credit throughout the year, eventually receiving crops in payment, for tobacco served as a substitute for money. Some large planters bought shares in ships, or opened sawmills, gristmills, iron mines, tanneries, and other enterprises often manned by slaves. A few planters even began to experiment with manufacturing items, such as shoes, or with new agricultural pursuits, such as growing wheat or raising large herds of cattle, hogs, and sheep.

Finally, of course, the families of well-to-do planters intermarried, consolidating their wealth among themselves. And they came also to monopolize governmental power. For a long time the high death rate prevented the emergence of a ruling class, but after 1700, election or appointment to county and provincial offices depended increasingly on the aspiring man's family name, connections, and high economic status. Wealth enabled the patriarchs of leading families to educate their sons and grandsons in the skills necessary to assume governmental posts, judicial responsibilities, militia officerships, and church positions that were created in increasing numbers as the society expanded and matured.

In this way, a native-born tidewater aristocracy developed, epitomized by some of the families that owned plantations in the vicinity of Wye Island in the eighteenth century. For example, the plantation called Stagwell, located on Wye Neck on the way to Wye Island, was acquired in 1706 by Richard Bennett, who upon his death in 1749 was described by the *Maryland Gazette* as "the Richest Man on the Continent." By a series of marriages and inheritances, Wye Island itself passed from the Lloyds to the Chews to the Bordleys and Pacas. The first three surnames rank at the forefront of colonial Maryland's merchant-planter caste, while the last is that of William Paca, a Revolutionary leader and the governor of Maryland from 1782 to 1785. Wye Plantation on the mainland was also acquired by the Pacas by marriage with yet another prominent family, the Tilghmans.

≈   ≈   ≈   ≈

AUTOMOBILE DIRECTIONS: Wye Island is located in Maryland near Wye Mills, 8 miles southeast of the Kent Narrows and 9 miles northwest of Easton. (See **Map 1** on page iv in the Table of Contents.)

To Wye Island from northern Delmarva and Interstate 95 near Newark, Delaware: From I-95 take Route 896 south

MAP 17 — Wye Island Natural Resources Management Area

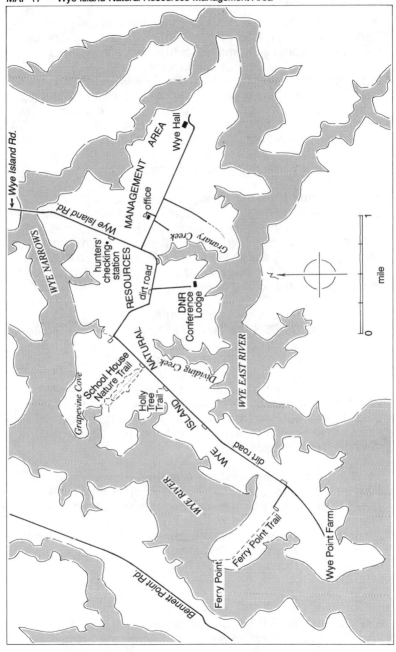

113

across Route 40 and over the Chesapeake and Delaware Canal. From there, follow Route 301 south, passing straight through an intersection where Route 896 bears left. In all, follow Route 301 south into Maryland for about 44 miles. Eventually, after passing exits for Route 305 and Route 304 near Centreville, take the exit for Route 213 south. At the top of the ramp, turn left and follow Route 213 south toward Wye Mills for 4.3 miles, then turn right (west) onto Route 50. Go 2.4 miles, then turn left onto Carmichael Road and follow it 5.1 miles to the bridge across Wye Narrows. (Near the end, the road changes name to Wye Island Road.)

To Wye Island from the Chesapeake Bay Bridge: After crossing the Bay Bridge, follow Route 50/301 across Kent Island. At the point where Route 50 and Route 301 split, fork right to follow Route 50, but go only 2.9 miles to an intersection with Carmichael Road on the right. Turn right and follow Carmichael Road 5.1 miles to the bridge across Wye Narrows. (Near the end, the road changes name to Wye Island Road.)

To Wye Island from southern Delmarva and the Chesapeake Bay Bridge-Tunnel at Norfolk: Follow Route 13 north into Maryland and past Pocomoke City and Princess Anne to the exit for Route 50 westbound near Salisbury, and from there take Route 50 west through Cambridge and Easton. After passing through the intersection with Route 404 near Wye Mills, continue on Route 50 for 3.9 miles, then turn left onto Carmichael Road and follow it 5.1 miles to the bridge across Wye Narrows. (Near the end, the road changes name to Wye Island Road.)

To Wye Island from Salisbury and the Delaware and Maryland seashore resorts: Follow Route 50 or Route 404 west to the intersection of these two roads near Wye Mills. From there continue west on Route 50 for 3.9 miles, then turn left onto Carmichael Road and follow it 5.1 miles to the bridge across Wye Narrows. (Near the end, the road changes name to Wye Island Road.)

≈   ≈   ≈   ≈

EXPLORING WYE ISLAND: Once you cross the bridge at Wye Narrows, you are on Wye Island, which for the most part is publicly owned, but includes some private areas, including Wye Point Farm at the extreme western end of the island and Wye Hall at the eastern end. **Map 17** on page 113 shows the island's roads, parking areas, trails, and other features. Please drive slowly and park in designated areas only.

≈   ≈   ≈   ≈

WALKING ON WYE ISLAND: There are three short foot trails. **The Nature Trail** (1 mile round-trip) follows a wooded belt and ends at Grapevine Cove. **The Holly Tree Trail** is only a few hundred yards long and leads to an exceptionally large holly tree. **The Ferry Point Trail** (1.5 miles round-trip) follows an arching arborway of Osage-orange trees to the site of an old ferry landing. Note that the trail starts at a narrow gap in a fence next to the parking area, and not at the rutted track at each end of the fence.

Since it carries little traffic, the **dirt road** itself provides some of the best walking at Wye Island, assuming that you use extra caution. From the parking area opposite the entrance to the DNR Conference Lodge, the distance to Ferry Point via dirt road and footpath is slightly more than 6 miles round-trip. Walk on the left, facing the oncoming cars, and step off the road as they pass.

You may also enjoy **wandering at large** on Wye Island, which will enable you to see more of the shoreline. The opportunity to walk through an agricultural landscape is a rare one, so please do not abuse the privilege by tramping across fields of standing or freshly-planted crops or by entering areas that are posted as closed. Even in winter, some fields may be planted in wheat, which at that season simply resembles grass. If in doubt, follow the edges of fields and the established tracks of farm vehicles.

Finally, a note about **hunting**: Each year the area's managers decide whether to allow hunting by special permit at certain times from mid-November to mid-January. During that period, wear orange and stay on the designated trails. Or, if you want to wander through fields and woods, either do your walking on Sunday, when hunting is prohibited, or first call or stop by the office to make sure that hunting is not underway.

8

PRIME HOOK NATIONAL WILDLIFE REFUGE
BEACH PLUM ISLAND NATURE PRESERVE

Prime Hook National Wildlife Refuge borders Delaware Bay a few miles northwest of the bay's mouth at Lewes and Cape Henlopen. In terms of size (approximately 9,000 acres), Prime Hook is in the same league with Delmarva's other major national wildlife refuges — Bombay Hook, Blackwater, and Chincoteague — all described elsewhere in this book. The main area for visitors at Prime Hook is shown on **Map 18** on page 127. For those who like to walk, there are four short trails (none longer than 1.5 miles round-trip) through marsh, farm fields, hedgerows, and piney woods. And when combined with the opportunity for up to 4 miles (round-trip) of beach walking at nearby **Beach Plum Island Nature Preserve** (shown on **Map 19**, page 131), the Prime Hook area offers bird watchers and hikers a wide variety of natural habitats. Although the refuge has not been developed with a dike-top tour road intended specifically for viewing waterfowl and shorebirds from your car, there are spaces to pull off onto the shoulder along Route 16 near Broadkill Beach, where the state road cuts through the refuge and overlooks water, marsh, and mud flats.

If you can bring a canoe, there is a launching ramp at the national wildlife refuge that provides access to **Prime Hook Creek,** which meanders for miles through the refuge. For more information about this outstanding canoe trail, see the discussion starting on page 128. Canoeing is also permitted on **Turkle Pond** and **Fleetwood Pond** within the national wildlife refuge.

Fishing and hunting are permitted at Prime Hook National Wildlife Refuge subject to the usual state and federal regulations and other special requirements. When deer hunting is in progress at the southern end of the refuge (the part described in this chapter), non-hunters are prohibited from entering, so call beforehand during fall and early winter to make sure that you will not run afoul of the hunting schedule. Of course, hunting is never permitted on Sunday.

Prime Hook National Wildlife Refuge is open daily from half an hour before sunrise to half an hour after sunset. Dogs must be leashed. The refuge is managed by the U.S. Fish and Wildlife Service; telephone (302) 684-8419.

Beach Plum Island Nature Preserve, which lies adjacent to the national wildlife refuge, is open all day every day from March through November. The southeastern end of the preserve is sometimes declared off limits, but usually at least a mile of beach is open. Vehicles with permits may drive on the beach for purposes of surf fishing. Dogs must be leashed. Beach Plum Island is managed by the Delaware Department of Natural Resources and Environmental Control, Division of Parks and Recreation; telephone (302) 645-8983.

FEATURING A BROAD RANGE OF HABITATS — sodden deciduous forest, piney (and relatively dry) woods, freshwater ponds and streams, meadows, cultivated fields, fresh and saltwater marsh, mud flats, dunes, beach, and Delaware Bay itself — Prime Hook National Wildlife Refuge and the adjacent Beach Plum Island Nature Preserve are together exceptionally good places to see a wide variety of birds at every season, although, of course, the periods of spring and fall migration are best.

Even for fledgling birders, identifying the approximately 270 species that have been seen regularly in recent years along the southern shore of Delaware Bay is easier than might at first be thought. Shape, size, plumage, and other physical characteristics are distinguishing field marks. Range, season, habitat, song, and behavior are other useful keys to identifying birds.

Range is of primary importance for the simple reason that many birds are not found throughout North America or even the eastern United States, and so can immediately be eliminated from consideration when birding in Delmarva. For example, the cedar waxwing and Bohemian waxwing closely resemble each other, so it helps to know that the latter is not seen here. A good field guide provides range maps based on years of reported sightings and bird counts. Of course, bird ranges are not static: some pioneering species, such as the glossy ibis and house finch, have extended their ranges during recent decades. Other birds, such as the ivory-billed woodpecker, have lost ground and died out.

Season is related to range, since migratory birds appear in different parts of their ranges during different times of year. The five species of spot-breasted thrushes, for instance, are sometimes difficult to distinguish from each other, but usually only the hermit thrush is present in Delmarva during winter and only the wood thrush is found here during summer. Again, the maps in most field guides reflect this sort of information.

Habitat is important in identifying birds. Even before you sight a bird, the surroundings can tell you what species you are likely to see. Within its range a species usually appears only in certain preferred habitats, although during migration some species are less particular. (In many cases, birds show a degree of physical adaptation to their preferred environment.) As its name implies, the marsh wren is seldom found far from cattails, rushes, sedges, or tall marsh grasses; if a wren-like bird is seen in such a setting, it is unlikely to be a house wren or Carolina wren or one of the other species commonly found in thick underbrush or shrubbery. The area where two habitats join, called an *ecotone*, is a particularly good place to look for birds because species peculiar to either environment may be present. For example, both meadowlarks and wood warblers might be found where a hay field abuts a forest. All good field guides provide information on habitat preferences that can help to locate a species or to assess the likelihood of a tentative identification. A bird list available at Prime Hook contains information on habitat preference and also seasonal occurrence.

Song announces the identity (or at least the location) of birds even before they are seen. Although some species, such as the red-winged blackbird, have only a few songs, others, such as the mockingbird, have an infinite variety. (Even so, mockingbird songs tend to follow certain characteristic patterns, such as the repetition of each phrase up to a half-dozen times, before moving on to another phrase.) Some birds, most notably thrushes, sing different songs in the morning and evening. In many species the songs vary somewhat among individuals and from one area to another, giving rise to regional "dialects." Nonetheless, the vocal repertory of most songbirds is sufficiently constant in timbre and pattern to identify each species simply by its songs.

Bird songs, as distinguished from calls, can be very complex. They are sung only by the male of most species, usually in spring and summer. The male arrives first at the breeding and nesting area after migration. He stakes out a territory for courting, mating, and nesting by singing at prominent points around the area's perimeter. This wards off intrusion by other males of his species and simultaneously attracts females. On the basis of the male's display and the desirability of his territory, the female selects her mate. Experiments suggest that female birds build nests faster and lay more eggs when exposed to the songs of males with a larger vocal repertory than others of their species, and the relative volume of their songs appears to be a way for males to establish status among themselves.

In a few species, including eastern bluebirds, Baltimore orioles, cardinals, and white-throated sparrows, both sexes sing, although the males are more active in defending their breeding territory. Among mockingbirds, both sexes sing in fall and winter, but only males sing in spring and summer. Some birds, such as canaries, have different songs for different seasons.

Birds tend to heed the songs of their own kind and to ignore the songs of other species, which do not compete for females nor, in many cases, for the same type of nesting materials or food. In consequence, a single area might include the overlapping breeding territories of several species. From year to year such territories are bigger or smaller, depending on the food supply. Typically, most small songbirds require about half an acre from which others of their species are excluded.

Bird calls (as distinguished from songs) are short, simple, sometimes harsh, and used by both males and females at all times of year to communicate alarm, aggression, location, and existence of food. Nearly all birds have some form of call. Warning calls are often heeded by species other than the caller's. Some warning calls are thin, high-pitched whistles that are difficult to locate and so do not reveal the bird's location to predators. Birds also use mobbing calls to summon other birds, as chickadees and crows do when scolding and harassing owls and other unwanted visitors. Birds flying in flocks, like cedar waxwings, often call continuously. Such calls help birds migrating by night to stay together.

The study of bird dialects and experiments with birds that have been deafened or raised in isolation indicate that songs are genetically inherited only to a very crude extent. Although a few species, such as doves, sing well even when raised in isolation, most birds raised alone produce inferior, simplified songs. Generally, young songbirds learn their songs by listening to adult birds and by practice singing, called *subsong*. Even so, birds raised in isolation and exposed to many tape-recorded songs show an innate preference for the songs of their own species.

Probably the easiest way to learn bird songs is to listen repeatedly to recordings and to refer at the same time to a standard field guide. Most guides describe bird vocalizations with such terms as *harsh, nasal, flutelike, piercing, plaintive, wavering, twittering, buzzing, sneezy,* and *sputtering*. Although these terms are somewhat descriptive, they do not take on real meaning until you have heard the songs themselves on records or in the field. Incidentally, bird recordings that are played slowly demonstrate that the songs contain many more notes than the human ear ordinarily hears.

Shape is one of the first and most important aspects to notice once you actually see a bird. Most birds can at least be placed in the proper family and many species can be identified by shape or silhouette, without reference to other field marks. Some birds, such as kestrels, are distinctly stocky, big-headed, and powerful-looking, while others, such as catbirds and cuckoos, are elegantly long and slender. Kingfishers, blue jays, tufted titmice, Bohemian and cedar waxwings, and cardinals are among the few birds with crests.

Bird bills frequently have distinctive shapes and, more than any other body part, show adaptation to food supply. The beak can be chunky, like that of a grosbeak, to crack seeds; thin and curved, like that of a creeper, to probe bark for insects; hooked, like that of a shrike, to tear at flesh; long and slender, like that of a hummingbird, to sip nectar from tubular flowers; or some other characteristic shape depending on the bird's food. Goatsuckers, swifts, flycatchers, and swallows, all of which catch flying insects, have widely hinged bills and gaping mouths. The long, thin bills of starlings and meadowlarks are suited to probing the ground. In the Galapagos Islands west of Ecuador, Charles Darwin noted fourteen species of finches, each of which had evolved a different type of beak or style of feeding that gave it a competitive advantage for a particular type of food. Many birds are nonetheless flexible about their diet, especially from season to season when food sources change or become scarce. For example, Tennessee warblers, which ordinarily glean insects from foliage, also take large amounts of nectar from tropical flowers when wintering in South and Central America.

In addition to beaks, nearly every other part of a bird's body is adapted to help exploit its environment. Feet of passerines, or songbirds, are adapted to perching, with three toes in front and one long toe behind; waterfowl have webbed or lobed feet for swimming; and raptors have talons for grasping prey.

Other key elements of body shape are the length and form of wings, tails, and legs. The wings may be long, pointed, and developed for swift, sustained flight, like those of falcons. Or the wings may be short and rounded for abrupt bursts of speed, like those of accipiters. The tail may have a deep fork like that of a barn swallow, a shallow notch like that of a tree swallow, or a square tip like that of a cliff swallow, or a round tip like that of a blue jay.

Size is difficult to estimate and therefore not very useful in identifying birds. The best approach is to bear in mind the relative sizes of different species and to use certain well-known birds like the chickadee, sparrow, robin, kingfisher, and crow as standards for mental comparison. For example, if a bird resembles a song sparrow but looks unusually large, it might be a fox sparrow.

Plumage, whether plain or princely, muted or magnificent, is one of the most obvious keys to identification. Color can occur in remarkable combinations of spots, stripes, streaks, patches, and other patterns that make even supposedly drab birds a pleasure to see. In some instances, like the brown streaks of American bitterns and many other species, the plumage provides camouflage. Most vireos and warblers are various shades and combinations of yellow, green, brown, gray, and black, as one would expect from their forest environment. The black and white backs of woodpeckers help them to blend in with bark dappled with sunlight. The bold patterns of killdeers and some other plovers break up their outlines in much the same manner that warships used to be camouflaged before the invention of radar. Many shore birds display countershading: they are dark above and light below, a pattern that reduces the effect of shadows and makes the birds appear an inconspicuous monotone. Even some brightly colored birds have camouflaging plumages when they are young and least able to avoid predators.

For some species, it is important *not* to be camouflaged. Many sea birds are mostly white, which in all light conditions enables them to be seen at great distances against the water. Because flocks of sea birds spread out from their colonies to search for food, it is vital that a bird that has located food be visible to others after it has landed on the water to feed.

To organize the immense variation of plumages, focus on different basic elements and ask the following types of questions. Starting with the head, is it uniformly colored like that of the red-headed woodpecker? Is there a small patch on the crown, like that of Wilson's warbler and the ruby-crowned kinglet, or a larger cap on the front and top of the head, like that of the common redpoll and American goldfinch? Is the crown striped like the ovenbird's? Does a ring surround the eye, as with a Connecticut warbler, or are the rings perhaps even joined across the top of the bill to form spectacles, like those of a yellow-breasted chat? Is there a stripe over or through the eyes, like the red-breasted nuthatch's, or a conspicuous black mask across the eyes, like that of a common yellowthroat or loggerhead shrike? Such marks are not merely peculiar to this or that individual (as is the case with a spotted horse) but rather are reliably characteristic of different bird species. From the head go on to the rest of the body, where distinctive colors and patterns can also mark a bird's bill, throat, breast, belly, back, sides, wings, rump, tail, and legs.

Finally, what a bird *does* is an important clue to its identity. Certain habits, postures, ways of searching for food, and other behavior characterize different species. Some passerines, such as larks, juncos, and towhees, are strictly ground feeders; other birds, including flycatchers and swallows, nab insects on the wing; and others, such as nuthatches and creepers, glean insects from the crevices in bark. Woodpeckers bore into the bark. Vireos and most warblers pick insects from the foliage of trees and brush.

All of these birds may be further distinguished by other habits of eating. For example, towhees scratch for insects and seeds by kicking backward with both feet together, whereas juncos rarely do, although both hop to move along the ground. Other ground feeders, such as meadowlarks, walk rather than hop. Despite the children's song, robins often run, not hop. Swallows catch insects while swooping and skimming in continuous flight, but flycatchers dart out from a limb, grab an insect (sometimes with an audible smack), and then return to their perch. Brown creepers have the curious habit of systematically searching for food by climbing trees in spirals, then flying back to the ground to climb again. Woodpeckers tend to hop upward, bracing themselves against the tree with their stiff tails. Nuthatches walk up, down, and around tree trunks and branches, seemingly without regard for gravity. Vireos are sluggish compared to the hyperactive, flitting warblers.

Many birds divide a food source into zones, an arrangement that apparently has evolved to ensure each species its own food supply. The short-legged green heron sits at the edge of the water or on a low overhanging branch, waiting for its prey to come close to shore. Medium-sized black-crowned and yellow-crowned night herons hunt in shallow water. The long-legged great blue heron stalks fish in water up to two feet deep. Swans, geese, and many ducks graze underwater on the stems and tubers of grassy plants, but the longer necks of swans and geese enable them to reach deeper plants. Similarly, different species of shore birds take food from the same mud flat by probing with their varied bills to different depths. Species of warblers that feed in the same tree are reported to concentrate in separate areas among the trunk, twig tips, and tree top. Starlings and cowbirds feeding in flocks on the ground show another arrangement that provides an even distribution of food: Birds in the rear fly ahead to the front, so that the entire flock rolls slowly across the field.

Different species also have different styles of flight. Soaring is typical of some big birds. Gulls float nearly motionless in the wind. Buteos and turkey vultures soar on updrafts in wide circles, although turkey vultures may be further distinguished by wings held in a shallow V. Some other large birds, such as accipiters, rarely soar but instead interrupt their wing beats with glides. Kestrels, terns, kingfishers, and ospreys can hover in one spot. Hummingbirds, like oversized dragonflies, can also hover and even fly backward. Slightly more erratic than the swooping, effortless flight of swallows is that of swifts, flitting with wing beats that appear to alternate (but do not). Still other birds, such as the American goldfinch and flickers, dip up and down in wavelike flight.

And now for a few practice puzzlers to illustrate and apply some of the points discussed above. All of the examples involve birds that you might see at Prime Hook or Beach Plum Island.

At a considerable distance across the hazy marsh in July, you spot a large, dark, long-legged, long-necked wading bird with a downward-curved bill. What is it? . . . . Of course, the vast majority of large, dark waders in Delmarva are great blue herons, but herons have straight bills. So your bird is probably a glossy ibis, which is also somewhat smaller than the great blue heron. The identification is confirmed when the creature flies off across the marsh with its neck outstretched. Herons and egrets fly with their necks folded back. The whimbrel, too, has a downwardly curved bill and flies with its neck outstretched, but its neck and legs are visibly shorter than those of the glossy ibis.

At the edge of Prime Hook's Turkle Pond in summer you observe a small bird that is all brown above and streaked with brown below. A long, pale-yellow stripe runs above each eye. As it walks the bird teeters and bobs. This is a . . . (I'm waiting for you to answer first) . . . a northern waterthrush, whose peculiar gait is shared by the somewhat larger spotted sandpiper, also seen on lakeshores.

At the edge of pine woods early in May, you hear a distinctive song: about eight buzzy notes ascending the chromatic scale, or that is, rising in a series of half tones. This song is enough to identify — what? Finally, you spot a small warbler with an olive back and yellow underparts, streaked black along the sides and having one black stripe through each eye and another below across each cheek. The bird bobs its tail. It is the misnamed prairie warbler, which is common in bushy pastures, saplings, and low pines. The palm warbler also bobs its tail, but it is brown above and in spring has a chestnut cap. Yet other birds with idiosyncratic tail tics include the eastern phoebe, which regularly jerks its tail downward while perching, and wrens, which often cock their tails vertically.

On a mud flat in spring you observe hundreds of birds probing and picking at the glistening muck. Most of them are small and brownish, so you dismiss them collectively as "peeps" — or that is, least, semi-palmated, western, Baird's, and white-rumped sandpipers. Your attention, however, is drawn by a few larger birds, as follows:

(1) A real eye-catcher is a bird whose body, neck, and head are black above and white below; it has long red legs and a needlelike bill.

(2) Another large bird has a tan head and neck and a black-and-white back; while feeding it sweeps its upwardly curved bill from side to side like a scythe.

(3) Also present are some speckled gray birds with long, thin, black bills and bright yellow legs — although some individuals appear to be distinctly larger than others.

(4) Similar in shape to #3 is a bird with bluish gray legs; when it flies its wings show a bold black-and-white pattern.

(5) Smaller than the other birds but still larger than the "peeps" is one whose breast is covered with many streaks running crosswise. It has greenish legs and a white eyebrow stripe. With its long bill it probes the mud with a rapid motion like a sewing machine.

(6) Slightly larger than #5 is a bird with a rich, rusty breast and a very long bill. It too feeds with a sewing machine motion, and when it flies, a long white wedge is visible on its back, pointing from the tail toward the head.

Answers: (1) Black-necked stilt. (2) American avocet. (3) Greater and lesser yellowlegs. (4) Willet. (5) Stilt sandpiper. (6) Short-billed dowitcher — whose bill is short only in comparison with the long-billed dowitcher.

≈ ≈ ≈ ≈

AUTOMOBILE DIRECTIONS: Prime Hook National Wildlife Refuge and Beach Plum Island Nature Preserve are located adjacent to Delaware Bay about 27 miles southeast of Dover and 7 miles northwest of Lewes. (See **Map 1** on page iv in the Table of Contents.)

To Prime Hook from northern Delmarva and Interstate 95 southwest of Wilmington: From Interstate 95 take Exit 4A for Route 1 south, and stay on Route 1 past a quick succession of exits. Follow Route 1 south past Dover and Milford toward Rehoboth and the Delaware beaches. For a period, Route 1 is congruent with Route 113. Eventually, after passing an intersection with Route 5, turn left off Route 1 onto Route 16 eastbound toward Broadkill Beach and Prime Hook National Wildlife Refuge. Follow Route 16 for only 1.2 miles, then turn left toward the refuge. Follow the refuge road to the parking lot by the visitor center, boat ramp, and Dike and Boardwalk trails.

To Prime Hook from the Chesapeake Bay Bridge: After crossing the bridge, follow Route 50/301 across Kent Island. At the point where Route 50 and Route 301 split, fork right to follow Route 50, but after only 7 miles, turn left onto Route 404 east toward Denton and Rehoboth. Follow Route 404 for 20 miles to the intersection on the left with Route 16 (3 miles after Route 16 intersects from the right). Turn left and follow Route 16 east for more than 29 miles, in the process crossing Route 13, Route 113, and Route 1. After crossing Route 1, continue on Route 16 for only 1.2 miles, then turn left toward Prime Hook National Wildlife Refuge. Follow the refuge road to the parking lot by the visitor center, boat ramp, and Dike and Boardwalk trails.

To Prime Hook from southern Delmarva and the Chesapeake Bay bridge-tunnel at Norfolk: After crossing the bridge-tunnel, follow Route 13 north into Maryland and past Salisbury. Continue on Route 13 north into Delaware and past intersections with Route 9 and Route 404, then turn right onto Route 16 eastbound. (Alternatively, from the vicinity of Snow Hill and Berlin, follow Route 113 north to Route 16, and there turn right.) Once you are on Route 16 eastbound, follow it to Route 1. After crossing Route 1, continue on Route 16 for only 1.2 miles, then turn left toward Prime Hook National Wildlife Refuge. Follow the refuge road to the parking lot by the visitor center, boat ramp, and Dike and Boardwalk trails.

To Prime Hook from Salisbury and the Delaware and Maryland seashore resorts: From the vicinity of Salisbury, follow Route 13 north, then take Route 16 east to the intersection with Route 1. From the seaside resorts, take Route 1 north to the intersection with Route 16. In either case, once you are at the intersection of Route 16 and Route 1, follow Route 16 east for only 1.2 miles, then turn left toward Prime Hook National Wildlife Refuge. Follow the refuge road to the parking lot by the office, boat ramp, and Dike and Boardwalk trails.

≈   ≈   ≈   ≈

WALKING AND BIRD WATCHING AT PRIME HOOK NATIONAL WILDLIFE REFUGE: As shown on **Map 18** at right, there are several short trails at Prime Hook.

MAP 18 — Prime Hook National Wildlife Refuge

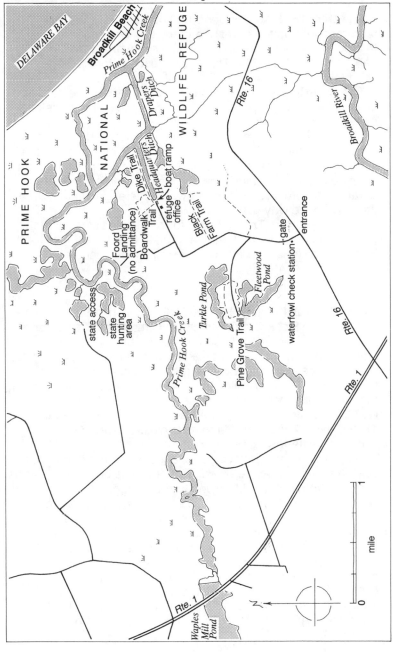

The Dike Trail (1 mile round-trip) starts next to the boat ramp and follows the edge of a canal (the Headquarters Ditch) to a point that provides a sweeping view over the marsh behind Broadkill Beach. This is the best trail for viewing waterfowl.

The Boardwalk Trail (0.5 mile) starts opposite the parking bays at the boat ramp. It forms a short circuit through fields, marsh, and wet woods.

The Black Farm Trail (1.5 mile round-trip) starts at a yellow gate by the side of the main refuge road 0.4 mile north of the spur road that leads to Turkle and Fleetwood ponds. Park on the side of the road and follow the trail (it is an old farm road attractively bordered by hedgerows) to the edge of the marsh, then return the way you came.

The Pine Grove Trail (1 mile) forms a circuit starting at the end of the spur road that leads to Turkle Pond and Fleetwood Pond. This is the best trail for viewing spring songbirds.

≈   ≈   ≈   ≈

CANOEING ON PRIME HOOK CREEK: Map 18 on page 127 shows Prime Hook Creek, which flows through the southern section of the refuge and usually is passable by canoe between Waples Mill Pond on Route 1 and the launching ramp by the refuge office. Between these two points the stream meanders for about 7 miles through forest, swamp, and marsh. Exploring this river makes a very enjoyable day's outing. However, during the period between October 15 and March 15, the river below Foord landing is closed in order to allow migratory waterfowl to rest undisturbed.

I suggest that you launch your canoe from, and return to, the boat ramp by the refuge office. Although it is possible to canoe one-way from Waples Mill Pond to the refuge office (or vice versa) you would, of course, have to arrange for someone to shuttle your car. Besides, for a few hundred yards below Waples Mill Pond, the stream is sometimes difficult during periods of low water. Also, the marshy, easterly section of the river is more interesting, so you might as well start there, provided that you go during the period mid-March to mid-October when the lower section of the river is open. (When it is closed, you can launch at Route 1 just below Waples Mill Pond and explore 4 miles of river downstream to Foord Landing.)

From the launching ramp by the refuge office, paddle along the Headquarters Ditch for about half a mile, then turn left at the first opportunity. Follow the channel past bayous on either side, then bear left in order to continue on the main channel upstream toward a series of hunting blinds. Paddle upstream as far as you want (bearing in mind that you must return the same way). Once you pass Foord Landing (which is simply a small dock and a shed), the character of the river is somewhat monotonous for several miles until it broadens out into a long, sinuous pond. At the extreme western end of this pond, take the left (southern) channel — it is very small — to reach Waples Mill Pond and Route 1. Return by the way you came.

As is evident from Map 18, it is also possible to canoe in a circuit about 2.5 miles long by turning right at the end of the Headquarters Ditch, then left into Drapers Ditch, then left again into Prime Hook Creek, and finally left once more in order to return to Headquarters Ditch.

≈   ≈   ≈   ≈

FROM PRIME HOOK TO BEACH PLUM ISLAND:
Immediately southeast of Prime Hook National Wildlife Refuge is the state of Delaware's Beach Plum Island Nature Preserve, which is not an island but rather a long spit of undeveloped beach and dunes sandwiched between the Broadkill River and Delaware Bay. The bold line on **Map 19** at right shows the way there. As you leave the Prime Hook refuge, turn left and follow Route 16 for 2.8 miles to the community of Broadkill Beach. (Toward the end of Route 16, there are a few places to pull off the road onto the shoulder in order to view birds on the marsh ponds and mud flats.) Within sight of Delaware Bay, turn right onto South Bayshore Drive and follow it for 1.9 miles to the entrance for Beach Plum Island Nature Preserve. Continue another 0.1 mile to the parking lot on the left.

≈   ≈   ≈   ≈

WALKING AT BEACH PLUM ISLAND NATURE PRESERVE:
A hike along the shore to Roosevelt Inlet (4 miles round-trip) is a pleasant excursion. However, depending on the season and on beach erosion, the lower half of the spit is sometimes closed.

MAP 19 — From Prime Hook Refuge to Beach Plum Island Nature Preserve

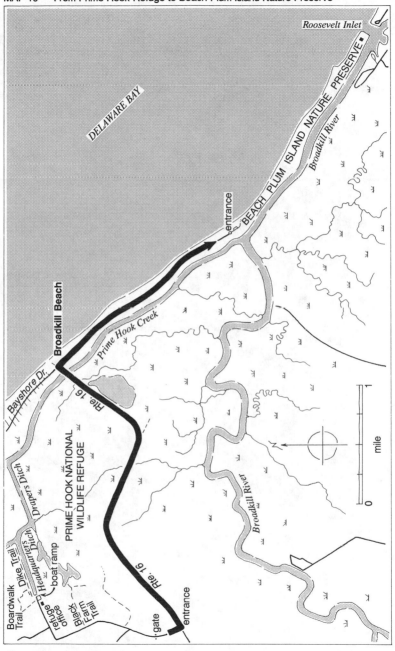

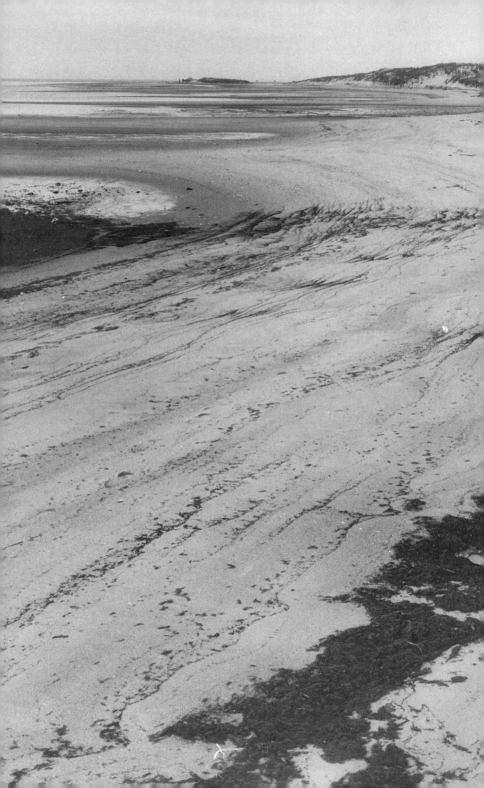

9

LEWES
THE CAPE MAY - LEWES FERRY
CAPE HENLOPEN STATE PARK

This excursion focuses on the vicinity of **Lewes** (pronounced Loo-iss), site of the first European settlement in Delaware. Shown on **Map 20** on page 141, the town is now an attractive resort, where many old houses have been renovated. Antique stores, galleries, specialty shops, and restaurants occupy the small business district, which is all the more interesting for the fact that it fronts not on the beach itself but rather on the Lewes-Rehoboth Canal a half-mile inland from Delaware Bay.

Near the center of Lewes is the **Zwaanendael Museum**, a scaled-down replica of the town hall in Hoorn, Holland, from which the chief sponsor of the early colony came. The museum was built in 1931 to commemorate the 300th anniversary of Dutch settlement. Devoted to local history, the museum is open Tuesday through Saturday from 10 A.M. to 4:30 P.M. It is administered by Delaware State Museums. Telephone (302) 645-1148 for information.

Next to the Zwaanendael Museum is the restored **Fisher-Martin House**, built about 1728 and now an information and exhibition center run by the Lewes Chamber of Commerce; telephone (302) 645-8073. During summer the house is usually open daily from 10 A.M. to 4 P.M. In winter it is open Monday through Friday.

A few blocks away from the Zwaanendael Museum and Fisher-Martin House is the **Lewes Historic Complex**, to which several old houses and other structures have been moved from nearby areas. Managed by the Lewes Historical Society, the buildings are open to the public from mid-June through the beginning of the Labor Day weekend, Tuesday through Friday, from 10 A.M. to 3 P.M., and on Saturday from 10 to 12:30 — and also for somewhat abbreviated hours in spring and fall. On the first Saturday in December, the historic complex is open as part of a Christmas house tour for all of Lewes. Also managed by the historical society is the nearby **lightship *Overfalls*** and the **Cannonball House Maritime Museum**, which are open on the same schedule (more or less) as the Lewes Historic Complex.

About a mile east of Lewes is the Delaware terminal of the **Cape May - Lewes Ferry**. For foot passengers who leave their cars in the parking lot at the Lewes terminal, a ride across Delaware Bay to New Jersey and back makes a very enjoyable ocean mini-cruise. The crossing takes about 70 minutes each way, but the duration of the round trip varies with the seasons because the boats do not run as often in winter as in summer. You may also want to allocate time to see the town of Cape May, reachable from the New Jersey ferry terminal via a shuttle bus that operates seven days a week during summer and on weekends during spring and fall. For information about the ferry schedule and fares, telephone 1-800-643-3779. To make sure the shuttle bus is running, call (609) 889-7201.

Finally, slightly east of the Lewes ferry terminal is Delaware's 4,000-acre **Cape Henlopen State Park**, shown on **Map 21** on page 144. The park has 6 miles of ocean and bay beaches (one area is lifeguarded during summer), a bathhouse and canteen, a fishing pier, a nature center, an observation tower and gun emplacements left from World War II, a campground that is open April through October, and excellent bird watching during spring and fall migrations. In addition to good beach walking, the park has foot trails that explore the dunes, forest, and marsh behind the beach. There are also paved hike-bike trails. Options for walking are discussed on 3pages 143-145.

Cape Henlopen State Park is open daily year-round from 8 A.M. to sunset. Dogs must be leashed and are altogether barred from Henlopen Point and also, May through September, from swimming areas. The park is administered by the Delaware Department of Natural Resources and Environmental Control, Division of Parks and Recreation; telephone (302) 645-8983. The park's Seaside Nature Center is also open year-round and provides programs, exhibits, and material on the cape's natural and cultural history; telephone (302) 645-6852.

IN 1609 THE ENGLISH NAVIGATOR Henry Hudson, at that time employed by the Dutch East India Company to search for a passage from Europe either northeast or northwest to the Orient, sailed his ship *Half Moon* into Delaware Bay before moving farther up the Atlantic coast to explore the river subsequently named for him. Although the

Delaware estuary had been visited before by other Europeans, Hudson's voyage, plus later explorations by other Dutch navigators, provided Holland with a claim to the region. After New Amsterdam (later New York City) was established in 1625, Captain David Pieterszen DeVries and other promoters in Holland organized an expedition to the Delaware estuary in order "to plant a colony for the cultivation of grain and tobacco as well as to carry on the whale fishery in that region." Leaving the Netherlands on December 12, 1630, thirty-two men (DeVries was not among them) were transported to the vicinity of Lewes, where they arrived in April 1631 and proceeded to establish the first European settlement in what is now Delaware. At the mouth of Lewes Creek, located a mile northwest up the coast of Delaware Bay from the present-day town, the Dutchmen built a communal dwelling house and trading post surrounded by a stockade on land that had been purchased by their agents from the Indians two years earlier. The Netherlanders called the place Zwaanendael (vale of the swans). After the colonists appeared to be secure and in a position to fend for themselves, their ship returned to Holland.

In December of the following year, DeVries arrived at Zwaanendael with more men to reinforce the outpost that was supposed to generate profits for himself and the other investors. He found it, however, a total loss, and that in the starkest terms. The settlement had been burned and all the Europeans massacred by Indians. The bones of men and cattle were found lying here and there in the open. DeVries was told by a native informant that the killings were the outgrowth of an incident in which an Indian had stolen a metal sign bearing the Dutch coat of arms. After the Netherlanders complained, the thief was executed by yet other Indians who were anxious to placate the Europeans, whereupon the thief's friends and kin revenged themselves on the Dutchmen.

The second DeVries expedition remained at Zwaanendael only a short time, but a quarter-century later, in 1658, the site was settled once more by Netherlanders. Financed by the Dutch West India Company, a fort and trading post were again built at the site of Zwaanendael, which came to be called Hoorn on the small river Hoornkill or Horekill. In 1663 the outpost was transferred to the sponsorship of the burgomasters of Amsterdam, and that same year the colony was greatly augmented by the arrival of forty-one Mennonite emigres from Holland led by Peter Cornelius Plockhoy. The settlement benefited too from the support of Fort Amstel at present-day New Castle, for at that time the Dutch were making a systematic effort to establish their power in Delaware Bay.

In 1664, however, during one of a series of three Anglo-Dutch wars fought between 1652 and 1678 for mercantile and maritime dominance, Great Britain seized control of the Delaware region. At Horekill an

English expedition destroyed the "quaking colony of Plockhoy to a naile." ("Quaking" because the Anglicans identified the Mennonites with Quakers and other pacifist sects.)

The Netherlanders who remained at Whorekill — as the English, exercising their inimitable penchant for corrupting names, called the place — were made British citizens. This fact, however, did not deter a detachment of forty Marylanders from again attacking Whorekill on Christmas Eve, 1673, during a brief period when Holland regained control of its New York and Delaware colonies. At Whorekill the Marylanders burned the settlement, leaving only one "thatch barne" standing to provide shelter for the approximately eight families and nine single men said to live in the village at that time. By some accounts the viciousness of this raid was motivated not so much by opposition to the Dutch as by the desire of Charles Calvert, the resident governor and future proprietor of Maryland, to assert his family's ownership of the Delaware coast. In this the Calverts ultimately failed, for although the grant from King Charles I to Cecilius Calvert in 1632 delineated boundaries that included what is now Delaware, the grant covered only "land hitherto uncultivated and occupied by savages." This clause, coupled with the fact of Dutch settlement in 1631, resulted in Delaware being carved out of Maryland and joined to New York after the Netherlands permanently relinquished claim to the region by treaty with England in 1674.

In 1680 the region administered from Whorekill was carved up to create a new county — Delaware's third — midway between New Castle and Cape Henlopen. The village at Whorekill (about then renamed Deale in Deale County) remained the court site for southern-most Delaware, a status it retained for over a hundred years until the seat of county government was moved to Georgetown in 1791. The courthouse stood in a corner of what is now the graveyard of St. Peter's Episcopal Church on Second Street in the center of Lewes. Its location there probably had something to do with the town growing up where it did rather than slightly to the northwest at the original site of Zwaanen-dael, for the early village was little more than a series of farms spaced at intervals along the creek and its adjacent road (now Pilot Town Road). In 1682, when the three counties of Delaware were transferred from the colony of New York to Pennsylvania (they subsequently gained their own legislature in 1704), names were again changed and the village became Lewes in the county of Sussex after the town of Lewes in Sussex, England.

The growth of Lewes — a gristmill was built in 1676 and a tannery in 1684 — did not, however, prevent the periodic despoliation of the community by raiders appearing without warning from the open ocean. In 1690 and again in 1698 the town was plundered by pirates who landed and went from house to house, taking whatever they considered of value. A pirate who came in peace, however, was Captain William Kidd; in 1700, while returning from the West Indies to New York with the intention of clearing himself of piracy charges, Kidd stood his ship off Lewes, from which some townspeople rowed out to barter for goods that had been looted from other vessels. (At his subsequent trial in England, Kidd unsuccessfully claimed that the ships he had seized were lawful prizes of war.) Ever since Kidd's visit, the sand dunes of Cape Henlopen have been associated with legends of buried pirate treasure.

In 1709 during the War of Spanish Succession, which was fought chiefly in Europe but spilled over into the American colonies as part of a series of French and Indian wars, Lewes was again sacked by about a hundred privateersmen sent ashore from a vessel authorized by the French government to attack and plunder English ports and shipping on a for-profit basis — just as Kidd had in fact been commissioned by the governor of New York to seize French vessels during the earlier King William's War. Marauding by pirates and by privateers continued in Delaware Bay until as late as the mid-1700s.

Lewes escaped damage during the Revolutionary War, although the nearby Cape Henlopen lighthouse, which had been erected in the 1760s, was burned on the interior by the English in 1776. (The lighthouse was refurbished and continued to serve until 1924; the following year the structure was toppled by erosion of the high dune on which it stood.) Also during the Revolution, several residents of Lewes had cattle stolen or extorted from them by British landing parties seeking supplies for their warships. In Lewes itself in 1776, Tories from the outlying area "cut the flagstaff down and sold the flag for 13d., and nearly did bodily injury to the Court," according to the report of a local patriot. Throughout Delmarva rural residents were often Loyalist in sympathy, while town folk usually were more radical. Lewes, in any case, supplied its share of soldiers and sailors to the revolutionary cause. Perhaps the most noteworthy patriot leader from Lewes was Colonel David Hall, a lawyer who in 1775 joined Delaware's executive revolutionary body, the Council of Safety. During the war, Hall was an officer in the Delaware Regiment. From 1802 to 1805 he served as the state's governor — the first of five Delaware governors from Lewes. Hall's house, built in the early eighteenth century and enlarged in 1790, stands at 107 Kings Highway (it is now a gift shop) opposite the front of the Zwaanendael Museum.

Lewes was yet again exposed to attack during the War of 1812. On April 6 and 7, 1813, three British ships bombarded the town after its inhabitants refused to supply the enemy with provisions. Perhaps because their view was obstructed by trees along the shore, the British inflicted only trivial damage. The Cannonball House, now a maritime museum on Front Street, was struck. Casualties of the bombardment totaled "one chicken killed, one pig wounded — leg broken," according to a contemporary account.

Not until nearly 130 years later, when Fort Miles was built at Cape Henlopen to help guard the entrance to Delaware Bay during World War II, did Lewes again see military action. German U-boats were active in the area immediately following America's entry into the war. Lewes gave succor to survivors — almost 250 in all — brought ashore from twelve ships sunk by U-boats between January and April of 1942. During that period nearly two hundred ships were sunk off the East Coast, often within sight of land. In response, the United States eventually instituted a system of coastal convoys, while at the same time our fliers and seamen gradually gained proficiency at tracking and attacking enemy submarines. By summer the U-boats rarely came closer to the United States than the middle of the Atlantic Ocean. However, on May 14, 1945 — nearly a week after VE Day — the German submarine U-858 was surrendered by its crew and towed into Lewes' harbor. Now Fort Miles is the site of Cape Henlopen State Park. From the beach huge bunkers are visible; they formerly housed 6-inch, 12-inch, and 16-inch guns, which never had occasion to be fired at enemy warships. A spectacular view of Cape Henlopen can be had from the top of one of the fort's observation towers and also from the Great Dune Overlook atop a massive gun emplacement.

Another facility at Cape Henlopen, in the area to the east of the present-day fishing pier, was the Delaware Breakwater Quarantine Station, where between 1885 and 1917, immigrants thought to have contagious diseases or to have been exposed to contagion were isolated for weeks or even months before being allowed to continue to Philadelphia or, as sometimes happened, being sent back to Europe.

Until tourism became the chief industry of Lewes during the second half of the twentieth century, the town's economy was based overwhelmingly on shipping (including ship building and ship chandlery), fishing, canning, and the piloting of large vessels up and down the Delaware. Although Lewes Creek may appear to be only a very minor river (it is now part of a canal linking Delaware Bay and Rehoboth Bay), in prior centuries it was a crowded roadstead that accommodated two-masted schooners and other small craft engaged in coastal trade, especially the shipping of farm products brought here from southern Delaware.

In 1828 the federal government began construction of the Delaware Breakwater just offshore from Lewes, and in consequence Lewes became an important harbor of refuge for ships entering and leaving Delaware Bay or passing up and down the coast. By 1840 about twenty-five vessels used the harbor daily, and over two hundred when gales threatened. Despite the breakwater, however, during two extraordinary storms in 1888 and 1889, dozens of ships were wrecked in Lewes Harbor. In 1901 another breakwater was completed two miles farther offshore from the Delaware Breakwater, so that together the two barriers now provide a harbor of refuge totaling about one thousand acres. However, this sheltered zone is shoaling in because of the northwestward growth of Cape Henlopen.

In 1869 a railroad spur was completed to Lewes, and by 1883 factories for drying and canning fruit and for processing menhaden into oil and fertilizer had been established near the depot. At the beginning of the twentieth century, Lewes engaged in a large trade in fruit and vegetables with northern cities. Two of the Atlantic coast's largest menhaden plants stood just east of what is now the ferry terminal. In 1953 the catch brought ashore at Lewes was approximately 360 million pounds, most of it menhaden.

Although the Delaware menhaden fishery declined during the 1950s and '60s and the fish factories closed, Lewes remains today an important center of sport fishing, as is apparent from the fleet of charter boats and head boats based in Lewes Creek. Also, another long-standing maritime tradition survives at Lewes, inasmuch as The Pilots Association for the Bay and River Delaware is still based here in the former U.S. Coast Guard station next to the ferry terminal. The largest employer in Lewes, however, is now the Beebe Medical Center, a regional hospital. Another major business operating out of Lewes is the Cape May - Lewes Ferry, which made its first run in 1964.

≈   ≈   ≈   ≈

AUTOMOBILE DIRECTIONS: Lewes and the nearby ferry terminal and Cape Henlopen State Park are located where the southern shore of Delaware Bay meets the coast of the open Atlantic. (See **Map 1** on page iv in the Table of Contents.) Note, however, that as you draw within a few miles of Lewes, the many roadside signs for the ferry designate a route that bypasses the old part of town, which it would be a shame to miss. The instructions below take you first to the center of historic Lewes and then to the ferry and state park.

To Lewes from northern Delmarva and Interstate 95 southwest of Wilmington: From Interstate 95 take Exit 4A for Route 1 south, and stay on Route 1 past a quick succession of exits. Follow Route 1 south past Dover and Milford toward Rehoboth and the Delaware beaches. Eventually, about 20 miles past the Route 1 - Route 113 split at Milford, turn left off Route 1 onto Business Route 9 toward Lewes. Go 2.5 miles to the Dutch-style Zwaanendael Museum. Turn right onto Kings Highway (it's just an ordinary street) and park as soon as you can in the vicinity of the museum and adjacent Fisher-Martin House.

To Lewes from the Chesapeake Bay Bridge: After crossing the bridge, follow Route 50/301 across Kent Island. At the point where Route 50 and Route 301 split, fork right to follow Route 50, but after only 7 miles, turn left onto Route 404 toward Denton and Rehoboth. For more than 44 miles, follow Route 404 east across Route 13 and Route 113 to Georgetown, and there go three-quarters of the way around a traffic circle and continue east on Route 9/404 for 12.2 miles. At an intersection with Route 1, continue straight ahead 2.5 miles on Business Route 9 to the Dutch-style Zwaanendael Museum. Turn right onto Kings Highway (it's just an ordinary street) and park as soon as you can in the vicinity of the museum and adjacent Fisher-Martin House.

To Lewes from southern Delmarva and the Chesapeake Bay Bridge-Tunnel at Norfolk: After crossing the bridge-tunnel, follow Route 13 north about 73 miles to the intersection (near Pocomoke City, Maryland) with Route 113, and there turn right onto Route 113 north toward Berlin and Ocean City. Follow Route 113 for about 57 miles to an intersection with Route 9, and there turn right toward Georgetown and Lewes. In Georgetown, go half way around a traffic circle and continue east on Route 9/404 for 12.2 miles to an intersection with Route 1. From there continue straight ahead 2.5 miles on Business Route 9 to the Dutch-style Zwaanendael Museum. Turn right onto Kings Highway (it's just an ordinary street) and park as soon as you can in the vicinity of the museum and adjacent Fisher-Martin House.

To Lewes from Salisbury and the Delaware and Maryland seashore resorts: From the vicinity of Salisbury, take Route 13 north, then Route 9 east through Georgetown to the intersection with Route 1, and there continue straight on Business Route 9 for 2.5 miles into Lewes.

From the seaside resorts, take Route 1 north to the intersection on the right — opposite Route 404 west — with Business Route 9. Turn right to follow Business Route 9 for 2.5 miles into Lewes. At the Dutch-style Zwaanendael

MAP 20 — Lewes

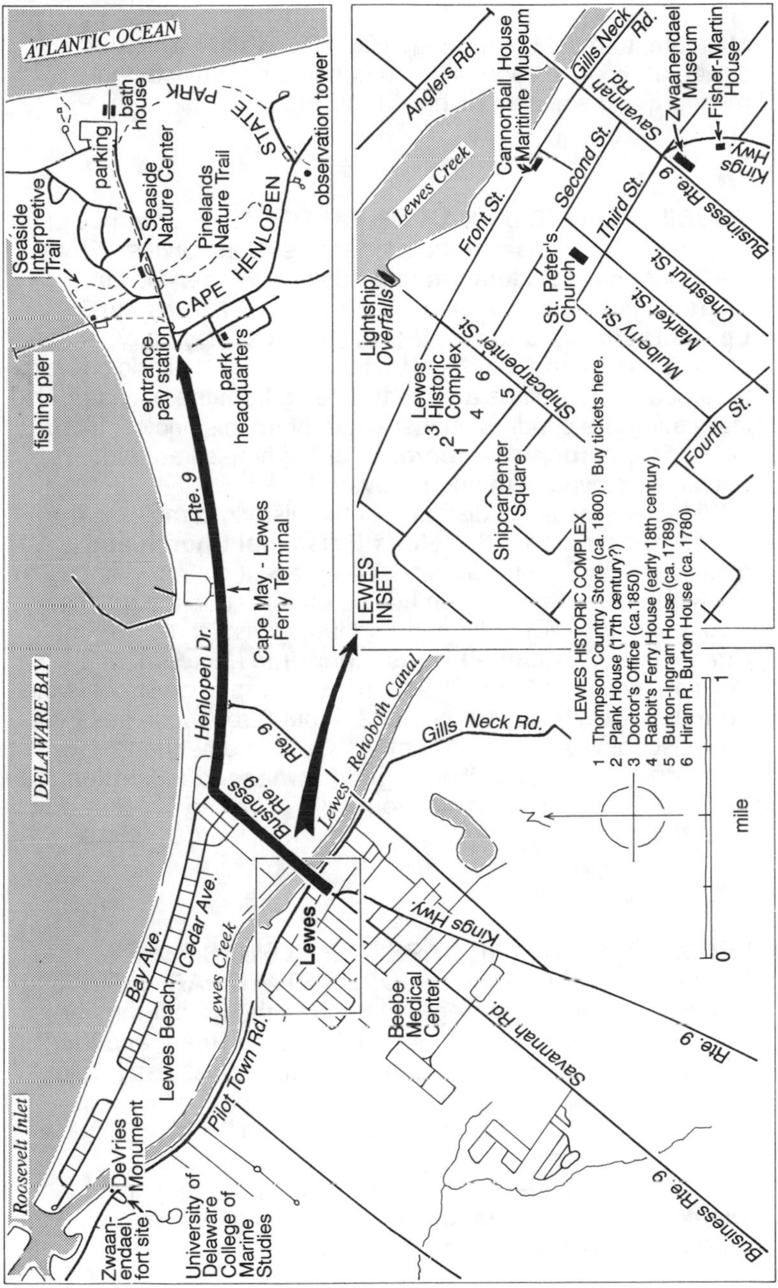

ATLANTIC OCEAN

bath house

parking

PARK

Seaside Nature Center

Pinelands Nature Trail

observation tower

Seaside Interpretive Trail

CAPE HENLOPEN STATE

entrance pay station

park headquarters

fishing pier

Rte. 9

DELAWARE BAY

Cape May - Lewes Ferry Terminal

Henlopen Dr.

Business Rte. 9

Lewes-Rehoboth Canal

Gills Neck Rd.

Bay Ave.

Cedar Ave.

Lewes Beach

Lewes Creek

Pilot Town Rd.

Lewes

Kings Hwy.

Beebe Medical Center

Savannah Rd.

Rte. 9

Business Rte. 9

Roosevelt Inlet

Zwaan-endael fort site

DeVries Monument

University of Delaware College of Marine Studies

LEWES INSET

Anglers Rd.

Cannonball House

Maritime Museum

Gills Neck Rd.

Savannah Rd.

Zwaanendael Museum

Fisher-Martin House

Kings Hwy.

Business Rte. 9

Lewes Creek

Front St.

Second St.

Third St.

Chestnut St.

St. Peter's Church

Market St.

Mulberry St.

Fourth St.

Lightship Overfalls

Lewes Historic Complex

1 2 3 4 5 6

Shipcarpenter St.

Shipcarpenter Square

LEWES HISTORIC COMPLEX

1 Thompson Country Store (ca. 1800). Buy tickets here.
2 Plank House (17th century?)
3 Doctor's Office (ca.1850)
4 Rabbit's Ferry House (early 18th century)
5 Burton-Ingram House (ca. 1789)
6 Hiram R. Burton House (ca. 1780)

mile

0   1

141

Museum, turn right onto Kings Highway (it's just an ordinary street) and park as soon as you can in the vicinity of the museum and adjacent Fisher-Martin House.

≈   ≈   ≈   ≈

TOURING LEWES BY CAR OR ON FOOT: Use **Map 20** on page 141 and its inset at the corner to explore Lewes. From the **Zwaanendael Museum** and adjacent **Fisher-Martin House**, drive or walk west on Third Street 0.2 mile to the **Lewes Historic Complex**, for which tickets may be purchased at the **Thompson Country Store**. Even if the historic complex is closed, the buildings are worth seeing from the outside. Also interesting is a subdivision just south of the historic complex; called **Shipcarpenter Square**, all of the houses are old structures moved here and renovated.

Within easy walking distance of the historic complex is the shopping district and **St. Peter's Episcopal Church and graveyard** on Second Street. (The present church was built in 1858 and is the third church edifice on this spot; the graves go back much further.) Within the shopping district at 118 Front Street is the **Cannonball House Maritime Museum**, and at the intersection of Front Street and Shipcarpenter Street is the lightship **Overfalls**. To the west, Front Street becomes Pilot Town Road, which leads 1.1 miles to a monument and cemetery at the **site of the original Zwaanendael settlement** opposite Roosevelt Inlet, as the mouth of Lewes Creek is now called.

≈   ≈   ≈   ≈

FROM LEWES TO THE CAPE MAY - LEWES FERRY TERMINAL and CAPE HENLOPEN STATE PARK: The long bold line on **Map 20** on page 141 shows the way. From the intersection of Business Route 9 (Savannah Road) and Front Street at the center of Lewes, drive east on Business Route 9 across the canal. Continue 0.4 mile to an intersection with Henlopen Drive, and there turn right and go 0.7 mile to the ferry terminal's foot-passenger parking lot on the left.

For Cape Henlopen State Park, continue straight past the ferry terminal for another 0.8 mile. From the park entrance, the main **ocean swimming beach** is straight ahead.

≈   ≈   ≈   ≈

WALKING AT CAPE HENLOPEN STATE PARK: Map 21 on page 144 shows the various trails and other features that make Cape Henlopen the Delaware shore's best place for walking.

The beach provides an opportunity for a short stroll or a round-trip hike of up to 10 miles. Because vehicles are permitted on the beach for purposes of surf fishing, walking along the shore is best from November through March, when fishing is poor and few vehicles are present.

The western beach and sandy tidal flats of **Henlopen Point** are a particularly interesting place to walk, but from March through September the area is closed in order not to disturb endangered piping plovers and other beach-nesting birds. During the rest of the year, an outstanding walk is to start at the **point parking lot** and follow the point's western flank north 0.7 mile, then continue around the point and down the ocean beach for as far as you care to go. To return to the point parking lot, use the pedestrian crossover straight from the ocean beach.

Another good place to start walking is at the oceanfront parking lot and overlook at **Herring Point** (also called the T Building), and from there hike north along the beach to Henlopen Point and back, for a round-trip distance of 6 miles. From the same lot south along the beach to a pair of observation towers is 2.7 miles round-trip.

The Seaside Interpretive Trail starts behind the west (left) end of the **Seaside Nature Center** and forms a circuit of 0.7 mile to the beach and back. A flyer discussing sights along the trail is available at the nature center.

The Pinelands Nature Trail starts across the road from the Seaside Nature Center and forms a circuit leading 1.6 miles through a sandy pine forest. Again, a booklet discussing sights along the trail is available at the nature center.

The Walking Dune Hiking Trail and Saltmarsh Spur provide good walking inland at Cape Henlopen State Park. The Walking Dune Hiking Trail leads to a high migrating dune, and the Saltmarsh Spur follows a low, wooded ridge that projects into a large marsh. This ridge is one of several parallel dunes that once trailed west from Cape Henlopen before the spit extended itself farther north. Fed by material swept northward by the longshore current from the vicinity of Rehoboth Beach and Dewey Beach, Cape Henlopen continues to build into Delaware Bay.

The trailhead for the Walking Dune Hiking Trail is a small

MAP 21 — Cape Henlopen State Park

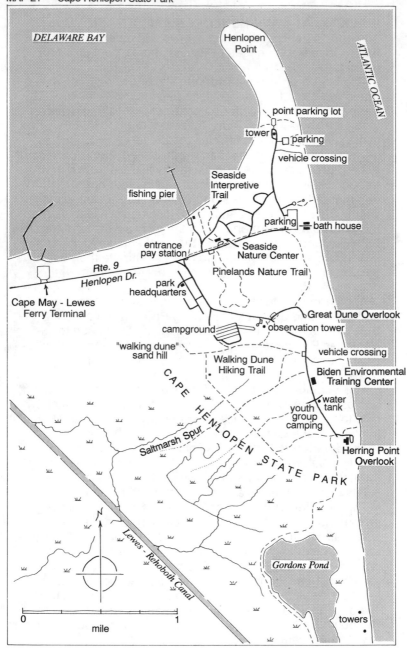

parking lot located 0.4 mile southeast along the road from an observation tower that is sometimes open to the public. From the parking lot the trail starts as an old asphalt road (closed to motor vehicles). Follow this road 0.5 mile to an intersection by a small chainlink enclosure on the left opposite a concrete bunker on the right. For the Walking Dune, continue straight; for the Saltmarsh Spur, turn left and go 0.5 mile to a four-way trail junction, and there turn right. As shown on Map 21, there is another less frequented spur trail into the marsh farther south.

Return by the way you came. Or, for a slightly longer walk, continue southeast, then east to the park road and Herring Point (the T Building) overlooking the ocean. Follow the path down to the beach, then walk north along the shore for half a mile to the vehicle crossing. Follow the rutted automobile trail back west through the dunes to your starting point.

A trail past Gordons Pond links the overlook at Herring Point (the T Building) with the park's southern entrance at Rehoboth. If you are prepared for a few wet places, a very attractive circuit of 5.5 miles is to take the trail south past Gordons Pond, then cross to the beach and follow the shore north past a pair of observation towers and back to the Herring Point Overlook, as described in greater detail below. This loop, however, is not possible May through August, when the beach opposite Gordons Pond is closed to protect nesting birds.

For the circuit around Gordons Pond, start at the Herring Point Overlook. At the entrance to the overlook area, cross the park road and follow a path 25 yards into the woods, then turn left on another trail marked with plastic stakes. Follow this trail as it winds through the back edge of the dunes, more or less parallel with the shore visible in the distance to the left. Eventually, descend from the dunes into piney woods. Continue through marsh, where the trail is often puddled. Follow the trail as it circles counter-clockwise around Gordons Pond. At a T-intersection with a sand road, turn right and go 75 yards to a large parking lot at the park's Rehoboth entrance. Turn left along the edge of the parking lot and cross to the beach. With the ocean on the right, follow the beach north past two observation towers. Pass below the high dune at the Herring Point Overlook. After crossing one groin — and before reaching another groin — turn left to follow a path leading up to the overlook parking lot.

10

EASTON
ST. MICHAELS
TILGHMAN ISLAND
OXFORD via ferry

The 60-mile car tour outlined on **Map 23** on page 155 links the chief towns of Talbot County, Maryland. **Easton**, the county seat, is shown on **Map 22** on page 153. The town features an historic district containing many attractive specialty shops, as well as the **Historical Society of Talbot County's museum** and the adjacent **James Neall and Joseph Neall houses** (early nineteenth and late eighteenth centuries, respectively). On the museum grounds there is also a re-creation of a seventeenth-century dwelling. The museum, which changes exhibits several times each year, is open Tuesday through Saturday from 10 A.M. to 4 P.M. and on Sunday from 12 to 3. Within those hours, tours of the adjacent museum houses start at 11:30 and 1:30; there is no morning tour on Sunday. And across the street from the museum is the historical society's **Tharpe House**, an early nineteenth-century dwelling where antiques and decorative arts are displayed for sale. For information on the historical society's various programs — including guided walking tours of Easton, for which reservations are required three days in advance — telephone (410) 822-0773. For a self-guided tour, simply pick up the historical society's pamphlet at the museum.

Also in Easton is the **Academy of the Arts**, offering exhibits of paintings, drawings, photographs, and sculpture, and a wide variety of other programs, including lectures, concerts, and classes. For information, telephone (410) 822-0455. The Academy of the Arts is open Monday through Saturday from 10 A.M. to 4 P.M. and Wednesday evening from 4 to 9. Another center of community life is the **Avalon Theater**, which hosts three or four events per week, including meetings of various civic groups, lectures, movies, concerts by classical, jazz, and folk musicians, and other entertainment. For information, telephone (410) 822-0345. Finally, Easton's main annual event is the Waterfowl Festival, held the second weekend of November.

Like Easton, **St. Michaels**, which is shown on **Map 24** on page 156, has numerous shops for crafts, gifts, and antiques, as well as several outstanding restaurants overlooking its attractive harbor, where the **Chesapeake Bay Maritime Museum** is located. The museum includes a comprehensive collection of bay boats and maritime artifacts. For most of the year, the museum is open daily starting at 9 A.M., but the closing time changes with the seasons. During January and February, the museum is open only on Friday, Saturday, Sunday, and Monday holidays. For information telephone (410) 745-2916. From April through October or early November, the **excursion boat *Patriot*** operates from the bulkhead in front of the museum's administration buildings, departing at 11:00, 12:30, 2:30, and 4:00 for cruises on the Miles River. Telephone (410) 745-3100 for information. Also in St. Michaels is the **St. Mary's Square Museum**, which is devoted chiefly to local history. It is open May through October on Saturday and Sunday from 10 A.M. to 4 P.M.

Tilghman Island, linked to the mainland by a drawbridge, is the next port-of-call on our car cruise. A large fleet of commercial fishing craft, including a few old sail-powered dredge boats, operates from the island. During the summer season, excursions are sometimes offered by the skipjack captains.

Oxford, which is shown on **Map 25** on page 159, is a quiet yachting village fronting on the Tred Avon River. During most of the year, it is served by the Oxford-Bellevue Ferry. However, the ferry does not operate from early December through February, so at that time of year you must drive the long way around to reach Oxford. In spring and fall, the ferry stops running at sunset; from June through Labor Day, the ferry stops running at 9 P.M.

ANYONE FAMILIAR with a map of the Chesapeake region has surely regarded with fascination the winglike landform that projects into Chesapeake Bay between the Miles River to the north and the Choptank and Tred Avon rivers to the south. (See Map 23 on page 155.) Here, in Maryland's Talbot County, are several interesting towns, each with its own flavor.

Easton grew up around the Talbot County Courthouse, established in 1711. Throughout most of the eighteenth century, the place was merely a tiny cluster of taverns and houses with a nearby race course where sometimes large crowds gathered — as in 1754, when about a thousand people came on horseback and in carriages to watch a race for a purse of £20 donated by Governor Horatio Sharpe. Not until after the Revolution was the town incorporated and formally laid out. Then in 1788 it was designated Maryland's administrative center for the Eastern Shore, and business boomed. (Incidentally, promotional literature for Easton often touts the town as the *colonial* capital of the Eastern Shore, which is false.) In 1790 the Eastern Shore's first newspaper was founded at Easton, and during the next four years the paper carried advertisements for ten general merchants at Easton, plus hatters, tailors, tavernkeepers, private schoolmasters, physicians, clockmakers, and other artisans and professionals, including a barber and bleeder, a dancing master, and a portrait artist. A new courthouse, paid for largely by the state, was built in 1794 (it still stands as the middle section of the present-day courthouse) and in it were located branch offices of the Annapolis government. Sessions of what is now the Maryland Court of Appeals were held alternately in Annapolis and in Easton, and even the federal circuit court sometimes convened at Easton from 1790 to 1796. In 1798 the *American Gazetteer* described Easton as the "chief town of Talbot County, Maryland," with "a handsome courthouse, a market house, about 150 dwelling houses, and several stores for the supply of the adjoining county."

During the nineteenth century, Easton was the most populous and important town on Maryland's Eastern Shore. As the century began, the town had two weekly newspapers. In 1805 the Eastern Shore's first bank was established at Easton, and starting in 1817 the first steamboat line linking Baltimore and the Eastern Shore ran to Easton Point (formerly sleepy Cow Landing) located a mile west of town at the head of the Tred Avon River.

After suffering from a long agricultural depression in the second quarter of the nineteenth century, the economy of Maryland's Eastern Shore began to revive in the years leading up to the Civil War as the region turned increasingly to supplying vegetables, fruit, and seafood to northern cities. Nonetheless, political sympathies among Talbot County's plantation-owning elite — descendants of the wealthy, powerful, and proud colonial gentry — were distinctly Southern. Although Talbot County voted 847 to 666 against secession in 1861, and although four times as many Talbot men served with the Union as with the Confederacy, the Civil War memorial in front of the courthouse in Easton is "To the Talbot Boys 1861-1865 CSA."

Easton's economy benefited from the arrival of the railroad in 1869, but other towns prospered still more. Toward the end of the century,

Easton was outstripped by Cambridge and Salisbury as those towns became major packing and shipping points for the Eastern Shore's farm products. Cambridge also did a large business in oysters and other seafood. During the heyday of oystering in the 1880s, even Crisfield was more populous than Easton. It was at about this time that a trend began in Talbot County that continued through the early twentieth century and the Depression years of the 1930s. Rich Northerners started buying waterfront plantations, and urban folk started coming by train and by steamboat for quiet vacations at local boarding houses.

Although Easton today has lost its former primacy among Maryland's Eastern Shore towns, it is still the commercial, financial, medical, and cultural center of an area that extends well beyond the limits of Talbot County. There is some light manufacturing at Easton and large regional retail strips along Route 50 and Route 322, which have taken business away from the center of town. Now the tone of the older part of Easton around the courthouse and along Washington, Harrison, Goldsborough, and Dover streets is set by the concentration of fashionable shops, antique stores, fine restaurants, stock brokerages, banks, and real estate brokers', accountants', and lawyers' offices that serve a disproportionately well-to-do population, including a large number of wealthy retirees and second-home owners whose properties are arrayed along Talbot County's six hundred miles of convoluted shore. Increasingly, too, expensive waterfront subdivisions are being occupied by those willing to commute long distances to jobs elsewhere in Delmarva and even to the Chesapeake's Western Shore.

Although Easton is far more than a tourist town, it has not neglected the tourist trade. In particular, the town hosts the annual Waterfowl Festival held on the second weekend in November. The festival is devoted largely to waterfowl art and artifacts, including prints, photographs, carved decoys, old guns, and other collectibles. All net proceeds from sales by the festival's vendors are donated to various conservation organizations. For information telephone (410) 822-4567.

≈   ≈   ≈   ≈

AUTOMOBILE DIRECTIONS: Easton is located on Route 50 about 15 miles north of Cambridge and 20 miles southeast of the Chesapeake Bay Bridge. (See **Map 1** on page iv in the Table of Contents.) The car tour to St. Michaels, Tilghman Island, and Oxford shown on **Map 23** on page 155 starts at Easton, so you should go there first.

To Easton from northern Delmarva and Interstate 95 near Newark, Delaware: From I-95 take Route 896 south across

Route 40 and over the Chesapeake and Delaware Canal. From there, follow Route 301 south, passing straight through an intersection where Route 896 bears left. In all, follow Route 301 south into Maryland for about 44 miles. Eventually, after passing exits for Route 305 and Route 304 near Centreville, take the exit for Route 213 south. At the top of the ramp, turn left and follow Route 213 south toward Route 50 and Easton for 4.3 miles, then turn left (east) onto Route 50 and follow it for 11 miles to a junction with Route 322 (Easton Parkway). Bear right onto Route 322, but follow it only 0.4 mile, then turn left onto Washington Street. Follow Washington Street 1.5 miles to the county courthouse at the center of Easton.

To Easton from the Chesapeake Bay Bridge: After crossing the bridge, follow Route 50/301 across Kent Island. At the point where Route 50 and Route 301 split, fork right to follow Route 50 for 16.4 miles to the junction with Route 322 (Easton Parkway). Bear right onto Route 322, but follow it only 0.4 mile, then turn left onto Washington Street. Go 1.5 miles to the county courthouse at the center of Easton.

To Easton from southern Delmarva and the Chesapeake Bay Bridge-Tunnel at Norfolk: After crossing the bridge-tunnel, follow Route 13 north into Maryland and past Pocomoke City and Princess Anne to the exit for Route 50 westbound near Salisbury, and from there take Route 50 west past Cambridge. From the northern end of the long bridge over the Choptank River, follow Route 50 for 10.5 miles to the junction with Route 322 (Easton Parkway). Bear left onto Route 322, but follow it only 0.5 mile, then turn right onto Route 565 toward Easton. Follow Route 565 (Washington Street) 2 miles to the county courthouse at the center of Easton.

To Easton from Salisbury: Take Route 50 west past Cambridge. From the northern end of the long bridge over the Choptank River, follow Route 50 for 10.5 miles to the junction with Route 322 (Easton Parkway). Bear left onto Route 322, but follow it only 0.5 mile, then turn right onto Route 565 toward Easton. Follow Route 565 (Washington Street) 2 miles to the county courthouse at the center of Easton.

To Easton from the Delaware and Maryland seashore resorts: From Ocean City take Route 50 west past Salisbury and Cambridge, then follow the directions in the previous paragraph.

From the vicinity of Rehoboth Beach, follow Route 1 north to the intersection near Lewes with Route 404 westbound, then follow Route 404 west through Georgetown and across Route 113 and Route 13 to the intersection with Route 50 near Wye Mills. Turn left onto Route 50 toward Easton and go 9.7 miles to the junction with Route 322 (Easton Parkway). Bear right onto Route 322, but follow it only 0.4 mile, then turn left onto Washington Street. Follow Washington Street 1.5 miles to the county courthouse at the center of Easton.

≈   ≈   ≈   ≈

TOURING EASTON ON FOOT: Use **Map 22** at right to explore Easton's historic district, which has many structures dating from the late eighteenth, nineteenth, and early twentieth centuries. The most interesting part of town is along Washington Street, Harrison Street, and some of the cross streets between the two. The **Museum of the Historical Society of Talbot County** is located at 25 South Washington Street, one block below the **Talbot County Courthouse.** The front part of the museum occupies a store built in the 1850s. Next door is the **James Neall House**, built between 1804 and 1810, and behind it at the far end of a federal-style garden is the **Joseph Neall House**, built in 1795. The Neall brothers were both Quaker cabinet makers. Across the street from the museum is the historical society's **Tharpe House**, built in 1810 (part is older). The **Avalon Theater**, which has a restaurant on its top floor, is located at the corner of Dover and Harrison streets. Two blocks south of the theater is the **Academy of the Arts** at 106 South Street. And about 0.6 mile south of the courthouse (off the bottom edge of the map and situated at the end of a long driveway entered from Washington Street) is the frame **Society of Friends Third Haven Meeting House**. It was started in 1682 and finished two years later — long before there was any town in the vicinity. The meeting house has now been meticulously restored. Many notable Quakers, including William Penn, have worshipped in this building. The nearby brick meeting house was built in 1880 and is used in winter.

≈   ≈   ≈   ≈

MAP 22 — Easton

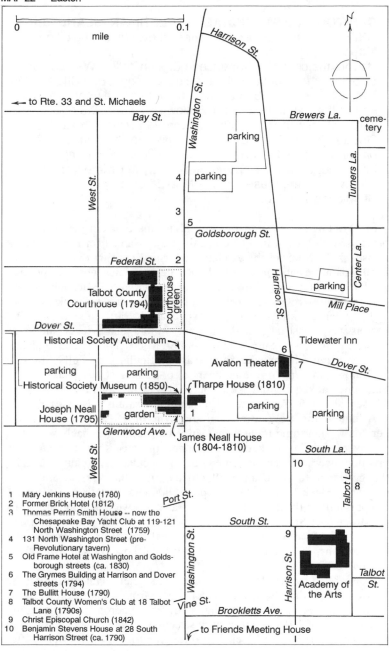

1 Mary Jenkins House (1780)
2 Former Brick Hotel (1812)
3 Thomas Perrin Smith House -- now the
   Chesapeake Bay Yacht Club at 119-121
   North Washington Street (1759)
4 131 North Washington Street (pre-
   Revolutionary tavern)
5 Old Frame Hotel at Washington and Goldsborough streets (ca. 1830)
6 The Grymes Building at Harrison and Dover
   streets (1794)
7 The Bullitt House (1790)
8 Talbot County Women's Club at 18 Talbot
   Lane (1790s)
9 Christ Episcopal Church (1842)
10 Benjamin Stevens House at 28 South
   Harrison Street (ca. 1790)

153

CAR TOUR TO ST. MICHAELS, TILGHMAN ISLAND, and OXFORD: This 60-mile car tour is shown by the bold line on **Map 23** at right.

From the county courthouse in Easton, follow Washington Street north about 0.1 mile, then turn left onto Bay Street. (On **Map 22** on page 153, the small arrow near the upper left shows the way out of town.) Follow Bay Street 0.5 mile to an intersection with Route 322 (Easton Parkway). Cross Route 322 and follow Route 33 west 9.4 miles to St. Michaels. After passing most of the way through St. Michaels, turn right onto Mill Street toward the **Chesapeake Bay Maritime Museum**. After visiting the museum, use **Map 24** on page 156 to explore St. Michaels on foot.

St. Michaels is located midway along the crooked peninsula that projects from Easton into Chesapeake Bay. Named for the Episcopal parish of St. Michael the Archangel formed here in 1672, the town itself was not established until about a century later, nor incorporated until 1805. Shipyards, however, were located at St. Michaels' harbor from the latter 1600s onward. Shipbuilding reached a peak in about 1810, when all kinds of bay boats, coastal craft, and ocean-going vessels were constructed and fitted out at more than a dozen shipyards in or near the town. Shipwrights from St. Michaels were active also at other leading Chesapeake shipyards, particularly at Fells Point in Baltimore. In terms of the numbers of boats built, Chesapeake Bay at that time ranked behind New England, but the average tonnage of Chesapeake craft greatly exceeded that of boats built in New England.

Although the Revolution and the War of 1812 were depressed periods for maritime trade, some ships built at St. Michaels served as highly profitable blockade runners and privateers — or that is, as privately operated warships fitted out on speculation and authorized by the governor to seize and sell enemy merchant vessels and their cargoes. Sleek two-masted clipper schooners — termed Baltimore clippers but built at other bay ports also — were among the ships constructed at St. Michaels during the early 1800s. Faster than any other ships afloat, these vessels made ideal privateers. Armed with a few cannons, they could chase down weaker boats or sail away from stronger craft.

Exasperated by the glaring success of American privateers during the War of 1812, when twenty-eight schooners from Talbot County alone operated against English shipping, a British squadron spent the spring and summer of 1813 in a tour of destruction up and down Chesapeake Bay, which the British blockaded throughout most of the war. After

MAP 23 — Car tour from Easton to St. Michaels, Tilghman Island, and Oxford

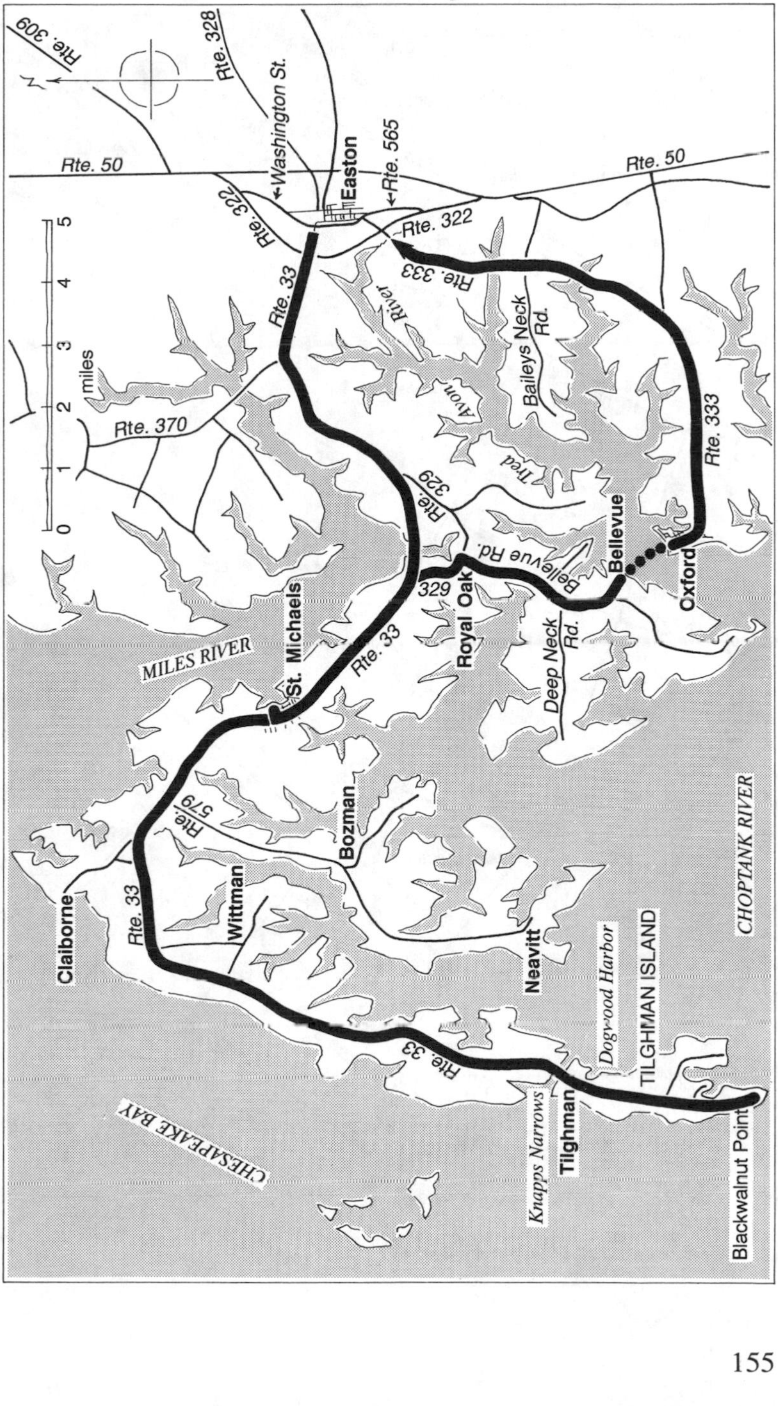

MAP 24 — St. Michaels

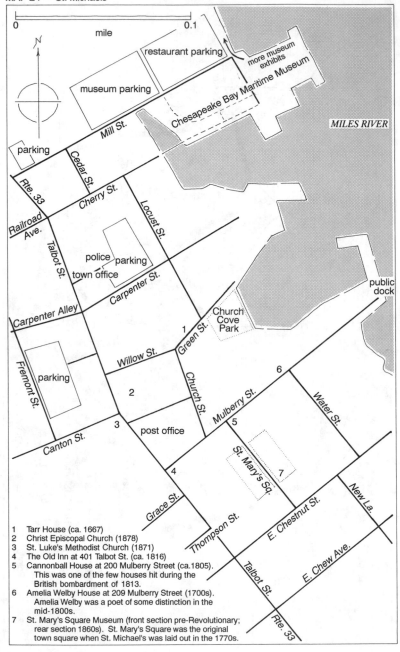

0   mile   0.1

N

restaurant parking

more museum exhibits

museum parking

Chesapeake Bay Maritime Museum

MILES RIVER

Mill St.

parking

Cedar St.

Rte. 33

Cherry St.

Railroad Ave.

Locust St.

Talbot St.

police   parking

town office

Carpenter St.

Carpenter St.

Carpenter Alley

public dock

Church Cove Park

Fremont St.

parking

Willow St.

Green St.

1

6

Church St.

Water St.

2

Mulberry St.

5

3   post office

Canton St.

St. Mary's Sq.

7

4

Grace St.

Thompson St.

New La.

E. Chestnut St.

Talbot St.

E. Chew Ave.

Rte. 33

1   Tarr House (ca. 1667)
2   Christ Episcopal Church (1878)
3   St. Luke's Methodist Church (1871)
4   The Old Inn at 401 Talbot St. (ca. 1816)
5   Cannonball House at 200 Mulberry Street (ca.1805).
        This was one of the few houses hit during the
        British bombardment of 1813.
6   Amelia Welby House at 209 Mulberry Street (1700s).
        Amelia Welby was a poet of some distinction in the
        mid-1800s.
7   St. Mary's Square Museum (front section pre-Revolutionary;
        rear section 1860s). St. Mary's Square was the original
        town square when St. Michael's was laid out in the 1770s.

burning Havre de Grace on the Susquehanna and Georgetown and Fredericktown on the Sassafras, the British attacked St. Michaels early on the morning of August 10. In the dark they sent ashore a landing party of about 300 soldiers who stormed an earthwork fort southeast of the town. The defenders fled but the British nonetheless suffered nineteen killed when the last militiaman to leave the fort fired a cannon into their ranks. Disheartened, the British spiked the fort's guns and re-embarked without taking the town. Then eleven British barges shelled St. Michaels for a period of hours but the bombardment was inaccurate and failed to damage the town or the ships under construction there.

Following the war St. Michaels suffered from the same loss of commerce that affected all small and middling Chesapeake ports as Baltimore and Norfolk became the main centers of trade. St. Michaels' shipyards were reduced to turning out brogans and log canoes from which local watermen tonged for oysters, plus an occasional bay schooner or pungy for carrying cargo among local ports. Frederick Douglass, who worked as a slave on a large plantation near St. Michaels, described the town in 1833 as "an unsaintly as well as unsightly place," where every oyster boat carried a jug of rum against the cold. But after dredging for oysters was legalized in 1865, St. Michaels' shipyards prospered by building two-masted, beamy, shallow-draft dredge boats called bugeyes and smaller single-masted dredge boats called skipjacks. (Examples of a wide variety of bay boats can be seen at the Chesapeake Bay Maritime Museum.) During the twentieth century, of course, the Chesapeake seafood industry has steadily declined, but the economic loss to St. Michaels has been counterbalanced by a rise in pleasure boating and tourism.

CAR TOUR continued (Map 23 — from St. Michaels to Tilghman Island): From St. Michaels, follow Route 33 west toward Tilghman Island. Go more than 12 miles to the drawbridge at Knapps Narrows, then continue south 3 miles through Tilghman to the end of the road at Blackwalnut Point.

Because **Tilghman Island** provides immediate access to Chesapeake Bay to the west and the Choptank River to the east, it has for generations been a watermen's community. Many workboats are based at Knapps Narrows and also at Dogwood Harbor a half-mile south of the drawbridge. A few sail-powered skipjacks also operate out of Dogwood Harbor. However, new yachting-oriented developments along the shore indicate that leisure activities and tourism may soon replace commercial fishing as the mainstay of the island's economy.

CAR TOUR continued (Map 23 — from Tilghman Island to Oxford via ferry): Remember, the Oxford-Bellevue Ferry does not operate from early December through February, so at that time of year, simply return to Route 322 (the Easton Parkway) and from there follow Route 322 south to Route 333 and Oxford. But during the rest of the year, proceed as follows:
Return on Route 33 from Tilghman Island to St. Michaels. From the intersection with Mill Street in St. Michaels, continue on Route 33 for 3.1 miles, then turn right onto Route 329. Follow Route 329 east for 1 mile to the village of Royal Oak, and there turn right onto Bellevue Road toward the ferry. Follow Bellevue Road 3.3 miles to the ferry landing. After crossing to Oxford, use **Map 25** at right to explore the town by car or on foot.

The **Oxford Customs House**, a small structure near the ferry landing, is a replica of the first federal customs house built in the 1790s, when Oxford no longer had any international trade to speak of. The **Oxford Museum**, located on Market Street near the corner with Morris Street, is open Friday, Saturday, and Sunday, 2 to 5 P.M., from mid-April through mid-October.

Oxford is one of Maryland's oldest towns. It appears on Augustine Herman's 1673 Map of Virginia and Maryland and was repeatedly mentioned as an official port in legislation of the period designed to consolidate trade at designated sites. Cecilius Calvert — second Baron Baltimore and proprietor of Maryland — and his son and resident governor, Charles Calvert, thought that the growth of towns was desirable for a number of reasons: to make commerce more efficient, to promote education, religion, and culture, and (not least) to facilitate the collection of the province's export tax on tobacco, half of which helped to pay the expenses of government, while the rest went to the Calverts.

Directives to establish port towns, including a town at what is now Oxford, were issued in 1669 and 1671. According to the Act for the Advancement of Trade passed by the General Assembly in 1683, "Noe merchant Factor or Mariner or other person whatsoever tradeing in this province" was to import or export goods except at designated ports; people who traded elsewhere were subject to "forfeiting all such goods & merchandizes." Oxford was one of four port towns that were to be established in Talbot County, and one of thirty in the colony. The following year a hundred lots were laid out at Oxford, but fewer than a

MAP 25 — Oxford

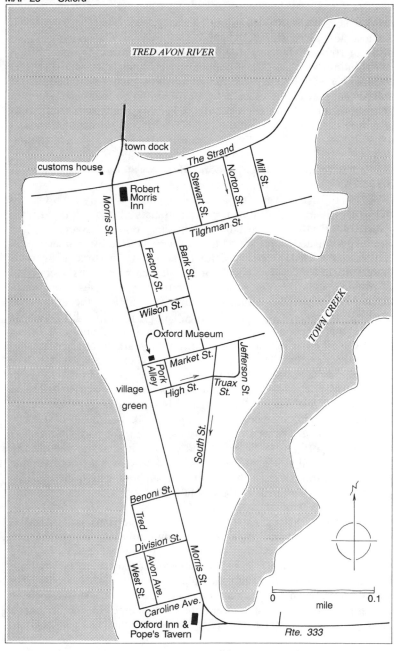

TRED AVON RIVER

town dock

customs house

Robert Morris Inn

The Strand

Stewart St.

Norton St.

Mill St.

Morris St.

Tilghman St.

Factory St.

Bank St.

Wilson St.

Oxford Museum

Pork Alley

Market St.

Jefferson St.

village green

High St.

Truax St.

South St.

TOWN CREEK

Benoni St.

Tred

Division St.

Avon Ave.

West St.

Morris St.

Caroline Ave.

Oxford Inn & Pope's Tavern

Rte. 333

N

0   mile   0.1

third were sold, and even many of those sales were later nullified because no houses were built, as required by law. Oxford was platted again in 1694, when it was briefly called Williamstadt in honor of the current king, William III. A collector of customs was installed there, and another one at Annapolis, so that all ships from abroad had first to call at one port or the other before proceeding to trade elsewhere in Maryland. In 1695 the high sheriff of Talbot County was required to reside at Oxford as a condition of office. In 1696 merchants who brought their families to live at Oxford were granted special trading concessions. In 1707 the town was platted yet again. Still the collection point for a very large customs district (though not as large as before), Oxford finally began to grow.

For about seventy years tobacco was exported directly from Oxford to Great Britain, and all manner of manufactured goods arrived from overseas. Commercial establishments in London, Liverpool, and Bristol established stores at Oxford that were headed by local agents or factors who traded merchandise for tobacco. At one time as many as eight British firms and an equal number of local merchants operated at Oxford. In addition to the merchants' private storehouses, there was a public warehouse for tobacco. In the first half of the eighteenth century, Oxford was second only to Annapolis in terms of the number of ships that stopped there. According to Jeremiah Banning, a Talbot County man of affairs and for twenty-two years a sea captain who sailed out of Oxford, "The storekeepers and other retailers both on the western and the eastern side of the Chesapeake repaired there to lay in their supplies. . . . Seven or eight large ships at the same time were frequently seen at Oxford delivering goods and completing their lading; nor was it uncommon to despatch a ship with 500 hogsheads of tobacco within twelve days of its arrival." Hides, wheat, salt pork, and lumber were also exported from Oxford. And yet the place never amounted to more than a small village of two or three hundred people perched on the edge of a uniformly rural hinterland, throughout which most of the colonists were scattered on their small plantations or farms growing tobacco and a few other cash crops.

The fact that the colonial government tried so hard and so persistently to legislate towns into existence shows only too clearly that such places were regarded as unnecessary by those who were to be required to do business in them. In the early years of the colony, ships from England traded directly with the tobacco growers by ascending the rivers, sailing from one plantation landing to the next. At first tobacco was simply sold to the ship's captains in exchange for goods, but as some growers prospered and acquired larger plantations, they sought to get a higher price for their crops by corresponding directly with British consignment houses, which sold the tobacco on commission. These large planters also bartered for the crops of the many small farmers in their vicinity, giving in exchange essential goods ordered from England and imported directly to their plantations, where the big growers set up their own stores. As a consequence of buying goods on credit, the smaller farmers became obligated to bring their crops to the larger planters, some of whom eventually acquired ships of their own, or at least chartered them.

Because of the comprehensive dealings of the large planters, a separate merchant class was slow to develop in the tidewater region, and so too were towns. Far more often than not, the official ports designated by law never came into being or were never more than trading outposts and warehouse landings were tobacco was gathered, inspected, and stored prior to shipment. Only at a few places like Oxford, where numbers of enterprising, well-financed, and well-connected merchants took the lead, did actual villages develop on the Eastern Shore. At Oxford the merchants gradually acquired the business of the larger planters by pitching their trade directly to them, buying tobacco outright in huge quantities, and supplying a broad range of merchandise and chattels, including not only items from Great Britain, but also indentured servants, convict laborers (particularly rebels from Ireland and Scotland), slaves from Africa or the Caribbean, wine from Madeira and the Canary Islands, and salt, sugar, molasses, and rum from the West Indies.

One Oxford merchant who rose to prominence in the eighteenth century was Robert Morris, the father of the financier of the American Revolution. The elder Morris arrived in Oxford in 1738 and proceeded to accumulate a fortune as chief factor for the large Liverpool trading house of Foster Cunliffe & Sons, which had branches throughout the Eastern Shore. Morris also engaged widely in trade on his own account. He had his residence and warehouse at the water end of Oxford's main street, now called Morris Street. A part of the house is incorporated into the present-day Robert Morris Inn.

Morris's influence extended throughout Maryland's tidewater region, where he introduced reforms that helped to improve and streamline the province's trade. Because the reputation and price of Maryland's tobacco suffered from the practice of adulterating good leaf with trash growth, Morris pressed for a tobacco inspection law, which finally was adopted in 1747, after Morris had already instituted a system of inspection in his own business and had gone a long way toward making other merchants do likewise. And in place of the old bookkeeping system by which debts and credits were expressed in terms of pounds of tobacco (so that entries constantly fluctuated in value with the price of the commodity), Morris introduced account keeping based on real money. Jeremiah Banning has left a description of Morris:

> His great natural abilities o'erleaped every other deficiency. As a mercantile genius, twas thought he had not his equal in this land. As a companion and bon vivant, he was incomparable. If he had any public point to carry he defeated all opposition. . . . He was a steady, sincere and warm friend . . . and had a hand ever open to relieve real distress. At repartee, he bore down all before him. [But he had also] a haughty and overbearing carriage, perhaps a too vindictive spirit, and . . . an extreme severity to his servants.

So great a role did the elder Morris play in Oxford's commercial affairs that some contemporaries regarded his death by accident in 1750 as precipitating a loss of trade at Oxford, although probably more significant were disruptions caused by the Seven Years War starting in 1756 and the Eastern Shore's shift from growing tobacco to growing wheat, which was a commodity that could not be traded to England because of prohibitive duties there. One after another, the English merchant firms sold their businesses at Oxford or moved them to Baltimore, which was emerging as the chief transshipment point for products of the Chesapeake region. The interruption in commerce caused by the War of Independence, during which British merchants fled the colonies, and the continued growth of Baltimore afterwards left Oxford with almost no international trade. In 1793 Jeremiah Banning, who served as Oxford's first United States customs collector during a period when very few ships arrived from foreign ports, described the town in elegiac terms:

> The poor, drooping, and forsaken Oxford, bereft of almost every comfort in life, hath nothing remaining to console it except its salubrious situation and fine navigation which may anticipate better times. Oxford, whose street and strands were once covered with busy, noisy crowds, ushering in commerce from almost every quarter of the Globe, and whose rich, blooming lots echoed with fat, glowing kine — alas, now is shaded by wheat, corn and tobacco. The once well worn streets are now grown up with grass, save a few tracks made by the sheep and swine; and the strands have more the appearance of an uninhabited island than where human feet have ever trod.

During the first two-thirds of the nineteenth century, Oxford quietly stagnated. Its population dropped to less than a hundred. But the boom in oystering that followed the Civil War revived shipbuilding at Oxford and provided business for scores of boats based in the town's harbor.

Packing houses sprang up, and at the beginning of each year's oyster season, hundreds of blacks and immigrants arrived by steamboat and by train (the railroad reached Oxford in 1871) to work during the winter at shucking, pickling, and canning oysters. A tomato cannery was also established and provided seasonal employment. By 1880 the population of Oxford had reached 750 and in 1890 the Oxford Saving Bank was opened. But Oxford's economy declined yet again at the beginning of the twentieth century as oyster harvests dwindled. Since then the town has experienced a gradual and almost complete cessation of commercial fishing and a corresponding reincarnation as a village in large part populated by well-heeled retirees and weekenders, with an emphasis on yachting.

CAR TOUR continued (Map 23 — from Oxford to Easton):
Follow Morris Street away from Oxford's ferry landing, then continue on Route 333 for 10 miles to Easton, where the car tour ends.

11

CAMBRIDGE
BLACKWATER NATIONAL WILDLIFE
REFUGE
DORCHESTER "EVERGLADES"
HOOPER ISLAND

The excursion outlined in this chapter starts in **Cambridge**, Maryland, which fronts on the Choptank River and is the seat of Dorchester County. (For a tour of Cambridge, see **Map 26** on page 180.) Workboats and pleasure craft crowd the riverfront boat basin and Cambridge Creek, and distinguished old houses line High Street between the river and the courthouse square. Within a few minutes drive of High Street is the Dorchester County Historical Society's **Meredith House** (circa 1760) and the adjoining **Neild Museum**. The former has been meticulously restored and the latter contains an outstanding collection of old tools and artifacts from everyday life. The site also includes an herb garden and a stable containing old carriages and sleighs. The buildings are open Thursday, Friday, and Saturday from 10 A.M. to 4 P.M. and by appointment; telephone (410) 228-7953.

Also in Cambridge is the **Brannock Maritime Museum**, devoted to the maritime history of Chesapeake Bay. The museum displays many old photographs and large models of locally built schooners, pungies, bugeyes, skipjacks, and other craft. The museum is open Saturday from 10 A.M. to 4 P.M., Sunday from 1 to 4, and by appointment; telephone (410) 228-6938.

Somewhat similar to the Brannock Maritime Museum is the **Richardson Maritime Museum**, open April through October on Wednesday from 1 to 4 P.M., on Saturday from 10 to 4, and on Sunday from 1 to 4.

Currently under development in Cambridge is **Sailwinds Park** on the shore of the Choptank River. Park plans call for a cultural and visitor center, a public beach, a waterfront amphitheater, and a wetlands boardwalk. The park also has facilities for festivals and shows, such as the Bay Country Festival during the week of July 4th and the Seafood Festival in mid-August. For information on the schedule of events, telephone (410) 228-1000.

From Cambridge the 90-mile car tour shown on **Map 27** on page 181 heads south to the 20,000-acre **Blackwater National Wildlife Refuge**, which is probably the best place in Delmarva to appreciate the immense number of migratory waterfowl that winter in the Chesapeake region. At any season the Blackwater refuge is also an excellent place to see bald eagles and a wide variety of other birds. As shown on **Map 28** on page 183, the refuge has two short hiking trails and a paved road for cars and bicycles that follows a dike overlooking marshes and freshwater impoundments. The road and trails are open daily from dawn until dusk. There is also a visitor center with an information desk, exhibits, and bookstore. The visitor center is open Monday through Friday from 8 A.M. to 4 P.M. and Saturday and Sunday from 9 to 5; it is closed federal holidays. The refuge is managed by the U.S. Fish and Wildlife Service; telephone (410) 228-2677. Bicyclists may also enjoy other local roads that cut through the refuge, as discussed at the beginning of the tour directions near the bottom of page 179.

From Blackwater National Wildlife Refuge, the excursion circles south through a marshy region that somewhat resembles the Florida everglades: so flat, so low, so wet, so broad, so *different* that at times traveling through this area has the quality of navigating in some substance intermediate between land and water. A drive here in **southern Dorchester County** is worthwhile at any time of year just to see the landscape. If you have the time and inclination, you can also tour **Hooper Island** (actually several islands, now linked to the mainland by bridges) before returning north to the vicinity of Cambridge.

IMAGES PRODUCED BY LANDSAT SATELLITE show the Delmarva Peninsula to be densely speckled with farm fields interspersed with relatively little forest. An exception, however, is southern Dorchester County, which even from outer space is visibly different from most of Delmarva. From on high, southern Dorchester lacks the freckled appearance produced by numerous, irregularly-shaped fields. Instead, the region resembles rumpled, blotchy velvet. Similar material occupies the coast of Delaware Bay, the area behind the Atlantic barrier islands, and the Chesapeake shore of Somerset and Accomack counties. In Chesapeake Bay itself, large, amoeba-like islands — Bloodsworth and Smith islands, for example — appear to be made of nothing but this amorphous stuff, across which, in some places, spread dark, snaky tentacles.

The "stuff," of course, is marsh. When you travel south from Cambridge into the region drained by the Blackwater River, farmland gradually gives way to forests of loblolly pine and then to an immense and utterly flat expanse of marsh grass that is interlaced by sinuous, sluggish creeks and dotted with occasional timber islands. It is more than just a big marsh; it is a region. In fact, according to the Dorchester County Office of Soil Conservation, as much as 46 percent of the entire county — and Dorchester is the largest county on Maryland's Eastern Shore — is non-tidal wetlands, including all hydric (that is, very wet) soils, some of which are farmed or used for growing trees. When tidal wetlands are added, Dorchester's wetlands area (almost 400 square miles) reaches 66 percent of the county.

Moreover, the region is very slowly getting wetter still as the level of the sea rises at a rate which, since the time of European settlement, has been about half a foot per century. Simultaneously, the land is sinking as the region's soft, thick mantle of silty, peaty soil compacts under its own weight. In southern Dorchester County some areas that once had villages — Lower Hooper Island, for example — are no longer habitable.

Counteracting and somewhat retarding the effects of the rising ocean and the sinking land are other forces tending to build up the marsh surface. Silt eroded from higher areas is carried downstream by the region's rivers and deposited over the whole marsh during periods of flood caused by extraordinary rains or exceptionally high tides. The leaves and roots of marsh grasses help to catch and hold the silt, producing a landscape as flat as the surface of the silt-bearing floodwater. And, of course, the decaying stems and leaves of the marsh plants add bulk to the land surface, building it upward.

The predominant marsh plant of southern Dorchester is Olney three-square, also called American three-cornered sedge. It is an important source of food for Canada geese. Growing about two feet high, it is easily identified by its stiff, spiky stems, which are triangular in cross-section. The prevalence of three-square reflects its ability to tolerate wide fluctuations in salinity, which in the marshes bordering the Blackwater River ranges from 2 percent to 42 percent of average sea salinity, depending on rainfall and the incursion of tides. Because of its importance as food for geese and other animals, three-square is maintained at Blackwater National Wildlife Refuge by annual burning in the

167

fall. Burning is not harmful to the three-square roots and rhizomes (which, after all, are buried in sodden earth), yet helps to prevent intrusion by other plants. Burning also produces fresh growth on which geese can graze during late winter and early spring, when other food is scarce.

Wild rice is another important marshland food plant, attracting blue-winged teals, red-winged blackbirds, soras, and bobolinks. In Maryland its seeds mature in early September. Wild rice is often found next to streams, so long as the salinity does not exceed one-fifth that of sea water. The appearance and disappearance of stands of wild rice from one year to the next provides a local clue to the relative balance of fresh water and salt water.

Other marsh plants are similarly indicative of salinity. Narrowleaf cattail prefers standing fresh water. Saltmeadow cordgrass, which is fairly short, dense, and soft-textured in appearance (but actually rather coarse to the touch) occupies brackish flats that are a little higher and drier than the extensive areas of three-square and narrowleaf cattail. Expanses of saltmeadow cordgrass are only rarely flooded by the tide, whereas the similar sounding saltmarsh cordgrass, which grows seven or eight feet high, is found along the lower reaches of tidal rivers.

Among the most abundant birds in the Blackwater region are wintering Canada geese, identified by a black head and neck, white cheeks and chin, and large size (about two and a half feet tall, with a wingspread of five to six feet). Peak concentrations of 25,000 to 35,000 geese occur in November, and about 20,000 geese are present all winter. These numbers are from the mid-1990s, but during the course of the twentieth century the population of wintering Canada geese at Blackwater and throughout the Chesapeake region has soared and then fallen steeply. For the first five years after Blackwater National Wildlife Refuge was established in 1932, no Canada geese wintered at the new sanctuary, and after ten years there were at most about 5,000 geese. But by the early 1960s the winter population had climbed to more than 100,000 Canadas at Blackwater, and the winter count stayed at that level during the 1970s before declining precipitously.

The rise in wintering Canada geese in the Chesapeake region during the century's middle decades was the result of changes in agriculture, principally the planting of more corn and soybeans starting in the 1930s and '40s and, at the same time, increased use of mechanical reapers. The harvesters leave substantial quantities of kernels and beans on the ground, where they are eaten by geese that graze on the stubble fields. The result has been so-called "short-stopping," meaning the tendency for goose populations that formerly wintered farther south in the

Carolinas to stop and stay for the winter in the Chesapeake region, as most Canada geese migrating along the Atlantic flyway now do.

Even as the Chesapeake region has become the favored wintering grounds of migratory Canada geese, the total flyway population of these birds has fallen from a peak of about 900,000 in the early 1980s to about 250,000 in the mid-1990s. Factors contributing to this steep decline include the loss of thousands of acres of Olney three-square to drought, salt water, and erosion, but the main cause was over-hunting, particularly on the Chesapeake's Eastern Shore, where marshaling hunting rights on private farm fields and accommodating and feeding visiting hunters became big business. Hunting was estimated to cause about 85 percent of deaths among Canada geese. Studies show that from 1962 to 1974, when the winter population of Canada geese was increasing in Maryland, the adult survival rate from one year to a subsequent year was about 82 percent; but during the mid-1980s, the survival rate dropped below 70 percent as Maryland attracted large numbers of hunters from other states. To counter the decline in wintering Canada geese, Maryland shortened the hunting season, set lower bag limits, and started a program (funded by revenues from non-resident hunting licenses) to pay farmers whose fields are not leased for hunting to leave crops standing in order to attract and feed geese in relatively safe places. Similarly, at Blackwater National Wildlife Refuge, cropland has been devoted to growing food for geese. As a result, the decline in the number of wintering Canada geese appeared to have been arrested in Maryland. However, responding in 1995 to a very poor breeding season, the federal Fish and Wildlife Service declared a moratorium, subject to annual review, that bars the hunting of Canada geese wintering along the entire East Coast.

Although a distinct subspecies of Canada goose is now fairly common in the Chesapeake region even during summer, migrating Canadas do not begin to arrive in great numbers until late September. Some continue farther south for the winter, and even within the Chesapeake area there is a good deal of movement throughout the winter, as flocks exhaust one food source and move to another.

Northward migration begins as early as the second week of February, and most migratory Canada geese are gone by mid-March. The path of migration is more or less straight north to the Ungava Peninsula east of Hudson and James bays, where the birds nest. The trip from the Chesapeake region is about 1,900 miles and lasts four to six weeks. Along the way the birds rest for two or three days at a time in preparation for the next flight.

Canada geese start breeding at the end of their third year. Pairs usually mate for life, although if one dies, the other mates again. Females lay five to eight eggs that require about twenty-eight days to incubate. The number of young that hatch and survive depends greatly on how early the snow and ice melt, but unseasonably late storms, predation by foxes, hunting by Innuit, and even the activities of caribou (which are known to eat goose eggs) are also factors. The geese stay at the nesting grounds until August, when they begin to mass along the shores of the bays for the flight south.

The recovery of banded birds has shown that the Canada geese that summer in Ungava and winter in the Chesapeake region form a sub-group (or subspecies or geographic race) among all those Canada geese that breed across the whole width of the continent. According to ornithologists, there are at least thirteen distinct populations of Canada geese. For the most part, they do not mix, and each population has its own breeding and wintering grounds and migration route between the two. The interaction of genetics and persistent behavior over thousands of years has led to substantial differences in the size of birds belonging to the different groups. Mid-continental Canada geese weigh up to eighteen pounds, while those seen in the Chesapeake region weigh up to nine pounds, and those found along the Pacific coast weigh just three pounds. The genetic differences that have developed among subspecies are both a cause and effect of the fact that young Canada geese adhere closely to family groups and learn from parent birds where to breed, where to winter, and where to migrate. Of geese that are banded in Maryland and later recovered, about 90 percent are found in the locality — often even the same pond — where they were banded one or more years earlier. Even so, geese are adaptable enough to react to changed circumstances, as demonstrated by the previously-mentioned fact that most of the geese of the Atlantic flyway shifted their wintering grounds northward to the Chesapeake during the mid-1900s, and yet other populations that winter in Pennsylvania, New Jersey, New York, and Connecticut are developing. If the geese are pressured by hunting, they will sometimes reverse their normal feeding schedule in order to browse in farm fields on moonlit nights.

Another recent phenomenon has been the increase among Canada geese that breed in the mid-Atlantic states, residing not only at wildlife refuges such as Blackwater but also at parks, golf courses, public reservoirs, and other places where they are safe from hunters — and where their browsing and their droppings are problematic. These year-round resident geese are another genetically distinct sub-group, somewhat larger than the Canada geese that breed in Ungava. In Maryland the population of resident Canada geese, which are sometimes called "street geese" because of the frequency with which they show up even in suburban residential areas, was estimated to be 50,000 in 1997, and Maryland has fewer than other East Coast states. On the East Coast as a whole, the stay-at-home geese are now thought to number nearly a million. Because they are present during the growing season, the resident Canada geese can do considerable damage to crops. To reduce their numbers, Maryland has instituted a short hunting season during the first half of September, before the migratory geese arrive.

In addition to the Canada geese seen in Delmarva are snow geese, of which there are two subspecies: greater and lesser. Estimates of the entire continental population of greater snow geese ranged from 300,000 to 600,000 in 1997. One thing is certain: the population is several times what it was thirty years ago. Greater snow geese winter along the Atlantic coast, mainly between Delaware Bay and Albemarle Sound, North Carolina. Because of their increased numbers, they are not only damaging the wildlife refuges meant to sustain them in winter but are also overgrazing their Arctic breeding grounds on Bylot Island and the northern shore of Baffin Island, where areas that have been stripped of food regenerate very slowly.

The number of lesser snow geese has also soared in recent decades. The continental population of lesser snows is thought to fall between three and five million, or in any case, about twice what it was in 1970. In some breeding areas, the multiple of growth has been far bigger. Only a few thousand of these birds winter in Delmarva, mainly in the vicinity of Blackwater National Wildlife Refuge. Most lesser snows winter in Louisiana and Texas and throughout the bottomlands of the Mississippi Valley, now converted to agriculture. Many migrate no farther south than Iowa. Their main winter food is waste grain and beans gleaned from fields of rice, soy, corn, and wheat. The abundance of food in winter, however, is not matched by what is available in the Canadian north during summer. On their nesting grounds located along western Hudson and James bays and as far north as Baffin and Southampton islands, the mid-continental lesser snows are destroying their own habitat as they root out rhizomes of marsh plants and denude broad areas. Some wildlife biologists anticipate that overcrowding and shortage of food in the degraded Canadian marshes will cause the population of lesser snow geese to crash. Ducks and shorebirds that share the same breeding grounds with the geese have already declined in numbers.

Somewhat confusingly, there are two color phases of the lesser snow goose. One is nearly all white, except for black wing tips, and thus resembles the greater snow goose. The other color phase of the lesser snow goose has a white head and neck and dark body; it is sometimes termed the blue goose. Both color phases of the lesser snow goose are usually seen together, and they interbreed on their nesting grounds. In contrast, greater snow geese and lesser snow geese frequent different areas and do not interbreed.

The lesser snow geese that winter in the Blackwater region congregate in September at staging areas in James Bay and southern Hudson Bay. They start their overland flight south early in October and arrive at the Blackwater refuge in October. In the Blackwater marshes they grub for rhizomes of three-square. Along with Canada geese and muskrats, the lesser snow geese are capable of digging up large areas termed eatouts. With Canada geese and tundra swans, they also graze in stubble fields of corn and soybeans or in fields of freshly-sprouted winter wheat.

Even more remarkable than the migratory movements of Canada geese and snow geese are the prodigious flights of tundra swans (formerly called whistling swans). During fall migration, these large, long-necked, white birds sometimes fly nonstop, night and day, for a thousand miles. Tundra swans breed in the northwest Arctic, and some of the tundra swans seen in winter at Blackwater National Wildlife Refuge and Eastern Neck Island have come from as far as the north coast of Alaska, having migrated across northern Canada, Alberta, Saskatchewan, North Dakota, and the Great Lakes to the mid-Atlantic coast, for a total distance of about 3,700 miles — the same as between New York and Paris. (I note that in England the word "swanning" is used as a verb synonymous with "jetsetting" — as in "swanning around the world.") There are other birds — Arctic terns, for instance — that migrate farther than tundra swans, but nothing beats the heavy swans for the amount of work performed in migrating to and from the mid-Atlantic coast. In January 1997 the Atlantic population of tundra swans was estimated at 86,000, of which about a quarter wintered in the Chesapeake region. The swans' main wintering grounds are the coastal bays of Virginia and North Carolina.

Arriving in the Chesapeake region during October and November and remaining here into March, the swans favor open water up to five feet deep, where, using their long necks, they can feed on submerged aquatic plants and thin-shelled mollusks. In fresh water, the swans browse on wild celery, and in brackish water they eat wigeon grass, sago pondweed, muskgrass, long clams, and Baltic macoma clams. As turbidity and pollution have reduced the supply of submerged aquatic vegetation in Chesapeake Bay, tundra swans have migrated farther south or have turned to grazing (along with Canada geese and snow geese) in fields of corn and soybean stubble and winter wheat.

Incidentally, also seen in the Chesapeake region is the mute swan, a European species introduced here. It does not migrate and is the only swan that breeds in the eastern United States or that is likely to be seen here in summer. The adult has an orange bill with a black knob. When swimming, it holds its neck in an S-curve, as compared to the straight-necked posture of our native tundra swan.

In contrast to the waterfowl that winter in the Blackwater marshes are those that breed here in spring and summer. For most of these birds, the height of the nesting season is the last week of May and the first week of June. Among the common breeding waterfowl is the black duck, so-called because of its dark, mottled body (although in flight the undersides of the wings are seen to be white). These important game birds most often nest in areas of saltmeadow cordgrass, although other sites, sometimes far from water, are not unusual. Their nesting season is long, starting in March and extending through August. Also common are mallards (males, of course, have green heads and white neck bands) which breed in large numbers in the Blackwater marshes, and are abundant during winter as well. Wood ducks, too, are commonplace during the breeding season, nesting in hollow trees and man-made boxes. Males are highly colored, with a swept-back crest and rainbow iridescence; females also have a crest, but are dull colored with a white eye patch. Finally, blue-winged teal breed in large numbers at Blackwater. Males are more easily identified by the white crescent on their cheeks than by the blue wing patches that give these small ducks their name. Like black ducks, blue-winged teal prefer to nest in the salt meadow, which — since it is slightly higher than other areas of the marsh — is less likely to be flooded.

More often heard than seen, bitterns and various rails (black, clapper, king, and Virginia) also nest in the Blackwater marshes. Several species of herons and egrets are common as well (in some cases year-round), but only the green heron and black-crowned night heron breed in the refuge. The most abundant breeding birds in the marshlands, however, are neither waterfowl nor waders, but rather the long-billed marsh wren, seaside sparrow, and — most numerous of all — the red-winged blackbird.

Among the most dramatic breeding birds of the Blackwater region is the bald eagle, easily identified by its white head, white tail, large, dark body, and wingspan up to seven feet. Bald eagles live for as long as thirty years and mate for life, although if one of a pair dies the survivor will often mate again. From February through May, one to three eggs are laid (usually two), taking seven weeks to hatch. Both eagle parents

173

care for their fledglings, and by the twelfth week after hatching, the young eagles are ready to fly.

Eagle nests are huge, nearly always located in the upper branches of trees that overlook the marsh or open water where the eagles hunt or scavenge. It takes both parents about thirty days to build a new nest, which typically measures five feet across. Nests are often reused and enlarged year after year. Some reports assert that nests that have been in use for many years measure as much as nine feet across and fifteen or even twenty feet from top to bottom and weigh about two tons. Much of the weight is from water, since at the core of the nest is a sodden mass of decaying compost. The debris recovered from fallen eagle nests consists mainly of sticks (some up to six feet long), clumps of sod, stalks of corn and cattails, marsh grass (with which the birds line their nests), and undigested food fragments such as muskrat bones, duck feet, and fish heads.

Bald eagles pick up most of these animals dead. Fish is their main food, and although most fish are scavenged dead, eagles also catch live fish by swooping close to the surface of the water and snatching them out with their talons. This manner of fishing is distinctly different from that of ospreys, which are slightly smaller than eagles and far more common; ospreys circle at a height of 50 to 150 feet, hover, then dive feet first into the water, from which they immediately emerge and take off. As it gains altitude, an osprey will interrupt its wing beats for a moment to shudder in mid-air like a dog shaking itself, and then — if it has not caught a fish — resume its circling.

Other large birds of prey of the Blackwater marshes are harriers (also called marsh hawks) and short-eared owls, both of which breed and feed in the salt meadows. They eat voles, shrews, and other small animals. Like eagles, harriers also sometimes eat muskrats that have been caught in traps; they are not known to capture muskrats on their own. The harrier is identified by its long tail with a white patch on top at the rump. It hunts by day, flying low over the marsh, veering from side to side with wings held in a shallow V. The short-eared owl similarly scours the marsh at dusk and at night, its wings tilted upward like the harrier's.

There are yet other large predatory birds that hunt in the marsh and nest in nearby woods. These include the red-tailed hawk (whose unbanded tail is dark red on the upper side and light pink on the lower side), the red-shouldered hawk (narrow white bands on the dark tail), and great horned, barred, barn, and screech owls. These owls are all night hunters, but (with the exception of the strictly nocturnal barn owl) are sometimes seen perched in woods during the day or perhaps even gliding over the marsh at dusk. Red-tailed hawks and great horned owls nest in pine woods, and red-shouldered hawks and barred owls nest in hardwood swamps.

The Blackwater marshes and bordering woods arc also home to numerous mammals, including muskrats, nutria, raccoons, otters, foxes, deer, meadow voles, and rice rats, but of chief interest to visitors is the endangered Delmarva Peninsula fox squirrel, so-called for its disproportionately large tail. The body, too, of the fox squirrel is bigger than that of the common gray squirrel, and its coat is more silvery. In its movements, the fox squirrel is slower and more deliberate than the gray squirrel, and it spends more time foraging on the ground. Fox squirrels usually build their nests far out on a branch, and their preferred habitat is mature piney woods, where they eat pine seeds. Piles of cone cores at the foot of loblolly pines is a sign of fox squirrels, which used to live throughout Delmarva, but now are found only in the Blackwater region, at Eastern Neck Island (Chapter 5), at Chincoteague National Wildlife Refuge (Chapter 19), and a few other places.

In economic terms, the most important mammal of the Dorchester marshes is the lowly muskrat, which is trapped for fur and for food. It is sometimes termed "marsh rabbit" when set on the table. In the mid-1960s, about 280,000 muskrats were caught annually in Maryland, but the number has declined drastically since then as the market for animal fur has declined. The coastal or Virginia muskrat found in the Blackwater region measures about two feet long, but it is nearly half tail and weighs only two pounds. It has two color phases: one black (and more valuable) and the other either red or brown. Although muskrats sometimes live in burrows dug in stream banks and entered through underwater tunnels, they more usually nest in dome-shaped houses or lodges scattered throughout the marsh and made of leaves, stalks, roots, and grass. The lodges can be up to six feet in diameter and four feet high. Most muskrat houses are in areas of three-square sedge, which is a prime muskrat food. Muskrats have at least two litters a year, with an average of five kits to a litter. If not kept in check by trappers and by other predators — chiefly raccoons and foxes, which break into muskrat houses to seize the kits — muskrat populations sometimes rise to the point where the animals denude large areas of the marsh.

Nutria are dark-brown rodents the size of beavers. Weighing about ten pounds (sometimes twice that much), they look like giant hamsters. They were introduced from Argentina to Louisiana in the 1930s and from there to the Blackwater region in the 1940s. Wildlife managers say that they have adapted all too well. Their numbers have soared, and by browsing on the roots of marsh grasses, they are capable of digging up annually hundreds of acres of marsh that then degenerate into mud flats or even sink to become brackish pools. Nutria formerly were valued for their fur, but not at present. Blackwater National Wildlife Refuge now has a program to pay muskrat trappers — who must first bid to trap within the refuge — a rebate for each nutria caught. The chief natural enemy of nutria is severe cold, for unlike muskrats, they nest in the open and in winter will form large huddles to try to stay warm.

≈ ≈ ≈ ≈

AUTOMOBILE DIRECTIONS: Cambridge is located where Route 50 crosses the Choptank River 30 miles northwest of Salisbury. (See **Map 1** on page iv in the Table of Contents.) South of Cambridge is the immense Blackwater National Wildlife Refuge, and still farther south is Hooper Island, separating the Honga River from Chesapeake Bay. The car tour of southern Dorchester County shown on **Map 27** on page 181 starts at Cambridge, so you should go there first.

To Cambridge from northern Delmarva and Interstate 95 near Newark, Delaware: From I-95 take Route 896 south across Route 40 and over the Chesapeake and Delaware Canal. From there, follow Route 301 south, passing straight through an intersection where Route 896 bears left. In all, follow Route 301 south into Maryland for about 44 miles. Eventually, after passing exits for Route 305 and Route 304 near Centreville, take the exit for Route 213 south. At the top of the ramp, turn left and follow Route 213 south toward Route 50 and Easton for 4.3 miles, then turn left (east) onto Route 50 and follow it for 28 miles. After crossing the Choptank River, turn right at the first traffic light onto Maryland Avenue toward downtown Cambridge. Follow Maryland Avenue 0.6 mile. After crossing the drawbridge at Cambridge Creek, turn right toward the historic area. In a few hundred yards, turn right onto brick-paved High Street.

To Cambridge from the Chesapeake Bay Bridge: After crossing the Bay Bridge, follow Route 50/301 across Kent Island. At the point where Route 50 and Route 301 split, fork right and follow Route 50 past Easton and across the Choptank River to Cambridge. At the first traffic light south of the Choptank River Bridge, turn right onto Maryland Avenue toward downtown Cambridge. Follow Maryland Avenue 0.6

mile. After crossing the drawbridge at Cambridge Creek, turn right toward the historic area. In a few hundred yards, turn right onto brick-paved High Street.

To Cambridge from southern Delmarva and the Chesapeake Bay Bridge-Tunnel at Norfolk: After crossing the bridge-tunnel, follow Route 13 north into Maryland and past Pocomoke City and Princess Anne to the exit for Route 50 westbound near Salisbury, and from there take Route 50 west to Cambridge. After Route 50 curves right in Cambridge, watch carefully for Maryland Avenue, and there turn left toward downtown Cambridge. Follow Maryland Avenue 0.6 mile. After crossing the drawbridge at Cambridge Creek, turn right toward the historic area. In a few hundred yards, turn right onto brick-paved High Street.

To Cambridge from Salisbury and the Delaware and Maryland seashore resorts: From the vicinity of Salisbury or from Ocean City, follow Route 50 west to Cambridge.

From the vicinity of Rehoboth Beach, follow Route 1 north to the intersection with Route 9 westbound near Lewes, and from there follow Route 9 west through Georgetown and across Route 113 to Route 13 southbound. Follow Route 13 south to Route 50, and then take Route 50 west to Cambridge.

As you enter Cambridge and Route 50 curves right, watch carefully for Maryland Avenue, and there turn left toward downtown Cambridge. Follow Maryland Avenue 0.6 mile. After crossing the drawbridge at Cambridge Creek, turn right toward the historic area. In a few hundred yards, turn right onto brick-paved High Street.

Cambridge was established in 1684, when Maryland's General Assembly authorized a port town "in Dorchester County Att Daniell Joansis plantation on the south side of Great Choptancke." This legislation, and other directives like it designating sundry ports, was intended to implement the prior year's Act for the Advancement of Trade. Taken together, the measures were supposed to promote the growth of centers of commerce and to facilitate the collection of tobacco taxes and custom duties by requiring that all trade in the colony be conducted at designated towns — most of which did not yet exist and, in fact, never came into being. Cambridge (like nearby Oxford) was one of the few specified sites that grew into a real town and (again like Oxford) was named for one of England's two great university cities.

In 1686 a courthouse was built at Cambridge, and the town has been the seat of Dorchester County ever since. Cambridge, however, still had few, if any, structures other than the courthouse and an Anglican church in 1706, when the oldest part of the town was laid out along High Street in accordance with procedures akin to present-day exercises in eminent domain. Land was taken for the town, lots were sold, and the prior owners were compensated. Buyers of lots — and these tracts might each contain a dozen or more acres — were required to build houses at least twenty feet on each side within one year, or forfeit their claim. Lots not improved with a house within seven years reverted to the original owners of the land.

From the time of the founding of Cambridge until the mid-1700s, tobacco was, of course, the main article of commerce there, as it was throughout the tidewater region. But by the late 1700s, a more diversified economy had evolved. Grain (wheat, corn, flax), livestock, salt meat (primarily pork), and timber became the main exports of the Eastern Shore, shipped out from Cambridge and other river towns. However, as Baltimore boomed following the American Revolution, trade declined in Maryland's smaller ports, although shipbuilding continued to be an important industry at Cambridge. Throughout the nineteenth century, shipyards in Cambridge built many vessels that became active in coastal trading as far south as the Caribbean. Even several whaling ships were built at Cambridge for the New Bedford, Massachusetts whaling industry.

After the Civil War, prosperity returned to Cambridge as the oyster trade flourished. Throughout the late 1800s and early 1900s, Cambridge was home port to a large fleet of sail-powered oyster dredgers, and even today a few are still based in Cambridge Creek. Seafood processing plants were built to handle the haul of shellfish and finfish caught in Chesapeake Bay and brought to Cambridge. Also during the late nineteenth and early twentieth centuries, Cambridge acquired a substantial canning industry for vegetables grown on the Delmarva Peninsula.

Since mid-century, however, the seafood and vegetable industries have shrunk at Cambridge. But this depressed community is slowly recovering, and today the town has a fairly diversified economy, emphasizing regional retailing, publishing, and the manufacturing of electronic circuitry, wire conveyor belting, fertilizer, and garments, as well as continuing, on a reduced scale, the processing of seafood, poultry, and vegetables. With the development of Sailwinds Park and a Hyatt resort and convention center on the shore of the Choptank River, Cambridge and Dorchester County hope to foster the tourist trade.

≈　　　≈　　　≈　　　≈

CAR TOUR OF CAMBRIDGE: The bold line on **Map 26** on page 180 shows the route of a car tour that provides a quick overview of Cambridge. The tour starts on High Street, where between the courthouse and the Choptank River, there are many handsome old houses. (Dates of construction are noted on the map.) From the riverfront area the route leads to the **Brannock Maritime Museum**, located on Talbot Avenue. From there the tour returns to the center of town at Church Street and High Street, where you may enjoy strolling in the old **cemetery of Christ Church**, burial place of five Maryland governors. The current church dates from 1883, but its site has belonged to the parish since about 1696, when the first church was built here. From Christ Church the tour route follows High Street south to the **Richardson Maritime Museum** at the corner with Locust Street, then turns left onto Poplar Street (opposite Locust). Poplar Street soon becomes Race Street. Formerly Cambridge's main retailing district, Poplar and Race streets retain much of the flavor of the early twentieth century, when many of the buildings were constructed following a fire in 1910. After turning left from Race Street onto Cedar Street, the route passes the end of **Cambridge Creek**, then turns left onto Trenton Street; the harbor here was once the site of numerous seafood packing houses but is now being developed with vacation condominiums and slips for pleasure boats. After turning right onto Maryland Avenue, the route continues just 0.3 mile to Dorchester Avenue, then turns left toward the **Visitor Center at Sailwinds Park** (scheduled for completion by mid-1998). Finally, after going back to Maryland Avenue and turning left, the tour route crosses Route 50 and ends at the **Meredith House** and **Neild Museum**.

≈   ≈   ≈   ≈

CAR TOUR OF SOUTHERN DORCHESTER COUNTY: The bold line on **Map 27** on page 181 shows the route followed by this 90-mile car tour, which leads first to Blackwater National Wildlife Refuge. A shorter alternative for bicyclists is to start at the refuge and, after touring its Wildlife Drive, follow Maple Dam Road south to the Blackwater River and back for a total of 22 very scenic miles. For a longer excursion of 30 miles, bicyclists can follow the car tour clockwise from the refuge, but then cut northeast on Route 335 in order to return to their

MAP 26 — Car tour of Cambridge

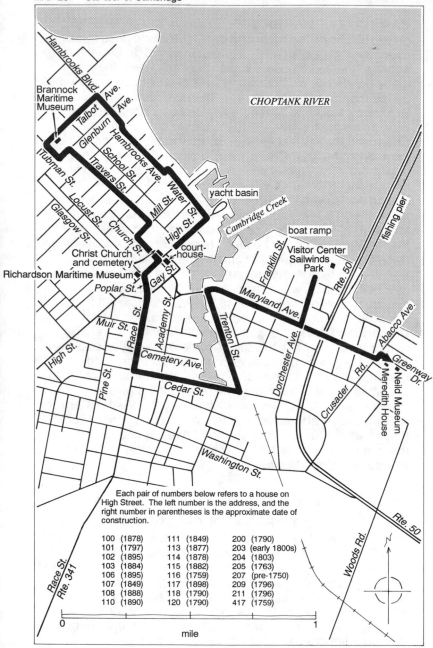

CHOPTANK RIVER

Brannock Maritime Museum

Talbot Ave.

Glenburn Ave.

Hambrooks Blvd.

Hambrooks Ave.

School St.

Tubman St.

Travers St.

Locust St.

Glasgow St.

Church St.

Mill St.

Water St.

High St.

yacht basin

Cambridge Creek

boat ramp

Franklin St.

Visitor Center
Sailwinds Park

Rte. 50

fishing pier

Christ Church and cemetery

court-house

Gay St.

Richardson Maritime Museum

Poplar St.

Race St.

Academy St.

Muir St.

Cemetery Ave.

Trenton St.

Maryland Ave.

Dorchester Ave.

Crusader Rd.

Abacco Ave.

Greenway Dr.

Neild Museum
Meredith House

High St.

Pine St.

Cedar St.

Washington St.

Rte. 50

Woods Rd.

Race St.
Rte. 341

Each pair of numbers below refers to a house on High Street. The left number is the address, and the right number in parentheses is the approximate date of construction.

100 (1878)	111 (1849)	200 (1790)
101 (1797)	113 (1877)	203 (early 1800s)
102 (1895)	114 (1878)	204 (1803)
103 (1884)	115 (1882)	205 (1763)
106 (1895)	116 (1759)	207 (pre-1750)
107 (1849)	117 (1898)	209 (1796)
108 (1888)	118 (1790)	211 (1796)
110 (1890)	120 (1790)	417 (1759)

0   mile   1

MAP 27 — Car tour of southern Dorchester County

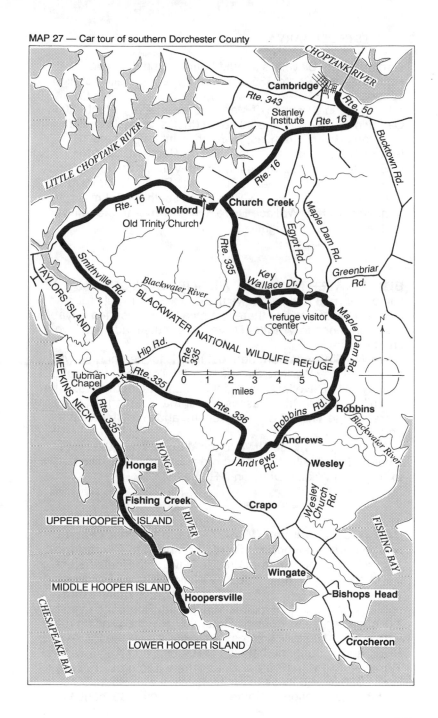

starting point. Bicyclists should bear in mind, however, that Route 336 and Route 335 are used by cars traveling at high speeds.

From the intersection of Maryland Avenue and Route 50 in Cambridge, follow Route 50 south (that is, away from the Choptank River) 1.4 miles, then turn right onto Route 16 toward the Blackwater refuge. Follow Route 16 west for 7.3 miles (passing at 3.2 miles the **Stanley Institute**, an old one-room school house), then turn left onto Route 335 toward the Blackwater refuge. Follow Route 335 south for 3.8 miles, then turn left onto Key Wallace Drive and go 1 mile to the refuge visitor center on the right.

≈   ≈   ≈   ≈

BLACKWATER NATIONAL WILDLIFE REFUGE: The bold line on **Map 28** at right shows the refuge's tour route for cars and bicycles, for which there is a small admission fee payable at the entrance to **Wildlife Drive**. The route leads past two short foot trails.

For Wildlife Drive, turn right out the visitor center driveway and follow Key Wallace Drive east 1.5 miles, then turn right onto Wildlife Drive just beyond the refuge headquarters. After 0.3 mile, Wildlife Drive passes a spur road leading left to the **Marsh Edge Trail** (0.3 mile in length) and an overlook at the end of the road.

Continue on Wildlife Drive to the **Woods Trail** (0.5 mile in length). Eventually, turn left in order to continue 1 mile before exiting from Wildlife Drive onto Route 355.

≈   ≈   ≈   ≈

CAR TOUR continued (Map 27 — from the Blackwater refuge south to Hooper Island, then back to Cambridge): Turn right out the exit from Wildlife Drive onto Route 335. Go 0.2 mile, then turn right onto Key Wallace Drive. Follow Key Wallace Drive 3.6 miles to a T-intersection, and there turn right. (This unmarked road is Maple Dam Road, but eventually it changes name to Robbins Road.) Follow the winding road for a total of 10.2 miles across the marsh, over the Blackwater River, and through the hamlets of Robbins and Andrews to a T-intersection with Route 336, and there turn right. Follow Route 336 for 4.8 miles to an intersection with Route 335.

At the intersection of Route 336 and Route 335, continue

MAP 28 — Blackwater National Wildlife Refuge

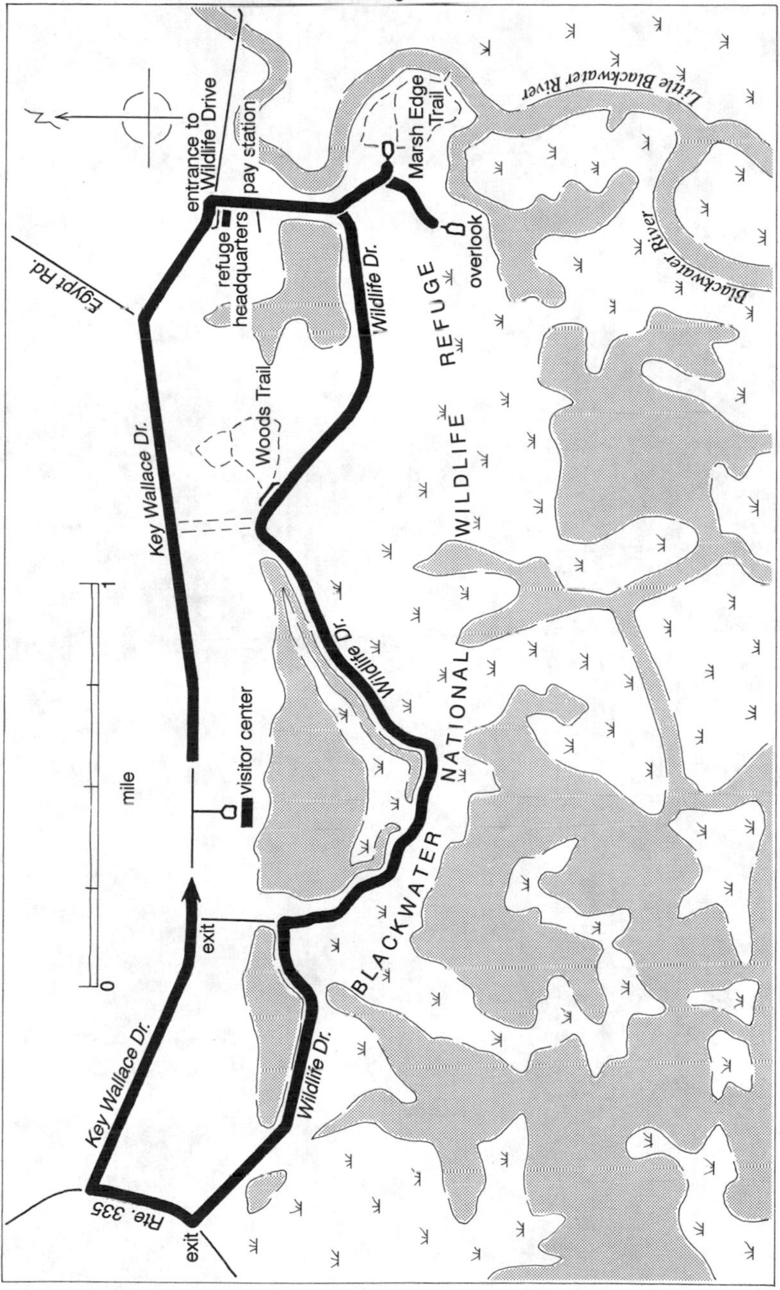

Little Blackwater River

Blackwater River

Marsh Edge Trail

overlook

entrance to Wildlife Drive

pay station

refuge headquarters

Wildlife Dr.

Egypt Rd.

Key Wallace Dr.

Woods Trail

WILDLIFE REFUGE

NATIONAL

BLACKWATER

Wildlife Dr.

mile

visitor center

exit

Key Wallace Dr.

Wildlife Dr.

Rte. 335

exit

183

straight ahead on Route 335 toward Hooper Island. You are soon, however, faced with a choice. If you do not want to see Hooper Island and its several fishing communities, go only 1.8 miles, then turn right onto Smithville Road and skip the next two paragraphs.

But if you *do* want to see Hooper Island (and of course you do), stay on Route 335 southbound. After 1.3 miles, pass **Tubman Chapel** on the right; it was built in the late 1760s and is the oldest surviving Catholic Church on the lower Eastern Shore; the parish now meets at the nearby St. Mary's Star of the Sea Catholic Church. Continue south across a high bridge to **Upper Hooper Island** and the town of **Honga**; the name is derived from the Honga River, previously known as the Hunger River. As for the name *Hooper*, Henry Hooper and his family settled on these islands from Calvert County in 1667 and at one time owned 2,300 acres. With the Hoopers came other Catholic families, including the Meekins (whose name survives in Meekins Neck, north of Hooper Island) and the Tubmans of Tubman Chapel.

From Honga continue south on the main road, at one point turning sharply right (so as *not* to go to Old House Point). Continue through the strung-out village of **Fishing Creek** (the island's main settlement) and across another high bridge to **Middle Hooper Island**. Follow the road until it simply peters out in the watermen's village of **Hoopersville**, then return the way you came. After leaving Upper Hooper Island, go 4.2 miles, then turn left onto Smithville Road.

To return to the vicinity of Cambridge, follow Smithville Road north 7.1 miles to a T-intersection with Route 16, and there turn right (east) and go 15.8 miles to Route 50; however, I strongly recommend that after 7.2 miles you stop by at **Old Trinity Church**, located off Route 16 just beyond the village of Woolford; watch for a sign on the left at the entrance to a long lane that leads to the church.

Built between 1670 and 1680 and meticulously restored in the 1950s, **Old Trinity Church** (shown at left) is said to be the oldest Episcopal Church in continuous use in the United States. It is beautifully situated on the shore of Church Creek. In its shady churchyard cemetery is buried Thomas King Carroll, elected governor of Maryland in 1829. Even if you cannot get into the church to see its intimate interior, which has box pews and a pulpit at the side (as was the case at many early churches), the diminutive size of the church serves to remind us of the small scale of society at the time it was built.

12

SALISBURY

More or less centrally located, **Salisbury**, Maryland is the Delmarva Peninsula's largest city and the seat of Wicomico County. The bold line on **Map 29** on page 195 shows a tour linking attractions that by any standard make a visit to Salisbury well worthwhile.

The tour starts at the **Main Street Downtown Plaza**, abutting the Wicomico River. Obviously, business activity is greatest on a weekday, but even on weekends, when banks, many stores, and most professional and government offices are closed, a stroll up and down the pedestrian mall between the 1878 county courthouse and the river provides a sense of Salisbury in the late nineteenth and early twentieth centuries (although the facades of some buildings are more recent). One establishment here is the **Art Institute and Gallery**, open Monday through Saturday from noon to 4 P. M.; telephone (410) 546-4748 for information on exhibits. You may also be interested in cruising the Wicomico River on the *Maryland Lady,* which operates March through December from the bulkhead across the river on West Main Street, about a block and a half from the bridge. Reservations are strongly recommended, especially for lunch and dinner cruises, but last-minute passengers can sometimes be accommodated; telephone (410) 543-2466.

From downtown Salisbury the tour route heads east to the outstanding **Ward Museum of Wildfowl Art**, which is devoted chiefly to the history of decoy carving and to bird sculpture, including contemporary pieces that have won the annual Ward World Championship Wildfowl Carving Competition. There are also other exhibits discussed on page 194. The museum is open Monday through Saturday from 10 A.M. to 5 P.M. and on Sunday (when the entrance fee is reduced by half) from noon to 5. For information on current exhibits, fees, classes, trips, and other programs, telephone (410) 742-4988.

Returing toward the center of town, the tour follows the Municipal Park along the East Branch of the Wicomico River and passes the small and very attractive **Salisbury Zoo**, featuring animals of the Americas. The zoo opens daily (except Christmas and Thanksgiving) at 8:00 A.M. From Memorial Day to Labor Day, it closes at 7:30 P.M. During the rest of the year, it closes at 4:30 P.M. For information telephone (410) 742-2640.

From the zoo the tour goes to the Newtown Historic District, along the way passing the Country House Store, which has an inventory of "country style" merchandise so large and varied that the place has become a tourist attraction in its own right; it is open Monday through Saturday from 10 A.M. to 5:30 P.M. And at Newtown there is the **Poplar Hill Mansion**, built at the beginning of the nineteenth century. With its large rooms and fine woodwork, the interior of this house is something special, open Sundays (except in January) from 1 to 4 P.M.; however, because the house is rented occasionally for parties and weddings, always telephone the resident curator beforehand at (410) 749-1776 to make sure that no private event will conflict with your visit. You may also want to call for information on the Newtown Fair, held the first Saturday in October, and during which some private homes and churches are open to the public.

The tour route ends at **Pemberton Historical Park**, site of **Pemberton Hall** (built in 1741 and shown on page 186) and the **Wicomico Heritage Centre Museum**. Fronting on the Wicomico River, the park is open daily from 8 A.M. to sunset and has a trail system outlined on **Map 30** on page 198. Pemberton Hall is usually open April through October on Sundays from 2 to 4 P.M.; telephone (410) 742-1741. The museum is open at the same time; telephone (410) 860-0447. Together, the park, house, and barn-styled buildings provide one of the best places in Delmarva to see an eighteenth-century riverfront plantation.

IN 1661 GOVERNOR CHARLES CALVERT of Maryland issued a proclamation to encourage immigration from Virginia's Eastern Shore northward into his family's proprietary colony, where the region between the Nanticoke River and Pocomoke Sound had almost no settlers. As an inducement, Calvert offered each male householder one hundred acres of free land for himself and as much again for his wife and each man brought to Maryland, plus fifty acres for each child. Settlers with money or tobacco could purchase additional land cheaply, and those who were friends of the Calverts or had rendered them services were often given large tracts. Although most of the settlers were Anglicans, some were Presbyterians attracted by Maryland's policy of religious freedom set by the Catholic Calverts and legislatively confirmed by the Toleration Act of 1649. Quakers also came, seeking to escape persecution in Virginia, which in 1660 had passed an act prohibiting the tenets and practice of Quakerism.

To promote and oversee the migration from Virginia, Calvert appointed three commissioners, all Virginians. Two were required to become permanent residents of Maryland, but the third, Colonel Edmund Scarburgh, was not expected to leave Virginia, where he was treasurer and surveyor general. Scarburgh, in fact, tried to double-cross Calvert by claiming, after his term as commissioner ended, that Virginia's territory extended as far north as the mouth of the Wicomico River. Scarburgh even assembled a force that invaded Maryland, coerced some settlers into swearing allegiance to the Old Dominion, and arrested one of the other commissioners. In response Calvert went to Jamestown and appealed to the governor of Virginia, Sir William Berkeley. After years of disputation during which Virginia issued patents for many thousands of acres in what is now Maryland, an agreement was reached in 1668, and the present-day boundary was surveyed in a line extending east from the mouth of the Pocomoke River, far below the Wicomico. (Perhaps intentionally, Scarburgh actually slanted this line slightly northward. By the time it transects the peninsula and reaches the ocean, the boundary includes in Virginia twenty-three square miles of what would be Maryland territory had the line been surveyed correctly.)

In any case, the process of settlement along the Pocomoke, Annemessex, Manokin, Wicomico, and Nanticoke rivers of Maryland's lower Eastern Shore occupied the 1660s, '70s, and '80s. Patents for tracts exceeding a thousand acres were common. Of course, land fronting on the water was claimed first, since Chesapeake Bay and its tidal rivers provided the chief means of transportation. In 1666 Somerset County was established, spanning the peninsula from the bay to the ocean — or that is, including present-day Somerset, Worcester, and Wicomico counties. As was customary, the justices of the county court not only heard criminal and civil cases but also enacted local legislation and administered the government. To speed settlement of the region, the high sheriff was authorized to issue land grants and to transact business that would otherwise have required the settlers to travel to the provincial capital at St. Mary's City on the Western Shore. In the wake of the first settlers came others in the late seventeenth and early eighteenth centuries, buying land from the original patentees, filling in the gaps, and pushing into the hinterland at a distance from navigable water.

In 1732 **Salisbury Town** was established, at least on paper, at the head of navigation on the Wicomico River. Landowners in the vicinity petitioned the Maryland General Assembly, which passed an act empowering commissioners to lay out and sell twenty lots, altogether totaling fifteen acres, and to compensate the owner, a minor named William Winder. His property, of which only a small part was taken for the town, was called "Pemberton's Good Will." Among the five commissioners was Colonel Isaac Handy, owner of nearby Handy's Landing, where he operated a lumber business and tannery. Handy also own a plantation at Pemberton Hall, located two miles downstream (see page 199).

Apparently Salisbury was a flop at first, like nearly all such paper towns. After all, the work of the vast majority of households was centered on farms scattered far and wide. At Salisbury most of the lots reverted to Winder because they remained unsold after seven years. Nonetheless, Winder and his family gradually sold off land in bits and pieces, so that the town developed in a haphazard manner unrelated to any platted plan. In 1741 William Venables built a dam and grist mill on the East Branch of the Wicomico River at present-day Division Street; the dam survived until 1909. (Dividing Street, as it was then called, took its name from the boundary running through the town after the eastern half of old Somerset County became Worcester County in 1742.) During the next forty years, a Methodist meeting house, an Anglican church, and a Baptist meeting house were built on tracts where today there are more recent incarnations of these early structures. By the end of the eighteenth century Salisbury was a locally important place for storing and shipping out tobacco, lumber, grain, flour, salt beef, and salt pork. It was also a mart where residents of the region could buy general merchandise. A map prepared in 1817 shows seventy-six irregularly shaped lots varying greatly in size and intricately fitted together on a few crooked streets.

Salisbury grew slowly but steadily during the nineteenth century. Major roads running down the spine of the Delmarva Peninsula and from bay to ocean passed through the town. In 1830 steamboat service to Baltimore was inaugurated. By mid-century a boat ran twice weekly, leaving from Cotton Patch Landing two miles below town because the river was too shallow for steamboats to reach Salisbury itself until a channel and harbor were dredged in the 1890s. Before then shallow-draft lighters ferried freight back and forth between the town and the landing during high tide. In 1879 boat service to Baltimore was increased to three times weekly, carrying passengers, livestock, farm produce, and other goods. The last passenger runs were in 1929, but even today there is still commercial traffic on the river in the form of barges loaded with fuel oil, stone aggregate, and grain.

During the latter 1800s, Salisbury emerged as the commercial center of Maryland's lower Eastern Shore. In 1860 the railroad from the north reached the town, making it the main gateway for military and commercial traffic to and from southern Delmarva throughout the Civil War. After the war other railroads were built running in all directions from Salisbury. The lumber business boomed, earning a Salisbury merchant named Elihu E. Jackson a fortune of $5 million and propelling him to the Maryland legislature and then the governorship in 1884. The town's dominance of the region around it provided the impetus for the creation of Wicomico County in 1867, carved out of Somerset and Worcester counties and seated at Salisbury. The strength of the local economy was evident in the speed with which Salisbury rebuilt after a fire in 1860 and an even greater fire in 1886 destroyed the center of town, which previously had mostly frame structures. As a precaution against another disaster, new buildings in the commercial district were required to be of stone, brick, or iron, with roofs of slate or other noncombustible material. Newtown, located just to the north of downtown and annexed to Salisbury in 1847, became the site of massive stone churches and substantial Victorian houses. Elihu Jackson built a forty room mansion called The Oaks which formerly stood at Division and Isabella streets, and he donated the money for construction of Trinity United Methodist Church at Division and High streets. His widow gave funds for the Jackson Memorial Building, located directly across Division Street from the church and used for classes and other activities.

The first census of the twentieth century showed that Salisbury had become Delmarva's largest town, with about 7,000 inhabitants. Growth was especially rapid during the 1920s. The development of motor vehicles and the construction of Routes 13 and 50 through Salisbury reinforced its role as a centrally-located transportation hub and a favorable site for trucking, retailing, manufacturing, food processing, medical services, entertainment, and higher education. Today the population of Salisbury is about 21,000. Wicomico County (including Salisbury) has about 75,000 residents. Lumber and the packing and shipping of fruits and vegetables remain important elements of the economy, but there is also a highly diversified roster of other businesses, including manufacturers of electronic components, cellular phones, pumps, boats, pharmaceuticals, and plastics. Poultry is one of the main industries. Purdue Foods has its corporate headquarters, a processing plant, and a feed mill at Salisbury. Vertically integrated giants like Purdue have since the 1930s made raising broilers and growing corn and soybeans for chicken feed the leading forms of agriculture on the Delmarva Peninsula.

As in many sprawling cities, Salisbury's central business district has during the last forty years undergone a cycle of decay followed by renewal. Much of the work of restoration and re-landscaping along Main Street and the waterfront has now been completed. Together with specific sites such as the Ward Museum, the zoo, Poplar Hill Mansion, and outlying Pemberton Hall, the downtown area and adjacent Newtown Historic District are the main places of interest to visitors.

≈ ≈ ≈ ≈

AUTOMOBILE DIRECTIONS: Salisbury is located in the middle of the Delmarva Peninsula where Route 13 and Route 50 cross. (See **Map 1** on page iv in the Table of Contents.) The tour route shown on **Map 29** on page 195 starts at the Downtown Plaza on Main Street in the center of Salisbury, so you should go there first.

To Salisbury from northern Delmarva and Interstate 95 southwest of Wilmington: From Interstate 95 take Exit 4A for Route 1 south, and stay on Route 1 past a quick succession of exits. Follow Route 1 south past Dover, then switch to Route 13 south toward Salisbury and Norfolk. After entering the outskirts of Salisbury, stay left in order to continue straight on *Business* Route 13 toward downtown Salisbury. Go 2.8 miles on Business Route 13 and then, after crossing straight over Route 50, turn right onto Main Street. Follow it 0.2 mile, then turn left onto Division Street and go a hundred yards to a four-way intersection. Turn right onto Circle Avenue in front of the library, then turn right again into a large parking lot behind the Downtown Plaza; the first hour is free.

To Salisbury from the Chesapeake Bay Bridge: After crossing the bridge, follow Route 50/301 across Kent Island. At the point where Route 50 and Route 301 split, fork right to follow Route 50 past Easton and Cambridge to the center of Salisbury. After passing the bridge at the Wicomico River (where there is a conspicuous sign for the Port of Salisbury), continue on Route 50 just 0.2 mile, then turn right onto Division Street and follow it 0.1 mile to a four-way intersection in front of the library. Turn right onto Circle Avenue, then turn right again into a large parking lot behind the Downtown Plaza; the first hour is free.

  Please note that after the Salisbury By-pass is completed to the north of Salisbury, the present-day Route 50 through the center of town is likely to be redesignated *Business Route 50*, and if so, that is the route you should take as you approach Salisbury.

To Salisbury from southern Delmarva and the Chesapeake Bay Bridge-Tunnel at Norfolk: After crossing the bridge-tunnel, follow Route 13 north into Maryland and past Pocomoke City and Princess Anne. As you approach Salisbury, stay right in order to continue straight on *Business* Route 13 toward downtown Salisbury and Fruitland. Follow Business Route 13 for 5.2 miles. After passing Vine Street and the Peninsula Regional Medical Center, turn left onto Carrol Street. Go just 0.1 mile, then turn right onto Division Street, left onto Circle Avenue, and right into a large parking lot behind the Downtown Plaza; the first hour is free.

To Salisbury from Ocean City and Bethany Beach: Take Route 50 west past the interchange with Route 13. Continue 3.5 miles, then (after passing Baptist Street) turn left onto Division Street and follow it 0.1 mile to a four-way intersection in front of the library. Turn right onto Circle Avenue, then turn right again into a large parking lot behind the Downtown Plaza; the first hour is free.

Please note that after the Salisbury By-pass is completed north of Salisbury, the present-day Route 50 through the center of town is likely to be called *Business Route 50*, and if so, that is the route to take as you approach Salisbury.

To Salisbury from Lewes: Follow Route 9 west through Georgetown and across Route 113 to Route 13 south. Follow Route 13 south into Maryland. After entering the outskirts of Salisbury, stay left in order to continue straight on *Business* Route 13 toward downtown Salisbury. Go 2.8 miles on Business Route 13 and then, after crossing straight over Route 50, turn right onto Main Street. Follow it 0.2 mile, then turn left onto Division Street and go a hundred yards to a four-way intersection. Turn right onto Circle Avenue in front of the library, then turn right again into a large parking lot behind the Downtown Plaza; the first hour is free.

≈   ≈   ≈   ≈

TOURING DOWNTOWN SALISBURY ON FOOT: The vicinity of Main Street at the center of Salisbury was rebuilt after the fire of 1886. A short and pleasant walk is to follow Main Street up and down between the county courthouse and the Wicomico River. In recent years there has been much renovation in this area, and two blocks have been converted to a pedestrian mall called the **Downtown Plaza.** Some shops face the plaza and others can be entered via two interior arcades at the Plaza Building and the Gallery Building (where the **Art Institute and Gallery** is located on the lower level).

≈   ≈   ≈   ≈

CAR TOUR TO VARIOUS SALISBURY ATTRACTIONS: The bold line on **Map 29** at right shows a tour that connects the sites described in the introduction to this chapter. The map can also be used to navigate directly to any single place in case you have no time for, or interest in, the others.

To reach the **Ward Museum of Wildfowl Art**, turn right out the parking lot behind the Downtown Plaza. Follow Circle Avenue across Market Street and the East Branch of the Wicomico River. Turn left onto Carrol Street and follow it 0.4 mile to a major intersection with South Salisbury Boulevard (Business Route 13) in front of the railroad. Turn right and go 0.2 mile, then turn left onto Vine Street. Continue straight as Vine Street becomes Schumaker Drive. Altogether follow Vine and Schumaker 1.5 miles to the Ward Museum on the left just beyond an intersection with Beaglin Park Drive.

The Ward Museum of Wildfowl Art has the world's most comprehensive collection of carved birds, ranging from utilitarian decoys to purely decorative sculpture. One gallery displays numerous antique decoys organized to show differences in style and technique among regions of the United States and Canada. Another is devoted to the brothers Lem and Steve Ward, two highly-regarded carvers from Crisfield, Maryland for whom the museum is named. There are exhibits on the history and paraphernalia of waterfowl hunting, and on conservation and habitat preservation. One gallery accommodates shows that change from time to time, featuring carving, paintings, and prints that run the gamut of nature study. And, finally, there is the Championship Gallery, exhibiting winners from the Ward World Championship Wildfowl Carving Competition held each August in Ocean City. Categories include Shootin' Rig, or that is, contemporary

MAP 29 — Car tour of Salisbury

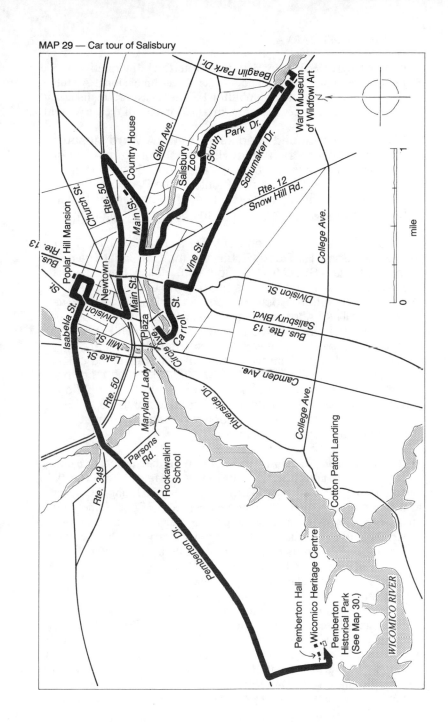

working decoys, Decorative Miniature Waterfowl, Interpretive Wood Sculpture (i.e., nonrealistic), and — like three-dimensional Audubon prints — Decorative Lifesize Wildfowl. These last are realistic and often very dramatic pieces that are virtuoso examples of the carver's art.

CAR TOUR continued (Map 29 — from the Ward Museum of Wildfowl Art to the Poplar Hill Mansion): Turn right out the museum driveway. Turn right again onto Beaglin Park Drive, then immediately turn left onto South Park Drive. Go 0.6 mile, then bear left at an intersection. If you are interested in the **Salisbury Zoo**, turn right into the parking lot; if not, just keep going.

From the zoo continue on South Park Drive 0.8 mile. Turn right onto Snow Hill Road (Route 12), then turn right again onto East Main Street toward Route 50. Follow East Main Street 0.6 mile, in the process passing the Country House Store on the left. At Route 50, turn left and follow the highway west 1.1 miles. After passing Baptist Street, turn right onto Division Street and follow it through the **Newtown Historic District**, developed as a well-to-do neighborhood after the Great Fire of 1886 destroyed nearly all buildings in the older part of the city to the south. Follow Division Street 0.3 mile past large Victorian churches and houses, then turn right onto Isabella Street. After just one block, turn left onto Poplar Hill Avenue, which reaches at T-intersection with Elizabeth Street in front of the Poplar Hill Mansion.

The **Poplar Hill Mansion** was built early in the nineteenth century, but by whom is not clear. Tradition favors Major Levin Handy, a veteran of the Revolutionary War whose family had long been prominent in the region. In 1795 Handy purchased a 357-acre tract on the outskirts of Salisbury, and he supposedly began construction of the house about five years later — but if so, work may have been curtailed by lack of funds. Shortly before Handy's death in 1804, Peter Dashiell, a member of another leading family of old Somerset County, purchased 229 acres of Handy's land at auction, and after Handy died, Dashiell bought still more land from Handy's widow early in 1805. Both purchases were for prices far too low to have included a large house that was anywhere near completion. In July 1805 Dashiell conveyed some of his land to his brother-in-law, John D. Huston, a wealthy physician who certainly had the means to build or to finish the mansion. In the foundation a brick bearing the date 1805 was discovered during restoration in 1974. Light may also be shed on the matter by a statement in the 1897 obituary of Isabella Huston: "Isabella was the daughter of Dr. John Huston, who purchased in 1800 Poplar Hill, then incomplete. Dr. Huston completed the property and made it the family home for over 50 years."

During Dr. Huston's lifetime the house was not yet known as Poplar Hill. The mansion was surrounded by farmland. The servants and farmhands were slaves who lived in quarters behind the main house. The estate inventory prepared after Huston's death in 1827 included seventeen slaves. In 1853 Huston's widow referred to the place as Poplar Farm, so-called because it was located at the end of a long avenue of poplar trees leading toward town. By surviving the fires that destroyed much of Salisbury in 1860 and 1886, Poplar Hill is now the oldest structure of note in the city.

With its symmetrical, five-bay facade ornamented with pseudo-classical forms such as the Palladian window over the door, Poplar Hill is in the Georgian tradition of the eighteenth century. Although beginning to be passé in major cities, this style (sometimes termed *Federal* when applied to houses built during the first thirty years of American independence) continued to be popular in the countryside. Other classical embellishments are a pediment above the fanlight, fluted pilasters flanking the door, and similar pilasters supporting an arch in the central hall. There is yet another Palladian window in back. Arranged on both sides of the hall, the six main rooms of the first and second floors have handsome fireplaces and carved moldings comparable to the best houses of the Federal period.

In 1971 the Poplar Hill Mansion was purchased by Wicomico County and restored with the aid of state funds. Since 1974 it has been owned and maintained by the City of Salisbury.

CAR TOUR continued (Map 29 — from the Poplar Hill Mansion to Pemberton Historical Park): Leaving the mansion behind on your right, follow Elizabeth Street (named for one of Dr. Huston's two daughters) west one block, then turn left onto Division Street. Go one block, then turn right onto Isabella Street (named for Huston's other daughter), and follow it 0.9 mile to Route 50, in the process passing the basin at the head of navigation on the Wicomico River, which is still used for transporting some bulk cargo, such as fuel oil and stone aggregate. Go straight across Route 50, but almost immediately fork left onto Pemberton Drive and follow it 2 miles, in the process passing (just after Pemberton Elementary School) the one-room **Rockawalkin School**, built about 1872, abandoned in 1939, and moved here in 1973. At the entrance to Pemberton Historical Park, turn left and follow the drive 0.6 mile to the parking lot.

MAP 30 — Pemberton Historical Park

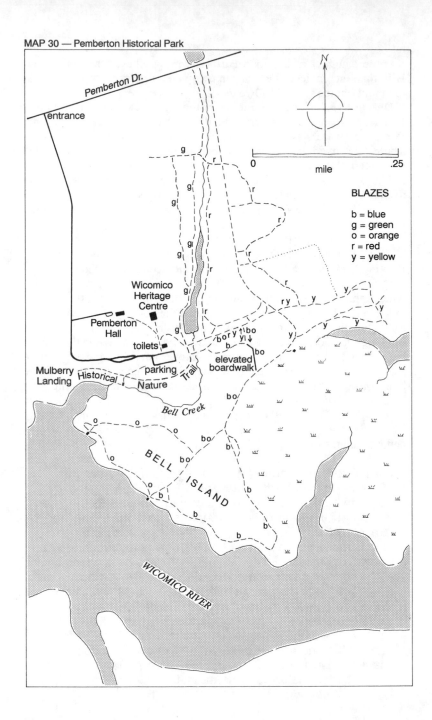

Pemberton Hall was built in 1741 by Colonel Isaac Handy, a planter, merchant, and shipmaster who started buying land at this site fifteen years earlier, principally from Joseph Pemberton, whose brother Thomas in 1682 had purchased nine hundred acres from the original patentee, Colonel William Stevens. In addition to growing tobacco at his Pemberton plantation, Isaac Handy operated a lumber business and tannery farther up the Wicomico River at Handy's Landing, where Salisbury was established in 1732. Handy served as one of five commissioners authorized to lay out the town. In addition, he was a militia officer and several times a delegate to the provincial General Assembly in Annapolis. Handy also had a wharf, called Mulberry Landing, at his Pemberton plantation, and even today an earth ramp descending to the river is plainly discernible near the right-angle bend in the park road. Sunk in the mud of the river bottom are wharf timbers thought to date from Handy's time. The river, of course, was the only way to carry out the tobacco, timber, salt meat, hides, and other products of the region, which Handy transported in locally-built sloops, such as the 40-ton *Ann* that he owned with a partner named James Blewer, and the 30-ton *Sally and Molly* owned jointly with his son George.

Pemberton Hall has Flemish-bond brickwork with glazed headers, as was typical of substantial houses of the time. The kitchen wing at one end is an addition. The main room has a high beamed ceiling, an immense fireplace flanked by hand-carved wood paneling, and two exterior doors to allow breezes to pass through in summer. Pemberton Hall is furnished in accordance with the inventory prepared following Handy's death in 1762. The house remained in the possession of Handy's descendants until 1835. From 1929 to 1960, it was occupied by tenant farmers. Exceedingly deteriorated, Pemberton Hall was donated in 1963 to Wicomico County, which has undertaken its restoration and the development of the surrounding historical park, where the Heritage Centre and even the building that houses the toilets are in the style of eighteenth-century tobacco barns.

WALKING AT PEMBERTON HISTORICAL PARK: A system of trails for hiking and horseback riding is shown on **Map 30** at left. Foot trails are marked with paint blazes. Off-road bicycling is prohibited.

You can join the trails by the pond spillway just below the end of the parking lot. The most interesting trails are those around Bell Island, along the edge of the marsh to the east, and up and down next to the pond.

13

BERLIN

As shown on **Map 31** on page 208, **Berlin** is located near the interchange where Route 50 and Route 113 cross, 7 miles inland from Ocean City, Maryland. The town's main attraction is its historic commercial district. Sober brick storefronts and a few more embellished facades, nearly all from the late nineteenth and early twentieth centuries, create a handsome streetscape. The buildings accommodate a mix of everyday businesses, antique stores, crafts and specialty shops, galleries, and restaurants. In addition to its own attractions, Berlin provides close proximity to other interesting places, including Assateague Island to the east (Chapter 18), Snow Hill and the Pocomoke River to the south (Chapter 14), and Salisbury to the west (Chapter 12).

Although it is not the purpose of this book to tout this or that business, it would be skew-jawed to talk about Berlin without mentioning at the outset the **Atlantic Hotel**, located at the center of town on Main Street. Built in 1895 and restored in the mid-1980s to turn-of-the century decor, the hotel and its two restaurants are by themselves sufficient reason to come to Berlin. Reservations are recommended on weekends; telephone (410) 641-3589.

Another attraction in Berlin is the **Globe Theatre**, cafe, bookstore, and gallery for contemporary crafts and art, located on Broad Street just around the corner from the hotel. The Globe offers a variety of events, including art shows, town tours, wine tastings, and concerts by recording artists. It is a well-established venue for acoustic music — mostly folk and blues — of the United States, Canada, and the British Isles. Telephone (410) 641-0784.

Like many Delmarva towns, Berlin's calendar of events includes a variety of fairs, festivals, parades, and other happenings, of which those with the most touristic interest are the Fiddlers Convention on the third Saturday in September and the Victorian Christmas throughout December. For information on local events or other matters, telephone the Chamber of Commerce at (410) 641-4775.

Finally, the **Taylor House Museum**, located on Main Street just north of downtown, is the former home of one of Berlin's leading citizens. It also has a gallery displaying local memorabilia. The house and museum are open mid-May through September on Monday, Wednesday, Friday, and Saturday from 1 to 4 P.M.; telephone (410) 641-1019.

LAND AT BERLIN was first patented by English settlers in the mid-1680s. Although the place was not on navigable water, it at least had the advantage of being located on a "road" — an Indian trail — that ran north and south along the Delmarva seaboard. In 1683 William Tompkins patented a 300-acre tract called "Burley" (later Burleigh Plantation) which the next year he sold to Colonel William Stevens. Formerly a soldier in Oliver Cromwell's army, Stevens had left England after Cromwell's death and the restoration of the monarchy. In about 1665 he settled at Rehobeth on the Pocomoke River and soon became one of the most prominent men on Maryland's lower Eastern Shore. He was among the first justices of Somerset County, which was established in 1666 and extended from Chesapeake Bay to the Atlantic coast, including present-day Worcester and Wicomico counties. Stevens was a delegate to the General Assembly, and he eventually became a member of Lord Baltimore's council and Deputy Lieutenant Governor. Given land warrants in recognition of his services, Stevens amassed a fortune as a very active claimant, buyer, and seller of land. In 1669 he patented a tract, which he later sold for 15,000 pounds of tobacco, at the future site of Snow Hill. Laid out as a town in 1686, Snow Hill became one of the Eastern Shore's chief ports. In 1670 Stevens established a ferry at present-day Pocomoke City. And in 1676 he patented land at Genesar, located on Sinepuxent Neck east of what is now Berlin. He sold this tract to the Whaleys, Ratcliffes, and Purnells, whose descendants long remained prominent in the region. Stevens and other Presbyterians directed a petition in 1681 to the Presbytery of Laggan in Ireland requesting "a godly minister to be sent to us." Two years later the Rev. Francis Makemie arrived and proceeded to establish congregations and churches up and down the Eastern Shore, including at Rehobeth, Snow Hill, and Accomac. One such Presbyterian meeting house was located about three miles south of present-day Berlin on Buckingham Plantation, owned by John White, Colonel Stevens' brother-in-law.

Throughout the eighteenth century, Berlin (called then Stevens' or Stephen's Cross Roads, after either William Stevens or nearby Stephen's Plantation) was merely a coaching stop on the Philadelphia Post Road, precursor of present-day Route 113. The place was located at a junction with the Sinepuxent Post Road. There was an inn, Burleigh's Inn, of which the name "Berlin" — pronounced with the accent on the first syllable — is supposedly a contraction. In 1757 the Buckingham Presbyterian congregation relocated its meeting house to a site at the south end of Berlin, although there was not then a village. The place is still occupied by the Presbyterian cemetery. A century later, after the meeting house collapsed in a blizzard, the congregation erected a new building at the center of town where the present-day church stands, the second on that site. In 1765 the Presbyterian minister established the Berlin Academy for boys, later called Buckingham Academy.

In the years leading up to the American Revolution, the gentry of Maryland's lower Eastern Shore, through their prestige and grip on the local government apparatus, secured the region for the revolution that eventually came, despite ambivalence on the part of many citizens and active opposition from some. Each Maryland county had a tight anti-imperial association of prominent citizens organized to resist the Stamp Act and the Townshend Acts and to enforce the boycott of British goods through the power of public opinion and occasional acts of intimidation and destruction. Eventually a Provincial Convention was elected, and by 1775 it and its executive arm, the Council of Safety, had assumed all the operations of the colonial government. The governor and other officials appointed from England held merely paper power. The election to the Convention in June 1776 was run mainly on the issue of whether to continue or sever colonial ties to England, and at the end of the month the newly-elected Convention authorized its delegates in Philadelphia to vote for independence. In the autumn, Maryland signaled its own independence by adopting a new constitution.

As the war got underway, there were loyalist plots, rallies, and raids on Maryland's lower Eastern Shore, but never a serious Tory threat to the revolutionary government. Worcester County, which had been carved out of Somerset County in 1742, organized three patriot militia battalions for local defense and military control. However, the county had difficulty filling its quota of recruits for service far from home in the Continental Army. Not infrequently men were pressed into service, and in 1781 a draft was instituted. Like all of Delmarva, the county was a source of grain and salt pork for revolutionary forces serving in the main theaters of action. General Levin Winder, later governor of Maryland during the War of 1812, was a Worcester County man. One person who sought refuge in rural Worcester County during the Revolution was the wife of an American naval officer named Stephen Decatur. Their son of the same name — later Commodore Stephen Decatur, hero of the Tripolitan War and of ship-on-ship victories during the War of 1812 — was born in a modest house at what is now Berlin in 1779. Hence Decatur Park and Tripoli Street.

At the beginning of the nineteenth century, Berlin was just a tiny hamlet, but over the course of the century it gradually developed into a major town. A post office was established in 1820. Three years later the place had eighteen houses and two stores. In 1825 St. Paul's Episcopal Church was built on present-day Church Street, supplanting a 1756 Anglican church at St. Martin a few miles to the north. By 1830 Berlin had about three hundred residents. A few homes from this period still stand, mostly along Main Street north and south of the business district; see Map 31 on page 208. Some of these early houses show the vernacular Federal style, with gable fronts and a few classical details, as in the case of Waverly, pictured at right.

In 1841 the Berlin Agricultural and Horticultural Society was organized. Items for which prizes were awarded at the first fair in 1842 indicate the region's chief farm products: wheat, oats, sweet potatoes, Irish potatoes, pumpkins, beets, onions, carrots, turnips, celery, cabbage, and of course cattle and pigs. The best milch cow and butter also took prizes, as did the best work horses (in pairs) and oxen. As for human labor, most of it, at least on the bigger farms, was done by slaves.* Locally owned schooners took on farm products, lumber, and shingles at coastal landings and transported the cargo to northern cities. Boats returning from New York brought limestone to be pulverized and applied to farm fields as fertilizer. The chief port for Berlin was Hays Landing, four miles south of town on Newport Creek, which empties into Chincoteague Bay.

During the Civil War, the seaside region of Delmarva was a corridor for the clandestine movement of men and contraband. Runaway slaves from Virginia and Maryland's lower Eastern Shore had for decades followed the swampy, forested Pocomoke River into Delaware. With its many Quakers and large population of free blacks, Wilmington was

---

*For a look at one plantation house, you may want to consider staying at Merry Sherwood, located immediately south of Berlin on Route 113 and now a bed-and-breakfast establishment; telephone (410) 641-2112. Built immediately before the Civil War, the house is an elegant Italianate mansion complete with Victorian furnishings and a few matter-of-fact reminders of slavery.

one of the few places where the semi-legendary Underground Railroad really existed as a loose organization that helped fugitives continue northward. Going in the opposite direction in the early months of the war were Confederate volunteers. As was the case in many border regions, Delmarva's communities and families were split, providing soldiers to both sides. Starting in the summer of 1861, Union troops occupied major towns on the Eastern Shore, including Snow Hill, Pocomoke City, Salisbury, and Accomac. Union cavalry patrolled the countryside, looking for Confederate recruiters and smugglers. Union ships, too, tried to intercept lighters and other small craft that slipped back and forth across Chesapeake Bay, transporting goods to the blockaded South. At one point detectives arrived in Berlin to arrest people accused of selling Confederate bonds and of sending money and contraband to the South. As the war dragged on and the federal government instituted a draft, many Worcester and Somerset men who were opposed to the North went into hiding. Hundreds took refuge in the Pocomoke swamps, living in shacks and leaving the woods only at night to pick up food left by friends at designated places. Some swamp refugees even supported themselves by making cypress shingles to barter for supplies from merchants.

Slaves, too, were recruited or drafted by the Union army and were promised freedom if they served. Their owners, if loyal to the Union, were supposed to be compensated, but the provision for payment meant little because the price of slaves plummeted in anticipation of an end to slavery after the war. Maryland, in fact, abolished slavery in October 1864, to the outrage of most whites on the Eastern Shore. In December several newly-established black churches in Worcester County were burned. In response the Union garrisons enforced a levy against whites in the vicinity to rebuild damaged or destroyed buildings.

Soon after the Civil War ended, the railroad reached Berlin, linking it with Salisbury and the major cities of the Northeast. In 1874 the line was extended to the nascent resort of Ocean City. For its first few decades (as again now) Ocean City created business for Berlin. Incorporated in 1868, Berlin emerged as the chief town of northern Worcester County. Local banks were organized, including the Calvin B. Taylor Bank, established in 1890 and still in business. Taylor also served as Berlin's mayor and as a delegate to the Maryland General Assembly. In the 1870s, J. G. Harrison and Sons Nurseries started growing fruit trees near Berlin and eventually became one of the world's largest suppliers of nursery stock, with huge landholdings in Worcester County and also in Delaware, western Maryland, and West Virginia. (After demise of the business in the 1930s and '40s, the Harrisons turned to resort development at Ocean City.) To replace the old Presbyterian Buckingham Academy and a young ladies' seminary, both of which had burned, Worcester County built the co-educational Buckingham High School at Berlin in 1885. Hotels and boarding houses sprang up, most notably the Atlantic Hotel, built in 1895. Vacationing families and sportsmen bent on fishing and hunting arrived by train and used Berlin as a base from which to make daily excursions. Traveling salesmen or "drummers" also frequented the hotels. They made their rounds of the town and the outlying villages and farms by horse and buggy hired from livery stables. In 1895 a fire broke out in a stable behind the Atlantic Hotel and consumed the center of Berlin. Other major fires occurred in 1901 and 1905, and in consequence new commercial structures were required to be built of non-combustible materials. The result is the concentration of buildings seen today, mostly dating from the turn of the century, similar in style, and made of the same locally-manufactured dark red brick.

At the end of the twentieth century, Berlin remains essentially what it was a hundred years ago: a place of general business and professional services for the seaside region of central Delmarva. A hospital and a large nursing home are in Berlin, and there are more than a few doctors and dentists. One of Worcester County's three high schools is still here, as well as two middle schools, an elementary school, and a private school. Although there are no longer any canneries, there is a lumber yard and a retailer of farm supplies. Agriculture is still at the core of the town's biggest businesses, which are a chicken processing plant, a manufacturer of dog food, and a feed mill. And there is tourism, generated by restoration of Berlin's historic business district starting in the mid-1980s, when there were as many as a dozen empty stores and several rundown buildings. Renovation was helped by the municipal government, state grants, and federal tax credits for historic preservation, but at bottom each project was possible only because local people invested their own money. For example, in 1986 ten businessmen from the area formed a partnership to buy, renovate, and operate the Atlantic Hotel, which had become a home for transients. The town government has also spent money. In 1994, at a cost of nearly $450,000, Berlin relocated overhead utility lines and installed Victorian-style streetlights. Perhaps this treatment, coupled with the proliferation of shops selling antiques, crafts, jewelry, and *objets*, offers a somewhat swank vision of the past, but it is nonetheless very successful and is perfect for Berlin's refurbished Main Street. And in any case, the boutiques are balanced by numerous utilitarian businesses, including some that have occupied the same spaces in Berlin since the early 1900s.

≈　　≈　　≈　　≈

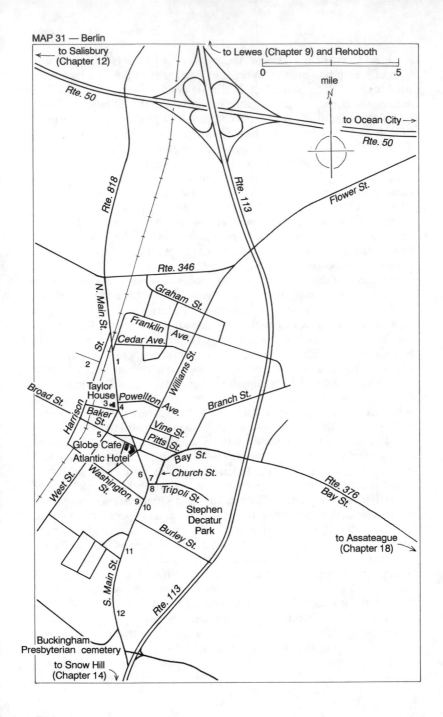

MAP 31 — Berlin

to Salisbury (Chapter 12)

to Lewes (Chapter 9) and Rehoboth

0 _____ .5
mile

N

Rte. 50

Rte. 50

to Ocean City →

Rte. 818

Rte. 113

Flower St.

Rte. 346

Graham St.

N. Main St.

Franklin Ave.

Cedar Ave.

Williams St.

Broad St.

Taylor House

Powellton Ave.

Branch St.

Harrison

Baker St.

Vine St.

Pitts St.

Globe Cafe

Atlantic Hotel

Bay St.

Church St.

Rte. 376
Bay St.

West St.

Washington St.

Tripoli St.

Stephen Decatur Park

Burley St.

to Assateague (Chapter 18)

S. Main St.

Rte. 113

Buckingham Presbyterian cemetery

to Snow Hill (Chapter 14)

1 2 3 4 5 6 7 8 9 10 11 12

1 The Thompson House at 217 North Main Street was built in the 1830s or '40s. With a Palladian window and gable facing the street, the house typifies the vernacular Federal style that was intended to suggest the outlines of a Greek or Roman temple. The porch has shallow dog's-tooth arches — a feature seen on several Berlin houses of this period.

2 Built in 1899, the Harrison House — also called Windy Brow — is an outstanding example of the ornate Queen Anne style, boldly unsymmetrical with decorative wood shingles, a wrap-around porch, a porte cochere, a turret, a gable with Palladian window, and an eyebrow window in the roof.

3 The Taylor House at 208 North Main Street is Berlin's municipal museum, open mid-May through September on Monday, Wednesday, Friday, and Saturday from 1 to 4 P.M. Built about 1832 in the Federal style, the house has a Palladian window, gable front, entrance flanked by fluted pilasters and columns that are topped by carved sunbursts and fans, and butterfly details on the brackets (or modillions) above the door and under the eaves. The two front rooms have handsome mantels, one of which repeats the elements of the front door.

4 The left-front section of the Stevenson-Chandler House at 125 North Main Street (on the corner with Powellton Avenue and bordered on the other side by Stevenson United Methodist church) dates from the 1790s, making it one of Berlin's oldest dwellings.

5 At 100 West Street (on the corner with Broad Street) is the Whaley House — also called Robin's Nest. The main section was built in 1801 and has a gable front and decorative Greek-motif cornice. The outbuildings behind the house include a granary, smokehouse, and "necessary."

6 Now near the center of town, Berlin's Buckingham Presbyterian Church (built in 1905) was preceded by a mid-eighteenth century meeting house at the site of the Buckingham Presbyterian cemetery, shown at the bottom of Map 31. The Buckingham congregation was one of several organized by the Rev. Francis Makemie in the 1680s. Presbyterian dissenters were among the earliest settlers of Worcester County.

7 Showing a vernacular treatment of the Queen Anne style of the 1890s, the Pitts-Bounds House at 23 South Main Street occupies the site of the Burleigh Inn, for which Berlin is thought to have been named.

8 Built about 1830, Kenwood at 101 South Main Street (at the corner with Tripoli Street) has a front entrance featuring Federal woodwork, with fluted pilasters, fanlight above the door, and other ornate carvings. The porch was added later.

9 The Keas House at 200 South Main Street (on the corner with Washington Street) was built in the 1880s.

10 Burley Cottage at 205 South Main Street was built in the 1830s. It has tall chimneys and a front porch with a bull's-eye window and sawtooth arches.

11 Built in 1832, Burley Manor at 313 South Main Street is a "hangover Georgian" house — that is, essentially eighteenth-century in style. The brick was stuccoed in the 1860s.

12 Waverly at 509 South Main Street (across from the Worcester Country School) is yet another Federal house. Its symmetrical gable end with Palladian window faces the street.

AUTOMOBILE DIRECTIONS: Berlin is located where Route 50 and Route 113 cross, about 7 miles inland from the southern end of Ocean City. (See **Map 1** on page iv in the Table of Contents, and also **Map 31** on page 208.)

To Berlin from northern Delmarva and Interstate 95 southwest of Wilmington: From Interstate 95 take Exit 4A for Route 1 south, and stay on Route 1 past a quick succession of exits. Follow Route 1 south past Dover, where Route 1 becomes congruent with Route 113. North of Milford, fork right to follow Route 113 south past Georgetown and into Maryland. Pass under Route 90, then cross Route 50. From the overpass at Route 50, continue just 0.5 mile, then turn right at a traffic light onto Route 346 west. Fork left almost immediately onto William Street and follow it 0.7 mile across Pitt Street to an intersection with Bay Street. Bear right a dozen yards to Main Street in front of the Atlantic Hotel in the center of Berlin.

To Berlin from the Chesapeake Bay Bridge: After crossing the bridge, follow Route 50/301 across Kent Island. At the point where Route 50 and Route 301 split, fork right to follow Route 50 past Easton, Cambridge, and Salisbury toward Ocean City. Stay on Route 50 past the exit for Route 90, then — just before the exit for Route 113 southbound — turn right onto Route 818 south. Go 1.3 miles to the Atlantic Hotel in the center of Berlin.

To Berlin from southern Delmarva and the Chesapeake Bay Bridge-Tunnel at Norfolk: After crossing the bridge-tunnel, follow Route 13 north about 73 miles to the intersection (near Pocomoke City, Maryland) with Route 113, and there turn right onto Route 113 north toward Berlin and Ocean City. Follow Route 113 for more than 26 miles, then turn left onto Main Street toward Berlin (opposite Germantown Road). Follow Main Street 0.8 mile to the Atlantic Hotel in the center of Berlin.

To Berlin from Salisbury: Follow Route 50 east toward Ocean City. Stay on Route 50 past the exit for Route 90, then — just before the exit for Route 113 southbound — turn right onto Route 818 south. Go 1.3 miles to the Atlantic Hotel in the center of Berlin.

To Berlin from the Delaware and Maryland seashore resorts: From the southern end of Ocean City, follow Route 50 west. Immediately after passing under the bridge at Route 113, turn left onto Route 818 and follow it south 1.3 miles to the Atlantic Hotel in the center of Berlin.

From the more northerly seashore resorts (and even from the upper end of Ocean City) go west to Route 113, then follow it south. After passing over Route 50, continue just 0.5 mile, then turn right at a traffic light onto Route 346 west. Fork left almost immediately onto William Street and follow it 0.7 mile across Pitt Street to an intersection with Bay Street. Bear right a dozen yards to Main Street in front of the Atlantic Hotel in the center of Berlin.

≈   ≈   ≈   ≈

SEEING BERLIN: The main area of interest is the center of town. Berlin's business district is a visually cohesive concentration of turn-of-the-century buildings. It is a very attractive place to stroll and browse. You may also want to use **Map 31** on page 208 to find and identify some of the town's old houses. The only house open to the public on a regular basis is the **Taylor House Museum** at 208 North Main Street.

If you are combining a visit to Berlin with an excursion to other nearby places, the directions around the border of Map 31 show the way toward Ocean City, Assateague Island, Snow Hill, Salisbury, Lewes, and Rehoboth.

14

SNOW HILL
POCOMOKE RIVER via canoe
FURNACE TOWN
POCOMOKE CITY
SHAD LANDING

The 55-mile car tour outlined in this chapter (and shown on **Map 35** on page 227) explores the vicinity of **Snow Hill** and **Pocomoke City**, both located on the Pocomoke River in southern Worcester County, Maryland. Snow Hill is the county seat and one of the Eastern Shore's oldest towns. The small business district does a large trade in antiques. In addition to its handsome streetscapes, churches, and waterfront, Snow Hill features the small but excellent **Julia A. Purnell Museum**, which displays clothes, tools, and artifacts from three hundred years of everyday life in Worcester County. The museum is open April through October, Monday through Friday from 10 A.M. to 4 P.M., and from 1 to 4 on Saturday and Sunday; telephone (410) 632-0515. For a quick overview of Snow Hill, see **Map 33** on page 223.

As for Pocomoke City, here is a major (and largely untouristed) Delmarva town of the present day, its past somewhat heavy on its hands. Once a prosperous river port, Pocomoke City is working hard to find new industries to replace those that formerly crowded its river front, and new businesses to replace those that have moved to the highway malls and away from the town's attractive but faded main street. For a discussion of the facilities and events that have made Pocomoke City an All-American City, see pages 230-231.

Near Snow Hill is **Furnace Town**, a re-created nineteenth-century village centered around the old masonry stack of the Maryland Iron Company. (See **Map 36** on page 228.) The buildings at Furnace Town are open daily from 11 A. M. to 5 P.M. during April through October; the grounds are open year-round. Furnace Town is also the access point for the **Paul Leifer Nature Trail** through Nassawango Creek Preserve. Telephone

Furnace Town Foundation, Inc. at (410) 632-2032 for information, including the annual calendar of events featuring music, dance, history, and activities for children.

For many people, however, the main attraction of this area is not its old, quiet towns along the Pocomoke, but the **Pocomoke River** itself, flowing from headwaters within a dozen miles of Ocean City southwest 50 miles to its muddy mouth (termed simply The Muds) at Chesapeake Bay. Like something transplanted here from the Gulf Coast, an extensive bald cypress swamp borders the Pocomoke and its tributaries in what is, in fact, the nation's northernmost stand of this quintessentially southern tree. The Paul Leifer Trail (mentioned in the previous paragraph), the Pocomoke City Nature Trail, and the Trail of Change at Shad Landing all provide opportunities to penetrate the bald cypress swamp on foot — without getting your feet wet. However, a far better way to see this exotic forest is from the water. Accordingly, a section of this chapter (see pages 224-226, including **Map 34**) is devoted to **canoeing on the Pocomoke River**, as is easily done because of the availabilty of rental canoes.

The car tour eventually ends at the **Shad Landing** area of the Pocomoke River State Park, where camping and marina facilities are available, and where the **Trail of Change** is located. (See **Map 37** on page 234.) The park is managed by the Maryland Department of Natural Resources; telephone (410) 632-2566.

Finally, bicyclists may enjoy a 25-mile ride that leads from Snow Hill through farmland and forest north of the Pocomoke River, passing Furnace Town and the **Pusey Branch Nature Trail** along the way. The bicycle route is shown on **Map 32** at right. It starts and ends with a short leg along Route 12, where bicyclists must be prepared for cars traveling at high speeds.

LOCATED AT THE HEAD OF NAVIGATION on the Pocomoke River, **Snow Hill** was platted as a town of one hundred acres by order of Maryland's General Assembly in 1686 and made county seat when Worcester County (pronounced Wooster) was carved out of Somerset County in 1742. During the colonial period, the town was a prosperous port of entry. Ships navigated the winding river by drifting with the tidal current while the crews used long poles to avoid shoals or colli-

MAP 32 — 25-mile bicycle tour from Snow Hill to Furnace Town, Pusey Branch Nature Trail, and Pocomoke State Forest

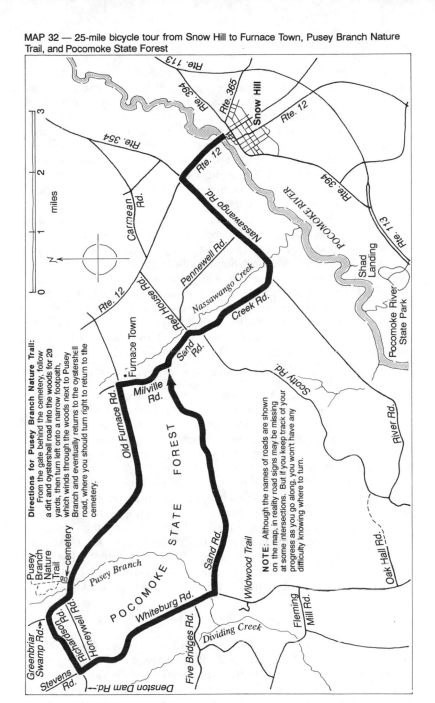

Directions for Pusey Branch Nature Trail: From the gate behind the cemetery, follow a dirt and oystershell road into the woods for 20 yards, then turn left onto a narrow footpath, which winds through the woods next to Pusey Branch and eventually returns to the oystershell road, where you should turn right to return to the cemetery.

NOTE: Although the names of roads are shown on the map, in reality road signs may be missing at some intersections. But if you keep track of your progress as you go along, you won't have any difficulty knowing where to turn.

sions with the bank. Snow Hill's merchants dealt directly with their counterparts in London and other centers of British commerce. From this town far up the Pocomoke, tobacco and furs were shipped to Great Britain and salt meat, corn, and other foodstuffs were carried to East Coast ports and to Caribbean plantations. To this town manufactured goods from England — fabrics, paper, household utensils, notions, books, tools, and other necessities of every description — were sent for eventual sale or barter by Snow Hill's merchants to the planters and farmers scattered throughout the hinterland. And from the Caribbean came sugar, molasses, salt, and rum.

During the nineteenth century, however, the rapid growth of Baltimore as the chief Chesapeake port relegated Snow Hill to the status of just another Eastern Shore town sending its products to the big city for transshipment there. Although Snow Hill continued to grow and prosper, its importance relative to nearby Pocomoke City and Salisbury shrank. After the Civil War, large steamboats plied the Pocomoke once or twice weekly, carrying freight and passengers to and from Baltimore, with stops too at Crisfield and Pocomoke City. A steamboat continued to make the Pocomoke run as late as the 1920s, and occasionally a showboat ascended the river. But long before steamboat service stopped, most local products, such as potatoes, canned vegetables, livestock, hides, cypress shingles, and large timbers, were taken from Snow Hill by railroad. In the 1890s the railroad brought a circus to Snow Hill twice yearly. Other popular events in Worcester County were the annual Pocomoke Fair at Pocomoke City, which early in the twentieth century eclipsed the fair at Snow Hill, and the yearly chatauqua (referred to as "culture in a tent"), which came to Snow Hill during the first quarter of the century.

In recent years Snow Hill has promoted itself as an antique mart, with several antique malls housed in old buildings in the town's turn-of-the-century business district. Snow Hill also remains an agricultural center. Its businesses include a feed mill, a chicken hatchery, a fertilizer plant, a lumber mill, and a plant that prints labels. The railroad is still important to the town's economy, but the Pocomoke River no longer carries any commercial products. Now, as a scenic and recreational river, it is popular with fishermen, canoeists, and boaters.

≈   ≈   ≈   ≈

FIVE MILES NORTHWEST of Snow Hill is **Furnace Town**, which was once a small company-owned village engaged in smelting iron. From our present-day perspective, the location of the furnace at this remote, swampy site bordering Nassawango Creek seems strange. The location, however, simply reflects the technology of iron-making

216

during the early nineteenth century. The essential ingredients were iron ore, charcoal fuel, and calcium carbonate for flux to help remove impurities in the ore. The Pocomoke region had all three. Since the late 1700s, beds of iron oxide (technically termed limonite but more prosaically called bog iron) were known to exist in the vicinity of Nassawango Creek, where they had been deposited in the still waters of the swamp after the ore was leached from throughout the watershed. Charcoal could be made from the region's extensive forests by partially burning cordwood in a slow, smoldering fire. And calcium carbonate was available in the form of the huge quantities of shells that were a by-product of the oyster and clam fisheries of Chincoteague and Chesapeake bays.

The Nassawango site offered other advantages as well. By the late eighteenth century it already had been developed with a dam and millpond to provide waterpower for a sawmill and gristmill. Also, the nearby Pocomoke River could serve to transport pig iron by schooner to Chesapeake Bay and from there to foundries in Baltimore and Philadelphia, and to carry back shells from the vicinity of Crisfield.

The furnace and village operated as the Maryland Iron Company from 1832 to 1847. As still seen today, the furnace consisted of a fat masonry stack that was hollow and lined with firebrick. As was typical of such furnaces, it was built at the bottom of a steep bluff, so that a trestlework charging ramp wide enough to accommodate a mule and cart could run from the top of the slope to the top of the stack.

When the furnace was in operation, charcoal, iron ore, and shells were carted up the ramp and dumped into the top of the stack, which also served as the chimney. The stack gases were nearly smokeless but occasionally streams of sparks shot out, and at night flames lit the sky and surrounding village. A water-powered bellows provided an intermittent blast of air that, with a heavy, pulsing roar, fanned the furnace fire. The rush of air was called a *hot blast*, because the air was preheated by passing through pipes exposed to the flames at the top of the stack. At Nassawango the hot blast apparatus was added in the late 1830s in order to increase the furnace temperature and to speed the rate of smelting as compared to the earlier cold-blast system. Hot-blast furnaces could also burn hard coal — not that coal was available at Nassawango.

Once fired, the furnace was kept in continuous blast for many months at a time, until supplies were used up or the furnace lining deteriorated to the point where it had to be replaced. Men known as fillers labored around the clock, feeding the furnace at regular intervals as the fuel, ore, and flux were consumed and the molten iron slowly sank to the crucible at the bottom of the stack. Working in the recessed casting arch at the foot of the furnace, the founder — a man of experience and judgment — occasionally opened the higher of two taps to draw off the molten slag that floated on the heavier molten iron. And by opening a lower tap, the founder could sample the iron itself and to some extent control its quality by calling for an adjustment in the proportion of ingredients and the blast of air. Then, two or three times a day, the founder released the molten iron into molds dug in the sandy floor of the casting house, which was a barnlike structure built around the opening of the casting arch. Typically, the molds consisted of nothing more than short, parallel troughs branching from a central channel. In the early days of iron making, the main pouring channel and the row of smaller molds were noted to resemble a sow with suckling pigs; hence the term *pig iron* for crude iron.

In addition to the workmen who actually operated the furnace were others, far more numerous, who supplied the necessary raw materials. With pick and shovel, diggers extracted bog iron from the swamp. Carters transported the ore to the top of the bank, as the bluff by the furnace was called. Other men loaded and unloaded the barges that were towed by mules along a canal that linked the town with a lock and landing at Nassawango Creek, which in turn led to the Pocomoke River. The barges were used to bring in oyster and clam shells and to take out the iron pigs once they were cast. Woodcutters supplied cordwood, which was needed in immense quantities, as indicated by an advertisement in the Snow Hill *Messenger* for May 20, 1833: "Wood Choppers Wanted at Naseongo Furnace. 50 good steady hands will meet with constant employment at forty cents per cord. Apply to manager at the Works." And after the wood had been cut, colliers converted it to charcoal.

Making charcoal was a laborious and painstaking process. First the cordwood was hauled to charcoal hearths scattered throughout the forest. These hearths were nothing more than large, circular clearings where first the wood was allowed to stand and dry for a few months. After the cordwood was seasoned, the colliers arranged the logs in a circular mass thirty or forty feet in diameter, with all the pieces standing on end and leaning toward a wooden chimney at the center. Another smaller layer of cordwood was placed on top of the first, and a third layer on top of that, until a rounded heap of wood was built. Then the colliers covered the logs with a layer of leaves and dirt. The chimney was filled with kindling and a fire set at the top.

For as long as two weeks the colliers, who lived in huts near their work in the woods, watched over the mound while the wood smoldered and turned to charcoal. Outbreaks of flame were quickly smothered with dirt. Blue smoke indicated that all was going well, but white smoke was a sign of too much combustion. The rate of charring was

controlled by opening and filling air holes. The most dangerous part of the job was "jumping the pit," which entailed climbing on top of the smoking heap and stamping on it to settle the coals and fill in air spaces. Finally, when the charring appeared to be complete, the colliers uncovered the mound a little at a time. The hot charcoal was loaded into metal-lined wagons, which then were hauled to the village and parked in a shed to protect the coals from rain. After the charcoal had cooled, it was added to the supplies stored in the charcoal house at the top of the bank.

Making charcoal was so time-consuming that it was a bottleneck in the entire iron-smelting process for many furnaces operating during the first half of the nineteenth century, especially after the introduction of hot-blast technology made possible the use of hard coal. Coal was far cheaper than charcoal, and labor costs for iron produced with anthracite were about 20 percent of labor costs for iron made with charcoal.

Although Nassawango Furnace suffered from a competitive disadvantage compared to furnaces located near coal fields, it continued in business during most of the 1840s, and, indeed, the furnace and village became a substantial operation. For married men and their families, there were about fifteen company-owned houses, plus several smaller cottages. Single men lived in a large and crowded boarding house. There were a general store with post office, a bank, a school, a Methodist meeting house, and the ironmaster's house called "the mansion," where for a period Furnace Town's owner lived. Other structures included several barns for draft animals, a blacksmith shop, a shoemaker's shop, and a shop for making patterns for iron castings. Assets included not only the furnace village but also five thousand acres of land.

The enterprise, however, was at best barely profitable, and became altogether unprofitable as time passed. About seven hundred tons of pig iron were produced annually — somewhat less than at comparable furnaces of the period. Costs were high and by some accounts the iron was marketable only at a low price because it was tainted with phosphorous. About 1840 the iron company was bought by Thomas A. Spence, who proceeded to pour the fortune of his wealthy, Baltimore-bred wife into the venture, but without good result.

By 1847 iron making at Nassawango Furnace had stopped, and during the following decades the village decayed and disappeared. By 1908 only the furnace, the ironmaster's house, and three cottages remained, and by 1978, when Furnace Town Foundation, Inc. was organized, the lone structure still standing was the massive masonry furnace stack. Since then Furnace Town has been the scene of ongoing restoration. The furnace itself has been stabilized and the charging ramp rebuilt. About a dozen buildings have been moved here in recent years in order to show the appearance and ancillary activities of a working iron village. (See **Map 36** on page 228.)

≈   ≈   ≈   ≈

AUTOMOBILE DIRECTIONS: For the various activities described in this chapter, go first to Snow Hill, which is located 17 miles southeast of Salisbury, where Route 12 crosses the Pocomoke River. (See **Map 1** on page iv in the Table of Contents.)

To Snow Hill from northern Delmarva and Interstate 95 southwest of Wilmington: From Interstate 95 take Exit 4A for Route 1 south, and stay on Route 1 past a quick succession of exits. Follow Route 1 south past Dover, then switch to Route 13 south through Maryland toward Salisbury and Norfolk. After passing the exit for Route 50 toward Ocean City, continue south on Route 13 to the next exit for Route 12 toward Snow Hill. At the bottom of the exit ramp, turn left onto Route 12 southbound and go a little more than 15 miles to Snow Hill on the Pocomoke River.

Alternatively, you may prefer to stay on Route 1 as it becomes congruent with Route 113 south of Dover. At Milford take Route 113 south and follow it past the interchange with Route 50. From there, follow Route 113 south about 15 miles, then fork right onto Route 394 toward Snow Hill. Follow Route 394 for 1.4 miles to the center of Snow Hill.

To Snow Hill from the Chesapeake Bay Bridge: After crossing the bridge, follow Route 50/301 across Kent Island. At the point where Route 50 and Route 301 split, fork right to follow Route 50 past Easton, Cambridge, and Salisbury. East of Salisbury, take Route 13 south toward Norfolk, but go only to the exit for Route 12 toward Snow Hill. At the bottom of the exit ramp, turn left onto Route 12 southbound and go a little more than 15 miles to Snow Hill on the Pocomoke River.

To Snow Hill from southern Delmarva and the Chesapeake Bay Bridge-Tunnel at Norfolk: After crossing the bridge-tunnel, follow Route 13 north about 73 miles to the intersection (near Pocomoke City, Maryland) with Route 113, and there turn right onto Route 113 north toward Berlin and Ocean City.

Follow Route 113 for 9.4 miles, then turn left onto Route 394
north toward Snow Hill. Follow Route 394 for 2.8 miles to the
center of Snow Hill.

**To Snow Hill from Salisbury and the Delaware and
Maryland seashore resorts:** From the intersection of Route
13 and Route 12 southeast of Salisbury, take Route 12 south
slightly more than 15 miles to Snow Hill on the Pocomoke
River.

From the Delaware and Maryland seashore resorts, first go
west to Route 113, then follow it south. From the interchange
at Route 113 and Route 50, follow Route 113 south about 15
miles, then fork right onto Route 394 toward Snow Hill. Follow
Route 394 for 1.4 miles to the center of Snow Hill.

≈   ≈   ≈   ≈

TOURING SNOW HILL: The bold line on **Map 33** at right
shows the route of a car tour that provides a quick overview of
Snow Hill, where there are more than a hundred century-old
dwellings. The tour starts on Green Street, near the clock at
the intersection with Washington Street (Route 12). Lined with
brick stores, many of which were rebuilt after a fire in 1893,
Green Street is Snow Hill's main business street. Follow
Green Street to a five-way intersection and then, in quick
succession, turn right onto Church Street, left onto Pettit Street
(vandals sometimes rotate this sign), and left again onto Water
Street, which will bring you alongside the **Julia A. Purnell
Museum**, where there are several parking spaces.

From the Purnell Museum, turn right onto Market Street and
follow it past Gunby and Morris streets, then turn left onto Ross
Street and left again onto Federal Street, where there are a
succession of handsome, mostly nineteenth-century houses.
At Washington Street, turn right , then (after two blocks) turn
right again onto Ironshire Street, which leads past the **Mt. Zion
One-Room School Museum**, which is open from mid-June
through Labor Day on Tuesday through Saturday from 1 to 4
P.M.

Just beyond the school museum, turn right onto Church
Street, then (after three blocks) turn right onto Market Street.
All Hallows Episcopal Church at the corner of Market and
Church streets was built over a period of seven years between

MAP 33 — Car tour of Snow Hill

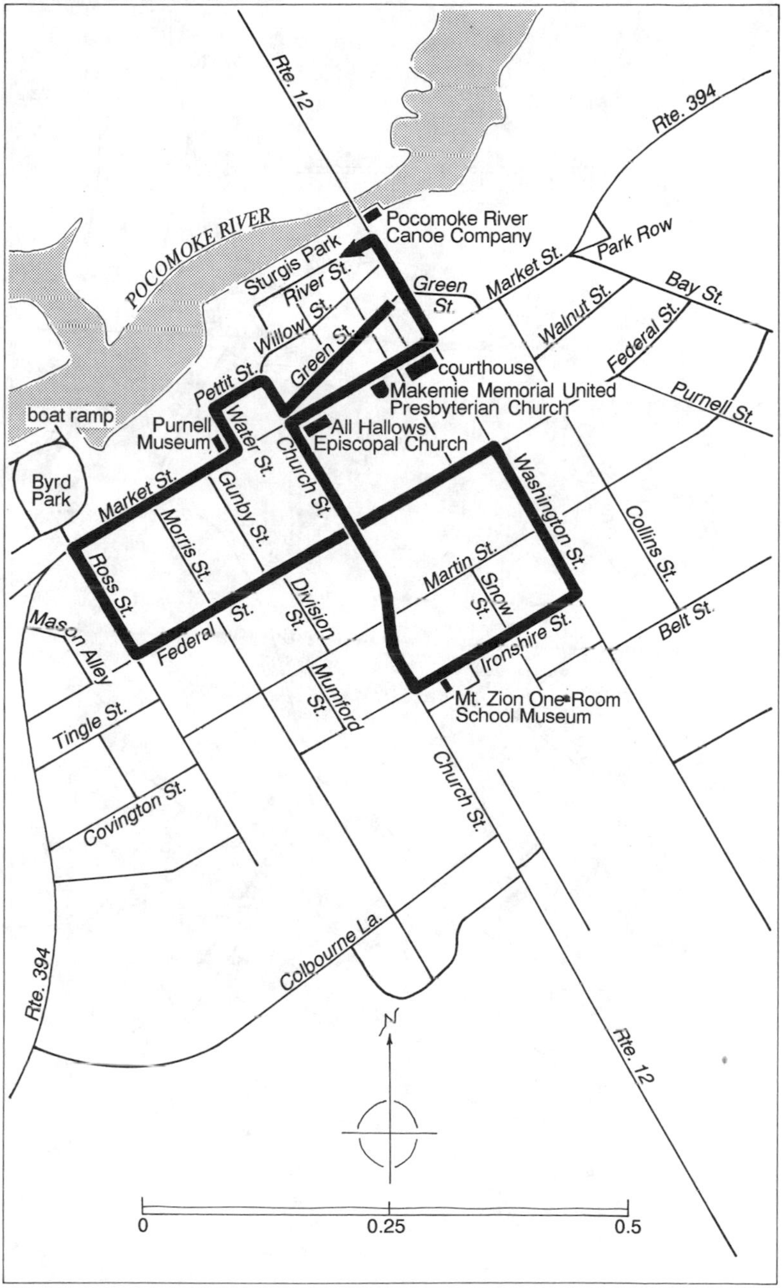

Rte. 12

Rte. 394

POCOMOKE RIVER

Pocomoke River
Canoe Company

Sturgis Park

River St.

Willow St.

Green St.

Green St.

Market St.

Park Row

Walnut St.

Bay St.

Federal St.

Purnell St.

Pettit St.

courthouse

Makemie Memorial United
Presbyterian Church

boat ramp

Purnell
Museum

Water St.

Church St.

All Hallows
Episcopal Church

Byrd
Park

Market St.

Gunby St.

Washington St.

Collins St.

Morris St.

Ross St.

Federal St.

Division St.

Martin St.

Snow St.

Belt St.

Mason Alley

Ironshire St.

Mumford St.

Mt. Zion One-Room
School Museum

Tingle St.

Covington St.

Church St.

Rte. 394

Colbourne La.

Rte. 12

N

0   0.25   0.5

223

MAP 34 — Canoeing on the Pocomoke River and Nassawango Creek

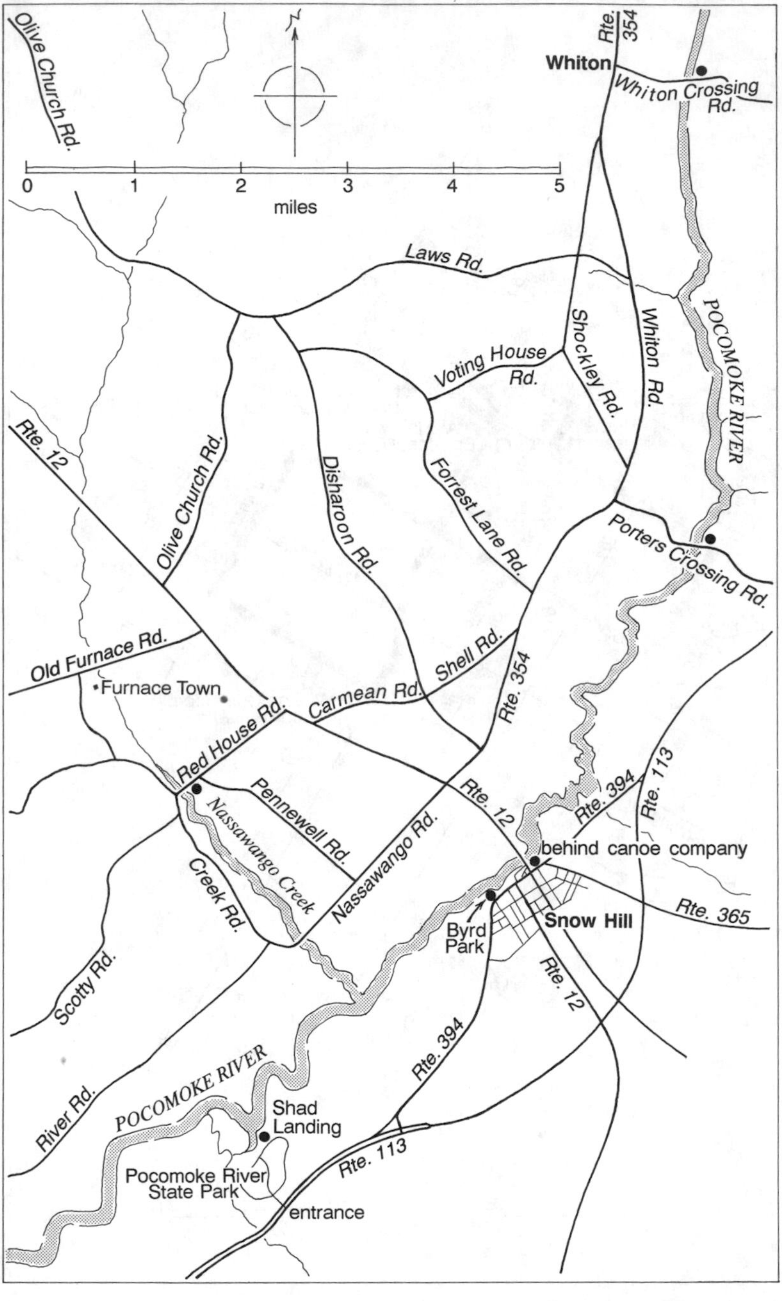

Olive Church Rd.

Rte. 354

Whiton

Whiton Crossing Rd.

0   1   2   3   4   5
miles

Laws Rd.

Shockley Rd.

Whiton Rd.

POCOMOKE RIVER

Voting House Rd.

Rte. 12

Disharoon Rd.

Forrest Lane Rd.

Olive Church Rd.

Porters Crossing Rd.

Old Furnace Rd.

Shell Rd.

Rte. 354

•Furnace Town

Carmean Rd.

Red House Rd.

Rte. 12

Rte. 394

Rte. 113

Pennewell Rd.

Nassawango Creek

Nassawango Rd.

behind canoe company

Rte. 365

Creek Rd.

Byrd Park

Snow Hill

Scotty Rd.

Rte. 12

POCOMOKE RIVER

Rte. 394

River Rd.

Shad Landing

Rte. 394

Pocomoke River State Park

Rte. 113

entrance

224

1748 and 1755; the interior was redone in the late 1800s.
Makemie Memorial Presbyterian Church was started in 1887
and finished three years later. Prior Presbyterian churches
stood in the old churchyard burial ground to the rear of the
present-day church, which serves a congregation that has
existed in this part of Maryland since the late 1600s.
Dissenters from the prevailing Anglican orthodoxy of the time,
many Presbyterians settled in the region just to the north of the
border with Virginia, which they had left for the more tolerant
atmosphere of Maryland. Lacking a minister, they petitioned
for aid from a Presbytery in northern Ireland, which sent out the
Rev. Francis Makemie. This energetic Ulsterman arrived in
1683 and organized several Presbyterian congregations
throughout Maryland's Eastern Shore.

   Just beyond the 1894 **Worcester County Courthouse**, turn
left onto Washington Street, then (after passing Green Street
and Willow Street) turn left onto River Street, which borders
Sturgis Park and, beyond it, the Pocomoke River. Across
Washington Street from Sturgis Park is the Pocomoke River
Canoe Company, discussed below.

≈   ≈   ≈   ≈

CANOEING ON THE POCOMOKE RIVER: Although the car
tour and foot trails described later in this chapter provide a look
at the swampy bald cypress forest that borders the Pocomoke
River and Nassawango Creek, a far better way to see this
unusual environment is by canoe. The meandering stretch of
river shown at left on **Map 34** provides the best canoeing that
Maryland's Eastern Shore has to offer.

   If you own a canoe, by all means bring it with you. However,
if you want to rent a canoe and gear, the Pocomoke River
Canoe Company is centrally located by the Route 12 bridge in
Snow Hill. This canoe livery is open daily from late March
through late December. For information telephone (410) 632-
3971 or write to the Pocomoke River Canoe Company, 312
North Washington Street, Snow Hill, Maryland 21863. From
mid-spring to mid-fall, canoes can also be rented from the
camp store at the Shad Landing area of the Pocomoke River
State Park; telephone (410) 632-2566. However, the river at
Shad Landing is less interesting than farther upstream.

   Various launching sites are shown by the dots on Map 34.
At Snow Hill, the most convenient is the bulkhead behind the

canoe company building, where there is a public parking area. Whether you bring your own canoe or rent one, the Pocomoke River Canoe Company can be hired to take you and your canoe upstream to Porters Crossing Road or Whiton Crossing Road, both on the Pocomoke River, or to Red House Road on Nassawango Creek, thus enabling you to paddle one way back to Snow Hill. Unless your interest is simply to paddle for an hour or two immediately upstream from Snow Hill (recommended for beginners), I suggest that you start at one of the places mentioned above. The trip from Whiton Crossing to Snow Hill is an all-day outing; from Porters Crossing or Red House Road to Snow Hill takes half a day. Even for a short outing, bring something to drink.

Finally, if you intend to explore the river's swampy, narrow sections, you will need insect repellent (although on the many occasions when I have been there during autumn, mosquitoes have not been a problem).

≈   ≈   ≈   ≈

CAR TOUR OF SOUTHERN WORCESTER COUNTY: This 55-mile car tour is shown by the bold line on **Map 35** at right. Although Worcester County seems determined to save money by omitting signs with road names at many intersections, you should have no difficulty if you follow the directions closely.

The tour starts at Snow Hill and goes first to **Furnace Town**. Follow Route 12 north out of town 3.8 miles, then turn left onto Old Furnace Road and go 1.1 miles to Furnace Town at the intersection with Milville Road. Furnace Town is discussed in the commentary for this chapter starting on page 216. As shown on **Map 36** on page 228, the town includes many old structures and also access to The Nature Conservancy's mile-long **Paul Leifer Nature Trail**. The trail starts behind the furnace stack and penetrates, via boardwalk, a swampy bald cypress forest bordering the old canal that linked Furnace Town with a landing on Nassawango Creek.

From the intersection of Old Furnace Road and Milville Road at Furnace Town, follow Milville Road south (i.e., leaving behind Furnace Town on your left). Go 0.9 mile, then bear left (this is Sand Road). Continue 0.6 mile, then turn right onto Creek Road, but after only 0.2 mile fork right onto Scotty Road. Follow Scotty Road 5.2 miles to an intersection where it joins

MAP 35 — Car tour of southern Worcester County

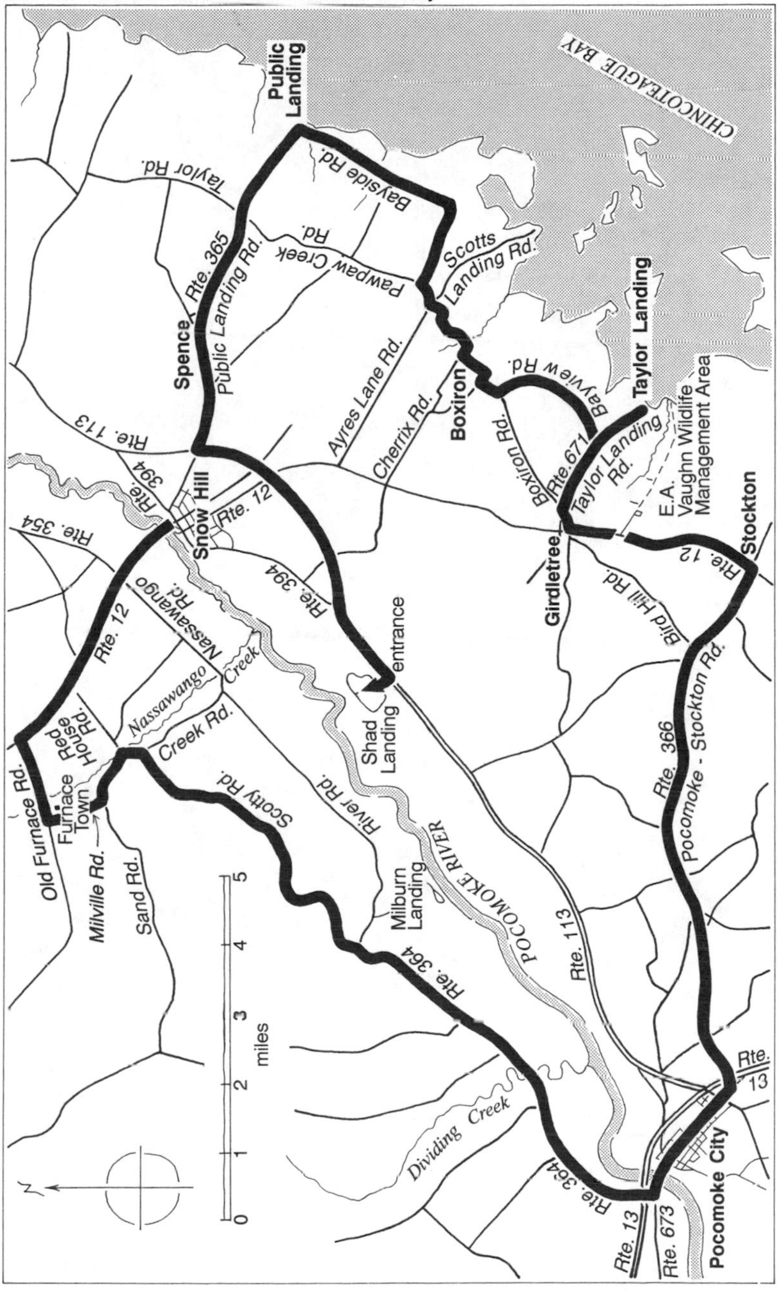

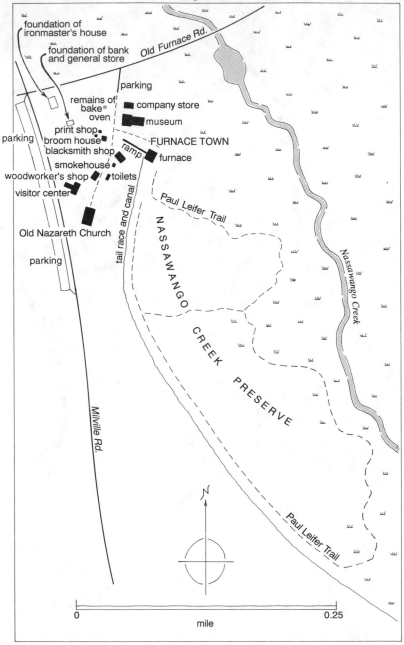

MAP 36 — Furnace Town and Nassawango Creek Preserve

foundation of ironmaster's house

foundation of bank and general store

Old Furnace Rd.

parking

remains of bake oven

company store

museum

print shop

FURNACE TOWN

parking

broom house

blacksmith shop

ramp

furnace

smokehouse

woodworker's shop

toilets

visitor center

tail race and canal

Paul Leifer Trail

Old Nazareth Church

NASSAWANGO

parking

CREEK

Nassawango Creek

PRESERVE

Milville Rd.

Paul Leifer Trail

N

0   0.25

mile

River Road, and there bear right to follow the main trend of the road, which soon becomes Route 364 south. Follow River Road/Route 364 south 6 miles to and straight across Route 13. Turn left at a T-intersection and go 1.9 miles across the Pocomoke River and through Pocomoke City on Market Street.

Like Snow Hill, **Pocomoke City** owes its existence and development to the Pocomoke River. Since 1670 there has been a landing here, known at first as Steven's Ferry, for Colonel William Stevens, who also helped to found Snow Hill and Berlin. In about 1683 or '84, the place was called Meeting House Landing, after a Presbyterian house of worship in the vicinity. In about 1700 a public tobacco warehouse was built, and for 120 years it stood at what then became known as Warehouse Landing. In 1780 the place was platted as Newtown and finally was incorporated as Pocomoke City in 1878, when both the river and the new railroad (which had arrived in 1872) seemed to guarantee a bustling future for the town.

Exploitation of the region's extensive bald cypress forests was a powerful stimulus to the village's economy. A steam-powered shingle mill — the town's first — was established in 1839. In 1845 two entrepreneurs from New Jersey arrived, purchased large tracts in the cypress swamps downstream from the town, and established a sawmill and shipyard. Writing nearly forty years later, the Rev. James Murray recounted that these men "aroused the citizens of New Town and the entire surrounding country to the idea of business which has never died out. They infused a spirit of industry and enterprise in all, from the day laborer to the merchant behind the counter and the farmer at the plow. They . . . produced an entire revolution in business life." At the time Murray wrote, Pocomoke City and the surrounding countryside had five sawmills, two flour and gristmills, three shipyards, and two marine railways. Among the ships built at Pocomoke City was the four-masted schooner *Lillian E. Kerr* and numerous coastal and bay craft. Shipbuilding continued at Pocomoke City well into the twentieth century.

The Rev. Murray's 1883 *History of Pocomoke City* is a veritable paean to local commerce:

> We have now eight large vessels sailing from Pocomoke City which are engaged exclusively in the bay trade. One and sometimes two steamboats plying between here and . . . [Baltimore] city and the railroad running daily to all parts north, by which facilities we have daily access to all the cities, doing an annual shipping business aggregating probably the round sum of $500,000. . . .
> [The] steamers are superseding, in a great measure, the sail vessels in carrying the produce of the Eastern Shore to Baltimore. . . . [T]hey have

first-class accommodation for passengers in their saloons, staterooms and cabins, and the viands upon their tables are selected from the best city markets. The writer having traveled on all of these steamers can say that the officers are polite and obliging, and passengers may be sure of being treated as ladies and gentlemen.

Our youthful readers cannot realize the advantages of steamboat travel to the same extent that some of us can, whose memory goes back to the time when there was no steamboat plying between Pocomoke City and Baltimore, and when it would require, at certain seasons of the year, two weeks or more for a sail vessel to make a trip from Pocomoke City to Baltimore and return.

Whereas with the present facilities of travel the trip can be made in thirty-nine hours, and give you eleven hours of that time to attend to business in the city. With these facts before us we can see clearly that progress is marching onward.

Indeed it is. Now the river carries very little commercial traffic — just an occasional barge taking out wood chips or sand and gravel aggregate — and the railroad too carries no passengers and relatively little freight compared to the past. Although timber remains a major industry in Worcester County, there are no longer any sawmills at Pocomoke City. The town's only timber operation is a chip mill for paper pulp. The oldest business in town is the small Robertson Bros. machine works, established in 1907 and now reduced to selling miscellaneous hardware and piping. Replacing the old businesses are new ones, most of which could be almost anywhere: a plant making clam chowder and other clam products, a gun manufacturer making police pistols (Beretta USA), three plastic manufacturers, a factory producing metal shelving and another making scuba and deep-sea diving suits, a candy manufacturer, a T-shirt printer, and a fish farm. To attract new businesses to its industrial park, the town offers very low-interest loans and has even built structures on speculation.

Pocomoke City has also worked hard to improve the center of town. In 1983 the city received a Certificate of National Merit from the federal Department of Housing and Urban Development for restoring Market Street to its appearance in the 1920s, when the central part of town was rebuilt "in the latest style" after a fire in 1922 destroyed 250 houses and businesses. Built in 1927, the Art Deco **Mar-Va Theater** still stands and efforts are underway to renovate it. In 1985 Pocomoke City was named an All-American City for redeveloping its waterfront, previously the site of shipyards, warehouses, and commercial docks, with a park, walkway, and facilities for recreational boating. More recently the town was named a Maryland Main Street Community for its efforts to preserve the vitality and architecture of its central business district, although some empty stores show the difficulty of competing against the malls and huge retail outlets on Route 50.

FOR A QUICK LOOK AT POCOMOKE CITY, take a walk up and down Market Street and along the riverfront boardwalk. There is a small parking lot located off Market Street at the city end of the bridge. Stretching upstream is **Cypress Park,** which leads to the **Pocomoke City Nature and Exercise Trail** just beyond the high Route 13 bridge. The trail itself runs 0.5 mile through woods and a cypress swamp to the nine-hole municipal golf course. The Victorian Italianate **Costen House** is located at 206 Market Street; telephone (410) 957-0678 or (410) 957-4364. Built in 1870 and now furnished with late Victorian pieces, the Costen House was the home of Dr. Isaac T. Costen, mayor of Pocomoke City from 1888 to 1892 and again from 1908 to 1912. The Costen House is open by appointment and on special occasions, such as the annual Pear Tree Festival, held the second Saturday in May. Late in August there is the Great Pocomoke Fair, which includes not only the usual rides, games, stage shows, and cooking and livestock contests, but also harness racing. And on the first Saturday in October there is River and Rails Heritage Day, featuring a train that runs south to Parksley (see page 337) — if the tracks are in good repair. For information on these these and other events, telephone City Hall at (410) 957-1333.

CAR TOUR continued (Map 35): After passing through Pocomoke City on Market Street, turn left to follow Route 366 east. Cross Route 13 almost immediately and continue on Route 366 for 8.2 miles to a crossroads with Route 12 in the decayed town of **Stockton** (formerly Stock Town, where in the middle of the nineteenth century cattle were gathered before being herded north to Wilmington and Philadelphia for slaughter). Early in the twentieth century Stockton had railroad service, three churches, several stores, a bank, a sawmill and lumberyard, a grist mill, a barrel factory, and a cannery.

Turn left in Stockton onto Route 12 and follow it 2.9 miles to a crossroads by the post office in the town of **Girdletree,** thought to be named for a farm called Girdle Tree Hill, whose owner removed a large beech tree by girdling it. As you approach Girdletree, you will pass the obscure entrance to the State of Maryland's **E. A. Vaughn Wildlife Management Area** on the right, located 2.2 miles north of Stockton.

WALKING AT THE VAUGHN WILDLIFE MANAGEMENT AREA: During the colder months when there are no mosquitoes, this area provides a very pleasant walk of about 3 miles round-trip to the marshes bordering Chincoteague Bay and back. The route is shown by the dashed line near the bottom of Map 35. Because this is a public hunting area, you should wear orange during the hunting season and stick to the main track, which starts by the gate next to the parking lot at the end of the entrance road. A worn track leads more or less straight through fields, woods, and marsh to the water's edge.

CAR TOUR continued (Map 35): At the post office in Girdletree opposite Onley Road, turn right and follow the main trend of the road 2.4 miles to the boat ramp at **Taylor Landing**, one of a dozen or more such Worcester County landings long used by oystermen and fishermen on Chincoteague Bay.

From Taylor Landing, return 0.8 mile, then turn sharply right onto Bayview Road. Follow Bayview Road 2 miles, then turn right at a T-intersection. Go 0.3 mile, then again turn right at a T-intersection. Continue 0.5 mile, then turn right at yet another T-intersection in the hamlet of **Boxiron** (a corruption of bog iron, after nearby Bog Iron Creek). At the next intersection, which is a skewed crossroads, bear slightly right (i.e. not hard right onto Scotts Landing Road) and continue 0.3 mile, then bear right onto Bayside Road and go 3.6 miles to a T-intersection in the village of **Public Landing** (also called Snow Hill Landing), and there turn right into the landing parking lot. The distance from here to the head of navigation on the Pocomoke River at Snow Hill is only 6 miles. Before the advent of railroads and steamboats, some products of the lower Eastern Shore were shipped up the Pocomoke River to Snow Hill, carried from there by wagon to Public Landing, then reshipped north by coastal schooners small enough to navigate the shallow channel at Chincoteague Inlet.

From Public Landing, follow Route 365 west 5.2 miles, then turn left onto Route 113 and continue 4.8 miles to the entrance to **Pocomoke River State Park — Shad Landing Area**. Follow the entrance road 0.5 mile, then turn right at a T-intersection and go 0.2 mile to the marina, where the car tour ends.

WALKING AT SHAD LANDING: Although this section of Pocomoke River State Park caters primarily to campers and boaters, there is also the mile-long **Trail of Change**, which

MAP 37 — Shad Landing Area of Pocomoke River State Park

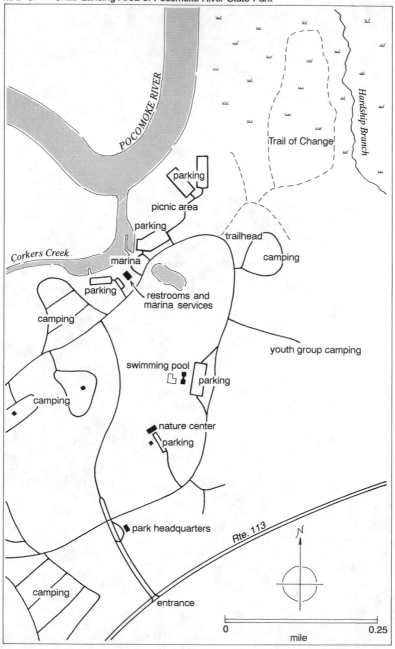

POCOMOKE RIVER

Hardship Branch

Trail of Change

parking

picnic area

parking

trailhead

camping

Corkers Creek

marina

parking

restrooms and marina services

camping

youth group camping

camping

swimming pool

parking

camping

nature center

parking

park headquarters

Rte. 113

N

camping

entrance

0   mile   0.25

234

provides a glimpse of a bald cypress forest. If you have not by now seen these trees, here is your chance.
The trail is shown at the upper-right corner of **Map 37** opposite. To reach the trailhead from the parking lot at the marina, follow the circle road clockwise about 180 yards to the Trail of Change on the left.

The "bald" in bald cypress derives from the fact that this conifer sheds its needles in autumn. Other distinguishing characteristics are the swollen, fluted base of the trunk, which helps provide stability in the sodden soil, and the woody "knees," which protrude from the ground or water and supply oxygen to the wide-spreading root system.

During the nineteenth century, logging for bald cypress was a major industry in Worcester County. Because bald cypress wood resists decay, it was particularly valued for shipbuilding, siding, and shingles — hence Shingle Landing on the Saint Martin River west of Ocean City, where shingles were shipped to Philadelphia and New York.

Virtually all stands of bald cypress seen today in the Pocomoke region are second growth. As the bald cypress forest reestablishes itself, the large size of the mature trees (100 to 125 feet tall) should eventually enable them to shade out competing species, principally red maple, and once again become the dominant swamp tree.

15

DEAL ISLAND
DAMES QUARTER MARSH
WHITEHAVEN via ferry
PRINCESS ANNE

Shown on **Map 38** on page 247, the 60-mile car tour outlined in this chapter explores northwestern Somerset County, Maryland, with a brief amphibious incursion into neighboring Wicomico County.

Deal Island, projecting into Tangier Sound but linked to the mainland by a high bridge, is a center of commercial fishing. The island's two harbors are home port for several skipjacks, such as those shown at left.

Inland from Deal Island is the immense **Dames Quarter Marsh**, shown on **Map 39** on page 249. Good vantage points for birding are accessible by car via Riley Roberts Road. And as shown by the two bold lines on the map, there are opportunities to walk comfortably for 4 or 5 miles round-trip through a sea of grass along dirt roads and dikes that are closed to cars. However, because **hunting** is permitted here in season, please read carefully the information at the bottom of page 248 before walking across the marsh. Dames Quarter Marsh is part of the Deal Island Wildlife Management Area, which is administered by the Maryland Department of Natural Resources; telephone (410) 651-2320.

Finally, after a digression via toll-free public ferry to the village of **Whitehaven** on the Wicomico River, the car tour ends at **Princess Anne**, seat of Somerset County and site of the handsome neoclassical **Teackle Mansion**, built at the beginning of the nineteenth century. Under the auspices of an organization called Olde Princess Anne Days, Inc., the Teackle Mansion is open year-round each Sunday from 1 to 3 P.M. and also, April through mid-December, on Wednesday and Saturday from 1 to 3. For information telephone (410) 651-1705. Behind the Teackle Mansion is a handsome boxwood garden that is always open.

Olde Princess Anne Days also sponsors an event of the same name held annually on the second weekend in October, during which many private houses are open to the public.

DEAL ISLAND WAS FORMERLY KNOWN as Devil's Island, supposedly because this low, marshy outpost at the head of Tangier Sound was considered by its earliest English settlers to be fit habitation only for the devil. The diabolic name, however, eventually was suppressed as incompatible with the new spirit of Methodism that spread throughout the Eastern Shore following the American Revolution. According to the Rev. Adam Wallace (writing in the middle of the nineteenth century), "Deal Island" came into use because the presiding Methodist elder of the district "used to insist on spelling the name in this way, lest there should seem to be a recognition of Satan's having some right to, or property in" the place.

Until the advent of Methodism, most of the rural population of the Delmarva peninsula in the late eighteenth century was virtually without organized religion. Many families worshipped (if at all) according to their own lights and traditions, frequently without the benefit of prayer books, bibles, or even literacy. Anglicanism, reorganized as Episcopalianism after the American Revolution, was strongest among the gentry and residents of towns. At the other extreme, the Anglican church was altogether absent from the remote island communities of watermen, shipwrights, and small farmers in the vicinity of Tangier Sound, who by the example of a few among them were tarred with a reputation for drunkenness, immorality, and lawlessness.

Shortly before the Revolution, Robert Strawbridge, Francis Asbury, and other Methodist missionaries from England started preaching on the Delmarva Peninsula. The Methodist preachers traveled and spoke everywhere — in houses, in barns, and in the open. For many years Asbury journeyed on horseback more than five thousand miles annually. Like John Wesley himself, the Methodist missionaries were ordained Anglican ministers, and their core beliefs were not much different from the religious mainstream. They stressed repentance, faith, and full salvation that was available to everyone. What set them apart was their evangelistic zeal, their urgency, and their program of spiritual and individual betterment. In the place of Episcopal ritualism, the Methodists had emotionally powerful meetings. Their services offered opportunities for all — even the unschooled and ineloquent, and even women — to testify about their personal trials and about the mental comfort and practical improvements that religion brought to their lives. Although grace was a gift that could not be purchased or even earned, Methodism stressed the importance of hard work, frugality, charity, and abstinence from liquor. A responsible life was part of the process of religious growth. Following the Revolution, a cadre of local lay "exhorters" helped itinerant preachers to spread the Methodist message at a time when the Episcopal church was in disarray: understaffed because most Anglican clergymen had returned to England or emigrated to Canada, and underfunded because it had lost its status as the established, tax-supported church. By 1820 Methodism had swept the Delmarva Peninsula, reaching even its farthest outposts. With its democratic spirit and emphasis on a direct, personal relationship between each individual and God, Methodism appealed in particular to the fiercely independent and traditionally undocile islanders, whose villages converted virtually to a man.

The eagerness with which the islanders embraced Methodism may have been, in part, a way of spurning the ruling class that had led Maryland and Virginia into the Revolution. During the war, Maryland's revolutionary government had oppressed the islanders, often confiscating their boats and their livestock and threatening the people with forced relocation because some of them aided the British by brokering supplies to their warships and by attacking and looting the landings, plantations, and vessels of patriot merchants and planters. One militia commander wrote that the free-booters based on the islands of Tangier Sound were "a set of Poor, Ignorant, Illitorate People, Yet they are Artful and Cunning as Foxes." Referring to the islanders, Colonel Joseph Dashiel of the Somerset Militia wrote to Governor Thomas Lee of Maryland, "I consider them . . . the most Dangerous Enemy we have to watch the motions of — and am Certain if they Can do us no other Damage they will rob & Plunder all they Can before they are removed." Although never carried out because of lack of means, the directive to forcibly remove the populations of Deal, Smith, and other nearby islands was in fact issued by the governor. Reviled by the peninsular aristocracy, the islanders after the war turned to Methodism and the belief, common in American culture, that local citizens, guided by their faith and supported by one another, could run their lives better than a government of outsiders.

In 1825 Joshua Thomas became a deacon of the Methodist church on Deal Island. Thomas was a waterman who had been converted to Methodism on the mainland at Annemessex (now Crisfield) in 1807 and had thereafter organized a series of very successful camp meetings on Tangier Island, where he lived until moving to Deal Island. Camp meetings were an opportunity not only to convert souls but also to prevent backsliding by reviving or fortifying the spirit. And, of course, camp meetings were an opportunity for reunions with friends and families within the larger Methodist community.

Eventually Joshua Thomas was dubbed "the Parson of the Islands," which is the title of Adam Wallace's famous biography of him. Rough, awkward, and stammering in ordinary life, Thomas nonetheless was capable of a remarkable flow of words when the spirit came over him. While continuing as a waterman, Thomas also served as a ferryman for visiting preachers, conveying them to and from the various island communities in his large log sailing canoe, *The Methodist*. At the services and camp meetings he attended, Thomas invariably testified, and soon he became a highly effective lay preacher, exhorting the residents of isolated villages up and down the lower Eastern Shore with parables drawn from fishing and oystering.

In 1828 Joshua Thomas was among those who spoke at the first annual camp meeting on Deal Island, which Thomas's biographer says became the site of "many of the most powerful meetings that perhaps have ever been witnessed since the day of Pentecost" — or that is (according to Acts 2) since the apostles first received from the Holy Ghost the power of speaking in diverse tongues of fire. For the occasion of these camp meetings on Deal Island, hundreds of sailing vessels plus various chartered steamships would converge on the place, carrying not only the faithful but also the curious and those who came merely to sell provisions and other goods to the assembled throng. Scores of permanent shelters were built in concentric semicircles facing the elevated outdoor pulpit. When Thomas spoke, "the multitude, congregated under the sound of his voice, would sometimes heave like the ocean in time of storm, before the power of Divine truth falling from his lips. . . ."

Thomas preached at Deal Island's annual camp meeting until almost the last year of his life in 1853. A chapel named for him and built in 1850 still stands on Deal Island behind the larger, present-day St. John's United Methodist Church, and immediately adjacent to it is Thomas's grave.

≈   ≈   ≈   ≈

IN ITS LIFE AND ECONOMY, Deal Island today resembles in many ways the nearby communities of watermen at Smith Island and Tangier Island (discussed in chapters 16 and 17). There is, however, at least one difference, and that is the fact that Deal Island is home port for a few skipjacks, Maryland's traditional sail-powered oyster dredgers.

The dredge itself which these vessels pull is a triangular iron frame with teeth to loosen the oysters from their bed, coupled with a bag of rope-and-chain netting to catch them. Each skipjack pulls two dredges — one on each side — and each dredge is attended by two crewmen who alternately pull in their dredge with a power winch and cull through the catch for oysters of legal size (three inches).

The survival of the skipjacks, which are the only sailing craft in North America still used for commercial fishing, is entirely the result of a state law dating from 1865. Oyster dredging had been introduced to Chesapeake Bay by New Englanders about 1800, but the practice was soon outlawed on the grounds that the dredges tore up the oyster beds. Many oyster beds, however, were too deep for traditional hand tongs, so in 1865 oyster dredging (or "drudging," as local usage has it) was again permitted, but only in deep water and from boats without motors. This was considered a compromise, but the new law set off a virtual gold rush as large fleets of sail-powered dredge boats were built.

Over the course of the following century, oyster harvests that at first were immense gradually became so relatively meager that in 1967 the law was amended to allow dredging on Monday and Tuesday while powered by an auxiliary "yawl" or pushboat, which is a small skiff equipped with a large inboard motor, usually a converted automobile engine. A yawl may also be used at any time to push its skipjack from port to open water and back, provided the dredge is not overboard. Cinched into place with its bow wedged against a bracket at the stern of the skipjack, the yawl propels its mother vessel from behind. When not in use, the yawl is suspended like a lifeboat from davits at the skipjack's stern. Because of the vagaries of wind, the skipjack captains have come to depend heavily on the two days of power dredging allowed them each week, and in fact some boats never sail. Yet even on days when dredging under power is allowed, the catch never approaches the daily limit of 150 bushels, and is often merely 25 or 30 bushels.

This somewhat bizarre system of restrictions and exceptions is intended as a conservation measure, not only to protect the depleted oyster beds from utter ruin by more efficient motorized dredgers, but also to preserve the skipjacks themselves, for which the captains and most Marylanders have a certain attachment. Ever since the law was changed to permit skipjacks to dredge under power on Monday and Tuesday, there has been talk of allowing conventional motorized work-boats to dredge also, subject to daily catch limits. But except for the opening of one small area near Smith Island to motorized dredgers, the law has not been liberalized further, in recognition of the fact that the skipjacks would be abandoned immediately if they did not retain their virtual monopoly on oyster dredging in Maryland waters.

Despite their favored status, however, the skipjacks are an endangered species. Most are old. They are, of course, expensive to maintain, and in recent years they have been only marginally profitable. As a result of pollution, poor reproduction, oyster disease, and a history of overharvesting, the annual oyster crop in Maryland's portion of Chesapeake Bay fell below 1 million bushels for the first time during the 1986-87 season and during the mid-1990s hovered at less than a quarter-million bushels.

In the 1880s, when the Chesapeake oyster fishery was at its peak of prosperity, 2,576 dredge boats were licensed on the bay, and these craft were not mere skipjacks but typically larger, two-masted, beamy bugeyes. Cheaper to build than bugeyes, skipjacks did not appear until oyster harvests began to decline in the 1890s, after the gross overharvesting of the previous decade, when fifteen million bushels were dredged up annually. During the early twentieth century, nearly a thousand skipjacks were in operation, but as of the late 1990s, fewer than ten were in use as working boats during the oyster season, which for dredgers lasts from November through March. During summer a few skipjacks are operated as tourist boats, and others are maintained as pleasure craft.

Apart from dredging, there are others ways to harvest oysters, and the most time-honored among these is tonging, a practice dating back to the mid-1600s. Hand tongs (also called shaft tongs) consist of a pair of rakes with handles twelve to thirty feet long, hinged together like scissors a quarter of the overall length above the iron tines. After anchoring above a shallow oyster bed (or "rock," as the beds are called) and lowering the tongs over the side of his boat, the tonger pulls the handles apart and pushes them together so as to open and shut the tines resting on the oyster bed. When the tonger feels a number of oysters clamped between the tines, he raises the tongs into the boat hand over hand — or perhaps hand *under* hand would be more accurate — and empties the catch onto his culling board, where he picks over the oysters and throws out those that are undersize. Done for hours on end, the work is very strenuous, so tongers now tie a cord to the tines and attach the other end to a power-winder that helps them to pull up the tongs.

Another form of tonging uses patent tongs, in which iron jaws without any long wooden shafts attached are suspended by a cable from a derrick-like mast and boom; the jaws are raised and lowered by a power winch. Obviously, patent tongs enable an oysterman to work in deeper water than do shaft tongs. A variation on patent tongs are hydraulic tongs, in which the jaws are opened and closed by hydraulic power.

Because shaft tongers can operate only in shallow water where their tongs reach the bottom, oyster dredging has long been prohibited in Maryland on rivers (such as the Chester, Choptank, and Potomac) where most shallow oyster rocks are located. This restriction has never sat well with Maryland's dredgers, and starting in the late 1860s, some dredgers organized poaching fleets that from time to time invaded the tongers' rocks. Soon tongers and dredgers were shooting at each other. During some particularly violent seasons, deaths were not uncommon. Often the dredgers engaged in all-out attacks on the tongers, ramming their small boats and driving them off. In some places, the tongers built forts armed with a few cannons on shore near the oyster rocks or at the river mouths, but these deterrents failed, as the dredge fleets slipped in at night or even seized the forts and carried off the guns. One waterman's account contained in Francis Dize's book *Smith Island, Chesapeake Bay* describes how the crew of a poaching skipjack simply stuffed a blanket in a cannonball hole and kept on dredging.

Although contemporaneous with the somewhat similar range wars of the West, such lawlessness on the Chesapeake in the latter 1800s seems scarcely believable today. But for poachers (who were said by most dredgers to be a minority) defiance of the law meant big profits, especially after oyster catches from the open bay began to decline because of overharvesting. Self-righteous and willful, the dredge boat captains regarded the law as unwarranted and meddlesome interference with their traditional, God-given right to make a living on the water as they saw fit. Besides, during the oyster boom of the 1870s and '80s, the dredgers, who altogether accounted for the vast bulk of the oyster harvest, were economically and politically powerful, whereas the tongers, although more numerous, were poor folk and of little account.

In 1868 Maryland's General Assembly created the Oyster Navy, precursor of the present-day Natural Resources Police, but for decades the small and underfunded Oyster Navy had little effect on the poachers, who simply sailed off when a police vessel was spotted. Often one dredge boat was stationed as a sentinel at a river mouth. Using lights or flags at the mast top, the sentinel signaled to the fleet of poachers when a police boat approached. Since the sentinel boat could not itself dredge, the other boats each contributed to it a set number of bushels of oysters.

Some hardened poachers, termed *oyster pirates* in their day, even took to shooting at the police, and there were occasions when the police refused to interfere with poachers because of fear of gunfire, or were beaten by poachers. In 1888, however, the police steamer *McLane* scored a notable success when it rammed and sank two poaching dredge boats and captured two more during a nighttime battle on the Chester River. Eastern Bay was soon subdued also. But on the Choptank and Potomac rivers, violence continued through the 1890s and into the twentieth century until gradually, as the oyster economy declined and the dredge fleets shrank, poachers simply became clandestine pilferers.

During the last three decades of the nineteenth century, some dredge boat captains operated outside the law in other ways also. At that time the crews included four men on each of the two hand-powered windlasses that were used to pull in the dredges. But these large crews were difficult to come by because the work was hard and living conditions on board the boats were poor. Blacks who at first did this work soon refused to sign on as crews because of the hardships, and so skippers turned to using immigrant laborers, mainly Irish, Germans, and some Italians, whom the captains indiscriminately termed Paddies. Agents in New York engaged these immigrants straight off the boat at Ellis Island by promising them jobs, ample food, and good pay. Most received tolerable treatment, as measured by the somewhat harsh standards of the time, but some were exploited mercilessly. Once underway, these hapless men were worked relentlessly all winter, despite common occupational maladies, such as lacerated and infected hands. For the entire season the crew might be kept on the boats and often even locked up at night to prevent their escaping. Many were subjected to a "company-store" system of charges by which they were said to be indebted to the skippers for the clothing, boots, food, and tobacco issued to them at exorbitant prices. Men who finally refused to work were beaten or put ashore in remote places without pay, and a few were even shot on the slightest provocation, afterward said to have constituted mutiny. Sometimes, especially as unpaid wages accumulated, men were murdered in a manner made to look like an accident — as by being knocked overboard by the boom, in which case the victim was said to have been "paid off with the boom."

It is hard to know how often such abuses occurred, but they were common enough so that eventually the Hibernian (or Irish) Society and German Society posted placards in the waterfront districts of New York, Philadelphia, and Baltimore warning their compatriots away from the dredge boats. In response, crimps — people whose business it was to lure or entrap men into shipping as sailors — resorted to shanghai methods, and victims were delivered to the dredge boat captains in a drunken stupor. In 1886 a federal marshal and his deputies destroyed several "Paddy shacks" on Hooper Island, where crewmen, presumably by then sobered up and wanting to leave, were imprisoned before being distributed to the boats. In 1908 the federal Shanghaiing Act was passed, but by then systematic abuse was waning. The development of small gasoline engines for winding in the heavy dredges greatly reduced the need for laborers, as did also the decline in the number of dredge boats themselves.

Every once in awhile, however, present-day abuses echo the past. For example, in July 1991, the American Civil Liberties Union of Maryland, acting of behalf of fifteen Mexican crab pickers, filed a suit in U.S. District Court in Baltimore describing a system of virtual peonage at a packing house in an Eastern Shore fishing town. At the trial, the owners of the packing house were found by the court to have held the workers in a sort of bondage at a one-bedroom house by confiscating their passports, visas, and work permits and threatening to tear up these documents if the workers broke the company rules, which included a prohibition on leaving the house without permission or talking to local residents. The Mexicans were paid $15 each for a workweek of fifty hours on the night shift, after their boss charged them for food and rent. In a subsequent and similar case, another Eastern Shore seafood packer settled with the plaintiffs before trial. Also, the fact that some Latin American laborers at Eastern Shore truck farms, orchards, plant nurseries, and packing houses are illegal immigrants (always unbeknownst to their employers) exposes these workers to exploitation by the middlemen who transport them and broker them jobs.

$$\approx \qquad \approx \qquad \approx \qquad \approx$$

AUTOMOBILE DIRECTIONS: Princess Anne is located on Route 13 about 14 miles south of Salisbury. (See **Map 1** on page iv in the Table of Contents.) The car tour to Deal Island, Dames Quarter Marsh, and Whitehaven shown on **Map 38** on page 247 starts just west of Princess Anne, so you should go there first.

To Princess Anne from northern Delmarva and Interstate 95 southwest of Wilmington: From Interstate 95 take Exit 4A for Route 1 south, and stay on Route 1 past a quick succession of exits. Follow Route 1 south past Dover, then switch to Route 13 south toward Salisbury and Norfolk. After passing east of Salisbury, continue south on Route 13 to the intersection with Route 363 (Deal Island Road) just west of the town of Princess Anne.

To Princess Anne from the Chesapeake Bay Bridge: After crossing the bridge, follow Route 50/301 across Kent Island. At the point where Route 50 and Route 301 split, fork right to follow Route 50 past Easton, Cambridge, and Salisbury. East of Salisbury, take Route 13 south toward Norfolk, but go only to the intersection with Route 363 (Deal Island Road) just west of the town of Princess Anne.

To Princess Anne from southern Delmarva and the Chesapeake Bay Bridge-Tunnel at Norfolk: After crossing the bridge-tunnel, follow Route 13 north into Maryland and past Pocomoke City to the intersection with Route 363 (Deal Island Road) just west of the town of Princess Anne.

To Princess Anne from Salisbury and the Delaware and Maryland seashore resorts: From the vicinity of Salisbury, follow Route 13 south to the intersection with Route 363 (Deal Island Road) just west of the town of Princess Anne.

From the vicinity of Rehoboth Beach, follow Route 1 north to the intersection with Route 9 westbound, then take Route 9 west through Georgetown and across Route 113 to Route 13 southbound. Alternatively, from the vicinity of Ocean City, follow Route 50 west to Route 13 southbound. In either case, once you are on Route 13, follow it south around Salisbury to the intersection with Route 363 (Deal Island Road) just west of the town of Princess Anne.

≈ ≈ ≈ ≈

CAR TOUR OF NORTHWESTERN SOMERSET COUNTY:
The bold line on **Map 38** at right shows the route of this 60-mile car tour, which leads first to Deal Island.

From the intersection of Route 13 and Route 363 just outside Princess Anne, follow Route 363 west 14.3 miles to and across the high bridge leading to Deal Island. Continue 3.6 miles on the main road as it twists and turns through the town of **Deal Island** to the end of the road in the village of **Wenona**, home port for a few skipjacks. The harbor at Wenona is immediately adjacent to the main road. For a comparable look at the waterfront in the village of Deal Island, turn off Route 363 at Ralph Abbot Road (just south of the high bridge) or at Haines Point Road (0.4 mile north of the bridge). On the outskirts of the town of Deal Island is St. Johns United Methodist Church, and behind it are the **grave of Joshua Thomas and a small chapel** built toward the end of his life.

Return from Deal Island the way you came. From the high bridge, follow Route 363 east 2.9 miles to Riley Roberts Road,

MAP 38 — Car tour of northwestern Somerset County

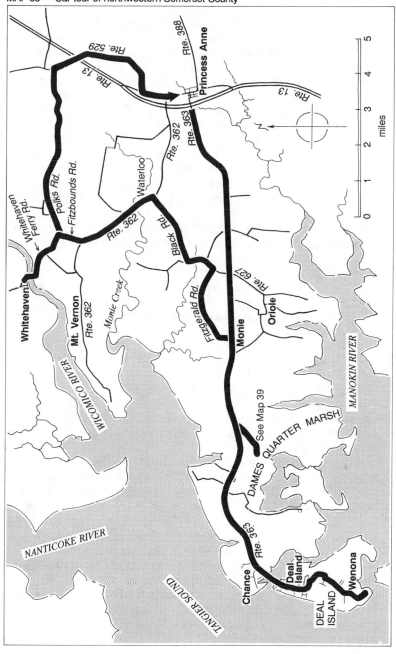

247

which is shown along the left edge of **Map 39**. To view waterfowl (best during late fall and winter) or simply to see the marsh, you can drive 6.2 miles round-trip down and back up Riley Roberts Road, although its lower half is rather rough.

Another road providing access to the marsh is off Route 363 about 2 miles east of Riley Roberts Road and is marked by a wooden sign saying (among other things) "Deal Island Wildlife Management Area — Wildlife Division — Maryland Department of Natural Resources." Turn sharply right onto this road and follow it (slowly) 1.4 miles to a boat ramp and parking lot that is marked on Map 39 as point A. This is a good spot from which to walk across **Dames Quarter Marsh**, as shown by the bold lines on Map 39, and as described below.

WALKING AT DAMES QUARTER MARSH: The marshy peninsula of Dames Quarter was formerly called Damned Quarter (as it appears on early maps), perhaps because it lies adjacent to Devil's Island, now Deal Island. A dike-top dirt road that is closed to cars provides a rare opportunity to walk comfortably far out into the marsh.

The bold lines on **Map 39** at right show two routes. One leads southeast almost to the water's edge at Broad Creek (Point B). This route is 5 miles round-trip; the last few hundred yards at Broad Creek are closed to the public. The other route zigzags west to Riley Roberts Road. It is 4 miles round-trip, although you can always walk farther by following Riley Roberts Road south to its end. The map also shows a path around the southern edge of the marsh, but this track is very rough and overgrown in places, and sections are sometimes closed to public use.

If you go walking at Dames Quarter Marsh, bear in mind that **hunting** for waterfowl is permitted occasionally during fall and winter. For more precise information about specified hunting days, call the Maryland Department of Natural Resources at (410) 651-2320. If hunting is underway, you are likely to know it from the coming and going of the hunters and the popping of their guns in the distance. On such occasions, confine your walk to the trail that leads southeast to Broad Creek. All but the first few hundred yards of this route lies within a sanctuary. On hunting days, stay off the trail leading west to Riley Roberts Road. Of course, even during the hunting season, you can have the marsh virtually to yourself if you go on a Sunday, when hunting is prohibited.

MAP 39 — Walking at Dames Quarter Marsh

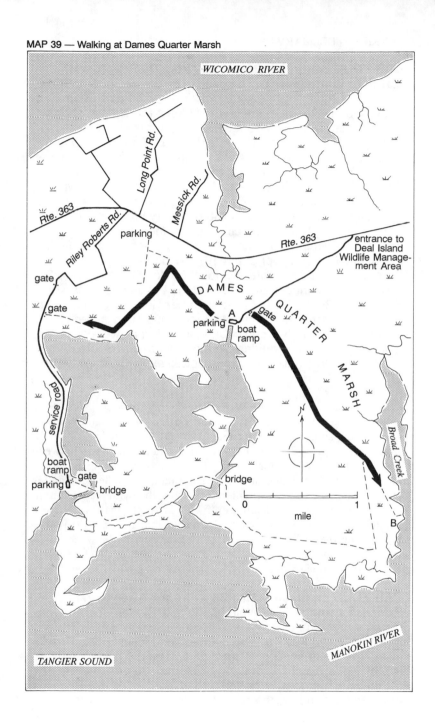

CAR TOUR continued (Map 38 — from Dames Quarter Marsh to Whitehaven): To continue on the car tour, return to Route 363 and follow it east 2.2 miles — or 3.1 miles from Riley Roberts Road. In the town of Monie (or at least, shortly after passing a sign announcing Monie), turn left onto Fitzgerald Road. Follow Fitzgerald Road 2.6 miles, then turn left at a T-intersection. Go 0.8 mile, then bear right onto Black Road. Follow Black Road 2.2 miles to a T-intersection with Route 362, and there turn left. After just 0.5 miles, you will reach **Waterloo Country Inn** on the right, occupying a plantation house built about 1750 by Henry Waggaman, one of Somerset County's leading citizens. In addition to accommodations, the inn has a restaurant serving breakfast, lunch, and dinner; telephone (410) 651-0883.

Continue west on Route 362 for 1.7 miles. Where Route 362 curves left, continue straight toward the Whitehaven Ferry on Fitzbounds Road. Go 0.7 mile, then bear left and continue 1.5 miles to the ferry, which operates year-round and is free of charge. Now a rarity, such cable-guided ferries were once far more numerous on the tidal rivers of the Eastern Shore. After crossing the Wicomico River, turn left to explore the village of Whitehaven.

Whitehaven, located on the Wicomico County (or north) side of the Wicomico River, was named for a port on the Cumberland coast of northwest England, from which came Colonel George Gale, leader of a group of settlers in 1701. Gale's three ships traded regularly between England and Maryland. Just south of the Wicomico River is Monie Creek, site of Gale's plantation called Tusculum, where he lived and is buried. Gale's first wife, incidentally, was the widowed Mildred Warner Washington, whose children included Augustine Washington, the father of George Washington. During the steamboat era, Whitehaven was an oyster landing and stop for boats plying between Salisbury and Baltimore. The village had its own fishing fleet, packing houses, a substantial shipyard, a hotel, and several popular saloons.

CAR TOUR continued (Map 38 — from Whitehaven to Princess Anne): From Whitehaven take the ferry back across the river and return 1.5 miles to the intersection with Fitzbounds and Polks roads. Turn left and follow Polks Road 5 miles to a T-intersection. Turn right and go 0.8 mile to and across Route 13, then continue on Route 529 for 2.5 miles. At a stop sign, merge with the main road leading left into Princess Anne and continue to the center of town.

Princess Anne, the seat of Somerset County, is named not for Queen Anne (who reigned from 1702 to 1707 and was the namesake of Queen Anne's County and of Annapolis) but rather for the daughter of King George II, the monarch when the town was founded in 1733. Princess Anne was a local port at the head of the Manokin River, which is now unnavigable because of sedimentation. Some aspects of life in Princess Anne during the 1830s and '40s are described in *The Entailed Hat*, a novel published in 1884 by George Alfred Townshend (or GATH, as he called himself). Today the town is, as ever, a rather still place where business focuses mainly on agriculture, lumber, poultry, and regional services. In addition to the various agencies of county government, the University of Maryland, Eastern Shore is located here, and nearby is the Eastern Shore Correctional Facility.

The town's Federal and Victorian houses give Princess Anne's residential streets a predominantly nineteenth-century appearance, but a few structures are older, and it is these that are most often open to the public. The **Manokin Presbyterian Church**, located on the main road (called Somerset Avenue or Alternate Route 13) two blocks north of Princess Anne's business district, has walls built in 1765; other features are more recent. The parish was organized by the Rev. Francis Makemie in 1683, and a church was built on this site by 1692. The **Washington Hotel** in the center of town was built in 1744; telephone (410) 651-2525 or, for the restaurant, (410) 651-2526. The bar and old, beamed dining room are a favorite local gathering place, especially on Friday and Saturday evenings. A formal **boxwood garden**, thought to have been laid out by General George Handy in the first half of the nineteenth century, occupies the corner of Somerset Avenue and Washington Street one block south of the 1904 **courthouse**. The **Teackle Mansion**, located on Prince William Street three blocks west of the courthouse, was built in 1801 by Littleton Teackle, Princess Anne's leading citizen. Teackle was a merchant, a banker (issuing his own notes or paper currency), and a shipowner — and ultimately a bankrupt. His mansion is modeled after a Scottish manor house and shows a rigorous and imposing symmetry, at least on the outside and in the central drawing room. **St. Andrew's Episcopal Church** is on Church Street one block south of Prince William Street. Its walls date from about 1770; the interior was remodeled in the nineteenth century.

CAR TOUR continued (Map 38 — from Princess Anne back to your starting point on Route 13): From the courthouse at the corner of Prince William Street and Somerset Avenue, follow Prince William Street west to the Teackle Mansion, and there turn right onto Mansion Street, then left onto Route 363. Go 0.1 mile to the intersection with Route 13.

16

SMITH ISLAND
JANES ISLAND STATE PARK
CRISFIELD

Smith Island, shown on **Map 40** on page 263 and located 10 miles west of Crisfield, Maryland, is actually a cluster of several islands that lie about as low in the water as an inhabited place can be. From a distance, the trees and houses of its three villages — Ewell, Rhodes Point, and Tylerton — appear to rise directly out of Chesapeake Bay, and, in fact, some streets and yards are often awash. Even from the vantage point of the island itself, dry land is a relatively minor component of the landscape, which consists mainly of tidal salt marsh, sky, and water. Although Smith Island has a couple of miles of open road linking Ewell and Rhodes Point, the island's many channels are its main streets, and boats are far more numerous than cars. The waterfront villages consist of narrow lanes bordered by frame houses and a few larger community structures, such as fire houses, churches, recreation halls, and an elementary school in Ewell. For grades eight through twelve, the students commute daily to Crisfield via school boat. Also in Ewell is the **Smith Island Center**, which is open April through October on Thursday, Friday, Saturday, and Sunday from 11 A.M. to 4 P.M. It serves as an information center and museum, featuring a movie and exhibits on the islanders' way of life. For information or group reservations, telephone (410) 425-3351.

A visit to Smith Island combines a pleasant excursion by passenger boat, perhaps a seafood lunch, and a chance to explore the island's villages, home to generations of watermen. Passenger boats to Smith Island operate daily, leaving Crisfield at 12:30 P.M. and returning late in the afternoon. There are several boats to choose from, as discussed starting on page 260. Within reason, bicycles can be transported on the boats, but there may be a small additional charge. If you want to stay overnight, telephone the Smith Island Center for information on accommodations.

Just outside of Crisfield immediately adjacent to the mainland is **Janes Island State Park**, where there are miles of narrow, wild beach fronting Tangier Sound. Shown on **Map 41** on page 264, Janes Island is worth a day's outing in itself. The park is open year-round from 8 A.M. to sunset. The trick, however, is getting to the island, which is separated from the mainland by a narrow channel. From April through October, the park offers — if the weather is good — rental canoes or even skiffs with outboard motors, but you should always call beforehand. Or you can use your own canoe or boat to reach the island at any time of year. (Strong winds, however, can sometimes make canoeing difficult, even in the narrow, protected channel leading to the island.) The park, which also has a campground and rental cabins, is managed by the Maryland Park Service; telephone (410) 968-1565. Pets are altogether prohibited.

Leave time to look around **Crisfield** itself, where after your excursion to Smith Island or Janes Island, you can enjoy a leisurely seafood dinner. The town's main annual event, held Labor Day weekend, is the National Hard Crab Derby and Fair at Somers Cove. Also located at Somers Cove is the **J. Millard Tawes Visitor Center and Museum**, where exhibits document the life of the governor from Crisfield, plus the history of the area's fisheries. For information about tourist events in Crisfield, call the visitor center at (410) 968-2500.

Finally, south of Smith Island is Tangier Island, which is discussed in the next chapter. In the course of time, both places are well worth visiting, but since you can only go to one first, I recommend Smith Island. With its three villages, its larger size, and its information center *cum* museum, Smith Island provides more to see.

ALTHOUGH THE CHESAPEAKE REGION was settled starting early in the seventeenth century, not until the middle of the nineteenth century did industrialization and rapid urban growth in the northern states, plus improved transportation by steamboat and rail, create major markets for all that the bay could be made to yield. Among the most productive areas for seafood since then has been Tangier Sound, where the watermen of Smith Island and other nearby communities have harvested (and in some instances, grossly overharvested) immense quantities of fish, eels, terrapin, oysters, clams, crabs, and waterfowl during the last century and a half, sometimes specializing in certain activities, such as catching and shedding soft crabs (as do Smith

Islanders today), or switching from one animal crop to another, depending on what is most abundant or profitable.

Despite a historic pattern of large fluctuations in crab catches from one year to the next, the main way of making a living on Smith Island remains crabbing from spring through autumn, although in October many watermen switch to oystering and continue at that through the winter. To earn a good income, the watermen must go out every day that the weather permits, usually beginning an hour or two before dawn and staying out until early afternoon, six days a week. To maximize their individual profit, the men often work alone, hauling in and repeatedly emptying a crab scrape (which is a lightweight dredge with a steel frame and twine bag pulled from a shallow-draft boat) or lifting oysters off the bottom with tongs suspended from a cable and boom. For crabpotting, they may be joined by a son or other youngster to help pull up, empty, and re-bait several hundred wire-mesh traps daily. For people who do not like the physical labor, perseverance, exposure to the weather, and long hours that this manner of life requires, or the unpredictable income that it provides, there is little alternative on the island, and so they move to the mainland, leaving behind those who, perhaps more mindful of tradition or simply unprepared for something different, choose to work the water or to raise a family on the island, as did their ancestors. As one elderly waterman told Francis W. Dize, author of *Smith Island, Chesapeake Bay*, "God gave us this island. He brought us here. He took care of our granddaddies and showed 'em how to use the water and the creatures in it, and this is where we belong." Accompanying this credo, however, is a subtext of uncertainty, summed up in the comment of a Smith Island crabpicker: "It is not a sure thing. You're just depending on the bay. It is scary."

Residents of Smith Island scoff, or even take offense, at some accounts in newspapers and magazines that have portrayed their way of life as "quaint" or "old-fashioned." After all, they say, don't their villages have sewers, electricity, and running water; don't their homes, or at least those of the younger folk, have all the usual household appliances; don't they watch the same television shows as the rest of America; don't they shop the malls and sometimes take vacations on the mainland like anyone else, and don't their teenagers like rock music? And if their cars sometimes are rattletraps, that is because it does not make much sense to bring a new car to the island, where there are only a few miles of road. The place for a good car is on the mainland, and most island families keep one there.

Certainly it is true that the island is not quaint in the sense of being artificially preserved or prettified. Its great visual interest is provided by the ongoing business of making a living from Chesapeake Bay. Along the waterfront, the paraphernalia and cast-off scrap and outright trash of commercial crabbing and oystering are everywhere. Lining the island's channels are the watermen's spindly docks, cluttered packing shanties, and bank floats, which are long, table-like rows of shallow basins through which bay water is constantly circulated by pumps. Because soft crabs fetch a far higher price than hard ones, many of the islanders keep crabs that show signs of shedding — or sell them to someone else who will keep them — until the crustaceans molt. First the crabs are sorted according to their stage in shedding their hard shells, then placed in the floats. From early morning until late evening during the spring and summer shedding season, the crabs are periodically inspected and transferred from one basin to the next as they approach molting, when they are pulled out and packed alive on beds of eel grass and ice in waxed cardboard cartons. Smith Island and some of the other fishing communities of Tangier Sound supply the market with tens of millions of soft crabs annually.

Although the main role of island women is that of homemakers, much of the work of sorting, shedding, and packing soft crabs is done by housewives, either together with their husbands when the catch is brought in, or while the men are out in their boats. Nearly every household is in business for itself, and family members help out in whatever way is necessary to make the family business go. Like crab shedding, picking the meat of hard crabs is another way to add value to what is caught, and the work of picking is done exclusively by women at one of the island's two packing houses. The picking and packing house in Tylerton is a co-op, administered by a board of directors that is elected by members who pay dues to use the facility. Each member picks her own crabs, steamed for her by the co-op's one employee, and sells what she picks to her own customers. In the future there may be some cooperative marketing. At the packing house in Ewell, a few women work for the owner and others rent seats where they pick their own crabs, selling the meat either to the packing house owner or to their own customers.

In addition to their specialized line of work, Smith Islanders show a remarkable homogeneity in other respects also. Nearly all are of English descent, and the majority share just five surnames — Tyler, Evans, Bradshaw, Marsh, and Marshall — that go back hundreds of years on the island, which was settled in the second half of the seventeenth century. In addition, ever since the Great Revival swept the Eastern Shore at the end of the eighteenth century and beginning of the nineteenth, virtually all the residents of Smith Island have adhered to a fervent Methodism, which provides the community with a touchstone of shared values and mutual support.

Methodism is more than a source of moral guidance and religious inspiration within this tightly knit community. The island's three churches are also the center of community life. The week-long camp meeting in Ewell late in July or early in August is not only a time of religious rededication but also the year's chief social event, when friends and family members who have left the island return for a visit. Christmas week too is a happy mix of church programs and other activities. Small children go "Christmas gifting" around the island early Christmas morning, receiving modest gifts of money from their adult neighbors. Other events include a church Christmas pageant, speeches by children, a visit by Santa Claus, and a banquet and Christmas dances, one for adults and another for teenagers, sponsored by the Ewell Volunteer Fire Department.

The churches are also the center of local government, although strictly speaking, there is no government here below the county level — no mayors or town councils. Instead, it is through the Methodist churches that many community projects on the island are conceived, debated, and supported, including streetlights, medical services, maintenance of public buildings and grounds, the Tylerton water system, and other traditional municipal services. (There are no police, and virtually no crime.) When the islanders must deal collectively with the county, state, or federal government or with private grant-making organizations, it is usually the church leaders who are chosen as spokesmen, called for the purpose the "Committee for Smith Island." Door-to-door collections sponsored by each village's church help to fund local projects and services, which is sometimes problematic because of the perception that not everybody contributes a fair share. And apart from money raised for local projects are the occasional special collections to help families who have suffered a death or a fire or some other misfortune. The Ewell M. E. Church, in fact, maintains an emergency assistance fund that is used as necessary.

Some visitors who have written about Smith Island speculate that the central role of religion in island life in part derives from the fact that the watermen rely so heavily on the bounty of nature or even on the mercy of nature. "Government won't save you from that big wave, won't make more crabs," the island's minister told Tom Horton, author of *Bay Country*. Horton also quotes Jennings Evans, an island waterman for forty-five years: "You've got to be thankful to someone. In the water business we never plant anything. We just harvest. Oysters, crabs, fish . . . it is just reap, steady reap. But you know, somebody's got to be doing some planting . . . there's got to be some system to it all somewhere."

To some extent, however, Smith Island's single-minded pursuit of crabs, oysters, and fish is changing. Since the 1910 census, when the island had about 800 residents, the population has declined to less than 400 as increasing numbers of young people have left and as older folk have died. In recent years, there has been an influx of part-time residents — retirees and owners of vacation homes — who, together with tourists, are an increasingly important part of the island's economy.

≈　　　≈　　　≈　　　≈

ALTHOUGH THE EXCURSIONS outlined in this chapter focus on Smith Island and unpopulated Janes Island, it is also appropriate to say a few words about **Crisfield**, the principal mainland town of Tangier Sound and the port from which the boats to Smith Island run. Most watermen in the vicinity of Tangier Sound send their catch of crabs, oysters, and fish to Crisfield for processing or transshipment, and yet even so the town is only a shadow of what it was a hundred years ago.

Previously called Annemessex and then Somers Cove, Crisfield was renamed in honor of John W. Crisfield, chief promoter and president of the Eastern Shore Railroad, which reached Crisfield in 1868. Arrival of the railroad ushered in an era of great prosperity and growth as scores of packing houses sprang up at Crisfield to handle the oysters that were brought ashore there, canned, and shipped throughout the country. Extraordinary hauls of oysters during the 1870s and '80s, when the bay's oyster beds were virtually strip mined by large dredge fleets, enabled the southern end of Crisfield, where the municipal wharf is located, to expand on a foundation of oyster shells into what was once marsh and water. By 1872 Crisfield was the center of the largest oyster trade in Maryland and was served by over six hundred sailing vessels harvesting several million bushels of oysters annually. Twenty to thirty railroad cars loaded with oysters left the town daily. The port was also served by three steamboats daily. After machines for making ice were invented, the harvesting, picking, and shipping of highly perishable crabs became another major industry.

In Crisfield's boomtown atmosphere, lowlife flourished. Saloons and brothels sprang up, and in some establishments and in some streets, brawling was common. In 1875 the town commissioners voted Crisfield dry in order to curb drunken lawlessness, and in response speakeasies proliferated.

The decline in oyster catches during the twentieth century, however, has led to a corresponding falling off of seafood processing at Crisfield. Even as early as the 1890s, packing houses and shucking operations started closing, as did burlesque houses and bars. The railroad into Crisfield was torn out in the late 1950s. (The tracks ran parallel to Route 413, where there are still a few old grain elevators and other structures left over from the railroad.) Somers Cove, formerly the site of many packing houses, was redeveloped as a yacht basin for pleasure boats starting in the 1960s.

≈   ≈   ≈   ≈

AUTOMOBILE DIRECTIONS: Smith Island lies in Chesapeake Bay on the state line between Maryland and Virginia — although all of the island's three villages are in Maryland. (See **Map 1** on page iv in the Table of Contents.) The island is reached by commercial passenger boats from Crisfield, which is located about 40 miles south-southwest of Salisbury. And just north of Crisfield is Janes Island State Park (discussed starting on page 262).

During summer a tourist boat runs to Smith Island from Point Lookout, Maryland, located at the mouth of the Potomac River; telephone (410) 425-2771 for information. The instructions below, however, take you to Crisfield, where there is year-round boat service to Smith Island.

To Crisfield from northern Delmarva and Interstate 95 southwest of Wilmington: From Interstate 95 take Exit 4A for Route 1 south, and stay on Route 1 past a quick succession of exits. Follow Route 1 south past Dover, then switch to Route 13 south toward Salisbury and Norfolk. After passing east of Salisbury and west of Princess Anne, turn right onto Route 413 toward Crisfield and go 14.6 miles to the end of the road at Crisfield's municipal dock.

To Crisfield from the Chesapeake Bay Bridge: After crossing the bridge, follow Route 50/301 across Kent Island. At the point where Route 50 and Route 301 split, fork right to follow Route 50 past Easton, Cambridge, and Salisbury. East of Salisbury, take Route 13 south toward Norfolk. Follow Route 13 past Princess Anne to the junction with Route 413, and there turn right toward Crisfield. Follow Route 413 for 14.6 miles to the end of the road at Crisfield's municipal dock.

To Crisfield from southern Delmarva and the Chesapeake Bay Bridge-Tunnel at Norfolk: After crossing the bridge-tunnel, follow Route 13 north into Maryland. From the intersection with Route 113 near Pocomoke City, continue straight on Route 13 for 3.8 miles to the intersection with Route 667 west toward Crisfield. Turn left onto Route 667 and follow it 11.5 miles to an intersection with Route 413. Turn left onto Route 413 and follow it 6 miles to the end of the road at Crisfield's municipal dock.

259

To Crisfield from Salisbury and the Delaware and Maryland seashore resorts: From the vicinity of Salisbury, follow Route 13 south past Princess Anne to the junction with Route 413, and there turn right toward Crisfield. Follow Route 413 for 14.6 miles to the end of the road at Crisfield's municipal dock.

From the vicinity of Rehoboth Beach, follow Route 1 north to the intersection with Route 9 westbound, then take Route 9 west through Georgetown and across Route 113 to Route 13 southbound. Alternatively, from the vicinity of Ocean City, follow Route 50 west to Route 13 southbound. In either case, once you are on Route 13, follow it south around Salisbury and past Princess Anne to the junction with Route 413, and there turn right toward Crisfield. Follow Route 413 for 14.6 miles to the end of the road at Crisfield's municipal dock.

≈   ≈   ≈   ≈

BOATS TO SMITH ISLAND: There are several different passenger boats from Crisfield to the island. Most of them leave from the municipal dock, and of these the largest and fastest is the *Island Princess*, which goes to Ewell, the island's main town. To make a reservation on the *Island Princess* (recommended on weekends in summer), telephone Captain Otis Tyler at (410) 968-3206 or the Harborside Restaurant at (410) 425-2201. At times when there is less demand, the *Island Princess* may be replaced by the smaller *Island Belle II*.

Other boats also depart from the municipal dock. Terry Laird's *Capt. Jason I* goes to Ewell and Larry Laird's *Capt. Jason II* goes to Tylerton, although sometimes one boat serves both places. Simply ask the captains where they are going, what the fare is, and where you should park your car. (One public parking lot is located a couple of blocks inland on the left as you head away from the water; it is entered from the next street over.) The boats to Ewell offer more scope for exploration than the boats to Tylerton, since Ewell is connected by road to the village of Rhodes Point. Tylerton, which is on a separate island within the Smith Island archipelago, is very small, which is both its special charm and its limitation.

The boats that run from Crisfield's municipal dock to Smith Island operate daily year-round, except during stormy weather or when ice obstructs the channel. They leave Crisfield at

12:30 P.M. and depart Smith Island at 4:00. Be sure, however, to ask your captain what time he plans to leave Smith Island, since actual times of departure may vary somewhat depending on the demands of the day — and even then be on hand ten minutes early. The trip takes about 45 minutes each way. There are also some excursion boats, of which the *Chelsea Lane Tyler* is largest. It is sometimes replaced or supplemented by the smaller *Betty Jo Tyler* and the *Captain Tyler*. They are owned by Smith Island Cruises and run between Somers Cove Marina in Crisfield and Ewell on Smith Island. One or more of these boats operates from Memorial Day weekend through October, leaving Somers Cove at 12:30 P.M. and leaving Ewell at 4:00. There are, however, disadvantages to the excursions boats. Unlike the boats that run from Crisfield's municipal dock (and which are used by the islanders themselves), the excursion boats are purely tourist oriented, and they are more expensive. Somers Cove Marina can be reached via Seventh Street off Route 413 (Main Street) 0.3 mile inland from Crisfield's municipal dock. Tickets can be purchased ahead of time at the Paddlewheel Motel at the corner of Main Street and Seventh Street. Always call (410) 425-2771 beforehand to make a reservation. During exceptionally stormy weather or on weekdays late in October, the excursion boat may not run.

During summer and early fall, most of the Smith Island boat companies provide their passengers (for a small additional charge) with a tour of the island via school bus. Tell your captain if you are interested.

The boat operators also, of course, hope that you will eat at restaurants on the island with which they are affiliated, but there is no obligation to do so. In any case, their restaurants are open only during the tourist season. The *Island Princess* docks at the Harborside Restaurant, patronized by a mixture of islanders and tourists seated in the conventional manner at tables of different sizes, so usually you can have your own table. The other boats dock at the county wharf opposite the Bayside Inn, which caters exclusively to tourists seated together at uniformly large tables. At both restaurants, you may order a huge family-style meal or just a few items. There is also Ruke's restaurant and seafood deck, located across the street from the Smith Island Center and serving fare that ranges from large seafood platters to sandwiches and subs of all kinds.

TOURING SMITH ISLAND: Map 40 at right shows the island and the three villages of Ewell, Rhodes Point (these two are linked by road), and Tylerton.

I have an opinion on how best to see the island, but it assumes that you would prefer to spend the few hours that you have there looking around on foot or on bicycle rather than eating a big meal at one of the restaurants. There probably isn't time for both, especially if you give the exhibits at the Smith Island Center the attention they deserve. And after all, you can always have a leisurely seafood dinner back in Crisfield after your trip.

Take a boat from Crisfield's municipal dock to Ewell. If you have a bicycle, by all means bring it along — for which there may be a small charge. After a quick crab sandwich at one of the island's restaurants (bring your own lunch October through May in case no eateries are open), spend your time exploring Ewell and Rhodes Point on foot or by bicycle, which necessarily involves hiking or biking back and forth 2 miles each way between the two villages. You will see far more this way than you would from the bus. If you are walking, be alert for cars; walk on the left shoulder, facing the oncoming vehicles. There is a fair amount of traffic on this road, but drivers are used to sharing the road with pedestrians and bicyclists.

≈   ≈   ≈   ≈

FROM CRISFIELD TO JANES ISLAND STATE PARK: Near Crisfield is Janes Island State Park, which by itself is worth a day's excursion.

As you approach Crisfield on Route 413, there are signs at Plantation Road and at Route 358 directing you to Janes Island State Park. Or, starting at Crisfield's municipal dock, you can refer to **Map 41** on page 264 and use the following directions: Take Main Street (Route 413) away from the Crisfield municipal dock for 1.3 miles, then turn left onto Route 358. For 1.1 miles, follow the twisty road, then turn left at a large sign for Janes Island State Park. After passing the park office, turn left at the first opportunity and follow the road past recycling bins and a storage area. Continue around to the right through a parking lot and then to yet another parking lot by the dock and launching ramp.

MAP 40 — Smith Island

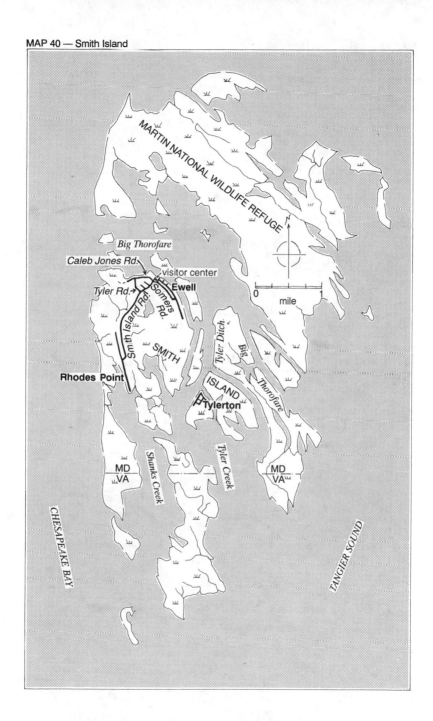

MAP 41 — Janes Island State Park

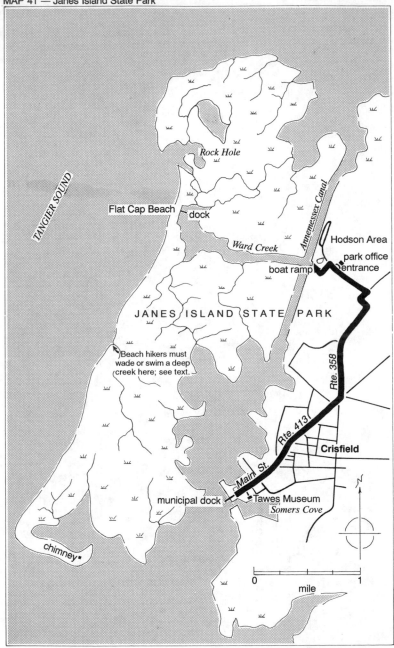

JANES ISLAND STATE PARK: The park has two distinct areas. The mainland portion (called the Hodson Area) is developed with a launching ramp, picnic grounds, camping sites, and a few rental cabins. Across the Annemessex Canal from the Hodson Area is Janes Island itself, undeveloped and consisting almost wholly of marsh bordered by a narrow ribbon of wild beach that extends for miles along the island's western shore. The island is a very attractive place, reachable only by boat via a mile-long channel (called Ward Creek) that starts opposite the mainland launching ramp and leads to the dock behind Flat Cap Beach. April through October, the park rents canoes and also skiffs with outboard motors — but always call (410) 968-1565 beforehand. Or you may use your own boat or canoe at any time of year. If you are inclined to explore the many sinuous channels through the marsh, a map showing canoe trails is available at the park office.

The best time for a visit to the island is the off season, not only because there is less of a crowd then, but also because there are fewer biting insects (but bring repellent just in case). I have gone several times late in September and early in October and have found the water still warm enough for swimming and the jellyfish gone for the year. If you don't care about swimming, you can go late into the fall and early in spring — or even during mid-winter if you first call on a weekday to make sure that the channel is not blocked by ice.

WALKING ON JANES ISLAND: Once you are on the island, it is possible to walk south along the shore 4 miles to the chimney and large rendering vats of an old fish factory at the island's lower end (see **Map 41** at left); however, doing so entails swimming or wading across the mouth of a small stream located at a point marked on the map. Clearly, this is something that you would only want to do during the swimming season (bring your suit) and if you are confident that you can handle the tidal current that you may find when you cross or re-cross the stream. Be conservative; only you know what the actual conditions are when you are there. Also, from Flat Cap Beach a shorter walk leads north to Rock Hole. Swimming is permitted from the beach, but there are no lifeguards, so extra caution is necessary. Finally, since there is no drinking water on the island, bring your own beverage, especially during hot weather.

17

TANGIER ISLAND

A visit to **Tangier Island**, which is located in Virginia's portion of Chesapeake Bay 12 miles southwest of Crisfield, Maryland, combines a pleasant cruise with a stopover at the village of Tangier, a centuries-old community of watermen. The island is shown on **Map 42** on page 274. Tangier's harbor provides a quick education in the paraphernalia of commercial crabbing, oystering, and fishing. The main street is a one-lane road bordered by white frame houses, a dozen stores, and a few community structures, all tightly packed together. Good eating is found at several seafood restaurants, and good walking is had by following narrow lanes that lead from the main village across marsh and tidal channels to outlying clusters of houses.

An excursion boat operates daily (including Sunday) from May 15 through October, leaving Crisfield at 12:30 P.M., arriving at Tangier at 1:45, departing Tangier at 4:00, and arriving back at Crisfield at 5:15. Because of stormy weather or lack of passengers (especially on weekdays in October), the boat sometimes does not go, so always telephone Tangier Island Cruises beforehand: (800) 863-2338 or (410) 968-2338. For more information about the excursion boat, see page 273.

There is also year-round service between Crisfield and Tangier via the mail boat, which leaves Crisfield at 12:30 P.M. but does not return until the next day, departing from Tangier at 8:00 A.M. (or 3:00 P.M. on Sunday). The mail boat is discussed further on pages 273-274.

In addition to the boats from Crisfield, there are yet other boats to Tangier Island that operate from Reedville, Virginia, located at the mouth of the Potomac River — call (804) 453-2628 for more information — and from Onancock, Virginia, on the Eastern Shore — telephone (757) 891-2240. The directions at the end of this chapter, however, assume that you are leaving from Crisfield, which provides the most frequent and reliable service to Tangier.

Because the various tour boats allow only a few hours on Tangier Island, you may want to stay overnight, which not only provides more time for leisurely and thorough exploration, but also enables you to see the island at periods when it is not jammed with other visitors and when the life of the community is more apparent. An overnight stay also provides time to hike along the long beach and sandy hook at the island's southern end. For lodgings, make a reservation at one of the following establishments: Located on the main north-south street, Chesapeake House is open April 15 through mid-October; telephone (804) 891-2331. As its name implies, Chesapeake House is simply a house; its accommodations are plain but adequate. There are no private bathrooms. In the realm of food, however, Chesapeake House is out of the ordinary — particularly its seafood lunches and dinners served family style at communal tables. On the western side of the island near the beach is Grace Brown's Sunset Inn, which is open year-round and serves a light breakfast. Most of the rooms are motel-style and include a private bath, air-conditioning, and cable TV; telephone (804) 891-2535. Also on the western side of the island is Shirley Pruitt's Bay View Inn, a handsome old bed-and-breakfast house with wraparound porches and small, motel-style outbuildings; telephone (757) 891-2396. If you plan to go during the colder half of the year, you may want to check first with your host to make sure that at least one of the island's sandwich shops will be open to provide you with lunch and dinner.

IN 1608, the year after Jamestown was founded, Captain John Smith explored Chesapeake Bay and noted the existence of the string of islands that includes Tangier. Not until the end of the century, however, was Tangier settled by a few families from Cornwall, the region of maritime villages at the extreme southwest end of England. According to tradition, the first settler was John Crockett, who moved to Tangier Island with his sons and their families in 1686. In the early 1800s, nearly half of the island's one hundred residents were named Crockett. Even today most of the approximately seven hundred islanders still bear the surnames of a few early settlers: Crockett, Pruitt, Parks, Dize (or Dise), Evans, and Thomas. The local accent is often said still to be reminiscent of the southwest of England (and if it helps tourism, who am I to say otherwise?) — although for the most part the intervening three centuries have produced a unique accent and body of colloquialisms that are the islanders' own.

During the War of 1812, Tangier Island was used for more than a year by a British squadron as a base of operations for raids against bayshore towns and plantations. In particular, the island was the staging area for the attack on Baltimore in September, 1814 — an attack which was doomed to failure, as Joshua Thomas, the "Parson of the Islands," pointedly told the British beforehand. Thomas was a waterman and resident of Tangier who had been converted to Methodism at a camp meeting on the mainland in 1807. As an exhorter (or lay preacher), he had thereafter helped to spread Methodism throughout the islands of Tangier Sound, in part by organizing camp meetings held at the southern end of Tangier Island. Here, before the war (and afterwards too until the middle of the nineteenth century) thousands of people came annually by boat from the nearby islands and from the Chesapeake's Eastern and Western shores for a week of religious convocation and preaching by itinerant Methodist preachers.

> The place suddenly assumed an attractiveness and importance which belonged to no other mustering ground [wrote Thomas's biographer, the Rev. Adam Wallace].
> Even before the war, its fame had become wide spread, and its popularity as a place of resort for all classes of people established. But who can write its stirring history? who tell its tremendous moral results? — or enumerate the thousands who were born for glory there; and the tens of thousands who were edified, sanctified, and established in the faith of the gospel, as years rolled on, for full half a century, on the famous beach at Tangier?

On this same sandy spit the British camped and built two forts when they seized Tangier Island in the summer of 1813. For their forts they cut down most of the trees near the encampment, but at the request of Joshua Thomas they spared the prayer grove where the camp meetings were held. During the British occupation, Thomas was allowed to minister to those among the troops who wished to hold Methodist services. Apparently the officers were impressed by Thomas, for before the British embarked to attack Baltimore, "they sent me word to be ready to hold a public meeting, and exhort the soldiers, on the campground," as Thomas later recalled. But to the chagrin of the British officers, Thomas shouted at the assembled infantry that "I could not bid them God speed in what I understood they were going to do."

> I warned them of the danger and distress they would bring upon themselves and others by going to Baltimore with the object they had in view. I told them of the great wickedness of war, and that God said, *"Thou shalt not kill!"* If you do, he will judge you at the last day; or, before then, he will cause you to "perish by the sword."

269

I told them it was given me from the Almighty that they *could not* take Baltimore, and *would not succeed in their expedition.*

I exhorted them to prepare for death, for many of them would in all likelihood die soon, and I should see them no more till we met at the sound of the great trumpet before our final Judge.

With this disheartening send-off, the British embarked for Baltimore, where in the first few minutes of the first day's fighting, the commander of their land forces, Major General Robert Ross, was killed. After two days, the British gave up the attack, and when they returned to Tangier Island, some officers told Thomas that "all the time we were fighting *we thought of you,* and what you had told us. You seemed to be standing right before us, still warning us against our attempt to take Baltimore."

Such, at any rate, are Thomas's recollections, and he was by all accounts a scrupulously honest, sincere man. Because of ongoing erosion from waves, however, the site of the British encampment and of the Methodist camp meetings on Tangier Island is now under water. During the last century and a half, the sandy hook at the island's southern end has shrunk drastically and shifted eastward about half a mile, just as the entire island has diminished considerably since it was first settled.

Today Tangier Island — which actually is several islands, as shown on Map 42 on page 274 — is only 3.5 miles long by 1.5 miles wide, and the habitable, or buildable, part is far smaller than that. Approximately 250 houses are clustered along three parallel "ridges," which, in fact, nowhere rise more than seven feet above sea level. Flooding from storms and high tides is not uncommon, and hurricane-driven waves have sometimes inundated most of the island. There are about three miles of roadway — typically one-lane streets — used by pedestrians and bicyclists, plus a few cars and trucks and a larger number of golf carts, motorcycles, and motorbikes, on which the young men buzz around the island in the evening "scooping up" (or giving rides to) the girls. A small airport provides quick transport to and from the mainland in the event of medical emergency, and also is the means by which many recreational flyers and hunters stop by for a visit.

Most transport, of course, is by boat, as would be expected on a small island where the vast majority of male residents are watermen, making a living by crabbing, oystering, and fishing. In a November 1973 article for *National Geographic*, Harold G. Wheatley, at that time the principal of the Tangier Island School, said, "Boats hold the same place in our lives that automobiles do for mainlanders. You've just got to have one: skiffs for the little ones, outboards for the youths, and work-craft for the breadwinners. . . . The sea is our life, our highway, our farm, our prison." This description is not much different than what is readily apparent today, or from what another observer wrote in the middle of the nineteenth century: "The inhabitants of Smith's and Tangier Islands may almost be called an amphibious race, for nearly all the men and boys spend fully half their time if not *in* yet *on* the water."

Once a young man gets a workboat — probably a used one at first — he is set to embark on an independent career "following the water." As one boy told Wheatley, "This is a good place to live, and I like to work on the water. My father's been taking me with him since I was ten. I've been growed up with it. On the land it seems like you're always under somebody, but on the water you do as you please."

Of course, in actuality, doing as one pleases means doing as the seasons and the work require, not just when the prospects of daily profits are high, but even when they are low, for everyone acknowledges that the only way to make a success at this sort of life is to go at it day in and day out for long hours. It is a career of hard drudgery and repetitive physical tasks. During summer the watermen labor alone, or perhaps with a school-age son or a hired hand, from 4 A.M. to early afternoon, tending as many as four hundred crab pots made of anodized steel wire formed into rectilinear cages. During winter some of the Tangier watermen tong for oysters, but most dredge for crabs, which requires a bigger, more expensive boat than summertime crabbing. For crab dredging, the captains and their crews of two men are away from home for six days at a time, working sometimes in freezing temperatures to dredge up female crabs that migrate annually to the mouth of Chesapeake Bay, where they bury themselves at the bottom. Crab dredging gives Virginia watermen a profitable winter fishery compared to their counterparts in Maryland.

The existence of crews clearly indicates that not all of Tangier's watermen have the wherewithal or the ambition to be their own boss. Apart from students, some crew members are young men still unsettled about their path in life, wondering whether to stay on the island, and a few are people who, although they have worked on the water for many years, have through bad luck or improvidence or lack of perseverance failed to join the ranks of the better capitalized independent watermen.

Finally, in case you read earlier in Chapter 16 about Smith Island, it is important to note that Tangier Island is different in several major respects. For one thing, Tangier is governed by a mayor and town council, with all the usual powers of local government, making it a more cohesive, more organized, and yet more ordinary place than Smith Island, with its three unincorporated villages. Also, Tangier's one school goes all the way through twelfth grade, graduating a very small class but nonetheless supported by the community because the local school is thought to minimize the out-migration of young people, at least compared with Smith Island, whose youngsters after seventh grade attend school on the mainland.

≈   ≈   ≈   ≈

AUTOMOBILE DIRECTIONS: Tangier Island lies in Virginia's portion of Chesapeake Bay, below Smith Island and the mouth of the Potomac River. (See **Map 1** on page iv in the Table of Contents.) The island is reached by commercial passenger boats from Crisfield, Maryland, which is located about 40 miles south-southwest of Salisbury.

To Crisfield from northern Delmarva and Interstate 95 southwest of Wilmington: From Interstate 95 take Exit 4A for Route 1 south, and stay on Route 1 past a quick succession of exits. Follow Route 1 south past Dover, then switch to Route 13 south toward Salisbury and Norfolk. After passing east of Salisbury and west of Princess Anne, turn right onto Route 413 toward Crisfield and go 14.6 miles to the end of the road at Crisfield's municipal dock.

To Crisfield from the Chesapeake Bay Bridge: After crossing the bridge, follow Route 50/301 across Kent Island. At the point where Route 50 and Route 301 split, fork right to follow Route 50 past Easton, Cambridge, and Salisbury. East of Salisbury, take Route 13 south toward Norfolk. Follow Route 13 past Princess Anne to the junction with Route 413, and there turn right toward Crisfield. Follow Route 413 for 14.6 miles to the end of the road at Crisfield's municipal dock.

To Crisfield from southern Delmarva and the Chesapeake Bay Bridge-Tunnel at Norfolk: After crossing the bridge-tunnel, follow Route 13 north into Maryland. From the intersection with Route 113 near Pocomoke City, continue on Route 13 for 3.8 miles to the intersection with Route 667 west toward Crisfield. Turn left onto Route 667 and follow it 11.5 miles to an intersection with Route 413. Turn left onto Route 413 and follow it 6 miles to the end of the road at Crisfield's municipal dock.

To Crisfield from Salisbury and the Delaware and Maryland seashore resorts: From the vicinity of Salisbury,

follow Route 13 south past Princess Anne to the junction with
Route 413, and there turn right toward Crisfield. Follow Route
413 for 14.6 miles to the end of the road at Crisfield's municipal
dock.

From the vicinity of Rehoboth Beach, follow Route 1 north to
the intersection with Route 9 westbound, then take Route 9
west through Georgetown and across Route 113 to Route 13
southbound. Alternatively, from the vicinity of Ocean City,
follow Route 50 west to Route 13 southbound. In either case,
once you are on Route 13, follow it south around Salisbury and
past Princess Anne to the junction with Route 413, and there
turn right toward Crisfield. Follow Route 413 for 14.6 miles to
the end of the road at Crisfield's municipal dock.

≈   ≈   ≈   ≈

BOATS TO TANGIER ISLAND: From Crisfield there are two
types of boat service to Tangier, each discussed below.

Excursion service is provided by Tangier Island Cruises
using the large *Steven Thomas* during the peak of the tourist
season or the smaller *Capt. Rudy Thomas* when there is less
demand. These boats dock behind the company's office
located at the corner of Tenth and Main Streets two blocks
from Crisfield's municipal wharf. The company's parking lot
can be reached from Tenth Street. The excursion boat leaves
Crisfield at 12:30 P.M. and departs from Tangier at 4:00 P.M.
It allows about two and a half hours on the island. If you plan
to stay on the island overnight, let the parking lot attendant
know so that your car won't be towed.

Mail-boat service is provided by the *Courtney Thomas*,
which docks at the Crisfield municipal wharf at the end of
Route 413 (Main Street). This boat, which is used by the
islanders themselves, leaves Crisfield at 12:30 P.M., but it
does not return until the next day, departing from Tangier at
8:00 A.M. (or 3:00 P.M. on Sunday). Obviously, this boat
entails an overnight stay on the island, which is the only option
November through mid-May. Buy your ticket on the boat. You
can park your car in the lot on Tenth Street behind the office of
Tangier Island Cruises. Again, let the attendant know that you
are staying overnight, so that your car won't be towed.

During the tourist season, the boat operators much prefer
that you take the excursion boat to Tangier, even if you are
staying overnight — and they will so direct you. If you take the
mail boat during the off season, you are asked to remain in the

MAP 42 — Tangier Island

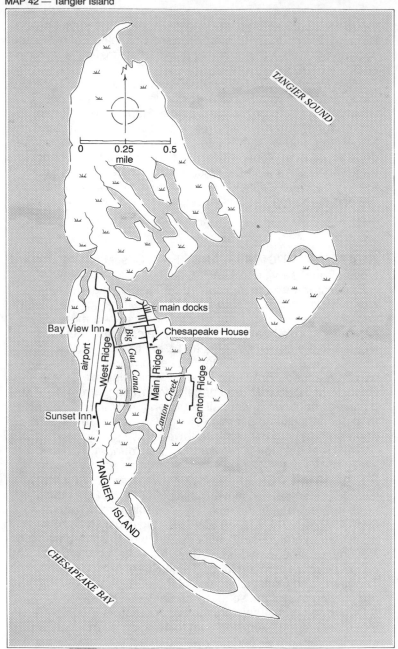

passenger cabin, out of harm's way from the supplies that are stacked loose on the deck and that sometimes shift and slide. For the return trip, when there is far less cargo, it is usually permissible to be on deck, but not at the bow in front of the helmsman. To summarize, if both the excursion boat and the mail boat are running, take the excursion boat, on which you are welcome to sit outside on the deck in the sun and breeze and to wander from place to place. If you stay overnignt on the island, you can take either the excursion boat or the mail boat back to Crisfield.

SEEING TANGIER ISLAND: Once the boat reaches Tangier Island, use **Map 42** at left to explore the town's narrow lanes on foot. Or, if you prefer, you can join a tour via golf cart. The golf-cart tours are quick and easy, but by walking you will have more freedom to explore and to pause where you want. Other options are to rent a bicycle, a golf cart, or even a canoe or a skiff with an outboard motor.

A standard feature of a visit to Tangier is a big seafood lunch at one of the restaurants. (I recommend the Chesapeake House, with its family style meals.) There is time for both eating and sightseeing if you don't linger excessively over your meal. Of course, if you stay overnight, you will have time to explore not only the town but also the long **beach** extending down the western shore below the airport and terminating at the sandy hook at the southern end of the island.

18

ASSATEAGUE ISLAND NATIONAL SEASHORE (northern section) ASSATEAGUE STATE PARK

This chapter describes the northern two-thirds of **Assateague Island** — the part, that is, in Maryland, which includes most of Assateague Island National Seashore and all of Assateague State Park, as shown on **Maps 43 and 44** on pages 286 and 287. The southern (or Virginia) section of Assateague Island is described in Chapter 19. Treating the northern and southern sections separately reflects not only the considerable differences between the two, but also the admirable fact that no public road on the island connects the two ends. As a result, the long midsection of Assateague is quite wild, especially in Virginia, where no vehicles are allowed on the beach between the state line and the Toms Cove Visitor Center.

The national seashore's northern section and Maryland's Assateague State Park have something for everyone. Most people come to swim at the two lifeguarded beaches. For walkers, there are three short trails at the national seashore, plus the opportunity to hike all day along the edge of the surf. North of the state park are 6 miles of beach accessible only on foot; south of the state park are 12 miles of beach open to off-road vehicles with permits. Most of the 5 miles of paved roads at the national seashore either are bordered by a bicycle path or at least have a bicycle lane, and there is even a separate bicycle bridge linking the mainland visitor center with the island.

Both the national seashore and the state park have facilities for car camping; in addition the national seashore has several remote campsites for backpackers and canoeists. Together the national seashore and state park also provide opportunities for surf fishing, surf boarding, crabbing, boat launching, and hunting. During summer, and to a lesser extent in spring and fall, the national seashore offers a variety of nature programs, such as slide shows and guided walks. For information about any of these activities, call the visitor center at (410) 641-1441.

Although the northern section of the national seashore is not as rich in wildlife as the southern section, it is still a good place for observing the many species of birds that frequent the offshore waters, beach, dunes, marsh, and Sinepuxent and Chincoteague bays. There are also, of course, the wild ponies, which you should never forget really are wild. Accordingly, please do not approach the horses closely or feed them; they can bite and kick, inflicting severe injuries.

The national seashore is open every day, all day, year-round. The admission fee entitles you to enter as often as you want for one week. Annual passes are also available. The state park is open daily April through November from early morning to sunset. During summer the parking lots fill early in the day, especially on weekends.

At the national seashore, pets must be on leashes no more than 6 feet long, and are prohibited at backcountry campsites and in the primitive area north of the state park, so by bringing a pet you are immediately barring yourself from the best place for beach walking. During summer the sand, sun, and insects can be very hard on dogs and other domestic animals, so the wisest thing to do is to leave your pet at home. And at the state park, pets are prohibited altogether, even on a leash and even in your car.

Assateague Island National Seashore is managed by the National Park Service; telephone (410) 641-1441 for general information and interpretive services at the Barrier Island Visitor Center or (410) 641-3030 for the campground office.

Assateague State Park is administered by the Maryland Department of Natural Resources; telephone (410) 641-2120.

AUTHORIZED IN 1965 and now one of the most visited public recreation areas on the East Coast, Assateague Island National Seashore is an outstanding park that very nearly never came to be. Its creation and management philosophy help to illustrate the evolution of national park policy over a period of more than a century.

Until the early 1960s, Congress had never authorized spending more than trivial amounts to buy land for national parks. Rather, our great national parks, starting with Yellowstone in 1872, were at first created from land already federally owned, with the minor exception of private inholdings, such as homesteads and mining claims, that existed when the parks were established, and some of which were bought by the government. (Many inholdings still exist today, and at least twenty-five national parks contain valid mining claims. Congress even permitted the establishment of *new* mining claims in some national parks until 1976.)

When the National Park Service eventually was established within the Department of Interior in 1916, it was put in charge of a dozen parks that had already been created. Most of the parks were huge (taken together, they were more than three times bigger than the state of Delaware) and all were in the West, where, of course, the overwhelming bulk of federal land was — and still is. According to standards formulated by the new park service, future national parks would be modeled on those already in existence. In brief, they were supposed to be vast, spectacular examples of unspoiled natural grandeur, like the Grand Canyon, designated a national park in 1919. As new parks were established, very few were near major cities, nor was the use of the parks intended to include more than low-keyed forms of nature appreciation, such as sightseeing, camping, horse trekking, and hiking.

Because all the early federal parks were in the West, the newly-established National Park Service recommended, and Congress authorized, a series of large national parks in the eastern United States. Here, however, the federal government owned little land, and for each new park that it authorized, a frugal and conservative Congress allocated no federal funds to buy land. Rather, the land had to be donated or bought with donated money. The states where the proposed parks were to be located served as intermediaries to assemble the land from gifts and from their own holdings, with the goal of eventually presenting the land to the federal government. In this way, Arcadia National Park was established in Maine in 1919, Great Smoky Mountains in 1930, Shenandoah in 1935, Mammoth Cave in 1936, and Isle Royale in Lake Superior in 1940.

Meanwhile, the responsibilities of the National Park Service were expanding rapidly, sometimes in directions that had little to do with its original mission. During the 1930s the park service was assigned, by transfer from other federal agencies, responsibility for managing many small historic sites (chiefly battlefields) scattered throughout the eastern states. In the decades that followed, the park service acquired numerous houses and other structures and even whole hamlets of historic value, such as Hopewell Furnace National Historic Site in Pennsylvania and Colonial National Historic Park, which includes Yorktown, Virginia. This growth was in addition to the stewardship the National Park Service already exercised over a lengthening list of "national monuments," consisting mainly of outstanding natural landmarks, like Devil's Tower in Wyoming, and areas of scientific interest, such as Dinosaur National Monument in Colorado and Utah. (Whereas national parks may be established only by Congress, the president has authority to designate national monuments, but, of course, no power to allocate funds for their acquisition if they are not already federally owned.) Thus during the second quarter of this century, the National Park Service became what might be described as a Smithsonian Institution of American land, charged with acquiring, preserving, and presenting to the public a diversified roster of scenically, historically, and scientifically important places.

Starting in the 1930s, a broader concept of recreation, beyond the National Park Service's traditional emphasis on nature appreciation, was also promoted by federal planners. In 1936 the first "national recreation area" was established to take advantage of the obvious opportunity for swimming and boating at Lake Mead, the reservoir created by the construction of Hoover Dam. During the 1940s and '50s, similar recreation areas, all administered by the National Park Service, were established incidental to other federal dam projects.

The nation's seashores, combining as they do striking scenery with vast potential for intensive recreation, also received attention from the National Park Service. After inventorying all the unspoiled beaches along the Atlantic and Gulf coasts, the park service in 1935 recommended twelve areas (including Assateague Island) for acquisition. Congress, however, approved only one such coastal park — the Cape Hatteras National Seashore in 1937 — and as usual authorized no funds for land. Over a period of decades, tracts totaling thousands of acres were assembled by the state of North Carolina, which in installments donated the land to the federal government. The federal government did, however, spend large sums at Cape Hatteras in an attempt to stabilize the shoreline — efforts which, with the benefit of hindsight, appear to have been futile and have provided a lesson for the management of other oceanfront parks that were established much later.

After authorization of the Cape Hatteras National Seashore, the possibility of creating a similar national seashore on Assateague Island gradually faded. During the late 1930s and throughout the '40s, legislation to create a seashore park at Assateague was repeatedly introduced in Congress, but without favorable result. Instead, a variety of other projects were implemented. Using funds derived from the annual sale of duck stamps to hunters, the federal government's Bureau of Sports Fisheries and Wildlife (now the Fish and Wildlife Service) purchased the southern third of Assateague Island — the part, that is, in Virginia — to create Chincoteague National Wildlife Refuge in 1943.

(See Chapter 19.) In 1940 and again in 1952, the Maryland State Planning Commission recommended that a state park be established on Assateague. Noting this interest, a developer who had bought most of the Maryland section of the island in the late 1940s gave the state a piece two miles long for an oceanfront park in 1961 in the hope that the state would then build a bridge to Assateague, as eventually was done. Meanwhile, the National Park Service stopped recommending Assateague for national seashore status after concluding in 1956 that the 60 percent of the island that was privately owned had been consigned irrevocably to resort development.

Assateague was, in fact, ripe for commercialization. The increase in national prosperity, urbanization, automobile ownership, and leisure time that followed World War II sparked booming development activity on the barrier islands of the mid-Atlantic coast. "Millions of Americans hungry for salt-air gratify their craving for ocean bathing and seashore recreation by patronizing the Nation's overcrowded beaches," declared a sales brochure for the nascent community of Ocean Beach on Assateague Island, and the brochure went on to tout the fifteen miles of pristine beach at the doorstep of Ocean Beach residents. More than 5,850 lots were actually sold on Assateague Island during the 1950s and early '60s as the developer of Ocean Beach embarked on a plan that included a dense grid of paved roads 130 blocks long, with shopping centers and hotel districts spaced at intervals. A paved road, Baltimore Boulevard, was built as far south as the state line, and many side streets were cleared as houses started to go up.

In March 1962, however, a nor'easter lasting three days literally swept over Assateague Island. Immense quantities of sand were shifted from the ocean front to the bay side of the island. For two or three miles south of Ocean City Inlet, the shoreline was moved more than four hundred feet westward. Much of Baltimore Boulevard was torn out. (Part of what remains can be seen at the Life of the Dunes Trail.) Of about fifty houses that had been built, all but eighteen were total losses. To protect the island against future storms, the developer of Ocean Beach sought assistance from the Army Corps of Engineers, but the government concluded that measures for erosion control would be excessively expensive and probably futile, so nothing was done.

Meanwhile, in 1961 Congress finally broke with the precedent that frowned on the use of federal funds to buy land for national parks. Elected in 1960, President John F. Kennedy successfully pushed for creation, in his home state of Massachusetts, of the Cape Cod National Seashore, to be pieced together almost entirely from private land purchased with federal tax dollars, plus inholdings that would be subject to various restrictions but not purchased. Similar authorization for Point Reyes National Seashore in California and Padre Island National Seashore in Texas followed in 1962.

Also in 1962, the Outdoors Recreation Resources Review Commission issued, after three years' study, its influential report *Outdoor Recreation for America*, which documented a lack of outdoor recreation areas — particularly waterfront areas — that were convenient to major cities. The report was embraced enthusiastically by Stewart Udall, Kennedy's secretary of interior, who initiated a policy of acquiring parkland in or near the nation's largest metropolitan regions, even if the sites did not entirely meet traditional National Park Service standards for large size, spectacular scenery, or lack of previous development.

To pay for the new acquisitions, Udall persuaded Congress to establish the Land and Water Conservation Fund, effective at the beginning of 1965 and presently scheduled to continue in existence until the year 2015. Revenue for the fund comes from national park user fees and a share of payments from offshore oil-drilling leases. The money is used not only for the acquisition and improvement of federal parks but also for a wide variety of other park and conservation purposes, including grants to state and local governments. Although much of the revenue — in fact, more than half between 1980 and 1997 — has not been allocated for parks and conservation and thus by default has gone to the government's general account, the Land and Water Conservation Fund nonetheless has helped to institutionalize the federal practice of buying land as a necessary and appropriate means to create some national parks.

Assateague is one of those parks. As a result of the recommendations embodied in *Outdoor Recreation for America*, the Department of Interior undertook to re-evaluate the island, where development had been temporarily thwarted and even in part eradicated by the 1962 storm. The result was a proposal to create the Assateague Island National Seashore, submitted to Congress in 1963 but not approved until 1965, the year after Maryland completed the Route 611 bridge and opened Assateague State Park.

As authorized, the new national seashore was to include construction of a road running along the island from one end to the other, plus other facilities for "maximum public recreation use," such as fishing piers, a marina, and a 600-acre concession area with a restaurant, a gift shop, and a motel with 500 units in twenty buildings. However, as tourist accommodations multiplied at nearby Ocean City and Chincoteague Island, a reaction set in. Not only did those resorts remove the necessity of providing similar tourist facilities at the national seashore, but also (it became apparent) visitors to Assateague wanted to see something different: a relatively wild barrier island and beach. In response to the burgeoning environmental movement and the renewed value placed by the public on undeveloped natural areas, Congress in 1976 amended the National Seashore Act to delete provisions for commercial development at Assateague, thus to some extent vindicating traditional National Park Service emphasis on conservation and nature appreciation. At Assateague today, the park service promotes the same low-keyed activities — camping, hiking, and wildlife observation — that have always been associated with our great national parks, while at the same time, of course, operating an intensively used bathing beach, plus accommodating the interests of hunters, surf fishermen, and those who simply want to drive on the beach for fun.

≈   ≈   ≈   ≈

AUTOMOBILE DIRECTIONS: Assateague Island is the long barrier island that stretches south of Ocean City, Maryland for 37 miles. (See **Map 1** on page iv in the Table of Contents.) The island's upper end, discussed in this chapter, is reached by the Route 611 bridge from the mainland and is not accessible directly from Ocean City to the north or from Chincoteague in the south.

To Assateague from northern Delmarva and Interstate 95 southwest of Wilmington: From Interstate 95 take Exit 4A for Route 1 south, and stay on Route 1 past a quick succession of exits. Follow Route 1 south past Dover, Delaware. Continue as Route 1 becomes congruent with Route 113, then at Milford take Route 113 south and follow it into Maryland. After passing over Route 50, continue south on Route 113 for just 1.3 miles, then turn left onto Route 376 east toward Assateague and Route 611. Go 4.1 miles to a T-intersection, and there turn right onto Route 611 south toward Assateague Island. Follow Route 611 for 3.1 miles to the national seashore's Barrier Island Visitor Center on the right.

To Assateague from the Chesapeake Bay Bridge: After crossing the bridge, follow Route 50/301 across Kent Island. At the point where Route 50 and Route 301 split, fork right to follow Route 50 past Easton, Cambridge, and Salisbury toward Ocean City. Stay on Route 50 past the exits for Route 90, Route 346, and Route 818, then exit onto Route 113 south toward Snow Hill. From the end of the exit ramp, follow Route 113 south only 1 mile, then turn left onto Route 376 east toward Assateague and Route 611. Go 4.1 miles to a T-intersection, and there turn right onto Route 611 south toward Assateague Island. Follow Route 611 for 3.1 miles to the national seashore's Barrier Island Visitor Center on the right.

To Assateague from southern Delmarva and the Chesapeake Bay Bridge-Tunnel at Norfolk: After crossing the bridge-tunnel, follow Route 13 north about 73 miles to the intersection (near Pocomoke City, Maryland) with Route 113, and there turn right onto Route 113 north toward Berlin and Ocean City. Follow Route 113 for about 28 miles to an intersection with Route 376, then turn right (east) toward Assateague and Route 611. Go 4.1 miles to a T-intersection, and there turn right onto Route 611 south toward Assateague Island. Follow Route 611 for 3.1 miles to the national seashore's Barrier Island Visitor Center on the right.

To Assateague from Salisbury: Follow Route 50 east toward Ocean City. Stay on Route 50 past the exits for Route 90, Route 346, and Route 818, then exit onto Route 113 south toward Snow Hill. From the end of the exit ramp, follow Route 113 south only 1 mile, then turn left onto Route 376 east toward Assateague and Route 611. Go 4.1 miles to a T-intersection, and there turn right onto Route 611 south toward Assateague Island. Follow Route 611 for 3.1 miles to the national seashore's Barrier Island Visitor Center on the right.

To Assateague from the Delaware and Maryland seashore resorts: From the southern end of Ocean City, take Route 50 east only 1.3 miles to the intersection with Route 611 at a traffic light, and there turn left (south) toward the Assateague parks. Follow Route 611 for 7.2 miles to the national seashore's Barrier Island Visitor Center on the right.

From the more northerly seashore resorts (and even from the upper end of Ocean City), the fastest route is first to go west to Route 113, then follow it south. After passing over Route 50, continue south on Route 113 for 1.3 miles, then turn left onto Route 376 east toward Assateague and Route 611. Go 4.1 miles to a T-intersection, and there turn right onto Route 611 south toward Assateague Island. Follow Route 611 for 3.1 miles to the national seashore's Barrier Island Visitor Center on the right.

≈ ≈ ≈ ≈

BARRIER ISLAND VISITOR CENTER: Here you can orient yourself, see films and various exhibits, and learn about the naturalist programs that are offered by the National Park Service at different seasons. You may also want to rent a tape cassette for a **Driving Tape Tour** of the Maryland portion of the national seashore. The tape runs about an hour, but you should allow more time in view of the likelihood that you will want to get out of your car at various exhibits and other points of interest. Exploring the three **Life of Assateague walking trails** passed by the car tour may occupy another hour or more. And then there is the **beach**, where the car tour ends, and where you can easily spend the better part of a day.

≈   ≈   ≈   ≈

NORTHERN ASSATEAGUE ISLAND is shown on **Maps 43 and 44** on pages 286 and 287. From the national seashore's Barrier Island Visitor Center on the mainland, continue east on Route 611 for 1.1 miles to an intersection beyond the bridge. For the state park, continue straight a short distance. For the national seashore, bear right and go 2.2 miles to the entrance station and North Ocean Beach parking lot, where a ranger station is located.

For **swimming** during the period from late June through Labor Day, there are lifeguarded beaches with bathhouses at the national seashore's North Ocean Beach and at the state park. Swimmers at the state park should leave their cars in the day-use lot (open until sunset) unless they are also camping.

WALKING AT NORTHERN ASSATEAGUE ISLAND: The northern section of the national seashore provides excellent opportunities for walking. However, to avoid areas where hunting is permitted from late autumn through January, hikers should stay on the trails or on the beach, as described below.

Life of the Dunes, Life of the Forest, and **Life of the Marsh** are the names of three short interpretive trails at the national seashore, each about 0.5 mile round-trip. (See **Map 43** on page 286.) A booklet called *The Life of Assateague* provides commentary on these trails and is sold at the Barrier Island Visitor Center. The marsh and forest trails are accessible by wheelchair.

The beach north to Ocean City Inlet provides an outstanding round-trip walk of up to 12 or 16 miles, depending on whether you start at the state beach (its parking lot is

MAP 43 — Northern Assateague Island: main visitor areas

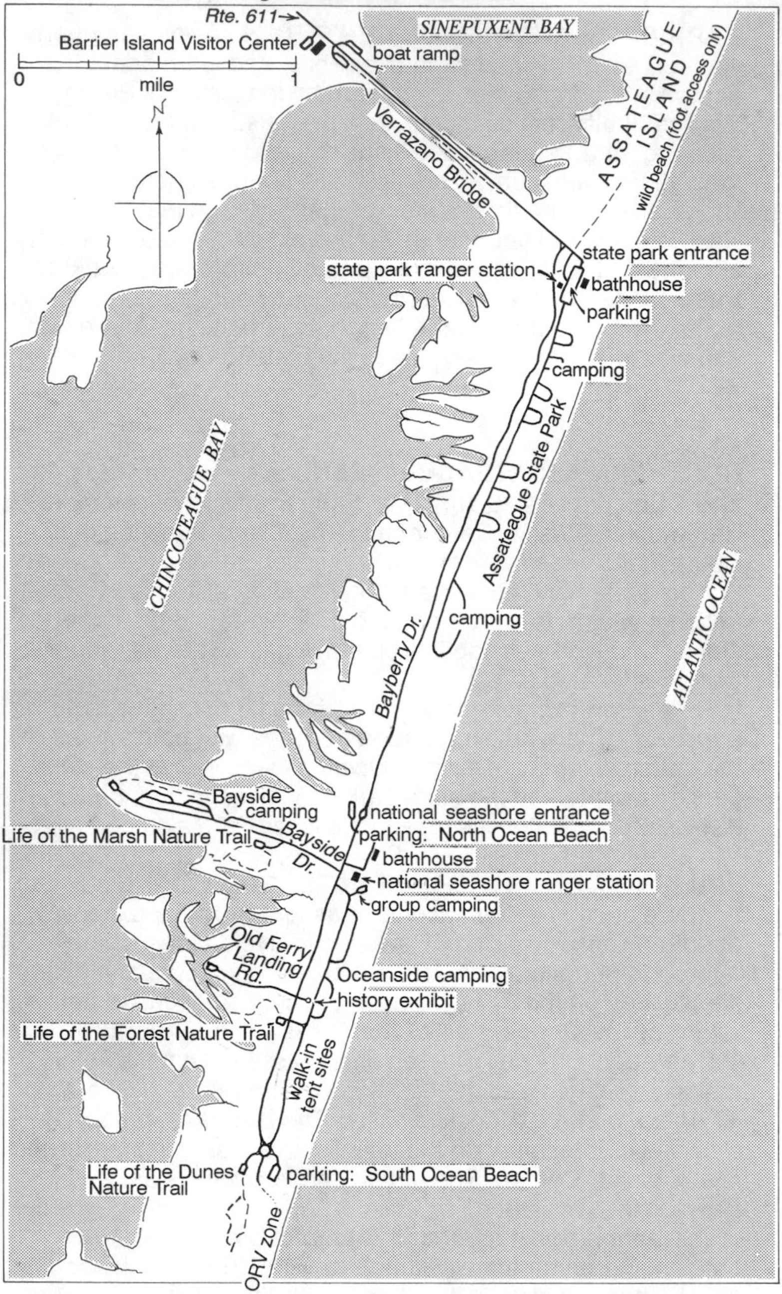

SINEPUXENT BAY

Rte. 611→

Barrier Island Visitor Center

boat ramp

0   mile   1

Verrazano Bridge

ASSATEAGUE ISLAND

wild beach (foot access only)

CHINCOTEAGUE BAY

state park ranger station

state park entrance

bathhouse

parking

camping

Assateague State Park

camping

Bayberry Dr.

ATLANTIC OCEAN

Bayside camping

Life of the Marsh Nature Trail

Bayside Dr.

national seashore entrance

parking: North Ocean Beach

bathhouse

national seashore ranger station

group camping

Old Ferry Landing Rd.

Oceanside camping

history exhibit

Life of the Forest Nature Trail

walk-in tent sites

Life of the Dunes Nature Trail

parking: South Ocean Beach

ORV zone

286

MAP 44 — Northern Assateague Island

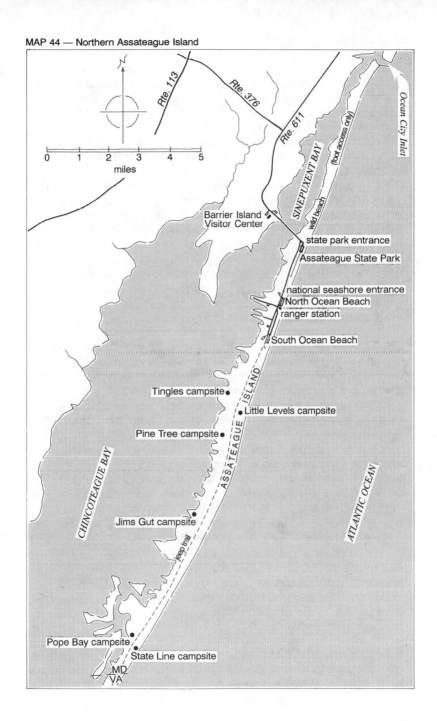

closed in winter) or farther south at the national seashore's parking lot. (See **Map 44** on page 287.) Because some areas at the northern section of Assateague consist of very low flats where storms or exceptionally high tides wash over the island, you may have to turn back before reaching Ocean City Inlet. Off-road vehicles are not permitted in the state park or to the north, whereas south toward Virginia, vehicular traffic on the beach can be heavy and detracts from a walk along the shore.

For a walk north toward Ocean City, allow plenty of time. If you park at the state beach and return after sunset, your car will be locked in, so you may prefer to park at the national seashore, where the lot never closes. As you set out, take a good look from the beach back toward the dune crossover, so that you will recognize it even if you return after dark. With the ocean on your right, walk north along the beach, which eventually ends at a boulder jetty at the Ocean City Inlet. Please observe signs indicating that hikers should stay on the low beach so as not to disturb nesting birds.

CAR CAMPING: There are campgrounds at both the national seashore and the state park. From mid-May to mid-October — and especially during summer — there is a strong demand for campsites, so call long ahead of time to reserve a spot.

At the national seashore, there are two campgrounds — Oceanside and Bayside — as shown on **Map 43** on page 286. Both campgrounds offer drive-in pads that can accommodate trailers, motorhomes, and tents. Both have drinking water, chemical toilets, and showers (cold water only), but no hookups for electricity or water. Some Oceanside tent sites are located a few hundred feet from parking spaces. For information telephone (410) 641-3030 or write to the Superintendent, Assateague Island National Seashore, Route 611, 7206 National Seashore Lane, Berlin, MD 21811.

The campground at the state park is open during the warmer half of the year and is equipped with drinking water, hot showers, bathhouses, and flush toilets. The campsites can accommodate trailers, motorhomes, and, of course, tents. For information on opening and closing dates and reservations, telephone (410) 641-2120.

BACKCOUNTRY CAMPING: An alternative to car camping is backpacking to remote campsites where there are picnic tables and chemical toilets but no water. The national seashore's

pamphlet on "Assateague Island Backcountry Camping" will help with your planning. To obtain a copy, call (410) 641-3030, or write to the address noted two paragraphs above.

The various backcountry campsites are shown on **Map 44** on page 287. The campsites at Little Levels and State Line are oceanside sites, open year-round and consisting simply of a bare expanse of sand behind the first ridge of dunes. Tingles, Pine Tree, Jims Gut, and Pope Bay are bayside campsites, closed for a few weeks during the hunting season. They are located among pine trees and are accessible by canoeists as well as by hikers. I recommend camping during a warm spell in late fall, winter, or early spring, when there are few mosquitoes, flies, or ticks and when the sun and heat are not oppressive. Of course, even if the forecast is for pleasant weather, you should be prepared for storms and cold.

Before setting out for backcountry camping, you must obtain a backcountry use permit at the national seashore ranger station at the North Ocean Beach parking lot on the day that you want to start. In order to allow enough daylight during which to reach your campsite, you are required to pick up your permit by specified times depending on the season and the destination. The deadline for Little Levels, Tingles, Pine Tree, and Jims Gut is 5 P.M. (3 P.M. when Standard Time is in effect), but if you are going to the distant State Line or Pope Bay sites, the deadline year-round is noon.

For backcountry camping, you must carry in your own water (allow a half-gallon per day absolute minimum for drinking) and carry out your own trash. If you plan to cook, bring a stove. Also, bring sunscreen, sunglasses, a hat, insect repellent, and extra-long, sturdy tent stakes, since ordinary pegs will not hold in the sand.

OFF-ROAD VEHICLES: If you have a car or truck suitable for off-road use, you may enjoy driving along the beach. The stretch of beach open to ORVs is about 12 miles long, extending from the vicinity of the national seashore's South Ocean Beach parking lot to the Maryland/Virginia line. (See **Map 44** on page 287.) An annual permit is required and may be obtained at the ranger station. Information about off-road vehicle permits, vehicle specifications, required equipment, and other regulations are set forth in a leaflet called "Assateague Island Off-Road Vehicles," available from the national seashore.

BOATING AND CANOEING: Trailered boats can be launched from the state park's ramp at the west end of the Route 611 bridge. (See **Map 43** on page 286.) Canoes can be launched at the end of Old Ferry Landing Road in the national seashore. This is a good spot from which to set out for the four bayside backcountry campsites or from which simply to explore the marsh. Be aware, however, that strong winds can sometimes make canoeing here very difficult.

Daily during summer, and on weekends during spring and fall, canoes (and also bicycles) can be rented from a private concession located at the end of Bayside Drive at the national seashore. Telephone (410) 641-5029 for information.

19

CHINCOTEAGUE NATIONAL WILDLIFE REFUGE
ASSATEAGUE ISLAND NATIONAL SEASHORE (southern section)

Despite its name, **Chincoteague National Wildlife Refuge** is located almost entirely on the Virginia portion of Assateague Island and is situated within the boundaries of Assateague Island National Seashore. Together, the federal refuge and seashore — shown on **Maps 45, 46, and 47** on pages 303, 305, and 306 — are among Delmarva's greatest natural areas. During fall and winter many thousands of waterfowl congregate on the refuge ponds, marshes, coves, and offshore waters, and some species are year-round residents, making southern Assateague a Mecca for bird watchers. (Seasonal fluctuations in waterfowl and wading birds more or less follow the same timetable as set forth in Chapter 3 on Bombay Hook National Wildlife Refuge.) Woods and scrubby brush provide habitat for other birds and wildlife, including sika deer (actually diminutive elk). And, yes, there are the wild ponies. I enjoy these animals as much as anybody, but still, in my opinion, they are among the least of the reasons to come to Chincoteague. Please do not approach the horses closely or feed them; they can bite and kick, inflicting severe injuries. The nationally-famous pony penning occurs the last Wednesday, Thursday, and Friday that fall in July.

For those who want to watch birds from their car, Wildlife Loop is open daily from 3 P.M. to dusk. For walkers there are trails of all lengths, from less than a mile to an overnight trek of two dozen miles. For bicyclists there are paved paths that are closed to motor vehicles, although as just noted, bicyclists must share Wildlife Loop with cars after 3 P.M. And for beach lovers, there are many miles of seashore, including a bathing beach with bathhouses and lifeguards during summer. The refuge and seashore also offer a variety of interpretive programs and opportunities for clamming, crabbing, surf fishing, hunting, and driving off-road vehicles.

Chincoteague refuge is open every day year-round. The times

at which the entrance gates are opened and closed change with the seasons and correspond roughly with pre-dawn twilight and nightfall. The admission fee entitles you to enter as often as you want for one week. Annual passes are also available. During summer the parking lots at the beach fill early in the day, especially on weekends. All pets are prohibited, even in your car. Rollerskating on the refuge roads and paths is also forbidden.

Chincoteague National Wildlife Refuge is administered by the U.S. Fish and Wildlife Service; telephone (757) 336-6122. The National Park Service provides recreational services and management in the Toms Cove area, which includes the lifeguarded beach; telephone (757) 336-6577.

BARRIER ISLANDS SUCH AS ASSATEAGUE occupy much of the Atlantic coast of the United States south of New England. These long, thin, changeable islands are a product of waves, longshore currents, tides, and wind acting on the unconsolidated sediments of the coastal plain and continental shelf, which really are one continuous apron of sand, silt, and clay eroded from the Appalachian and Piedmont highlands to the west. Also contributing to the mile-thick mantle of deposits along the mid-Atlantic coast are immense quantities of gravel, sand, and rock flour scoured by continental glaciers from regions farther north and carried to the sea by huge rivers of meltwater that today survive in the relatively trivial trickle of the Hudson, Delaware, and Susquehanna rivers.

Together the coastal plain and continental shelf slope slightly eastward, and across this surface the shoreline has advanced and receded repeatedly as the ocean has risen and fallen, depending on how much of the planet's water is amassed in the polar ice caps and in continental ice sheets. Since onset of the Pleistocene Epoch, or Ice Age, about two million year ago, there have been four episodes of continental glaciation in North America. The most recent incursion of northern ice to reach what are now New York, New Jersey, and Pennsylvania lasted from about 70,000 to 12,000 years ago, and during that period sea level was as much as three hundred feet lower than now. Even today the Ice Age continues at higher latitudes, where enough ice remains in the polar ice caps and the Greenland ice sheet to raise the ocean another 130 feet if the ice were to melt, as no doubt some of it will.

The rising sea level of our present geologic time has helped to create barrier islands in several different ways. For one thing, the rising ocean has resulted in massive and relentless erosion of the shore, and in this environment barrier islands have often originated as long spits of silt, sand, and pebbles trailing downcurrent from an eroding headland. Because the longshore current is simply the result of wind-driven waves striking the shore at an angle, the direction in which a spit grows reflects the region's dominant onshore winds interacting with the general orientation of the coastline. For example, the vicinity of Bethany Beach, Delaware, is an eroding headland — a visibly truncated peninsula bound by Indian River Bay to the north, Assawoman Bay to the south, and the open ocean to the east. (See Map 1 on page iv in the Table of Contents.) Both above and below Bethany, the coast angles slightly westward, like a boomerang or chevron pointing toward the ocean. Arriving from the east, incoming waves that strike above Bethany Beach produce a longshore current that washes sand along the coast toward the northwest, ultimately producing the spit at Cape Henlopen. Striking the shore below Bethany Beach, waves from the east wash material along the coast toward the southwest, producing the long coastal barrier consisting of Fenwick Island, Ocean City, and Assateague, which together trail downcurrent from the eroding Bethany headland.

Such spits can eventually grow so long that they may reach another headland or curve inland, thus nearly impounding the water behind them, as has occurred at Chincoteague Bay. When this happens, storm-driven waves and tide may rise so fast on the ocean side of the sandy barrier that the sea breaks through, creating an inlet and turning the spit into a narrow island or string of islands. Similarly, after a storm surge has partly inundated a low barrier island and has overfilled the bay behind it, the outgoing rush of water as the tide ebbs and the wind slackens may quickly carve a gap across the barrier. During the first third of this century, Assateague was linked to Ocean City, but a hurricane in 1933 blew so much water into Chincoteague, Sinepuxent, and Assawoman bays that the water broke out just south of the city, carving a channel across the spit and turning Assateague into an island. Normally, such gaps eventually fill in with sand swept laterally along the beachfront by the longshore current, but the inlet at Ocean City proved to be so convenient for boats that long jetties were constructed in order to keep the gap open. By blocking the natural southward movement of sand, these jetties have caused the northern end of Assateague to be starved of sand and have contributed to severe erosion.

Other forces are also at work. Because the coastal plain and continental shelf slope eastward at such a low gradient, the water offshore is shallow. In these shallows waves break, dissipating their energy and depositing their load of churned-up sand. As a shoal or bar develops, more and more sand is deposited behind the bar where the waves break. Eventually, the shoal may merge with an existing island or it may even by itself build upward above sea level, at which point vertical growth is augmented by wind-blown sand that is captured and anchored by grasses and other plants that colonize the new land to form dunes rising five or ten or even as much as thirty feet above the ocean. At the same time, a very gradual rise in sea level — about a half-foot per century, geologists say — floods the shallows behind the sandy barrier, resulting in a bay of considerable width and depth separating the island from the mainland. Such a scenario can by itself lead to the creation of barrier islands in areas where there is a substantial and continuous input of sand, as near a river mouth.

The growth of spits and shoals and their transformation into barrier islands are processes that have actually been observed over long periods of time. A third way for barrier islands to originate is more speculative. It is possible that some long, narrow barrier islands started simply as rows of high dunes along the coast of the mainland. Over time these sandy ridges may have been isolated by the rising sea, which flooded the low areas behind the dunes to create wide lagoons and bays. This process could explain, for example, the Outer Banks of North Carolina in the vicinity of Cape Hatteras, where the narrow barrier islands, now spectacularly far offshore, may once have been high dunes along the mainland coast when sea level was three hundred feet lower than at present.

Even a cursory glance at old (and not so old) maps shows that barrier islands such as Assateague are constantly changing. Inlets form and heal or move under the influence of the longshore current. For example, Martinet's 1885 Map of Maryland, which includes also the bordering areas of Virginia, shows only a rudimentary spit at the southern end of Assateague, but during the last hundred years this spit has grown about three miles to form Toms Cove Hook. (See Map 45 on page 303.) In fact, during the last five years, during the interval between the publication of the first and second editions of this book, the lower part of the hook has added many acres of sand flats along its southern shore while the hook's "shank" below Toms Cove Visitor Center has narrowed.

Over the longer term — at least during the period of rising sea level that has been under way since the retreat of the last continental glacier — the barrier islands of the mid-Atlantic region have been migrating westward under the influence of occasional major storms. The biggest storms may wash entirely over some of the low islands, such as those of the Delmarva Peninsula, eroding the side that faces the sea and at the same time burying in sand the marshes along the islands' western margins. In fact, long, low, narrow islands such as Assateague are sometimes termed washover barriers, and there are large parts of Chincoteague National Wildlife Refuge at southern Assateague that occupy areas that are called wash flats.

Evidence that much of Assateague Island is retreating westward toward the mainland is plain to see. At some places on Assateague, beds of peat that were formed in what was once marsh along the island's back shore have been exposed by waves on what is now the ocean front. Similarly, stumps from forests of cedar and pine that once grew on the western side of the island have on occasion been revealed by erosion at what is now the beach. The fact that Assateague and similar barrier island are retreating westward does not necessarily mean, however, that the bays behind the islands are shrinking or that the islands will one day merge with the mainland. Rather, in most places the mainland shore is also retreating westward as the sea rises, so that an expanse of water between the mainland and barrier islands is maintained.

Although washover has historically been a common phenomenon at Assateague, the formation of inlets is a more usual process by which sand from the ocean front is transported to the back shore of a barrier, resulting in westward movement of an island or spit. When a storm carves a new inlet, that event alone often involves the displacement of an immense quantity of sand, some of which may be swept into the bay behind the barrier. And as long as the gap remains open — which could be merely for a season or for a period of years — the inlet intercepts sand carried by the longshore current. Waves and tide wash the sand into the bay, where it settles in the relatively still waters and forms a delta-like complex of shoals and channels that persist even after the inlet heals at the beachfront. At Assateague, ample evidence of former inlets is readily apparent along the back side of the island. For example, Map 43 on page 286 in Chapter 18 shows various channels and delta-like formations of old inlets along the western side of the island. Such bayside shoals provide the foundation for the growth of marshes and ultimately of dry land as wind and washover bury the marsh in yet more sand. In this way the island grows on the west side as it erodes on the east, resulting in retreat toward the mainland, which is itself retreating as the sea rises.

When the first European settlers arrived at Assateague in the mid-1600s, they found waterfowl "in millionous multitudes," according to one colonist's account. At that time, nobody lived year-round on Assateague, but the testimony of the Europeans shows that Indians

from the mainland regularly hunted and gathered shellfish on the island.

By the last quarter of the seventeenth century, English settlers were using Chincoteague and Assateague islands for grazing livestock, and it is probably from some of their horses that the wild ponies seen on Assateague today are descended. The islands were considered to be good places for grazing cattle and horses because no fences were needed and the marsh and dune grasses provided ample fodder. Several small settlements were established by stockmen and by those who fished or hunted for a livelihood. This pattern continued through the eighteenth and nineteenth centuries.

The largest settlement on Assateague Island was Assateague Village, located in the vicinity of the lighthouse built in 1867 near what was then the southernmost tip of the island. At the beginning of the twentieth century, Assateague Village had a population of about two hundred people, engaged in commercial fishing, clamming, and oystering, as well as grazing sheep, horses, and cattle. From 1912 until it burned in 1916, there was a fish factory where as many as fifty workers were employed processing menhaden into oil and fertilizer. (The foundations of this factory are still visible on the southeast shore of Toms Cove.) Another fish factory operated from 1919 to 1929. However, as the hook grew in length and the cove filled with sand, large boats could no longer land there, so the factory was closed and the houses of the village, or at least most of them, were moved by barge to neighboring Chincoteague Island. The abandonment of Assateague Village prepared the way for the creation in 1943 of Chincoteague National Wildlife Refuge, occupying the southern third of Assateague Island.

Please keep in mind, when you visit Chincoteague National Wildlife Refuge, that the priorities here mandated by law are first to protect endangered species, then to promote waterfowl and other native animals, and only lastly to accommodate visitors. If we cannot behave responsibly during our visits, in the future we will simply be barred from many activities and areas within the refuge that we presently enjoy.

≈　　≈　　≈　　≈

AUTOMOBILE DIRECTIONS: Chincoteague National Wildlife Refuge occupies the Atlantic coast in Virginia just south of the boundary with Maryland. Only a very small part of the Chincoteague refuge is on Chincoteague Island. Most of the refuge occupies the southern third of Assateague Island, which is the long barrier island that stretches south of Ocean City Inlet for 37 miles. (See **Map 1** on page iv in the Table of Contents.)

To Chincoteague Refuge from northern Delmarva and Interstate 95 southwest of Wilmington: From Interstate 95 take Exit 4A for Route 1 south, and stay on Route 1 past a quick succession of exits. Follow Route 1 south past Dover, then switch to Route 13 south through Maryland toward Salisbury and Norfolk. Stay on Route 13 past Salisbury, Princess Anne, Pocomoke City, and the junction with Route 113 (which provides an alternative approach from the north, inasmuch as Route 1 merges with Route 113 below Dover). After crossing the state line into Virginia, continue south on Route 13 for 4 miles to the intersection with Route 175, and there turn left (east) toward Wallops Island, Chincoteague, and Assateague. Go 10.4 miles, although along the way you may want to stop at the visitor center for NASA's Wallops Flight Facility. At a T-intersection in the town of Chincoteague, turn left to follow Route 175Y north toward Assateague. Continue 0.4 mile, then turn right onto Maddox Boulevard toward Assateague. Go 2.1 miles — at one point passing almost half-way around a traffic circle, beyond which are the Refuge Waterfowl Museum and the Oyster and Maritime Museum, both on the left. Continue to the entrance station for Chincoteague National Wildlife Refuge and Assateague Island National Seashore.

To Chincoteague Refuge from the Chesapeake Bay Bridge: After crossing the bridge, follow Route 50/301 across Kent Island. At the point where Route 50 and Route 301 split, fork right to follow Route 50 past Easton, Cambridge, and Salisbury. East of Salisbury, take Route 13 south toward Norfolk. Follow Route 13 past Princess Anne and Pocomoke City. After crossing the state line into Virginia, continue south on Route 13 for 4 miles to the intersection with Route 175 and there turn left (east) toward Wallops Island, Chincoteague, and Assateague. Go 10.4 miles, although along the way you may want to stop at the visitor center for NASA's Wallops Flight Facility. At a T-intersection in the town of Chincoteague, turn left to follow Route 175Y north toward Assateague. Go 2.1 miles — at one point passing almost half-way around a traffic circle, beyond which are the Refuge Waterfowl Museum and the Oyster and Maritime Museum, both on the left. Continue to the entrance station for Chincoteague National Wildlife Refuge and Assateague Island National Seashore.

To Chincoteague Refuge from southernmost Delmarva and the Chesapeake Bay Bridge-Tunnel at Norfolk: After crossing the bridge-tunnel, follow Route 13 north from the toll plaza for about 64 miles, passing (toward the end) through Temperanceville and Oak Hall. Continue to the intersection with Route 175, and there turn right (east) toward Wallops Island, Chincoteague, and Assateague. Go 10.4 miles, although along the way you may want to stop at the visitor center for NASA's Wallops Flight Facility. At a T-intersection in the town of Chincoteague, turn left to follow Route 175Y north toward Assateague. Continue 0.4 mile, then turn right onto Maddox Boulevard toward Assateague. Go 2.1 miles — at one point passing almost half-way around a traffic circle, beyond which are the Refuge Waterfowl Museum and the Oyster and Maritime Museum, both on the left. Continue to the entrance station for Chincoteague National Wildlife Refuge and Assateague Island National Seashore.

To Chincoteague refuge from Salisbury and the Delaware and Maryland seashore resorts: From Salisbury follow Route 13 south. From the Delaware and Maryland beach resorts, go west to Route 113 and follow it south. In either case, go to the junction of Route 13 and Route 113 near Pocomoke City, and from there continue south on Route 13. After crossing the state line into Virginia, continue south on Route 13 for 4 miles to the intersection with Route 175, and there turn left (east) toward Wallops Island, Chincoteague, and Assateague. Go 10.4 miles, although along the way you may want to stop at the visitor center for NASA's Wallops Flight Facility. At a T-intersection in the town of Chincoteague, turn left to follow Route 175Y north toward Assateague. Continue 0.4 mile, then turn right onto Maddox Boulevard toward Assateague. Go 2.1 miles — at one point passing almost half-way around a traffic circle, beyond which are the Refuge Waterfowl Museum and the Oyster and Maritime Museum, both on the left. Continue to the entrance station for Chincoteague National Wildlife Refuge and Assateague Island National Seashore.

≈   ≈   ≈   ≈

CHINCOTEAGUE REFUGE AND ASSATEAGUE

SEASHORE: Map 45 at right shows the roads, visitor centers, parking lots, bicycle paths, foot trails, and other facilities at the southern end of Assateague Island.

The main refuge road leads 2.7 miles to the beach, where there are several large parking lots, some bathhouses, and the **Toms Cove Visitor Center** (administered by the National Park Service). Along the road are places to pull over for viewing waterfowl from your car.

The **Chincoteague Refuge Visitor Center** (administered by the Fish and Wildlife Service) is located next to the parking lot at the entrance to Wildlife Loop, which is open to cars from 3 P.M. to dusk. Wildlife Loop is also a popular walkway and bicycle path, so drive very slowly.

Swimming draws large crowds to the national seashore during summer and early fall. From mid-June through Labor Day, lifeguards are on duty from 9:30 A.M. to 5:30 P.M. daily at the beach by the Toms Cove Visitor Center. Although you may swim elsewhere or at other hours if you wish, it is clearly safer to swim at the lifeguarded beach.

A wide range of **wildlife tours and programs** are offered at Chincoteague National Wildlife Refuge. A concessionaire provides a 1.5-hour Wildlife Safari via a large, bus-like trailer. This tour explores the back roads of the refuge, including the service road that stretches north from Wildlife Loop. For information and reservations call (757) 336-6155, or write to Assateague Island Tours, P.O. Box 252, Chincoteague, VA 23336. Schedules change with the seasons. If you have not secured a reservation before you arrive, you can inquire in person at the tour booth located at the Chincoteague Refuge Visitor Center. The refuge and park staff also provide a variety of naturalist activities, including auditorium programs and guided nature walks. Information about these activities is available at the refuge visitor center or at the park service's Toms Cove Visitor Center.

WALKING AT CHINCOTEAGUE REFUGE AND ASSATEAGUE SEASHORE: Assateague Island provides

some of the best walking on the East Coast.

Wildlife Loop (see **Map 45** at right) is a paved road 3 miles long around Snow Goose Pool. It is open to pedestrians, bicyclists, and — from 3 P.M. to dusk — to cars also. Park at the Chincoteague Refuge Visitor Center just west of Snow Goose Pool.

MAP 45 — Southern Assateague Island: main visitor areas

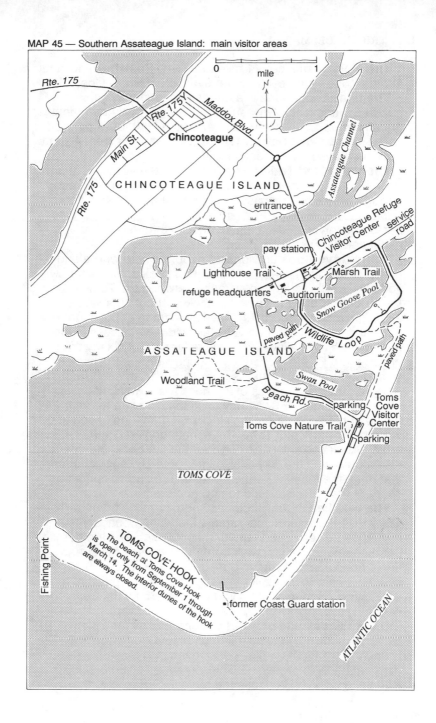

The Marsh Trail leads 1 mile round-trip from the parking lot at the refuge visitor center to an overlook at Snow Goose Pool.

The Lighthouse Trail is a pedestrian loop only a few hundred yards long. On weekends during the warmer months, there may be exhibits of wildlife art at the lighthouse oil shed.

The Toms Cove Nature Trail is another short loop; it starts opposite the southern beach parking lots.

The Woodland Trail is a paved loop 1.6 miles long. It is open to pedestrians and bicyclists. The loblolly pine forest through which the trail passes is the best area to see the endangered Delmarva Peninsula fox squirrel. The trail also has an observation deck that overlooks a marsh where you might see wild ponies or deer.

Toms Cove Hook provides an opportunity to walk along the ocean beach to Fishing Point and then back again by the way you came. The round-trip distance between the Toms Cove Visitor Center and the tip of the hook is about 10 miles, although you can lop off 1.5 miles by starting at Lot 4 farther down the beach. Off-road vehicles also have access to the hook. In order to allow tern's and plovers (particularly the endangered Piping Plover) to nest undisturbed, the hook is closed to hikers and vehicles from March 15 through August 31, and the interior dunes of the hook are always off-limits.

Looking at Map 45, you may think that you can return from the tip of the hook by circling clockwise along the beach and following the shore of Toms Cove, but I don't recommend this route. At places along the north side of the hook, the beach disappears, and the way is also interrupted by several streams that drain the marsh. Furthermore, on hunting days the north shore of the hook is closed to non-hunters.

The wild beach that stretches north 11 miles from the Toms Cove Visitor Center to the Virginia-Maryland boundary is a hiker's paradise. (See **Map 46** at right.) Vehicles are not permitted here. As you walk north, you will see fewer and fewer people, and if you go during winter, you can have the beach virtually to yourself. In gauging how far you want to walk, simply remember that you must return by the way you came.

D Dike Crossover provides the opportunity for a circuit of 7 miles, as shown by the bold line on **Map 47** on page 306. This is one of my favorite walks, passing through most of the different habitats present at Chincoteague National Wildlife Refuge. However, because the route in part follows the

MAP 46 — Southern Assateague Island

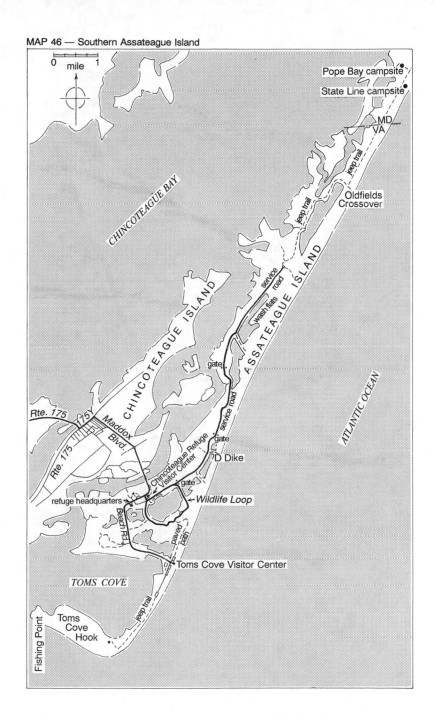

MAP 47 — Southern Assateague Island: D Dike walking tour

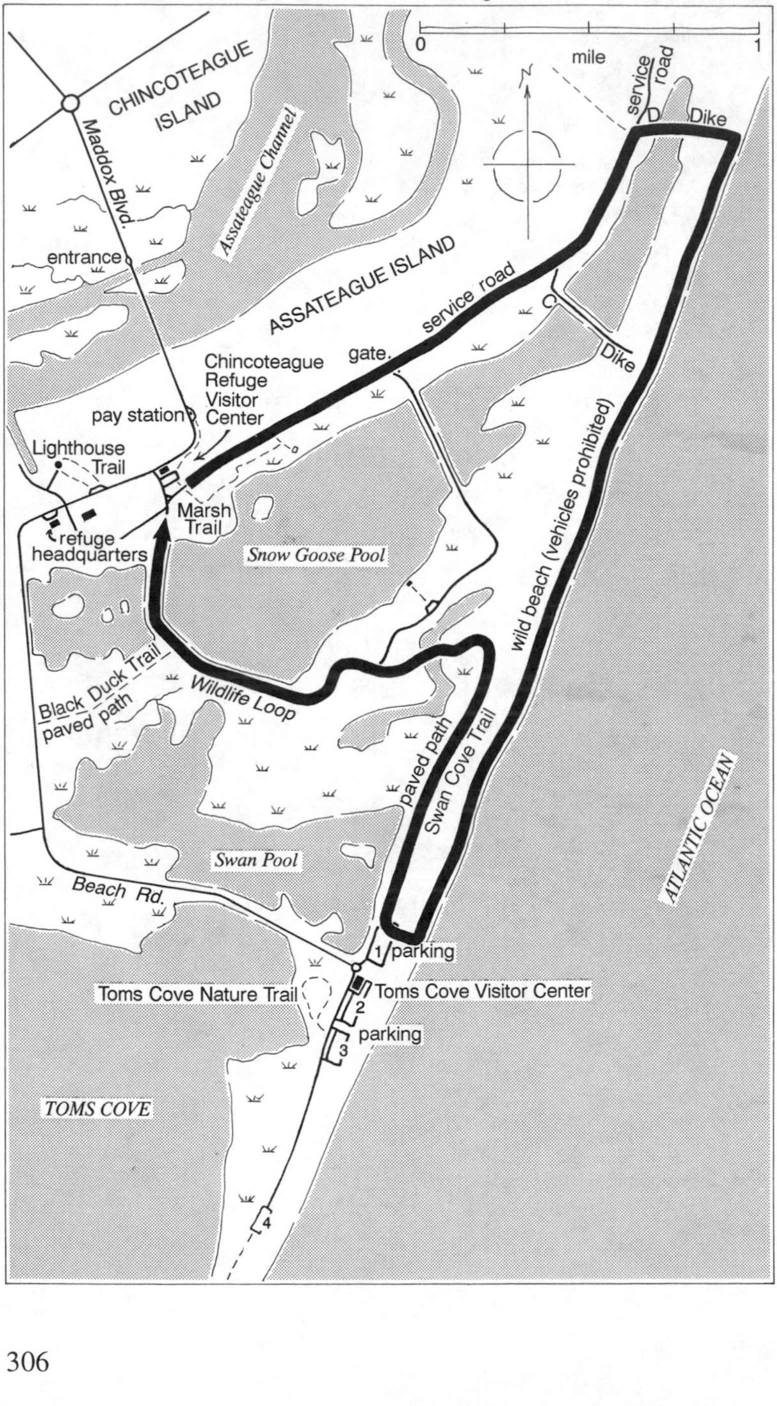

CHINCOTEAGUE ISLAND

Maddox Blvd.

Assateague Channel

0   mile   1

service road

D Dike

Dike

entrance

ASSATEAGUE ISLAND

service road

gate

Chincoteague
Refuge
Visitor
Center

pay station

Dike

Lighthouse
Trail

Marsh
Trail

Snow Goose Pool

refuge
headquarters

wild beach (vehicles prohibited)

Black Duck Trail
paved path

Wildlife Loop

paved path

Swan Cove Trail

ATLANTIC OCEAN

Swan Pool

Beach Rd.

1/parking

Toms Cove Nature Trail

2   Toms Cove Visitor Center

3   parking

TOMS COVE

4

306

service road for a mile, please read also the paragraph on hunting and other hazards starting near the top of page 308 For D Dike Crossover, park in the lot by the Chincoteague Refuge Visitor Center just west of Wildlife Loop. Enter the drive and turn left in order to follow the paved road north, with woods on your left and — after a few hundred yards — the marsh and Snow Goose Pool on your right. (Watch for cars after 3 P.M.) Where the paved road veers right across the water, continue straight past a gate and go about 1 mile on the dirt service road through piney woods. Bear half-right at the second dirt road intersecting from the right. (This is the D Dike road, and sometimes it is marked as such, but signs have a way of falling down in the sand or being vandalized.) Follow the D Dike road to and across the dunes; then — with the ocean on your left — follow the beach south about 3 miles. When you reach railings leading inland over the foredunes, cross to a large parking lot.

To return to the Chincoteague Refuge Visitor Center west of Wildlife Loop, locate the paved hiker/biker path (called the Swan Cove Trail) at the northwest corner of the beach parking lot. Follow the trail along a backdune and to the left through the woods. Merge with Wildlife Loop and continue straight. (Watch for oncoming cars.) Pass a paved path (the Black Duck Trail) intersecting from the left. About 75 yards after passing a dirt road that intersects from the left, bear left to the parking lot where you started.

The service road, which is open to pedestrians but closed to bicycles and all but authorized vehicles, extends along the western side of Assateague Island. (See **Map 46** on page 305.) For the most part, the service road is a well-graded dirt road terminating at a turn-around 7.5 miles north of the Chincoteague Refuge Visitor Center. From the turn-around, the service road continues half-left as a rutted jeep trail, leading another 3 miles to the Oldfields Crossover, which is the only place, other than D Dike, where it is permissible to cross back and forth between the service road and the beach.

With certain caveats mentioned in the next paragraph, the service road provides outstanding walking. Of course, you do not have to hike all the way to the Oldfields Crossover. In gauging how far you want to go, simply remember that you must return by the way you came, unless you *do* walk all the way to the Oldfields Crossover, in which case you can return via the beach to the D Dike Crossover, for a total of about 21 miles. For strong walkers, this is an outstanding day's outing. The only difficulty, apart from the distance, is locating D Dike as you walk down the beach. To do this, you may want to examine the D Dike Crossover on the way north (it is only about two hundred yards from the service road) so that you will recognize it from the beach on your return trip south.

In planning a walk along the service road, bear in mind that **hunting** in this area is allowed on weekdays (except Wednesdays) during certain periods in fall and winter, and on those occasions non-hunters are barred from the service road and many other areas. Call (757) 336-6122 for information about hunting dates. If you do not want to bother to call, simply go on Saturday, Sunday, or Wednesday, when hunting is prohibited. Also, hikers are barred from the service road on Thursday, Friday, Saturday, and Sunday of Thanksgiving. From noon through 3:30 P.M. during this four-day period, the service road is open to general traffic for people who want to see the area from their cars. Finally, from mid-April through November, bring insect repellent.

To start your walk on the service road, park in the lot for the Chincoteague Refuge Visitor Center just west of Wildlife Loop. Enter the drive and turn left in order to follow the paved road north, with woods on your left and — after a few hundred yards — the marsh and Snow Goose Pool on your right. (Watch for cars after 3 P.M.) Where the paved road veers right across the water, continue straight past a gate on the dirt service road.

BACKPACKING AND CAMPING: These activities are permitted, but only if you are willing to hike 12.5 miles to the State Line backcountry campsite, located a mile north of the boundary with Maryland. (See **Map 46** on page 305.) The State Line campsite consists of nothing more than an expanse of sand behind the foredunes, a picnic table, and a chemical toilet. There is no nearer campsite, and camping at undesignated points is prohibited. The national seashore's pamphlet on "Assateague Island Backcountry Camping" will help with your planning. To obtain a copy, call (757) 336-6577 or (410) 641-3030, or write to the Superintendent, Assateague Island National Seashore, Route 611, 7206 National Seashore Lane, Berlin, MD 21811.

If you are in reasonably good physical condition, hiking north to the State Line campsite makes a memorable overnight excursion, allowing ample time to enjoy the bleak and pleasant

ambiance of the surf, beach, and low dunes. But remember, hiking in soft sand with a heavy pack is hard work, requiring more time and effort than walking on firm ground. I especially recommend camping during a warm spell in late fall, winter, or early spring, when there are few mosquitoes, flies, or ticks and when the sun and heat are not oppressive. Of course, even if the forecast is for pleasant weather, you should be prepared for storms and cold.

For backcountry camping, you must obtain a backcountry use permit at the Toms Cove Visitor Center before 2 P.M. (or before noon from November through February) on the day that you want to start. You must also carry in your own water (allow a half-gallon per day absolute minimum for drinking) and carry out your own trash. If you plan to cook, bring a stove. Also, bring sunscreen, sunglasses, a hat, insect repellent, and extra-long, sturdy tent stakes, since ordinary pegs will not hold in the sand.

When you set out for the State Line campsite from the Toms Cove Visitor Center, the ocean, of course, will be on your right. The State Line campsite is located about a mile north of a fence that marks the boundary between Maryland and Virginia. A small sign showing a hiker marks the campsite.

For your return from the State Line campsite, you may want to hike along the service road. (See Map 46 and the discussion starting on page 307). The area through which the road passes is very scenic, and I strongly recommend it. From the beach, the service road can be reached via the Oldfields Crossover, located 1.7 miles south of the fence at the state line and marked (maybe) by tire tracks issuing from the dunes and also (maybe) by a post near the dunes. Of course, at its southern end, the service road terminates at Wildlife Loop, so from there you must follow Wildlife Loop left to the paved bicycle path (Swan Cove Trail) that leads to the Toms Cove Visitor Center. Or you can cross over to the beach at D Dike. Either way, the distance from the state line to Toms Cove Visitor Center is 13 miles — slightly greater than along the beach, but from the service road you will see far more birds and also deer and horses.

Finally, long-distance hikers may be tempted by the prospect of **walking along the beach from one end of Assateague Island to the other**, camping along the way. I have done this, and it was a disappointment. Between the state line and the North Ocean Beach access point (see **Map 44** on page 287 in

Chapter 18) all but the last mile of beach is open to off-road vehicles, so that progress for the hiker is measured by marching from one fisherman's motor vehicle to the next parked at intervals of a few hundred yards along the heavily rutted beach, while yet other cars and pickup trucks zoom by at fairly frequent intervals. This goes on for 13 miles. Even if the fish are not running, there can be a lot of traffic on this section of the beach, making it unattractive to hikers, especially compared to the marvelous wild beach south of the state line or at the northern end of Assateague Island.

20

ACCOMACK and NORTHAMPTON COUNTIES

This chapter explores the -va in Delmarva, or that is, the small piece of Virginia occupying the extreme southern end of Chesapeake Bay's Eastern Shore. So long and narrow are Virginia's Accomack and Northampton counties (see **Map 1** on page iv in the Table of Contents) that in themselves they form a peninsula appended to the lower end of the larger Delmarva Peninsula.

For many people, this is an utterly blank place on their mental map of the Atlantic seaboard. Although Assateague Island National Seashore and the resort town of Chincoteague are well known, they occupy the extreme northeastern corner of this part of Virginia and are described separately in Chapter 19. As for the rest of Virginia's Eastern Shore, it is an agricultural region characterized by numerous farm hamlets, many dating from the colonial period, as well as a few larger Victorian towns created by the railroad. More recently, some commercial strips have been spawned by Route 13, the main north-south highway. At the ends of the roads that extend east to the marshes and channels behind the barrier islands of the Atlantic coast, there are a series of wharf-villages devoted to commercial and sport fishing. And at places on or near the navigable tidal creeks that penetrate inland from Chesapeake Bay are various faded villages and a few larger towns going back hundreds of years, in some cases derived from this or that tavern, general store, tobacco warehouse, court, or church built in the seventeenth century.

The 95-mile car tour outlined on **Map 49** on page 326 starts at the **town of Accomac** (seat of Accomack County), where there is an attractive historic district best seen on foot (per **Map 48** on page 323). From Accomac the route leads past **Wachapreague** and **Willis Wharf** (two fishing towns) to **Brownsville Farm**, which offers outstanding walking through woods, past cultivated fields, and across marsh bordering Hog Island Bay, as shown on **Map 50** on page 331. Brownsville Farm is part of The Nature

Conservancy's Virginia Coast Reserve; telephone (757) 442-3049. The Nature Conservancy allows walkers who do not make a nuisance of themselves to enter the property between dawn and dusk. Because **hunting** is sometimes permitted at Brownsville Farm, please see page 330 for a note on safety.

Still trending south, the car tour eventually reaches **Eastville** (seat of Northampton County), where a museum consisting of the colonial courthouse, the clerk's office, and the debtor's prison is open on weekdays from 9 A.M. to 5 P.M. Almost next door is the eighteenth-century Eastville Inn, which may be renovated and reopened as a visitor center.

From Eastville the car tour heads north along the bayside stage road, passing through such ancient villages as **Bridgetown** and **Pungoteague**, sites of the two oldest churches on Virginia's Eastern Shore. At **Onancock** the sumptuous mansion at **Kerr Place** is open Tuesday through Saturday from 10 A.M. to 4 P.M.; it is closed during January and February. Kerr Place is the headquarters of the Eastern Shore of Virginia Historical Society; telephone (757) 787-8012.

The car tour ends at the Victorian railroad town of **Parksley**, where the **Eastern Shore Railway Museum** and the **Antique Auto Museum** are open Monday through Saturday from 10 A.M. to 4 P.M. and on Sunday from 1 to 4 — although during late fall and winter, the museums are closed on Tuesday and Wednesday. They are also closed on Thanksgiving, Christmas, and New Year's Day. For information, telephone (757) 665-7245.

Finally, the Eastern Shore of Virginia has an annual Garden Week Tour on the last Friday and Saturday of April, when many private houses are open to view. For information telephone the Chamber of Commerce in Melfa at (757) 787-2460.

ENGLISH SETTLEMENT on the Eastern Shore of Virginia started in 1614, when seventeen men were sent from Jamestown to operate a salt works on a tract of land facing Cherrystone Creek just north of the present-day town of Cape Charles, which in turn is a dozen miles above the actual Cape Charles at the mouth of Chesapeake Bay. Periodically a ship from Jamestown brought supplies to sustain the outpost and took away the barrels of salt produced by evaporating sea water in large kettles over wood fires. By 1617, however, the outpost had been abandoned.

For strategic reasons the colony's leaders at Jamestown were anxious to control both sides of Chesapeake Bay, and accordingly in 1620 another settlement was established at Cherrystone Creek when seventy-five men were sent out under contract with the Virginia Company to work company-owned land. The Virginia Company (originally called the London Company) was the commercial venture that sponsored and governed the colony from the time Jamestown was founded in 1607 until 1624, when the company's charter was annulled because of mismanagement and lack of profits. Thereafter Virginia was a royal colony, subject to an ill-defined balance of power between the governor, who was appointed by the king and answerable only to him, and the locally elected House of Burgesses, which had been established in 1619.

In 1624 the English population of Accomack Plantation, as the settled area of Virginia's Eastern Shore was called, was only seventy-nine people, and the following year it dropped to fifty-one after the employees on the Virginia Company's land were transferred to the Western Shore of the Chesapeake. The land books sent to England that year listed only three owners of private tracts east of the bay. Presumably the rest of the adult population of Accomack Plantation were tenants on the company land (which had been subdivided and leased after removal of the company's men), settlers in the process of perfecting title to land, and indentured laborers.

Land policy was intended to promote rapid yet orderly settlement. Under the headright system, a settler received fifty acres of land for each person (including himself) whom he transported to Virginia at his own expense to live and work on his land for a stipulated period. The colony's various local courts, meeting monthly at private houses or taverns, had authority to issue certificates allowing a settler to move onto unclaimed land with his workers. After the claimant had improved the property with a house, garden, and orchard and had cleared and planted some fields, and after he had the land surveyed (which was sometimes delayed for years because of the shortage of qualified surveyors), he could exchange the certificate for a patent granting him title to the land. To prevent settlers from scattering far and wide in search of the most fertile land, the courts could — and sometimes did — refuse to issue certificates for sites that were considered by the authorities to be too distant for collective defense and convenient government.

Part and parcel of the land system was the practice of indentured servitude, by which immigrants without money bound themselves to work for a master for a term of years in exchange for being transported to the New World and provided with food, lodging, clothing, and tools during the period of servitude, plus a modest premium at the end of their term. By 1641, when the population of Virginia was about 7,500, three-fourths of the settlers had come from England as indentured servants, most of whom worked as field hands. After about 1670, however, the influx of indentured immigrants declined, and instead labor was increasingly performed by African slaves. At first slaves were imported primarily from Caribbean plantations, but after the beginning of the eighteenth century, they were brought in large numbers directly from Africa.

The population of Virginia's Eastern Shore in 1641 was about 700 people. The entire region was one county, established in 1634 and at first called Accomack County and then, after 1643, Northampton County. Nearly all the population was confined to the southern half below Occahannock Creek. The county had its own court, whose commissioners (typically the leading citizens) not only adjudicated minor civil and criminal cases but also issued local laws and regulations. By the end of 1642, the region had two churches, each with its own minister, who like every other man was also a tobacco planter, supported in part by his glebe or farm owned by the parish. There was also a commander of the militia, in which all men served without pay. The county was divided into six military districts, and drills and target practice were held regularly. Occasionally the militiamen were alerted in response to perceived threats from Indians, conflicts with foreign powers (mainly the Dutch), or the appearance of pirates in Chesapeake Bay. Compared, however, to the area along the upper James River, where there were major massacres by the Indians and bloody reprisals by the settlers, the Eastern Shore was peaceful.

Every Virginia planter grew tobacco, which was used as a substitute for money (debts and prices, for example, being expressed in pounds of tobacco). Raising cattle, pigs, and sheep was also common. Marked by brands or by various ways of slashing and cropping the ears, the livestock were allowed to wander freely in the woods. Each planter was responsible for erecting a fence conforming to legal standards in order to keep livestock out of his fields; if the animals broke through such a fence, their owner was accountable for the damage they did. Salt meat, cheese, hides, and wool were exported to England and also to other colonies; some food was sold to reprovision ships. For the most part, however, effort was so concentrated on growing and exporting tobacco that in 1647 the Burgesses enacted a law requiring that every planter also grow, as a precaution against famine, three acres of corn for each of his tithables — or that is, people on whom taxes were paid.

By 1663 settlement of Virginia's Eastern Shore had spread over such a large area that the region was divided into two counties. The name Northampton was retained for the lower county, and the old name Accomack was revived for the upper county, although the dividing line was placed somewhat south of the present-day boundary that runs from the vicinity of Belle Haven on the west side of the peninsula to Willis Wharf on the east. Three years later, the pace at which vacant land was patented increased greatly when the headright system was replaced by a new set of requirements for acquiring title. Large tracts could be patented merely by building a tiny house (twelve by twelve feet minimum), putting someone in it for a year, and fencing one acre for an orchard and garden. However, such patents were subject to a rent, payable to the king, of two shillings per year for each fifty acres. The new land system favored those who had the capital to pay the rent while the land was brought into production, or who could possibly make the land immediately profitable by putting herds of cattle on it. Under the new land system, immense tracts were patented in the northern part of Accomack County, including the coastal marshes and Atlantic barrier islands. These remote and isolated areas were used for grazing livestock because the animals could not easily wander away or damage farm fields.

During Bacon's Rebellion in 1676, William Berkeley, the royal governor at the time, fled from Jamestown to Virginia's Eastern Shore, where he established a stronghold and temporary capitol at the residence of John Custis II on Old Plantation Creek, south of the present-day town of Cape Charles. The Eastern Shore militia remained loyal to the governor, who retained the sympathies of the tidewater planters against Bacon's frontiersmen. Bacon sent a ship with soldiers to seize Berkeley, but it was boarded and captured by the governor's forces. From the Eastern Shore Berkeley led an expedition to reinstall himself at Jamestown, but Bacon attacked and burned the town, and Berkeley again fled. After Bacon died of malaria, the rebellion collapsed, and early in 1677 Berkeley returned from the Eastern Shore to the region along the James River. There he executed many of Bacon's followers before being recalled to England by King Charles II, who is said to have remarked of Berkeley, "The old fool has put to death more people in that naked country than I did here for the murder of my father."

By the beginning of the eighteenth century, the settlement of Virginia's Eastern Shore was as far advanced as any other part of the colony's tidewater region. Virginia's Eastern Shore had a population of 6,000 people, as compared with 70,000 for all of Virginia. Almost 90 percent of Northampton County and 80 percent of Accomack County were patented. Ferries sailed twice weekly from Kings Creek to the ports of York and Hampton on the Western Shore. Although most of the creeks of Virginia's Eastern Shore were too shallow to accommodate large ships, many smaller vessels came and went. A few major ports, through which all goods shipped into or out of the colony were supposed to pass, had collectors of customs, and even minor ports had ballast overseers to supervise the unloading of stone, gravel, and sand ballast onto land, rather than allowing it to be dumped overboard where it might hinder navigation.

Virginia's Eastern Shore in 1700 had two roads, one bayside and the other seaside, each running from Cape Charles to the Maryland line, plus in Accomack County a middle north-south road. There were also many cross roads, leading to churches, meeting places of the courts, public wharves, tobacco warehouses, and mills. Along these roads tobacco was either hauled in carts or rolled in large barrels called hogsheads, through which an axle was run like a lawn roller. To construct and maintain roads, every freeman was required to supply laborers in proportion to the number of tithables he had, and owners of land adjacent to roads were responsible for keeping the ways free from fallen trees.

During the years leading up to the Revolutionary War, the Eastern Shore of Virginia participated in the widespread opposition to England's attempts to raise more revenue from the American colonies. Resolutions denouncing the Stamp Act were adopted by the courts of Accomack and Northampton counties, and people who chose to ignore the Stamp Act were not prosecuted. When actual fighting broke out, the two counties supplied seven companies of soldiers to the Continental Army. Because the British blockaded the mouth of Chesapeake Bay, supplies from France and from neutral countries were landed at Metompkin and Chincoteague creeks on the Atlantic coast, then brought overland and reloaded onto small craft that evaded the British barges operating in the bay. Occasionally during the war, British raiding parties seized flour, livestock, and poultry to replenish the supplies of their warships. Operating from remote outposts along the Chesapeake shore, bands of loyalists — or in some cases merely piratical opportunists called picaroons — ransacked and burned the plantations of known patriots and seized their slaves and ships. Except for this nasty guerrilla war, however, the Eastern Shore was relatively peaceful compared to the Western Shore, where Portsmouth was burned and the war eventually reached its climax at Yorktown.

Throughout the eighteenth century, tobacco and livestock were the principal sources of wealth, but by the beginning of the nineteenth century, when the population of Virginia's Eastern Shore was more than 22,000, cotton began to be grown, and for a few decades it replaced tobacco as the chief money crop. Cotton, in turn, gave way to vegetables shipped to rapidly expanding cities, especially after 1829, when completion of the Chesapeake and Delaware Canal across the isthmus at the northern end of the Delmarva Peninsula greatly reduced the distance from Chesapeake Bay ports to northern markets. Sailing vessels carried farm products and seafood from Delmarva to Norfolk, Washington, Baltimore, Philadelphia, and New York. On Virginia's Eastern Shore, the transition to producing and shipping perishable foodstuffs accelerated when steamboats went into service in the early 1840s.

By the beginning of the Civil War in 1860, the Eastern Shore of Virginia was growing mainly sweet potatoes, Irish potatoes, corn, oats, and some cotton. The fact that Union forces completely controlled the region and all of Chesapeake Bay throughout the war reinforced the orientation of local markets toward northern cities. Extension of the railroad southward from Maryland in 1884 to a terminus at the new town of Cape Charles provided further stimulus to an economy based on shipping vegetables, strawberries, and seafood.

The twentieth century has seen yet other shifts in the Eastern Shore's agricultural economy. As has occurred nationally, farm population and the number of farms has steadily decreased since the early 1900s, while the size and efficiency of farms has increased. During the first third of the century, potatoes were the main cash crop, but as with all agricultural commodities, overproduction caused prices to plummet during the Great Depression of the 1930s, just as the price of tobacco had periodically collapsed during the colonial period. During the Depression, soybeans were introduced as a new crop, and by 1960 led in acreage, followed by a variety of vegetables harvested by migrant laborers.

Probably the most important development on Virginia's Eastern Shore in the latter half of the twentieth century has been construction of the 17.6-mile Chesapeake Bay Bridge-Tunnel at the southern tip of the peninsula. Completed in 1964, it has greatly increased traffic passing up and down the peninsula and has stimulated tourism and light industry, although the economy of the region remains primarily agricultural. Linking Cape Charles and Norfolk, the bridge-tunnel caused immediate abandonment of the automobile ferries that used to serve Virginia's Eastern Shore. Just as building the railroad in the nineteenth century stole business from the old towns on the stage roads and created a new locus of commercial activity, so the advent of motor vehicles, the building of Route 13 (finished in 1931), and construction of the bridge-tunnel have caused a relocation of business away from the railroad towns to the vicinity of the highway. The tour outlined below, however, largely ignores Route 13 and follows instead some of the region's oldest roads through areas unseen by most visitors.

≈   ≈   ≈   ≈

AUTOMOBILE DIRECTIONS: Accomack and Northampton counties in Virginia occupy the extreme southern end of the Delmarva Peninsula. (See **Map 1** on page iv in the Table of Contents.) Together, they comprise all of the portion of Virginia that is located east of Chesapeake Bay. The car tour shown on **Map 49** on page 326 starts at the town of Accomac, so you should go there first.

To Accomac from northern Delmarva and Interstate 95 southwest of Wilmington: From Interstate 95 take Exit 4A for Route 1 south, and stay on Route 1 past a quick succession of exits. Follow Route 1 south past Dover, then switch to Route 13 south through Maryland toward Salisbury and Norfolk. Stay on Route 13 past Salisbury, Princess Anne, Pocomoke City, and the junction with Route 113 (which provides an alternative approach from the north, inasmuch as Route 1 merges with Route 113 below Dover). After crossing the state line into Virginia, continue south on Route 13 for nearly 22 miles. Pass an exit for Business Route 13 toward Accomac, then (after 1.5 miles) turn left toward Accomac at a crossroads with Route 764. Go 0.4 mile, then park in the center of town near the courthouse.

To Accomac from the Chesapeake Bay Bridge: After crossing the bridge, follow Route 50/301 across Kent Island. At the point where Route 50 and Route 301 split, fork right to follow Route 50 past Easton, Cambridge, and Salisbury. East of Salisbury, take Route 13 south toward Norfolk. Follow Route 13 past Princess Anne and Pocomoke City. After crossing the state line into Virginia, continue south on Route 13 for nearly 22 miles. Pass an exit for Business Route 13 toward Accomac, then (after 1.5 miles) turn left toward Accomac at a crossroads with Route 764. Go 0.4 mile, then park in the center of town near the courthouse.

To Accomac from the Chesapeake Bay Bridge-Tunnel at Norfolk: After crossing the bridge-tunnel, follow Route 13 north from the toll plaza for more than 46 miles. Pass an exit for Business Route 13 toward Accomac, then (after 1.1 miles) turn right toward Accomac at a crossroads with Route 764. Go 0.4 mile, then park in the center of town near the courthouse.

To Accomac from Salisbury and the Delaware and Maryland seashore resorts: Follow Route 13 south from the vicinity of Salisbury, or Route 113 south from the vicinity of the Delaware and Maryland beach resorts. In either case, go to the junction of Route 13 and Route 113 near Pocomoke City, and from there continue south on Route 13. After crossing the state line into Virginia, continue south on Route 13 for nearly 22 miles. Pass an exit for Business Route 13 toward Accomac, then (after 1.5 miles) turn left toward Accomac at a crossroads with Route 764. Go 0.4 mile, then park in the center of town near the courthouse.

Accomac, spelled without a k at the end, is the seat of Accomack County. Although Accomack County was established in 1663, the area that had been settled by the English did not at that time reach as far north or as far inland as the present-day town of Accomac. So for fifteen years the county court met at Pungoteague, farther south and closer to Chesapeake Bay; then for a few more years court sessions alternated between Onancock, which was the county's chief port and center of commerce, and Metompkin (now Accomac), which was selected for its central location. Travel distance to court was an important consideration because county residents had many reasons for going. Court was not only where litigants resolved disputes, but also where all freemen voted (and were fined if they failed to vote), where residents petitioned for this or that government act or improvement, where wills were probated, where land transactions and sales of costly chattels were recorded, and even where divine services were sometimes held.

In 1693 the court of Accomack County was established permanently at Metompkin, meeting at first in a tavern. In 1710 a wooden courthouse was built (and for ten years was used also as a place of worship). But not until 1786 did the Virginia General Assembly, in response to a petition from residents of Metompkin, pass legislation providing that "ten acres of land, the property of Richard Drummond, adjoining Accomack Courthouse, shall be laid out into lots of half an acre each, with convenient streets, and together with twenty other half acre lots already improved shall form a town by the name of Drummond." Trustees were empowered to sell the lots in order to pay Richard Drummond. The purchaser of each lot was required to build a house at least sixteen feet on each side within two years. In addition to its two dozen houses, Drummondtown at that time also had a tavern, a saddle shop, at least one store, a courthouse that had been rebuilt in brick in 1756, a wooden jail, and a brick house for the jailer.

During the late eighteenth century and the first half of the nineteenth century, Drummondtown prospered, as is readily apparent from the handsome churches and houses that were built during this period (and which are detailed in the walking tour described below). In 1835 the town was described as follows in *A New and Comprehensive Gazetteer of Virginia and the District of Columbia*:

> Accomack Court House, or Drummondtown, besides a brick courthouse and jail, contains a Methodist house of worship, 39 dwelling houses, 1 common school, 3 mercantile stores, 1 tannery, 2 saddle and harness makers, 3 tailors, 3 cabinet makers, 1 watch and clock maker, 1 carriage maker, and 2 boot and shoe factories. There are 3 grist mills in the vicinity. The population is 240, including 4 attorneys and 2 physicians. County courts are held on the last Monday of every month. . . .

In 1893 the name of Drummondtown was changed to Accomac. By then the village, which had been bypassed by the railroad in 1884, was threatened with relocation of the county seat to the new town of Parksley on the railroad. Although the county's voters rejected the move in 1895, Accomac again suffered economic loss when the town was bypassed by Route 13 in the 1920s.

Today Accomac is a small and quiet place. Although the town's commercial main street is somewhat decayed, the courthouse green (with its clustered lawyer's offices) and the nearby residential streets possess an air of prosperity and historic continuity derived in large part from the ongoing business of county government.

≈   ≈   ≈   ≈

WALKING TOUR OF ACCOMAC: This short tour, which entails little more than a walk around the town's oldest block, is shown by the bold line on **Map 48** at right.

Start at the county office building, which is located on Courthouse Avenue (Route 764) near the intersection with Front Street (Business Route 13). Across Courthouse Avenue from the county office building is the **Debtors' Prison**, built in 1783 as a home for the county jailer and converted in 1842 to use as a place where insolvent debtors were confined separately from criminal prisoners. As small as it is, this structure — which has two lower rooms and a loft — is substantially larger than the minimum 16 by 16 feet required for houses when the town was laid out in 1786. A sign on the door explains current arrangements for gaining entry to the prison, where there is a small museum.

MAP 48 — Accomac walking tour

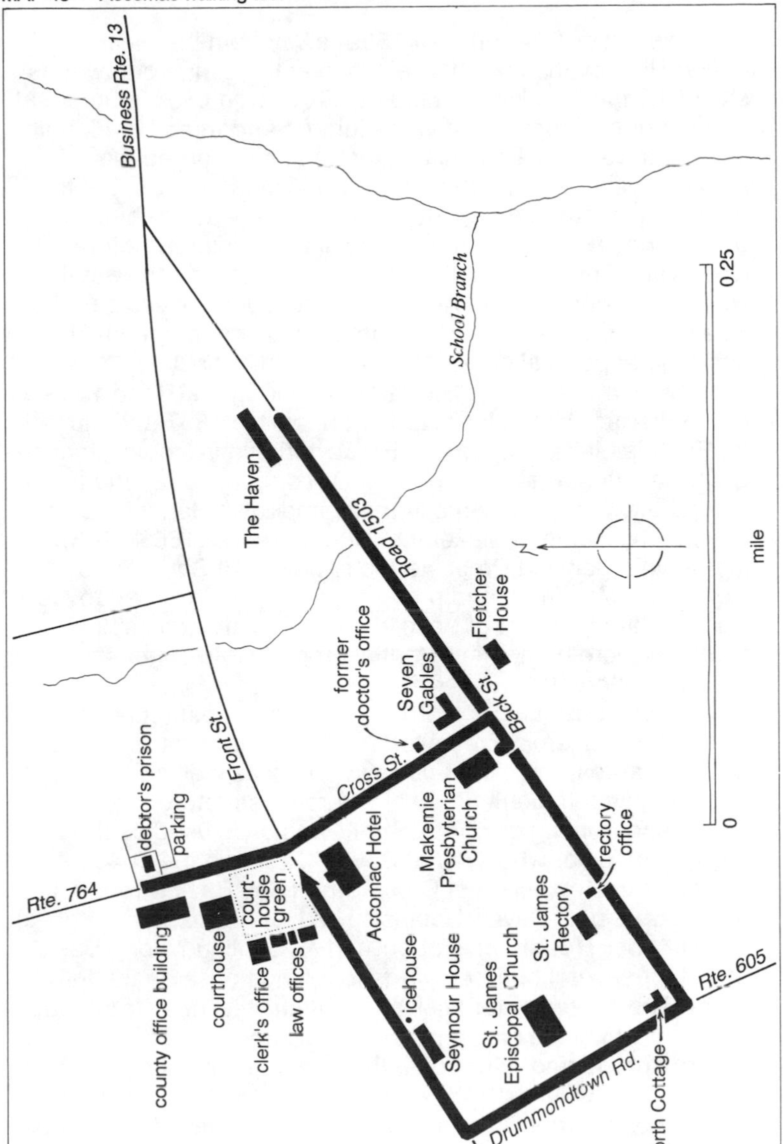

Business Rte. 13

School Branch

0.25

mile

0

N

The Haven

Road 1503

former doctor's office

Seven Gables

Fletcher House

Back St.

Cross St.

Front St.

debtor's prison

parking

Rte. 764

county office building

courthouse

clerk's office

law offices

court-house green

Accomac Hotel

Makemie Presbyterian Church

icehouse

Seymour House

St. James Episcopal Church

St. James Rectory

rectory office

Rte. 605

Drummondtown Rd.

Bloodworth Cottage

Business Rte. 13

Follow Cross Street (Road 1502) away from the main intersection by the courthouse green at the center of town, as shown by the bold line on Map 48. The large brick structure at the corner on Front Street is the former **Accomac Hotel**, built in 1922 to replace a colonial tavern that had burned the previous year. As noted on the historic marker in front of the hotel, the tavern that previously stood here was the birthplace of Henry A. Wise, governor of Virginia immediately before the Civil War. One of his last official acts was to sign the death warrant of John Brown. Although opposed to secession, Wise was commissioned a Confederate brigadier general and, unlike some other political generals, served with distinction.

At the corner of Cross Street and Back Street (Road 1503) is the **Makemie Presbyterian Church**, built in 1837 and named for Francis Makemie, the first Presbyterian minister in America. Both the exterior (see the photograph on page 312) and the interior are very handsome in their simplicity. Behind the church is a statue of Makemie. During his life (1658-1708), Makemie organized Presbyterian churches at Snow Hill and Rehobeth, Maryland, and preached from the Carolinas to New York. When he was not traveling, he lived in Accomack County, where he had substantial property and various business interests.

On Cross Street at the corner with Back Street (opposite the side of the Makemie Presbyterian Church) is a house called **Seven Gables**, the oldest part of which was built near the end of the eighteenth century. The one-room structure next to the house and fronting on Cross Street was once used as the office of a doctor who lived at Seven Gables in the 1840s.

From the intersection of Cross Street and Back Street, follow Back Street past Seven Gables. The first house on the right is the **Fletcher House**, built about 1817. Continue along Back Street for several hundred yards to a long house on the left called **The Haven** and consisting of eight sections strung out in a row, of which the oldest part was built about 1794.

Turn around and return past the front of Makemie Presbyterian Church. Half way down the block on the right side of Back Street is the small clapboard **office of St. James Episcopal Church**, and next beyond it is the brick **rectory**, built about 1811. The office, like that next to Seven Gables, was originally used by a doctor. Throughout the Civil War, when Virginia's Eastern Shore was occupied by Union forces, their commander made the rectory his headquarters; what is now the church office was his telegraph office. Although the

Episcopal church was unscathed by the war, the town's Methodist and Presbyterian churches were damaged by federal troops who used them for barracks and stables. Turn right at the corner with Drummondtown Road (Route 605), past **Bloodworth Cottage**, built in the late 1700s. Next on the right is **St. James Episcopal Church**, constructed in 1838 in the Greek Revival style and containing inside, on the altar wall, *trompe d'oeil* architectural effects first painted about 1855 and recently restored.

Turn right at the T-intersection with Front Street (Business Route 13). The second house on the right (set back only a dozen feet from the road) is the **Seymour House**, of which the oldest part was built in 1791. The arrangement of distinct sections, commonly described as "big house, little house, colonnade, and kitchen," was fairly common on Virginia's Eastern Shore in the early 1800s. Also popular at that time was the more modest double house, featuring a passage joining two somewhat larger but nearly identical sections. (There is a double house about 0.3 mile farther north along the road, on the right-hand side.) Still other houses, termed step or telescope houses, have sections that are progressively bigger or smaller.

In the yard just beyond Seymour House, notice the round **ice house**, set low in the ground and with a conical roof.

Leaving behind Seymour House on the right, continue straight ahead to the courthouse green, where the walking tour ends.

≈   ≈   ≈   ≈

CAR TOUR OF ACCOMACK AND NORTHAMPTON COUNTIES: The bold line on **Map 49** on page 326 shows the route followed by this 95-mile car tour.

From the intersection next to the courthouse green at the center of Accomac, follow Business Route 13 southwest. (That is, start with the courthouse green on your right.) Go only a few hundred yards, then turn left onto Route 605, which is part of the old stage road along the ocean side of Virginia's Eastern Shore. After 4.4 miles you will enter the hamlet of **Locustville**.

At the northern edge of Locustville is the **Locustville United Methodist Church**, built in 1923, and across the road is **Locustville Academy**, which operated as a private school from 1859 until 1879,

MAP 49 — Car tour of Accomack and Northampton counties

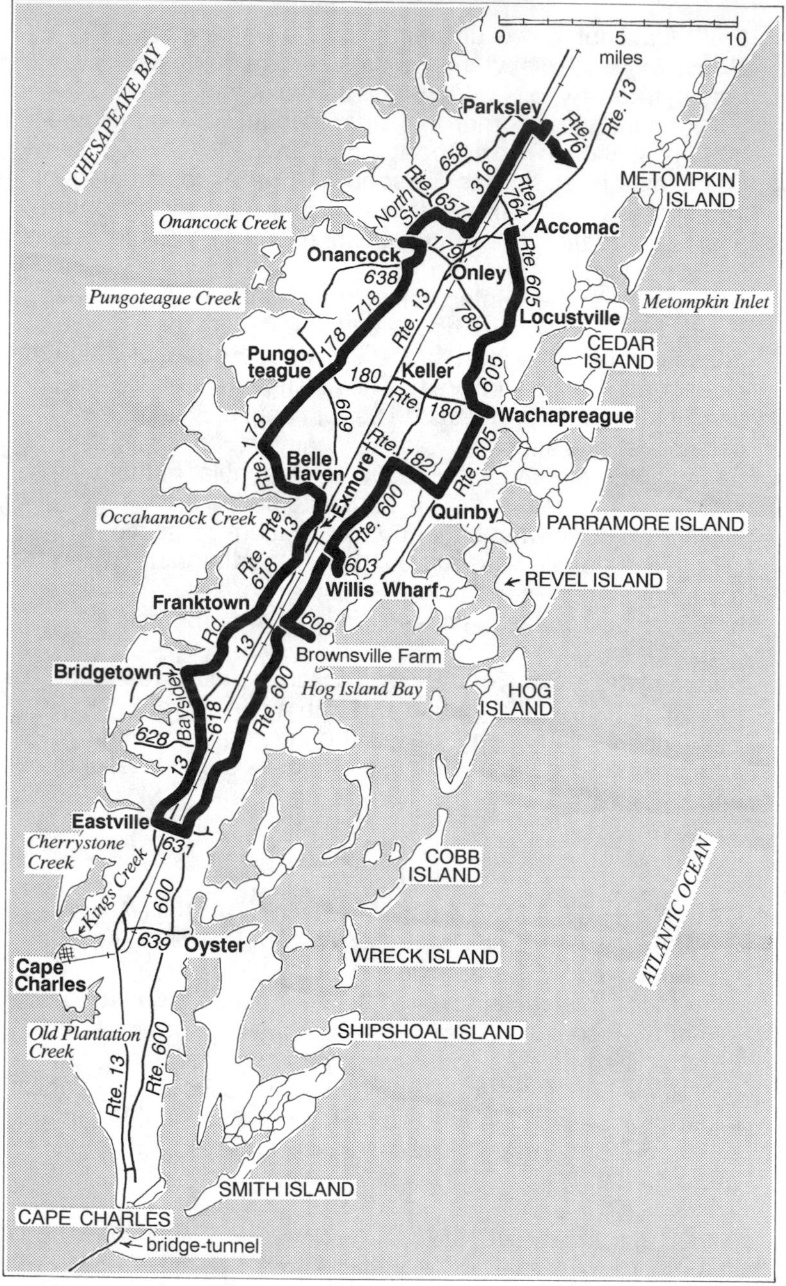

CHESAPEAKE BAY

0   5   10
miles

Parksley

Rte. 176

Rte. 13

658

316

657

764

Rte. 605

METOMPKIN ISLAND

Onancock Creek

North St.

179

Accomac

Onancock

638

718

Onley

Metompkin Inlet

Pungoteague Creek

Rte. 13

789

Locustville

178

718

Rte. 605

CEDAR ISLAND

Pungo-teague

180

Keller

180

Wachapreague

178

609

Rte. 182

Exmore

Rte. 600

Rte. 605

Belle Haven

Rte. 13

Rte. 13

Quinby

Occahannock Creek

Rte. 618

603

Willis Wharf

PARRAMORE ISLAND

Franktown

608

Brownsville Farm

← REVEL ISLAND

Rd. 13

Bridgetown →

618

Rte. 600

Hog Island Bay

HOG ISLAND

628

Bayside

13

Eastville

631

COBB ISLAND

Cherrystone Creek

Kings Creek

600

639   Oyster

WRECK ISLAND

Cape Charles

Old Plantation Creek

Rte. 13

Rte. 600

ATLANTIC OCEAN

SHIPSHOAL ISLAND

SMITH ISLAND

CAPE CHARLES

← bridge-tunnel

326

when it was acquired by the county school board. Girls used the first floor and boys the second. Locustville Academy prepared its male students for business careers or college. Subjects included not only the usual reading, writing, and arithmetic, but also Greek and Latin and, for girls, such accomplishments as piano and drawing.

Locustville proper is located another 0.3 mile beyond the academy on Route 605. This hamlet is typical of many small Eastern Shore villages of the nineteenth century. By all means find an excuse to stop in at the **general store**, even if only to buy a snack. Across Route 605 are two double houses, and about 70 yards farther along the road from the general store is the old **Locustville Hotel**.

CAR TOUR continued (Map 49): From Locustville continue south on Route 605 about 4 miles to a T-intersection with Route 180, and there turn left. Go 0.8 mile to the waterfront village of Wachapreague.

Although a wharf, shipping firm, and village were established at **Wachapreague** in 1872, it was not until construction of the thirty-room Hotel Wachapreague in 1902 that the town became a resort for waterfowl hunters and sport fishermen attracted by advertisements in northern newspapers and national outdoor journals. From the nearest railroad station at Keller, visitors were conveyed to Wachapreague by the hotel's carriages. In the 1920s the town's attractions included a dance hall, a poolroom, a drugstore with soda fountain, and a movie theater. Although the resort business gradually tapered off and the hotel itself burned in 1978 (there is now a motel-style Wachapreague Hotel across the street from the old hotel site), the town is still a base for charter boats and recreational fishermen.

CAR TOUR continued (Map 49): From the waterfront in Wachapreague, follow Route 180 for only 0.4 mile out of town, then turn left onto Route 605 (Bradfords Neck Road). Follow Route 605 for 4 miles to the intersection with Route 182 on the outskirts of the town of Quinby, with occasional glimpses to the left of wooded Parramore Island in the distance. Turn right onto Route 182 (Quinby Bridge Road) and go 2.3 miles to a crossroads with Route 600 (Seaside Road), and there turn left. Follow Route 600 (again part of the old stage road running down the eastern side of the peninsula) for 4.8 miles to a crossroads with Route 603 (Willis Wharf Road), and there turn left. Go 1.1 miles; after crossing a bridge, turn left into a parking lot for a boat basin, where there is a good view back toward the Willis Wharf waterfront.

In contrast to Wachapreague, which caters to recreational fishermen, the village of **Willis Wharf** is a base for commercial oystering and clamming. Although most of the old processing plants have been closed or torn down, some have been replaced by hatcheries for shellfish aquaculture, which has been moderately successful here. Oyster and clam seedlings (or spat) are raised in tanks. When the shells are thumbnail size, they are set out in beds leased by the operators or their affiliates and located in the nearby tidal bays and creeks. Aquaculture has given new life to the local shellfishing economy, which had been in decline because of overfishing and depletion of oyster reefs and clam bottoms.

Called Downings Wharf in the early 1800s, the village was renamed for Edward Willis, who moved here in 1850 and built the **Willis Store**, which still stands at the corner where Route 603 meets the waterfront. The store also includes a restaurant. Many homes in Willis Wharf were moved from Hog Island in the 1930s when rising sea level caused the island village of Broadwater to be abandoned.

CAR TOUR continued (Map 49): From Willis Wharf return on Route 603 by the way you came to the crossroads with Route 600, and there turn left to continue south on the old Seaside Road. Go 4.2 miles, then turn left on Route 608 (Brownsville Road) in order to visit The Nature Conservancy's Brownsville Farm. After 1.1 miles, turn sharply right into a white oystershell driveway that leads to a parking area for the office of The Nature Conservancy's Virginia Coast Reserve.

The Nature Conservancy is an international, nonprofit organization devoted to preserving ecologically important areas, which also, of course, often have great scenic and recreational value. Among The Nature Conservancy's largest and most spectacular holdings is the **Virginia Coast Reserve**, which has its headquarters at **Brownsville**, a 2,846-acre working farm named for John Brown, who patented this land in 1652.

Brownsville Farm is merely a small part of the Virginia Coast Reserve, which extends for sixty miles along the Atlantic coast and consists of fourteen islands, vast saltmarsh tracts, and adjacent mainland sites altogether totaling 45,000 acres. With funding from the Mary Flagler Cary Charitable Trust of New York and other donors, The Nature Conservancy has since 1969 acquired most of the barrier islands of Virginia's Eastern Shore, and those that it does not own are (with the lone exception of Cedar Island) the property of the state and federal governments. In addition to buying land outright, The Nature

Conservancy tries to protect its core holdings by working with nearby landowners to devise acceptable conservation easements. The conservancy works also with local governments to help formulate zoning ordinances that balance conservation and development.

Except for Parramore, Shipshoal, and Revel's islands, the barrier islands of the Virginia Coast Reserve are open to the public during daytime for such uses as hiking, birding, fishing, and nature study. During spring and summer, visitors are asked to use extra care in order to avoid plover nesting sites and bird colonies on the beaches and in the dunes and marshes.

Since they are accessible only by boat, the barrier islands are not discussed further here except to note that The Nature Conservancy itself occasionally offers field trips to the islands. For information call the Virginia Coast Reserve at (757) 442-3049 or stop by the office. Trips fill early, so make reservations well in advance. The office also has information for people who wish to provide support by becoming members of The Nature Conservancy or Friends of the Virginia Coast Reserve, as is well worthwhile. One of the advantages of membership is receiving the Virginia Coast Reserve newsletter, which provides early notice of trips.

WALKING AT BROWNSVILLE FARM: First, a few words of caution. Brownsville is private property; walkers are welcome only to the extent that they do not hinder ongoing research and farm operations, so stick to the farm roads and trails and be alert for farm vehicles. Also, with the permission of the Virginia Coast Reserve, deer hunting occurs at Brownsville during fall and early winter. Usually hunters are barred from the area through which the route described below passes, but sometimes hunters are present, so it is wise to wear orange. Even during the deer season, you can avoid hunters by walking on Sunday, when hunting is prohibited.

Map 50 at right shows Brownsville Farm, where shell roads and foot trails pass through woods and skirt cultivated fields that in turn occupy a peninsula jutting into the marsh. A boardwalk and dike enable walkers to cross the marsh to some timber islands — **the Hammocks** — fronting on Hog Island Bay. A round-trip walk to the Hammocks, as shown by the bold line on Map 50, totals 4 miles.

Starting at the office parking lot, cross the large grassy area diagonally toward the left (away from the office). Pass through the woods on a boardwalk, then turn right onto a rutted farm road, which leads nearly a mile to a screened shed.

MAP 50 — Walking at Brownsville Farm

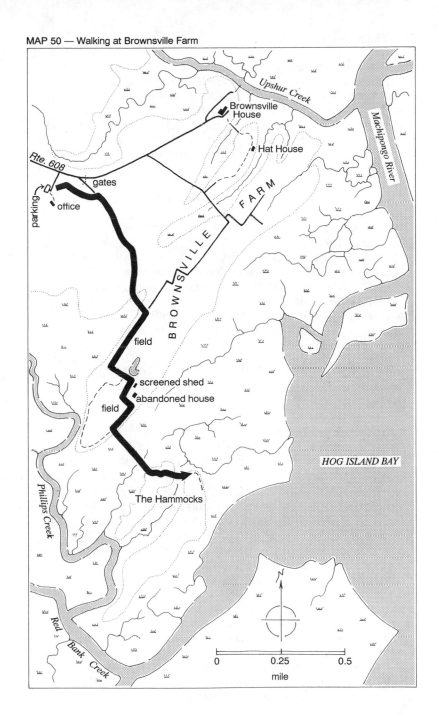

After passing behind the screened shed, the path becomes rougher. Go several hundred yards as the path bends left, then right. As you continue along the rutted farm track with a field on the right, watch for a gap in the hedgerow to the left, where a small footbridge and a dike lead across the marsh to the Hammocks. Follow the path across the marsh, then across one timber island to another island. There the trail peters out — although you can continue along the shore several hundred yards for a view out across Hog Island Bay. Hog Island itself is 8 miles distant and has such a low profile that it is barely visible.

After returning from the Hammocks via the dike, you may want to circle clockwise around a large field for a view out over the marsh at Phillips Creek. Eventually, return from the screened shed to the office by the way you came.

As shown on Map 50, Brownsville Farm also includes **Brownsville House**, built in 1806 by a member of the locally prominent Upshur family, into which John Brown's granddaughter married about 1690. Brownsville House has been restored by The Nature Conservancy and serves as the residence of the director of the Virginia Coast Reserve. If you want to tour this handsome house, inquire at the office for information about the infrequent occasions when it is open to the public.

CAR TOUR continued (Map 49): From the Virginia Coast Reserve office at Brownsville Farm, return on Route 608 by the way you came to the intersection with Route 600 (Seaside Road). Turn left onto Route 600 and follow it south 10.8 miles to a crossroads with Route 631 (Indiantown Drive) and there turn right. For 1.3 miles, follow Route 631 past the old Eastville Station and across Route 13 to a T-intersection with Business Route 13 in Eastville. Visible to the right is the courthouse green; to the left is the Eastville Inn, which may be renovated for use as a visitor center. Turn left, then immediately right in order to park.

Eastville is the seat of Northampton County. After a courthouse had been erected farther south at Kings Creek in 1663, residents from the north end of the county complained that they were inconvenienced and in 1677 requested that the court meet at a more central location. Later that year the court convened for the first time at "the Hornes," as the vicinity of Eastville was then called, supposedly because several creeks penetrate the area like the prongs of antlers.

Gradually the Hornes evolved into the permanent seat of county government. At first court was held in a "victualling house" or tavern — a precursor of the 1724 **Eastville Inn** — but beginning in 1690 the justices gathered in a new courthouse erected by the tavern keeper at his own expense in order to induce the court to continue to meet at the Hornes. In 1731 a brick courthouse was built; termed the **Old Courthouse**, it still stands on one side of the courthouse green, where it was moved in 1913 to make room for the Confederate monument. Another, larger courthouse was built in 1795, and the Old Courthouse was leased for use as a store. Now the Old Courthouse, the adjacent **Old Clerk's Office** (probably built in the third quarter of the eighteenth century) and the **Debtor's Prison** (located behind the Old Clerk's Office) are maintained as a museum to which keys may be obtained on weekdays during business hours from the current clerk's office in the 1899 courthouse, which also faces the courthouse green.

In 1773 the owner of twenty acres adjacent to the courthouse divided his tract into forty half-acre lots and offered them for sale. During the following half-century, the courthouse village acquired considerable commercial importance, as described in 1835 in *A New and Comprehensive Gazetteer of Virginia and the District of Columbia*:

> Eastville P.V. [Post Village] and seat of justice is in about the middle of the county and two miles from the Chesapeake Bay and the Atlantic Ocean. Eastville has 2 principal streets running at right angles to each other. Besides the usual county buildings it contains 21 dwelling houses, 4 mercantile stores, 2 taverns, 1 new and handsome Episcopal church, and 1 common school and 1 Bible society. The mechanical pursuits are : 1 coach factory, which completes about $6,000 worth of work annually; 1 harness maker, 1 cabinet maker, 2 blacksmiths, 2 boot and shoe manufacturers, 3 tailors, 1 house and sign painter and 1 hatter.
>
> There are in Eastville 3 castor oil manufactories and 2 others in the county. The county exports about 20,000 gallons of oil annually. The principal commerce is with Baltimore, Philadelphia, and New York.

The "new and handsome Episcopal church" mentioned in the gazetteer is **Christ Episcopal Church**, built in 1828 and containing stained glass windows from Germany. It is located on the north edge of town, where you may want to stop briefly as you drive out.

In 1884 the railroad was constructed a mile east of Eastville, prompting residential and commercial development in the area between the village and its station. The new railroad towns of Exmore and Cape Charles, however, grew far more rapidly than Eastville, which in the second half of the twentieth century has declined as a commercial center. Today this attractive historic village is sustained entirely by the presence of the county government.

CAR TOUR continued (Map 49): From the intersection of Business Route 13 and Route 631 in Eastville, follow Business Route 13 north 1.3 miles to an intersection with the main Route 13, and there turn left. Follow Route 13 north only 2.4 miles, then turn left onto Route 628 and immediately turn right onto Route 618 (Bayside Road), which is part of the old stage road following the western side of the peninsula. Follow Bayside road north as straight as possible, ignoring the fact that its number designation keeps changing. After 3.7 miles, turn right into the driveway of Hungars Episcopal Church in the now nearly non-existent hamlet of Bridgetown, where there was a settlement as early as 1660.

Hungars Episcopal Church was built in 1742 on the site of an earlier church dating from about 1680. Its furnishings are supposed to have been very rich; it even had an organ, one of the earliest in the colonies. Yet following the American Revolution, the church was abandoned as most Anglican clergymen refused to affiliate themselves with the new American Episcopal hierarchy and also as much of the population turned to Methodism. The church eventually was reopened in 1819. In serious need of repair, the structure was slightly shortened in 1851, when the front was rebuilt in the same Flemish bond pattern as the original. At the same time, side doors were eliminated.

CAR TOUR continued (Map 49): From Hungars Episcopal Church, turn right out the driveway and continue north on Bayside Road. (Again, ignore the fact that the number designation changes from one segment of the road to the next.) Continue as straight as possible on Bayside Road for 7.9 miles, in the process passing through **Franktown**, which in the 1800s was considered an important village, with a post office and tavern on the stage road. Eventually, turn left (north) onto Route 13, but follow it only 1.7 miles, then turn left onto Route 178 (Belle Haven Road). Go 1 mile, then turn left in Belle Haven to continue on Route 178 northbound for another 8 miles to the hamlet of Pungoteague. For a bit of local color and perhaps a snack, take the time to stop in at the general store located at the intersection of Route 178 and Route 180 in Pungoteague.

With its old frame houses and stores (now boarded up), sleepy **Pungoteague** is a quintessential nineteenth-century crossroads village. But its history goes back much further, as evidenced by the presence here of **St. George's Episcopal Church**, the oldest church building on

Virginia's Eastern Shore. (The church is located on the left side of Route 178 as you leave town going north; be sure to stop by.) Started in 1738, St. George's was constructed nearly in the shape of a Greek Cross — or that is, with arms almost equal. This is not what is seen today, however, because during the Civil War the building was badly damaged by Union soldiers, who used it to stable their horses. All interior wood was ripped out and even one wing of the brick shell was torn down. What survives is a rectangular structure patched together from the opposing arms or transept of the original church.

St. George's was built on the site of a still earlier church erected in 1678, but even before that Pungoteague was a place of note, where in 1664 the court of the newly-formed Accomack County met in the house of the area's first English settler. The court continued at or near Pungoteague for fourteen years.

An historic marker on the northern outskirts of Pungoteague marks the site of **Coles Tavern** (also called **Folkes Tavern**), where the county court met in 1667. That same year there was presented at the tavern a play called "The Bear and the Cub" (said to be the first dramatic performance in England's American colonies). The play turned out to be grist for the court's mill after a member of the audience (a certain John Martin) complained under oath that the presentation was indecent. In response the court ordered "that Cornelius Watkinson, Philip Howard and William Darby do appear in those habiliments that they then acted in, and give a draught of the speeches and passages they used." Darby, the author, was even held without bail until the play was acted before the court, whose justices decided that there was no indecency and assessed against Martin the court costs, including board for Darby while in jail.

In 1835 *A New and Comprehensive Gazetteer of Virginia and the District of Columbia* described Pungoteague as having "20 dwelling houses, 1 Methodist house of worship, 1 Episcopal house of worship, 1 common school, 1 tavern, 1 mercantile store, 1 tannery, 1 boot and shoe maker and 1 blacksmith shop. The trade from Pungoteague Creek employs 5 regular coasting vessels. The population is 100 including 1 physician." In all likelihood, this summary is apt for Pungoteague throughout most of the nineteenth century — until, that is, construction of the railroad down the middle of the peninsula in 1884 demoted Pungoteague to the status of a back-roads residential village.

CAR TOUR continued (Map 49): From Pungoteague continue north on Route 178, which after 1.9 miles suddenly becomes Route 718. Continue straight on Route 718 for 4.2 miles to a T-intersection with Route 638 (Cashville Road), and there turn right toward Onancock. Go 1.1 miles, then turn left at a T-intersection with Market Street in Onancock. After only 0.5 mile, turn right into the driveway of **Kerr Place**, which is marked by a sign, or perhaps more noticeably by a white fence with large pointed posts. Built by John S. Kerr (pronounced Carr) at the end of the eighteenth century on what was then the outskirts of Onancock, the brick mansion now houses a collection of period furniture, paintings, and costumes that altogether make Kerr Place a "must see."

From Kerr Place turn right out the driveway and continue along Market Street, eventually passing the old town square on the right, followed by several old houses on the left. Continue as Market Street reaches the waterfront and curves right past the **Hopkins & Bros. Store**, which is worth a visit and includes a restaurant. An excursion boat for Tangier Island leaves from here June through September; ask for a brochure or call (757) 891-2240 for information. (See also Chapter 17.)

Onancock is the result of legislation, passed in 1680 by the Virginia House of Burgesses, calling for the establishment of a port of entry in every county to facilitate trade and the collection of export and import duties, as required by the authorities in England. At each port, fifty acres of land were to be purchased by the Virginia government and laid out in half-acre lots. For the port of Accomack County, a site at the head of navigation of Onancock Creek was selected, and the land was purchased from Charles Scarburgh in 1681. The purchasers of lots were required to pay one hundred pounds of tobacco and to build a house at least twenty feet long within four months. At first the place was named Port Scarburgh, but within ten years the settlement was being called Onancock Town. All tobacco shipped from Accomack County was supposed to be loaded at Onancock Town, and all goods imported for sale in the county were to be unloaded there.

For three centuries Onancock (now more or less amalgamated with Onley and the large shopping center on Route 13) has been Accomack County's chief commercial center. Between 1681 and 1693 the county court met here on and off in a courthouse that presumably stood on the present-day town square. By 1800 Onancock was spreading eastward from its original boundaries. During the nineteenth century, ships built and owned locally by such merchants as Stephen Hopkins sailed regularly to other Chesapeake ports and even the West Indies. Toward the end of the century, when Onancock was at the height of its prosperity, steamboats took on huge quantities of potatoes, onions, strawberries, and other Eastern Shore produce at the town wharf, and even as late as the 1920s there was daily steamer service from Onancock to Baltimore.

CAR TOUR continued (Map 49): As Market Street curves past the front of the Hopkins & Bros. Store, it turns into King Street. Follow King Street 0.4 mile away from the waterfront and past more old houses built before the Civil War. Again pass the town square on the right. At a T-intersection with North Street, turn left and continue out of town 1.8 miles, then turn right at a T-intersection with Merry Branch Road. Go 2.1 miles, then turn left at a crossroads with Route 316 (Greenbush Road). Follow Route 316 north 5.4 miles. After entering Parksley, turn right across the railroad onto Route 176 (Bennett Street). Go one block, then turn left onto Dunne Avenue and follow it to the Melvin L. Shreves, Jr. Center on the left (in the restored J. Fulton Ayres Produce building), where the Welcome Center for the Eastern Shore Railway Museum is located. The tour that you can get here also includes the Antique Auto Museum. A parking lot for museum visitors is located slightly farther up the street.

The **Eastern Shore Railway Museum** includes an interesting collection of railroad cars and a small station (moved to Parksley from Hopeton) that contains a clerk's office and two racially segregated waiting rooms.

It is fitting that there be a train museum in **Parksley**, since the town was created entirely in response to the railroad. While the tracks were being laid in 1884, Henry R. Bennett, a traveling salesman, saw the possibility of a new town here on the farm of Benjamin Parks. With his friends and relatives, Bennett organized the Parksley Land Improvement Company, which bought 160 acres from Parks and laid out streets in a grid pattern on both sides of the tracks. Bennett's planned community had legal provisions for concentrating commercial establishments near the railroad in the center of town, for setting aside the sites of parks, schools, and churches, for barring the sale of liquor, and for segregating blacks in a separate district to the southwest, which later was placed outside the town limits. Parksley grew rapidly, with the result that there is more Victorian residential architecture here than in most other towns on Virginia's Eastern Shore, as can be seen by touring Parksley's residential streets, particularly west of the railroad.

CAR TOUR continued (Map 49): From the intersection of Route 176 (Bennett Street) and Dunne Avenue at the center of Parksley, follow Route 176 east out of town for 2.5 miles to the intersection with Route 13, where the car tour ends a few miles north of the starting point at Accomac.

DRINK
Pepsi-Cola

ICE
COLD
Coca-Cola

**QUAKER
STATE
MOTOR OIL**
CERTIFIED   GUARANTEED

Coca
TO BE GOOD

BEVERAGE

FREE GRANKCASE
SERVICE
REFILL WITH
TEXACO MOTOR OIL

Sky Chief
Su-preme

GASOLINE
PETROX

HOWE SCALES

AUTHORIZED
DEALER AGENCY

Let us
Mobiloil
your Car
ENGINE · CHASSIS · GEARS

Socony-Vacuum
CREDIT CARDS
Honored Here

KELLY
Springfield
TRACTOR TIRES

ICE

Ta

INDEX OF FEATURED SITES, including places, buildings, and excursions

IF YOU LIKE THIS BOOK, you may also enjoy some of the other guidebooks listed below. All follow the same format. These guides are widely available at bookstores, nature stores, and outfitters, or you can write or call Rambler Books for current prices and ordering information: 1430 Park Avenue, Baltimore, MD 21217; telephone (410) 523-5257.

COUNTRY WALKS NEAR WASHINGTON

Dozens of outings explore the national, state, and local parks and hike-bike trails located within an hour's drive of the national capital. Each chapter includes an overview, detailed directions, one or more maps (there are sixty in all), and extensive commentary. All material has been checked and revised for this expanded second edition.

"Cream of the local outdoors-guide crop" —*Washington Post* • "The happy union between a utilitarian and historically informative guide" —*Washington Times*

COUNTRY WALKS NEAR BALTIMORE

Like *Country Walks Near Washington*, this book includes directions, maps, and substantive essays, all of which have been updated for the third edition. Some of the trails are suitable for bicycling, including the Northern Central Railroad Trail, one of the best rails-to-trails conversions in the mid-Atlantic region.

"Fisher's books, with his own photos illustrating them, are models of pith and practicality. . . . The maps for '*Country Walks*' excel."—*Baltimore Sun*

COUNTRY WALKS & BIKEWAYS IN THE PHILADELPHIA REGION

This guidebook explores the Delaware Valley's parks, wildlife refuges, and trail networks from Wilmington in the south to Easton in the north, including eighty-five miles of canal trails along the Delaware River.

COUNTRY WALKS NEAR BOSTON

"An invaluable paperback."—*Boston Sunday Globe* • "The best few dollars you could ever spend . . . . This is my favorite trail guide. . . . Unlike the others, it features a lot of social, cultural, and natural history" —*Boston Phoenix*

COUNTRY WALKS NEAR CHICAGO

"A handy guide. . . . The general information sections — which, if combined, constitute three-fourths of the book — are excellent."— *Chicago Tribune*